30 DAY Rapidex Cookery Course

Written by
Ms. Rita Sharma
and
P.P. Bhalla

Designed and illustrated by
Prabhjot Mundhir

PUSTAK MAHAL®

Published by:

PUSTAK MAHAL®

J-3/16, Daryaganj, New Delhi-110002
☎ 23276539, 23272783, 23272784 • *Fax:* 011-23260518
E-mail: info@pustakmahal.com • *Website:* www.pustakmahal.com

Sales Centre

- 10-B, Netaji Subhash Marg, Daryaganj, New Delhi-110002
☎ 23268292, 23268293, 23279900 • *Fax:* 011-23280567
E-mail: rapidexdelhi@indiatimes.com
- 6686, Khari Baoli, Delhi-110006
☎ 23944314, 23911979

Branch Offices

Bengaluru: ☎ 080-22234025 • *Telefax:* 080-22240209
E-mail: pustak@airtelmail.in • pustak@sancharnet.in

Mumbai: ☎ 022-22010941, 022-22053387
E-mail: rapidex@bom5.vsnl.net.in

Patna: ☎ 0612-3294193 • *Telefax:* 0612-2302719
E-mail: rapidexptn@rediffmail.com

Hyderabad: *Telefax:* 040-24737290
E-mail: pustakmahalhyd@yahoo.co.in

ISBN 978-81-223-1210-2
Edition : 2012

Printed at : Gopsons Paper Ltd., Noida, UP

Foreword

Food is not timeless, it lives in a social, national and international context. Food of a nation has its own values and draws from its environment.

Food forms the basis of not only a healthy nation but meanders down into healthy families and individuals who lay the foundation of respectable societies.

In today's day and age it is important to cook by yourself where you are in total control of what you are cooking with a stable state of mind. Prabhjot has outlined the importance of this crucial but most important skill required for being a good cook in her book which guides you through this culinary journey.

Prabhjot in her book "*30 Day Rapidex Cookery Course*" touches upon all the aspects related to healthy cooking which is so important in the present day context of living. Food today is not only meant to be tasting great and presented well. What is even more important is the foundation of good culinary skills which is the metamorphosis of good cooking. This issue has been addressed well by the author in her book.

I wish Prabhjot all the best for her book and future endeavours.

To happy reading, healthy eating and gourmet appetites,

Cheers!

Manjit S. Gill, WCC
Corporate Executive Chef
ITC Hotels Division

Preface

Dear Readers,

The book *30 Day Rapidex Cookery Course* is one of the unique books on cookery which not only gives you the practical knowledge of various cooking methods, advice on food storage and handling of important ingredients but it also imparts the theoretical knowledge of cooking, which is very essential to make your cooking basics strong. It teaches you how to handle basic products like milk, wheat, rice, variety of herbs and spices, pulses, vegetables, fruits, meat products and seafood. It also makes you conversant with the use of basic products in Indian, Western, Chinese and Italian cuisine.

Whereas, the theory and practical knowledge of cooking are the integral parts of this course, garnishing and presentation of the various dishes are also not ignored. That is why various cooking methods are included here and are well illustrated by coloured photographs.

Here, I must clarify one thing that the theory of this book was written by Ms. Rita Sharma, who, unfortunately, suddenly left for her heavenly abode as she was suffering from cancer. Later, the responsibility of re-editing, adding, and writing the content of the course was assigned to Sri P.P. Bhalla by the publishers. I, being an author of many books on cookery for Pustak Mahal, was asked to design and illustrate the course with photographs and to add a section of selected recipes. I have tried my level best to do the needful. While providing the recipes from my own treasure, I have tried to give authentic recipes of national and international cuisine. I am grateful to the organizations like Huns Cookwares, Kalsi's Bakehouse and Diamond Farm Products at Pune, and Ambrosia and Natural Ice Creams in Mumbai, who allowed my team to take shots of their products in their units.

I am really thankful to my photographers Kanika Gulzar, Sanjay Yadav and Abhijeet. I am also grateful to Mr Malhotra and family for sparing time for modeling for the book. And of course, I can't ignore my husband's efforts in improvising the required things while shooting. Easy to follow recipes required for everyday meals and a variety for the special occasions are included at the end of each chapter.

We cook many traditional dishes of day-to-day use in a microwave oven with the idea that along with mastering the traditional methods of cooking, you also learn how to use this high-tech gadget in your kitchen properly so that not only cooking becomes easy and interesting for you, but also saves your valuable time spent in the kitchen. Since a microwave is an important timesaving device and an asset in todays modern kitchens, it should not be reduced to just a gadget to reheat the food.

Hope you will appreciate our efforts and make the best use of this cookbook.

Enjoy your experiments with cooking.

Prabhjot Mundhir

Contents

Contents

Contents

Contents

Welcome to

30 DAY Rapidex Cookery Course

Welcome

Heartiest congratulations for choosing to learn cooking by opting for **30 Day Rapidex Cookery Course.**

The selection of this course is the evidence of your interest in cooking. If you are new to it, you will become well acquainted with cooking a variety of dishes in the next 30 days. If you are already into cooking, this will help you to become an expert.

At the outset, let us get to know each other. We are a team of culinary experts, who have been in this field for the past several years. We have been conducting cookery classes for women belonging to different age groups. During these interactions, we were overwhelmed with a number of common problems that women face everyday while cooking. This inspired us to pool our talents and develop a course, that would touch upon all aspects of cookery. Our special concern has been the doubts and problems that people face in everyday cooking.

Cookery is a wide subject. It is only after pooling our technical expertise, research on the subject and putting together our vast experience that we have been able to give you the '**30 Day Rapidex Cookery Course**'.

What makes the course unique?

The study material of this course is based on two principles. The first, learn by doing it yourself. It is a hands-on practical course where complete details are provided to you, to do things by yourself.

The second, it has been written in such a way that it is easily understandable. Many activities have also been illustrated. So, enjoy every bit of it and have fun while learning.

Get ready for all the appreciation that awaits you, as your family and friends will enjoy the wonderful dishes set before them.

Cooking is an art

Cooking is a creative art, but since it is done primarily at home, it is rarely appreciated like the other art forms. However, with the popularity of cookery shows on television, it is gaining importance.

A variety of programmes on the culinary art are being aired on different channels. Their inimitable style, knowledge and dexterity displayed during the presentation showcases cooking as a form of art, that is scientifically researched. One does not cook only with hands. The heart is involved, too. Once you become familiar with the mechanics of cooking, adaptations and improvements can be enhanced as you progress. You need not always follow the same regime of cooking. Innovation is the key. Bring about variations in your cooking. This way, you would not only avoid monotony in the daily chores but also earn appreciation.Your experimentation with food will boost your morale and will also be great fun for you and your family!

What makes a great cook?

Don Bradman, the legendary Australian cricketer once said, "Everyone cannot be a great cricketer. But everyone can look like a great cricketer." Clothes make all the difference. They create a feeling of being a great cook. Everyone needs to dress for the occasion, so you, too, need to get yourself a cook's apron to look like a great cook. It will protect your clothes and you will not be afraid of trying anything in the kitchen. Remember, all great cooks wear aprons while cooking.

For your cookery skills to be accepted as great, you must understand the exact needs of the persons for whom you are cooking. There are two distinct aspects of this issue.

1. To understand the biological need for food and nutrition for all human beings, you must understand food chemistry, too.
2. Individual liking and taste of the people for whom you are cooking differs from person to person, as the variety of food is vast.

The **'30 Day Rapidex Cookery Course'** is devoted to thirty lessons on concepts and food that one needs to master, to learn basic cooking. You can take one lesson each day.The lesson has two parts, the theoretical and the practical. Both are equally

important. While the theoretical knowledge is important to create a strong foundation, the practical exercises prepare you to master the art of cooking. In the next thirty days, you will get an opportunity to learn the basics of cooking and handle a variety of dishes.

After every **six days** there is a **Progress Checklist**. Do not ignore it. Answer the questions in the checklist. The answers to all questions must be 'yes'. When in doubt, refer to the relevant lesson. If you have missed out on the practical work, complete it.

Self-learning is based upon personal discipline. If you want to be successful, complete your work everyday.

ICONS (How to use icons to learn easily)

Some essential tips which can be helpful while cooking.

Things you must keep in mind.

Every lesson concludes with several practical things to be done. Do not skip these. If it is not possible to do all in one day, do those that interest you more. Even within the lessons, recipes for cooking several dishes are discussed. Try cooking these dishes.

Interspersed between individual subjects, you will come across 'Cooking Methods', which describe the principles of cooking that are common to a variety of food. These are provided at intervals throughout the course depending upon their application in everyday cooking.

Throughout the course, you will come across relevant cooking tips. These tips will help you to make your task easier. You will also find 'Expert Cook' Suggests. These are the suggestions shared by experienced cook. Use them wherever you can. Collect such suggestions from columns in newspapers, magazines and from television shows, and implement them in your cooking.

Why do I need this course?

You need food to eat. This food has to be cooked. If you want the food to be well cooked, you will have to be a good cook.

Prehistoric man did not cook food. He ate it raw. It did not matter whether he ate tender leaves, grains or berries, he knew no better way than to eat them uncooked. Even meat was eaten raw just as animals still do. But man soon realised that food tasted better, could be eaten more comfortably, and was more digestible when cooked.

Earlier, cooking was very basic. It involved boiling or cooking food directly on an open fire. The addition of salt or a few herbs (which started much later) enhanced the taste. Today, cooking is far more complicated. The modern man is very fussy about his food. Therefore, each and every homemaker or anybody else who wants to enjoy good food needs to learn cooking.

Who make better cooks, men or women?

The answer to this is 'both'. Women handle the bulk of cooking in their homes, and are also traditionally responsible for cooking. Men dominate the scene at the institutional level. Some of the finest chefs in the hotels, all over the world, are men. With the changing scene at the workplace where both men and women work, it is better that both are well acquainted with cooking techniques.

In the traditional joint family everyone learnt from each other. Food habits and knowledge

were passed on from one generation to the other. With the joint family being replaced by the nuclear family, most young girls and brides are deprived of the vast knowledge of cooking that could have easily been learnt from the elders.

This course is a sincere effort to benefit those who have not yet been initiated into the art of cooking.

This do-it-yourself course is for those who need to cook but are unaware of the technicalities involved. It is also for those who are acquainted with the art of cooking but are keen on improving their skills. Since cookery is a subject with no end, and new ideas emerge everyday, much can be learnt by new and old alike constantly.

How will this course help me?

This is a practical course in cookery. We will take you through a vast field of knowledge within the next thirty days. But just as you cannot learn to drive a car by reading a book, you cannot learn to cook just by browsing through the course. At every step, we will give you practical assignments. Please do not skip them. If you do, you are taking shortcuts. They seem good, but can take you to a wrong destination.

Do not hurry with the reading material. Unless you have the basic knowledge, very often you will be faced with wrong results when you start cooking a dish. Once you have your fundamentals right, you will not need the recipes. You will be creating new dishes on your own.

From time to time, we will be providing you with ideas and hints. Take special note of them. They have helped in reducing cooking problems for others. You, too, will benefit from them.

Our purpose is to familiarise you with the basics of cooking. We would like to help you build self-confidence. We do not promise to make you an expert overnight. But we can assure you that you can become a great cook gradually.

How will the course make me a great cook?

People often wonder why one becomes a great cook and the other remains ordinary, despite all the efforts and work. You do not need an answer. Just look around yourself. You will find mediocre people in every field. It is not that they cannot become great in their work. They simply lack commitment and dedication and belief in their own abilities. They get what they believe in – mediocrity!

So, one thing is clear that to become an expert, one needs to develop self-confidence. Just as a little baby does not start running soon after birth, you cannot develop this confidence overnight. One gains confidence from doing small things successfully. Nothing succeeds like success. Each success prepares you for a bigger success until you reach your goal.

Understanding the need for nutrition

The human body is a complex structure that requires a variety of food to meet its nutritional requirements such as carbohydrates, proteins, fats, minerals and vitamins.

Carbohydrates appease hunger. We get them through sugar and starchy food such as rice, flour and also from some root vegetables such as potatoes and beetroot.

Proteins help us grow. They replenish worn out tissues and build muscles. They also appease hunger. We obtain our need for protein from milk and milk products, pulses and legumes such as pulses, grams and peas, and from animal food such as eggs, meat, fish, etc.

Fats are a rich source of energy. Since our system can utilise them only in small quantities, we consume them in form of butter, and as a cooking medium such as ghee or vegetable oils.

'You can do it if you believe that you can!'

Dry Fruits

Vitamins and minerals are required in very small quantities. They are very important for maintaining good health and are available in cereals, vegetables and fruits. We could easily fulfil our daily needs from these sources, but many times they are lost in cooking. While minerals are referred to by their chemical names, the vitamins have alphabetic names such as A, B, C, etc. It is important that our daily diet contains minerals and vitamins because they influence some intricate functions in the body. Vitamins are either water-soluble, or fat-soluble. For obvious reasons they cannot be stored in the body and must be provided daily. The B and C group of vitamins are water-soluble. They must form a part of the daily diet to keep one healthy.

The human body follows an intricate mechanism. It requires a certain amount of energy to keep the main functions in good order. Even when we are sleeping, and not indulging in physical activity, we are still consuming some amount of energy. We require more energy when we think, work and do other things. Whatever we do, energy is used.

For convenience; this energy is calculated in Calories. Calorie is heat required to raise the temperature of one cubic centimeter of water by one degree centigrade. Thousand such calories represent one Calorie as used in dietary calculations.

'You are what you eat'

An average man requires 2000 to 3000 calories per day. An average woman requires 1800 to 2700 calories. An average child requires 1500 calories. The requirement varies with the amount of physical activity done by different persons. While a person with a sedentary lifestyle will require fewer calories, a person who does manual labour will require a greater amount. Teenagers and growing children may require more than a manual labourer because they need energy not only to meet the normal daily requirements, but also to build bones, muscles and fat.

Proteins should form an important part of the meal. Carbohydrates should be taken in proportion to the physical work put in everyday. Fat should be consumed in small quantity as a cooking medium. Minerals and vitamins can be taken in the form of fruits and vegetables. They should form the main part of the meal. This is important because the intestines require roughage to function well.

We cannot weigh and analyse all the food we eat. We can only eat according to our appetite. If a balanced meal is eaten, and one is able to maintain a steady weight, it may be understood that the food consumed is right. If one tends to put on weight, one may need to change the diet by cutting down on calories. Excess energy is stored as fat. If one feels tired, irritated, more prone to sickness accompanied by a general feeling of fatigue, the chances are that the diet is not balanced. There may be a need to add more protein, or supplement it with vitamins, particularly the water-soluble vitamins B and C.

THE LIKING AND TASTE FOR FOOD

For food preferences, you must understand that like other habits, individuals develop distinct food habits. They like or dislike food mentally according to the likes or dislikes in their childhood. It is, therefore, necessary that children should be taught to try variety of food, even though they may develop special preferences. People who have travelled widely, will tell you that there are regional and national preferences for different kinds of food. Both rice and wheat are cooked in innumerable ways all over the world. The variety of cooking should not disconcert you but challenge you just as it has challenged people all over the world.

Your immediate concern while cooking should be the preference of food items of the people for whom you are cooking. When eating, people forget the nutritional aspects. Their appetite and senses of sight, smell and taste guide them. To attract one immediately, the dish must delight one mentally and visually. It is for this reason that presentation of food is given great emphasis. Many times the presentation of food scores over its taste. The aroma of the food is next to set the salivary glands flowing. With the mouth watering, the desire for food increases. Finally, when the food comes in contact with the taste buds in the mouth, the cooking receives the final approval.

THE SPIRITUAL ASPECT OF FOOD

Kadha Prasad

There is yet another aspect of cooking that you must understand. You can call it the spiritual aspect. If every human being is connected to the great spirit called God, then every human being is a part of Him. Therefore, when one cooks for the family, one is actually cooking for the children of God. While cooking if one remembers this then he/she is not simply cooking but is preparing *'Prasad'* – an offering for God. This ensures cleanliness and wholesome fare. Those who eat it as *'prasad'* offered to God, benefit equally from the spiritual nutrition.

Even in the ***Bhagavad Gita;*** food is mentioned as being *Sattvic, Rajasic* and *Tamasic*. While *Sattvic* food is desired and consumed by those of noble thoughts and actions, *Rajasic* food is attractive to worldly people with taste and position.*Tamasic* food is for crude and base people.

STEPPING STONES TO SUCCESS

Finally, a few words of caution: You are on your way to become a great cook. Sometimes, if you slip, do not loose confidence. Making mistakes is a part of life. Take them in your stride. When Edison, the greatest inventor of all times, after having failed to make the incandescent bulb after 2000 trials, was asked what he had gained from his futile effort, he simply said, "I have found 2000 ways that do not work." You may not need to persevere that hard. Mistakes should not be a deterrent to further action. They should be stepping stones to success. Every mistake is an added experience. We see it everyday. Cooking is no exception.

INDIAN CUISINE

Indian cuisine is rich in diversity and variety because of its rich cultural heritage. In the process of evolution, different groups, particularly the Mughals and the British have influenced it greatly. Indian cooking can basically be divided into four categories: northern, eastern, western and southern.

Each region has its distinct flavour and specialities. Regional spices and condiments have lent them their distinct identity.

1. *Murg Badami*

North is identifiable with spicy-rich food. Baked tandoori rotis and naans, shallow and deep-fried plain and stuffed parathas and puris are eaten with *Butter Chicken* and *Shahi Paneer*. The legacy of the exotic food of *Nawabi Dastarkhan* is a part of the rich heritage.[1*]

2. *Machh Bhat*

Fish and rice form the staple diet of people in **East**. These are combined with deep-fried vegetable preparations and *paneer* based desserts that are famous all over.[2*]

3. *Poha*

Western India has earned a distinction for its tangy and spicy fast food called *chaat*, which is an assortment of various spices and toppings. *Pao-Bhaji*, which is bread-like buns fried in butter and eaten with mashed vegetables, cooked in butter and spices, is very popular. In several areas the simultaneous use of salt and sugar is notable. There is an assortment of regional sweetmeats to choose from.[3*]

4. *Idli Sambhar*

Tamarind, coconut and rice are indispensable to **South Indian** cuisine. The food is hot and tangy. Go to any part of India and you will surely find South Indian specialities such as *Dosa, Idli, Sambhar* and *Vada*, etc.[4*]

Though there are distinct and marked regional differences in the cuisine, the basic Indian food consists of dals, vegetables, rice, chapatti or roti, yogurt and fruits. The method of cooking varies from one region to another.

Wheat is the staple food of north. Rice is the popular cereal in southern and eastern India. In West, both rice and wheat are consumed. Wheat flour is used to prepare roti, paratha and puri. The use of bread is popular all over India because of the British influence. Rice is usually boiled or steamed and then consumed. Both wheat and rice are used to make snacks and sweets. As a meal, they are served with dals, vegetables, yogurt, pickle, chutney and *papad*. Non-vegetarian dishes are equally popular. They are prepared in various forms and eaten with keen interest with wheat and rice preparations.

Practical things to be done

As we said earlier, this is a practical course. So let us answer the following questions by ticking one of the options:

1. I firmly resolve to become:
   - ❑ A cook.
   - ❑ A great cook.
   - ❑ An expert cook.
2. To remind myself of my resolution I will:
   - ❑ Place it on a tent card on my table.
   - ❑ Paste it on the mirror in my room.
   - ❑ Think about it.
3. To look like a great cook:
   - ❑ I already have a cook's apron.
   - ❑ I will get one today.
   - ❑ I will think about it.
4. Go to the market. Look around the shops of vegetable and fruit vendors. Can you notice the variation in quality? Can you choose the fresh from the stale?
   - ❑ Yes
   - ❑ No
   - ❑ May be

PURCHASING FOOD ITEMS

In the next thirty days we will be discussing a lot about food, and various cooking styles. Before you begin to cook, you need to buy the ingredients required to prepare the dish. We will discuss the qualities of individual ingredients as we come to the relevant parts of the course. However, here are a few suggestions that you must keep in mind.

1. Buy your requirements from one or two reliable stores. When you buy from different stores, you cannot be too sure about the quality. The quality of ingredients finally decides the quality of the dish you cook.
2. Buy some of your requirements on a monthly basis. This way you keep a check on both the consumption and the expenses. You can immediately pinpoint any wastage.
3. When you go out to buy household requirements, do not rely upon guesswork. Check your store. Make a list of what you require. When you enter a store with a list, the salesman knows that you mean business. He gives you prompt attention.
4. When in a store, look out for new ideas and new products. Progress depends upon innovation. Do not be hasty in buying. First be convinced by its utility and then buy.
5. Do not always accept the salesman's recommendations about new products. He may be offering it to you because he gets a better margin. Buy what you need. Use your judgement before trying a new product.
6. Vegetables and fruits are best bought fresh. It may not be practical to buy them daily. Buy according to your need. Store appropriately in a refrigerator to avoid spoilage.
7. Buying fruits and vegetables is an art. Do not buy them from anyone and anywhere. At the market check the quality at various shops. You will soon realise why quality is important.
8. Milk and milk products have a short life. Buy only as much as you require. Store in a refrigerator.
9. Buy meat, chicken and fish from a reliable butcher's shop. Patronise a single shop and you will get the right quality.
10. Store meat, chicken and fish in a deep freezer as they have a shorter shelf life.

DAY 01

Planning a Meal

Before we get down to practical cooking, there are a few other considerations that need to be understood. We have discussed the nutritional aspects of food and the constituents of food i.e. carbohydrates, proteins, fats, vitamins and minerals. We also discussed that the energy in the food is calculated in calories. Ideally, a nutritionist can plan a meal that is near perfect. However, individuals are governed by the taste for food developed in childhood, and by their appetites that vary from one day to another. It is, therefore, important for the cook to delve deeper into the intricacies of each meal.

Digestibility:

Some food items are easily digestible compared to others. Cooking helps make many food items easily digestible, particularly with the addition of condiments and spices.

Variety:

Cooking enables a person to present food in different ways. Rice and wheat, two staple items of food all over the world, have literally been cooked and presented in hundreds of ways. It is the same with other food items as well.

Nutritive value:

A good cook appreciates the nutritive value of all kinds of food, and ensures that there is least loss of nutritive value while cooking. In many cases, cooking enhances the nutritive value by making it easily digestible.

Safety:

Food is a source of good nutrition not only for human beings, but also for a variety of bacteria and other disease causing organisms. During cooking, the bacteria and harmful organisms are killed due to the heating involved in the process.

A WELL-PLANNED MEAL

A satisfying well-planned meal must be:

- Attractive
- Delicious
- Nutritious

Since carbohydrates, proteins and fats are all good sources of energy, it would appear that one could derive energy from any of these forms. However, in reality, it is not so. The body has complex requirements, and to fulfil those, one needs to eat a balanced diet which constitutes a mixture of carbohydrates, proteins and fats along with the necessary vitamins and minerals. Besides these; a certain amount of bulk is important to keep the bowels functioning well.

While planning a meal, the cook needs to understand all these factors. Sugar, starches and cereals constitute carbohydrates. All kinds of meat, eggs, pulses and cheese constitute proteins. Butter, ghee, lard and cooking oils constitute fats. Vitamins and minerals come partly from the cereals and fats, but a major source is fresh fruits and vegetables. Milk is a complete food, and has a little of all these.

To make it easier for the cook to plan a meal, we can divide our food into four distinct groups:

- Cereals
- Meat and pulses
- Vegetables and fruits
- Milk and milk products

Cereals: Rice and wheat form the staple diet of people all over the world. These two cereals have literally been converted into thousands of food items that are eaten at all times of the day. Maize, sorghum and other cheaper varieties are no less important than food. From the morning 'bowl of cereals' to roti, puri, paratha, and a variety of biscuits, cookies, breads and cakes are all made from cereals.

Meat and Pulses: The body muscles require protein that comes from all kinds of meats including poultry, fish and seafood. The vegetarians derive their requirement of protein from legumes and pulses. Soyabeans, peanuts and a variety of other nuts are also rich in protein. All over the world, at least one item from the protein group along with cereal, is included in the meal.

Vegetables and Fruits: Every meal must have as many vegetables and fruits as possible. These not only provide the much-needed vitamins and minerals to the body, but also provide bulk. A large part of these is cellulose, which is indigestible. It helps keep the bowel movements regular, and the intestines clear. A regular intake of vegetables and fruits keeps the skin clear and bright.

Milk and Milk Products: Milk is a complete food in itself. An infant depends entirely upon it. Milk is used to prepare innumerable delicacies. However, milk in its natural form, as whole milk, toned milk, low fat milk, skimmed milk, dried milk and condensed milk continues to be popular. Yogurt, ice cream and cold desserts using milk still remains everyone's favourite.

After understanding the four groups of food, and their nutritional value, it becomes easier to plan the meals by including food from each of the four groups everyday. This ensures balanced nutrition.

To understand this concept of planning meals, look at any typical Indian meal. There will be a cereal dish of wheat (roti, puri or paratha) or rice, a dish of meat or pulses, at least one vegetable dish, some salad and yogurt or any other milk product. If one item is missing in one meal, it might be made up at another. For example, some do not like yogurt, but may drink milk with cereal at breakfast or buttermilk with a meal. Another consideration for planning a meal is the different meals that one consumes everyday. In general, everyone has three meals a day: **Breakfast, Lunch, Dinner.**

Breakfast from Different Regions of India

This is the first meal of the day. Since the gap between dinner and breakfast is almost twelve hours, it is advisable to have a good breakfast. Soon after breakfast, one sets out for work. If you have eaten well, you will be in a good mood and shall keep going for a long time. This meal varies from home to home. While some prefer to eat a regular meal with roti and vegetables, many like parathas or *puri-aloo*. Cereals and milk, bread, butter and eggs are favourite in some homes. In South, *idli* or *dosa* are preferred for breakfast.

Indian Style Lunch

Most people prefer a light lunch. Men are mostly out at work, therefore prefer a quick bite. Even those at home have a light meal of rice and dal, or roti and some vegetables. All over the world, sandwiches, soups, salads and items like rolls and frankies dominate the scene at lunchtime.

Stuffed Paratha and Dahi

Upma

Dalia

Puri Sabji

Chana Bhatoora

Khatta Meetha Kaddu and Roti

Paneer and Fruit Salad

Matar Pulao

Continental Dinner

This is the main meal where all the members of the family get an opportunity to sit and eat together. This is a heavy meal with almost all the four groups of food served. Since digestion requires time, it is advisable that one should not eat dinner late. When taken early, it gives time for the body to digest the food and one can sleep comfortably afterwards.

Continental Dinner

Chicken Kebab

Fruit Cream

Spinach and Mushroom Salad

Grilled Chicken pattice

French Onion Soup

COOKING METHOD # 1

In between these three main meals, people take beverages such as tea and coffee with some sweet and salty savouries. In summers, cold drinks substitute for tea and coffee.

Water, Heat and Steam

All of us are aware of the need for clean water for cooking. Water, as we see, does not directly cook food. Besides helping in washing food items, to get rid of extraneous matter that may carry disease germs, water is used to help soak food items such as rice, legumes and pulses to swell them for softening easily while cooking. Use of water in cooking helps distribute salt and sugar uniformly. It also helps in even distribution of heat to cook the food uniformly.

Adding heat makes water an important cooking medium. It is used for poaching, stewing, simmering and boiling a variety of food items. Eggs are both poached and boiled. So is fish. Legumes and pulses and many other food needs to be simmered to soften and then cooked. Water and heat together help soften and cook vegetables, meat and poultry.

Steam adds further benefits to water as a cooking medium. Steam at 100°C is a stronger cooking medium than water at 100°C, as additional heat is required to convert the boiling water at 100°C to steam at 100°C. Steam penetrates deeper, helps food soften and speeds up cooking. Covering the pan helps generating and accumulating steam. The use of a pressure cooker has made steam a safe and convenient way of cooking. Steam is used to cook all kinds of food. Food like *idli* and *dhokla* are totally dependent upon steam.

Cooking Method # 1.1

Steaming:

This means cooking with steam, either with or without pressure. Steam cooks faster than boiling water because it contains more heat. When steam is under pressure, the temperature increases to 250°F, and cooking is even more rapid. Steaming vegetables is an excellent way to retain colour, flavour, and nutrients without the use of any fat.

A few tips to follow while steaming:

Place the steaming-basket in a pot with a little boiling water and cover. Cook until the vegetables are just tender. Alternatively, place the food in the separator of a pressure cooker. Place the grid in the cooker; pour in one-cup water, place the separator on the grid and close the lid placing the weights on. Steam.

Watch the cooking time carefully to prevent overcooking the food. If cooking in a pressure cooker, follow the instructions given in the instruction manual for cooking different kind of food.

Cooking Method # 1.2

Boiling:

To cook by boiling, we need to bring the liquid to a boiling point. Food to be boiled is then lowered into it. This method is used for boiling rice, noodles, pasta, lobsters, crabs and starchy or root vegetables such as potatoes, turnips, corn cobs, pre-soaked beans or chick peas (*kabuli chana*), etc.

A few tips to follow while boiling:

The liquid left after boiling can become a tasty broth soup, base for a sauce, used in curries or used to knead *atta* (dough) for chapatti or paratha.

Keep a watch so that the liquid does not boil over.

Once the liquid reaches boiling point, the flame can be reduced and that saves fuel.

Cooking Method # 1.3

Simmering:

It means cooking in a liquid that has just boiled and has bubbles rising slowly to the surface. Examples of simmered food include soups, sauces and stews.

A few tips to follow while simmering:

Bring the liquid to a boil, then reduce the heat to simmer.

Watch closely so that it does not boil over.

Stir frequently for even cooking.

Cooking Method # 1.4

Poaching:

It means to cook in a hot liquid that is bubbling on the bottom of the pan but is otherwise calm. This liquid may be chicken stock, meat or fish stock, vegetable stock, water or dry white wine. Examples are, poached eggs or fish.

A few tips to follow while poaching:

Never let the liquid boil.

The liquid should just cover the food.

The poaching pan or pot should be partially uncovered so that the steam can escape and the liquid does not simmer or boil.

Cooking Method # 1.5

Braising:

This is cooking food in a small amount of liquid, in a covered container at a low heat of 300°F to 350°F. It is a combination of baking and steaming. It is used mainly for meat that needs longer cooking time to become tender. The amount of liquid will vary, but it often covers from one-third to two-third of the food. The part of the food that is uncovered, is cooked by hot-steamy air in the covered container. You can braise food in a covered container placed in the range or in the oven. Oven braising tends to cook more evenly. We cook most of our food by this method on the cooking range. Braised food includes pot roast, stew and braised vegetables.

A few tips to follow while braising:

Braised meat is usually seared or browned first. Brown in a small amount of oil or its own fat.

For more flavour, simmer meat in meat or poultry broth, wine or a combination of both. Add vegetables and herbs for an aromatic blend of flavours without salt.

The longer the food cooks, the more tender it will be.

Stir frequently.

If braising meat or poultry, do it one day before it is served. You can refrigerate it overnight and remove the fat that congeals on top.

Day 02

Rice

So far we have been discussing some of the basics of cooking. Since it is a vast subject, we will resume our discussion later. This is a practical course in cookery, so, let us get down to it. Nothing gladdens the heart more than having cooked a dish well. It makes one happy to see the appreciation on the faces around you.

Some Basic Facts About Rice

Rice is the staple diet of more than half of the world's population. Wheat follows it, as the next most important food item in cereal.

It is commonly believed that rice was known and cultivated in China more than 3000 years ago. However, later, researchers established that the rice plant may have originated in Southern India and, thereafter, it spread gradually across the globe.

Rice grows as paddy. When the husk, which accounts for almost 25 percent of the weight of the paddy, is removed, we get a grain covered with a light brown fine covering. This is removed by polishing the rice. The light brown coating is rich in oil and protein. After removing the oil through a solvent process, the de-oiled bran is used as cattle and poultry feed. What we see in market is the polished rice.

The rice sold in the market is either raw or parboiled. Raw rice is obtained by removing the husk from the paddy and then polished. The broken portion of rice is sieved out. New rice is white in colour but with age, it turns creamy.

Parboiled rice is obtained first by steeping the paddy in water for a few days and then subsequently boiling it. It is then dried and milled to obtain parboiled rice. This process toughens the outside of the rice grain. There is lesser breakage during milling and polishing processes. Parboiled rice is translucent and cooks better. Almost half the rice available in the market is parboiled rice.

From the nutrition point of view, brown rice (unpolished rice) is the best. However, it is sticky to cook and not attractive to look at. It is not as tasty as the polished rice. Nutritive value of raw and parboiled rice is similar. Rice contains Vitamin K, which is lost during washing and cooking of the grain. The rice we eat is about 78 percent starch and 7 percent protein. The rest is moisture and a little fat, ash and fibre.

Kinds of Rice

We have already discussed that rice could be raw milled or parboiled. Rice is graded according to the length and thickness of the grain. It is classified as long-grain, medium-grain and short-grain rice.

The narrow kernel easily identifies **long-grain rice**, which is four to five times as long as it is wide. It becomes longer when soaked; tender and fluffy when cooked and the grains are separated. Some varieties have a wonderful aroma. The longer and finer varieties sell at a higher rate.

Among the aromatic varieties of long-grain rice, **Basmati rice** is highly priced. It is popular for making *pulaos* and biryanis. It is grown in the foothills of the Himalayas. Aging improves the flavour of this variety. It must be soaked before cooking. The grains swell and become manageable to stand cooking.

The substitution of one variety of rice for another generally causes no problems but long-grain or medium-grain rice should never be substituted for short-grain. This is because certain recipes require specific variety of rice.

When cooked, almost all varieties of rice swell to twice its size. The volume depends on the variety and the age of the rice. Aged rice absorbs more moisture than the freshly harvested one. New rice is white, requires less water to cook, but tends to stick on account of the presence of an enzyme. This enzyme becomes ineffective when rice is aged.

Rice must be cleaned and washed before cooking. However, not all the rice require being soaked before it is cooked, unless the recipe demands it. Aged rice must be soaked. All methods of cooking rice release starch. This can cause the grains to stick together. When a fluffy rather than a creamy texture is required, some recipes may ask you to rinse and drain the rice thoroughly after cooking.

RICE IN EVERYDAY COOKING

Perhaps no other food item has been cooked and used as food in as many ways and varieties as rice is. As one travels around the world, one can see it in innumerable forms. It is good food any time of the day.

Rice is always eaten cooked. It may be served either hot or cold. Here are a few popular preparations of rice we come across in everyday life.

- **Rice as whole grain:** Served boiled or steamed, as *pulao*, biryani, *khichdi* and *kheer*.
- **Wet ground rice:** Used to make *dosa*, *idli* and *cheela*.
- **Dry ground rice:** Used to make rice *poli* and *phirni*.
- **Rice flakes:** Used as breakfast cereal, *poha* and *chewda*.
- **Puffed rice**: Used as breakfast cereal and in a variety of snacks.

STORING RICE

Rice can be stored in airtight containers at room temperature up to one year. Buying and storing rice depends entirely on the space available. Many people believe in bulk buying whenever prices are low. Rice is one of the easiest grains to store. But with constraints of space in all homes, buying 15-20 kilograms of rice at a time is advisable. Buy the best quality that you can afford. In most homes, two varieties are purchased, one for everyday use and the other for special occasions.

Clockwise: Rice, Rice Flakes, Dry Ground Rice, Puffed Rice

Medium-grain rice is shorter, but as thin as the longer varieties. This variety is commonly used for everyday cooking. Basmati and the longer varieties are reserved for special occasions.

Short-grain rice, often referred to as pearls, is short and plump. It contains more starch than the other two varieties. When cooked, it becomes quite sticky. Although eaten as boiled rice by most people, it is the perfect choice for puddings and *kheer*.

COOKING RICE

Rice can be cooked in a number of mediums such as water, meat or vegetable stock, oil or milk. The art of cooking rice is to ensure that the grains remain firm and separated. Except pre-treated and pre-cooked rice, all rice should be washed thoroughly in running water and drained properly before cooking. Rice can be cooked in a variety of ways. Though we will take up each recipe in detail later on, let us discuss the basic methods.

BOILING RICE

The cleaned and washed rice is poured into an open vessel containing two or three times its volume of boiling water. It is then brought back to

Boiling Rice

Rice on Boiling Point

Rice Being Strained

Boiled Rice

boil, cooked uncovered and then drained. To test if the rice is done, take a ladle or fork and dip it into the boiling rice to bring out a grain. Gently press this grain between your thumb and index finger. If you are able to crush it completely, the rice is done.

Place a lid over the vessel, and hold the lid and the vessel together. Tilt it gradually over the kitchen sink to drain out all the liquid. Then, gently toss the vessel a few times to separate the grains.

Alternatively, you could use a large colander with a fine mesh to drain out the water from the rice. Though, getting it back into a serving dish may prove a little difficult.

You could also use two cloth clips, the kind you use to hang out your washed clothes, to secure the lid to the vessel while draining the rice. This will do away with the juggling act you have to perform keeping the lid tight on the vessel to prevent the rice grains from falling out.

Note: Always use kitchen gloves to keep from burning your finger. A kitchen hand towel could also serve as well.

Steaming Rice

This could be done in a heavy-bottomed cooking pan, an electric rice steamer or a pressure cooker. If you are using a heavy-bottomed cooking pan, pour the cold water of double the volume of rice; place cleaned and washed rice into the vessel; bring the rice and water to a boiling point and then lower the heat. Allow the contents to simmer, the pan should be firmly covered till the liquid is completely absorbed. Toss the pan a couple of times to separate the grains.

When using a steamer, the washed rice is placed in the steamer over boiling water for 20-30 minutes, depending on the variety of rice used.

In a pressure cooker, steam the rice in the cooker or in the separator specially designed for the purpose. The water should cover 1½ inch above the rice. The pressure is allowed to rise. After two whistles, switch off the heat. Allow the cooker to cool. When you use a separator in the cooker, the procedure to be followed is the same.

Boiling and steaming are the common methods used for preparing rice for a normal family meal. Fried rice, *pulaos*/biryanis and desserts such as

Clockwise: Soaked Rice, Steaming Rice, Cumin and Fried Onion Added, Cooked Steamed Rice

kheer and *phirni* are cooked on special occasions. We will learn about them a little later.

How much to cook?

All new cooks often wonder what would be an appropriate quantity to cook. Given below are portions required for each adult for different items.

Main dish – boiled or steamed rice	60-70 gm or 1/2 cup
Pulao, biryani, fried rice	40 gm or 1/3 cup
Kheer, phirni, zarda, sweet pulao	20-25 gm or 2 tablespoons
Dosa, idli	25-30 gm or 1/4 cup

Rice Preparations

Steamed and boiled rice is served with dal, curried vegetables or meat, fish, eggs or poultry, dry vegetable preparations, salad, curd, pickles and *papads*.

Fried rice, *pulao* and biryanis are ideally served with salad and curd (yogurt) preparations such as raitas.

Sweet preparations such as *kheer*, *phirni* and *zarda* are served as desserts, after the main meal, mostly on special occasions.

Here are some useful tips for cooking rice:

- Cook rice in the end. It tastes the best when served hot.
- While boiling or steaming rice, add a pinch of salt and a tsp of vegetable oil or ghee to it. The salt adds flavour and whitens the rice grains and the oil will ensure that the grains do not stick together.
- If the rice is excessively boiled or is sticky, rinse it in cold running water. Drain well. Toss in a vessel with the lid on. This will wash away the stickiness and separate the grains.

Setting Faults Right

If your rice is undercooked, follow any of these instructions:

- Put the rice in the separator of a pressure cooker; place the grid in the cooker body; pour in a cup of water; cover the separator with aluminium foil and steam the rice till one whistle. Let the cooker cool and remove the separator. Your rice will be done.
- Steam in a covered vessel over boiling water for 5 minutes.
- Place the rice in an ovenproof casserole and cover with aluminium foil. Place it in a moderately hot oven: 100–150°F for 5 minutes. Switch off the oven but let the dish stand for 5 minutes in the oven and then remove it. Keep the foil on till served.

Cooking Utensils

In most Indian homes a **cooking vessel** (*pateela*) or a **pressure cooker** is most commonly used to cook rice. It is preferable that the cooking vessel is heavy-bottomed. Stainless steel is the best but brass or aluminium ones are also commonly used.

Pressure cookers of all kinds are also suitable for making rice.

Rice cookers are popular in homes where rice is cooked frequently for 6 to 8 persons.

Steamers are specially designed twin-containers, one fitting into the other. The larger one holds the water while the smaller one, having a fine mesh, holds the rice grains. It has a fitted lid.

Fancy Rice Preparations

Although, majorly rice is eaten boiled, or steamed, it can be cooked in a variety of fancy items such as *pulaos* and biryanis, and cooked in combination with a variety of vegetables, pulses and meat. It is also used to make snacks. Cooks around the world have used their imagination in presenting rice in innumerable forms. Look out for others to see how they innovate. Try your own ways.

Practical things to be done

1. Boiling Rice

Utensils used: 1 cup, a large tray, a bowl for washing and soaking rice, an open cooking pan with a lid, a ladle or a large spoon.

Portion: ½ cup rice per person. We are cooking for two.

To boil rice, follow this simple procedure:

1. Take 1 cup rice in a tray. Push all the rice to one side of the tray. Taking a small portion at a time, spread it out in the centre. Pick up the stones or dirt if any. Repeat the process till you have cleaned up all the rice.
2. Place the rice in enough water in a bowl; gently rub them with your fingers to shake off the dirt; drain the cloudy water and repeat the washing process till the water runs clear.
3. Soak rice in double the volume of water for 30 minutes or a little more. All long-grained rice must be soaked before cooking. Use clean drinking water to cook the rice.
4. Pour rice and water into the cooking pan. Add a pinch of salt and half a tsp of any vegetable oil or ghee.

5. Place the cooking pan on the gas. Bring it to a boiling point on high flame and let it boil uncovered till the water reaches the level of the rice and then reduce the flame.
6. Stir rice occasionally, otherwise the grains will be sticky. One cup of rice should take about 10-12 minutes to cook. With a ladle or big spoon, take out a grain of rice; press it between your thumb and index finger to test if it is done.
7. Place the lid over the cooking pan. Holding the lid and the cooking pan, tilt it over the kitchen sink to drain out all the liquid. Alternatively, you can drain it through a fine mesh of a colander.
8. With the lid on, toss the rice a couple of times to ensure that the grains separate nicely. Your rice is ready to be served.

TIPS: To reheat leftover rice, put in a pan that fits into a pressure cooker. Pour a cup of water into the cooker. Put the lid on without the weight. As soon as steam comes out of the snout of the cooker, switch off the heat. Your rice will once again be like freshly cooked rice.

2. Steamed Rice

Utensils used: In addition to the ones used for boiling rice, a griddle or *tawa* is used here.

Portions: The same as for the boiled rice.

To steam rice, follow this simple procedure:

1. Clean and soak the rice as mentioned earlier.
2. Pour the rice and water into the pan. Place on the gas stove. Bring to a boil, keeping the pan half covered.
3. As soon as the water rises to the level of the rice, reduce the flame. Cover the pan completely. Put the *tawa* under the pan.
4. Cook on low heat for about 12-15 minutes or till the rice is done. Open the lid. You will see small holes on the surface of the rice.
5. Fluff up the rice with a fork using a light hand and serve it hot. Reheat if required.

Expert cook suggests...

1. When storing large quantities of rice, add one gram of boric powder for every kilogram of rice. This keeps the insects away.
2. Add two bay leaves when boiling rice, it will impart a fine aroma.
3. For fluffier rice, add a tsp of vinegar to the boiling water.
4. Add a few drops of lemon juice to rice to avoid stickiness.
5. When rice becomes too soft, allow it to cool. Grind in an electric mixer; add chopped onions, minced fresh coriander, green chillies, salt, pepper and a little lemon juice; mix; divide into equal portions; form flat '*tikkies*'; roll in breadcrumbs and deep fry. Serve hot.

Day 03

Wheat and Wheat Products

Next to rice, wheat is the most important cereal used all over the world to make a wide variety of items. It is the staple source of carbohydrates for most people. It was a little known in southern and eastern India until the shortage of rice compelled people to turn to it as food. Wheat flour is widely used to make rotis, naans, puris and parathas. Refined flour is used to make all kinds of breads, biscuits, cookies, cakes and a variety of sweets.

Wheat is a hard, light brown grain. If one removes the thin outer covering, we see the inside grain which is white. The outer covering is called bran. It is rich in protein, fibres and ash, and is used as cattle feed. The white inner grain is grounded to be made into refined flour that is used for human consumption in a variety of ways.

After the wheat grain is ground, the flour is sieved to separate the bran. The rest is used as flour. This way the finer bran would also be sieved as part of the flour, and though nutritious, it gives its light brownish colour to the flour. To overcome this, wheat millers now polish the wheat grain just as rice grains are polished. This removes the bran, leaving behind the white grain, which is then grounded into flour. This flour is white, but not as nutritious as the conventional flour.

Wheat is used in everyday cooking

Wheat is not used as bran and flour only. Coarsely crushed, baked or cooked, wheat is used as nutritious porridge and as puffed grains as breakfast cereal. Besides the conventional flour used in everyday cooking, the coarser flour known as semolina (*sooji*) is used for making *halwa* and other sweet dishes. The finest flour (refined flour, also known as baker's flour) is used for making biscuits, cookies and cakes. You will soon realise that wheat has innumerable uses for preparing food items.

- **Broken wheat grains:** Cooked to make porridge (*daliya*), *kheer*, *upma*, and *khichdi*.
- **Coarse wheat flour (*sooji, rawa*):** Cooked to make *upma*, *idli*, *halwa*, *dosa*, and *kheer*.
- **Wheat flour:** Cooked to make roti, chapatti, puri, paratha, tandoori roti, and *halwa*.
- **Fine wheat flour (*maida*):** Cooked to make *luchi*, naan, *kulcha*, *bhatura*, *jalebi*, and a variety of biscuits, cakes and snacks.

Nutritional value of wheat

The wheat grain constitutes of three distinct portions. The light brown outer layer (bran), the inner white grain (endosperm) and the wheat germ (embryo), which sprouts to form the wheat plant when wheat is sown. Whereas the bran constitutes 14.5 percent of the grain, the endosperm is 83 percent, and the embryo

Clockwise: Wheat Grains, Wheat Flour, Broken Wheat, Semolina, Refined Flour

2.5 percent. The bran has high proportions of protein, fiber and ash. The endosperm is mainly starch. It is poor in protein. The embryo is rich in protein, fat, vitamins and minerals. The bran and the embryo are the most nutritive portions of the wheat grain. Therefore, many prefer to eat flour made of the whole grain, with the least amount of bran sieved out, as bran helps in reducing constipation. This explains the popularity of brown bread.

The finer flours are mainly the endosperm portion of wheat with low quantities of vitamins and minerals.

Sprouted wheat

Sprouted wheat is also used to make flour. It is rich in proteins, vitamins and minerals. To sprout wheat, soak the required quantity of wheat for 24 hours in water; drain the water by hanging the grains in a piece of cloth; leave the grains in the cloth; and keep the cloth moist by sprinkling water on it when required. When you see little white spots on the grains, which are the germinating embryo or wheat germs, it is ready for consumption. You can consume sprouted wheat as it is, with a little salt or lemon. You may fry it for use or you may dry and pound it, and mix it with the usual wheat flour to make it more nutritious.

Storage

In many homes wheat is purchased in bulk and stored in drums or big containers for future use. When required, a portion is taken out, cleaned and milled into flour. This can be problematic as in many homes there are space constraints. Wheat attracts insects that damage it. Keeping this in mind, many prefer to buy wheat flour in smaller quantites. So it is wiser to replenish your stock of wheat flour than buying in bulk. This can solve the problem of wastage due to attack of weevils. If you are a family of four and consume more wheat in your daily diet, buy 5 kilos of flour at a time. Store it in an airtight container. Always buy freshly milled flour from a reliable store. Branded flours are more expensive, but offer good value. Buy *maida*, *sooji* and *daliya* in smaller quantites as and when required. Do not store them for longer periods.

Khaja

Basket of Phulkas

COOKING METHOD # 2

Using Flour

Like rice; rotis, puris and parathas form the staple diet in most Indian homes. Many families serve both rotis and rice together at meals. They are eaten with dals, curries, vegetables and other dishes. The basic ingredient for making rotis, puris and parathas is flour.

Apart from wheat, millets such as *jowar, bajra, makka* (corn or maize) and Bengal gram (*kala channa*) are also converted into flour and used to make roti or a variety of other items.

To convert flour into rotis, puris, parathas, etc., the flour is kneaded into dough. Of all grains, wheat is the most suitable to make dough as it contains a unique protein called gluten. This lends elasticity to the dough. Dough made out of other cereals is not elastic. Of the 10 to 13 percent protein in wheat, 8 to 10 percent is gluten. While kneading, wheat flour requires water more than half its weight. Some varieties take in as much as two-thirds of its weight. Gluten gives it the sticky, rubbery and extensible quality. Different varieties of wheat yield dough of different characteristics. This determines their suitability for making different food items.

The flour is first kneaded with water and salt into a dough of varying stiffness for various products, for example, for making chapatti/roti, a little soft and pliable dough is required, whereas for making puris, stiff dough is needed. Sometimes, the dough is kneaded along with some raw or boiled vegetables, or boiled pulses or spices to make it wholesome. The kneaded dough is then put through different processes of baking, shallow frying or deep-frying to make tastier food items.

Cooking Method # 2.1

Kneading the dough

1. Four fold a kitchen napkin on the platform and sieve 2 cups wheat flour with 1/2 tsp salt in a trough.
2. Add 1 cup water in it and mix.
3. Mix the flour and water with your fingers. Knead and gather it.

4. Knead it with your hand and the back of your fist till smooth.
5. Change its side and knead it again, form a ball and keep it covered for 30 minutes. Use it the way you want.

Roti Maker

Roti maker is a modern electric gadget for prepairing the traditional roti. It is easily available in the market. Not only it is useful in rolling out the rotis out of dough but also helps in cooking them on hot electric plate. However, do not buy one immediately. Learn how to roll out rotis with your hand. Only after you gain some experience, and feel that a Roti maker can ease your work, you should consider buying one.

Cooking Method # 2.2

Rolling the dough

Let us now take up the method of rolling out rotis from the dough.

You will need:

- A rolling board or clean working platform
- A rolling pin
- Some dry flour

Knead the dough again for half a minute. Set aside and proceed as follows:

1. Divide the dough into equal parts and roll each part into a ball. Roll it in the dry *atta* and flatten it with your fingers.
2. Place the flattened roll in the centre of the rolling board or on the platform.
3. Place the rolling pin over it and start rolling out gently, changing the sides. The dough will elongate and might stick to the pin. Pick up the dough from the board gently and dust both sides with dry flour.
4. Place it again on the rolling board and now start rolling the narrow portion of the elongated dough to get a round shape.

Using dry heat

Dry heat plays an important role in cooking. We often see roadside vendors roasting corncobs on coal cinders. At home, there is the barbeque, roasted chicken, kebabs, *paneer* and vegetables. The heat can be direct, or may be through a metal pan or griddle or *tawa*. The heat that passes through the *tawa* helps to cook chapattis. They are finally puffed up on the direct flame. Dry heat is also utilised to make rotis, naans and parathas in a tandoor, or clay oven. It is heated up, and uncooked rotis are directly placed on the hot walls until cooked. The clay oven has been replaced by an electric tandoor in the cities for convenience.

Use of dry heat for cooking has given us puffed corn, wheat, rice and soybeans. We also have roasted *chanas* or chickpeas. In the winters, roasted pistachios and peanuts are popular everywhere.

Application of heat not only helps in cooking food, but when some spices are roasted on dry heat, the heat helps generate special flavours, and many recipes recommend roasting of spices before using them to flavour food.

Cooking Method # 2.3

Making rotis

You will need:

- A *tawa*
- A clean piece of cloth or a pair of tongs

To make rotis, follow this simple procedure:

1. Heat a *tawa*/griddle over a gas stove. Keep the flame low.
2. After you have rolled out the dough, pick it up from the board and remove extra flour by placing it on your palms with your fingers stretched around the contours of the roti.

3. Transfer it gently onto the *tawa* in one go so that it falls in the centre.
4. Turn the heat to the maximum. Soon you will find tiny mounds appearing on the surface of the roti. Pick it up and turn its side.
5. When tiny mounds appear on the other side and it gets light brown marks, turn the side of roti and lower the flame. Pick it up with tongs and cook directly on the flame.
6. The roti will puff up and attain brown flecks over it. Remove the roti from the *tawa*, either serve it hot or store in a casserole lined with folded cloth to keep it warm. Repeat the process with the remaining rolled out dough.

If your rotis turn out crisp, or have a burnt texture, do not be disheartened. In the beginning, everyone is bound to make mistakes. When you persevere, you will succeed. Just keep trying. Soon you will be making excellent rotis.

Besides wheat flour, rotis can also be made from grains such as maize (*makka*), *bajra, jowar* and gram turned into flour.

TIPS After preparing rotis and parathas, it is important to keep them fresh. Even after storing them in a casserole, they turn soggy. Therefore, it is advisable to line the container (in which you are storing them) with a folded cotton cloth and then keep the rotis on it. Alternatively, you can also wrap them in aluminium foil.

Note: While deep-frying puris, *luchis* and *bhaturas*, follow a similar procedure. Roll out puris and *luchis* on the rolling board. If you find it difficult to roll out *bhaturas* with your hand, you can grease the underside of a plate. Place the roll of dough over the greased area. Spread it out with your fingertips according to the required thickness.

Or use puri maker to flatten the rolled out balls into the round discs.

Cooking Method # 2.4

Deep-frying puris

You will need :

- A *kadhai* or a deep frying pan.
- A perforated ladle with a long handle.
- Oil/ghee for frying.

To fry puris, follow this simple procedure:

1. Divide the dough into equal parts. Roll each part with the rolling pin or press it on the puri maker.
2. Pour enough ghee or oil into the *kadhai* so that the puri is able to swim well in the oil. To test if the oil is heated enough, drop 4-5 mustard seeds into the oil. If they pop and splutter, the oil is heated to the required temperature.

3. Pick up the rolled out dough into round disc from the rolling board and slide it gently into the oil from the side of the *kadhai*. The puri first goes down to the bottom, but will slowly emerge on the surface of the oil.
4. Press it gently with the perforated ladle and change its side. The puri puffs up and will turn golden brown.
5. Take it out from the oil with the perforated ladle. Let the excess oil in the puri drain off by holding it against the side of the *kadhai* and place it on the kitchen oil absorbent paper. Serve hot.

Luchis and *bhaturas* are also deep-fried the same way on the full flame. Just as practice is the only way to perfection when it comes to making rotis, it is the same for *luchis* and *bhaturas*.

Important: while frying puris, the flame should always be high.

When to prepare what?

Rotis and parathas are prepared regularly in most Indian homes. Puris and *luchis, etc.*, are heavy on the stomach and are prepared on special or festive occasions. Wheat preparations are served with dals, vegetables, meats, pickles, yogurt or raita and *papad*, etc.

The table (1.1) will give you an idea about ingredients that go into the preparation of the dough of Indian breads and also the way they are cooked.

Table 1.1

Food Item	Quantity	Required/Cooking Method
Roti – two	1 cup flour (*atta*)	Baked on *tawa*
½ cup water		
¼ tsp salt		
Paratha – three	1 cup flour (*atta*)	Shallow fried on *tawa*
½ cup water		
¼ tsp salt		
2 tbsp ghee or oil		
Tandoori Roti – two	1 cup flour (*atta*)	Baked in a clay tandoor
½ cup water		
¼ tsp salt		
2 tbsp ghee or oil		
a pinch of baking soda		
Naan – four	2 cups flour (*maida*)	Baked in a clay tandoor
½ cup warm water		
1 tsp yogurt (*dahi*)		
2 tsp ghee or oil		
¼ tsp dry yeast		
1 tsp sugar		
Puri – six	1 cup flour (*atta*)	Deep-fried in *kadhai*
½ cup water		
¼ tsp salt		
Oil for frying		
Bhatura – four	2 cups flour (*maida*)	Deep-fried in *kadhai*
½ cup warm water		
½ cup yogurt (*dahi*)		
½ tsp salt		
½ tsp baking powder		
Oil for frying		
Luchi – six	1 cup flour (*maida*)	Deep-fried in *kadhai*
½ cup warm water		
½ tsp salt		

TIPS: After kneading the dough, cover it with a moist cloth. Keep aside for 20-30 minutes. This time is known as the standing period of the dough. This helps to make dough more pliable and soft and good rotis are prepared.

In some cases, ghee/oil is mixed with the dough to lend crispness to the preparation. For making naans, dry yeast is mixed with sugar and warm water. It is allowed to rise and mixed into the flour (*maida*) to make pliable dough. The dough is left to rise again. Then shaped into naans with the hand and baked in a tandoor.

Dahi and warm water in the *bhatura* dough help the fermentation process. The dough is kept aside for few hours till it rises. It is rolled with the hands and deep-fried in a *kadhai*/deep frying pan.

Kneading can also be done with the help of a food processor. The instruction manual that comes with the equipment provides instructions for the kneading of *atta* and *maida* according to the required stiffness.

Expert cook suggests...

1. When making 'chapatti dough', use hot boiling water to mix the flour. The chapattis will turn out soft and tasty.
2. To reheat stale 'chapattis' or 'Parathas', wrap them in a clean cloth and pack into an airtight container that can fit into the pressure cooker. Pressure cook for a couple of minutes. The chapattis will be fresh.
3. To ensure that chappatis stay soft and warm for those who eat late, wrap them in a cloth and place over the rice in the pan.
4. Use whey instead of water to knead the flour for chapattis. They will taste like 'naan'.
5. Chapattis will stay soft for a long time if you mash a small boiled potato with the chapatti dough.

DAY 04

Spices, Herbs and Condiments

Spices, herbs and condiments lend Indian food an aromatic characteristic. We cook the same vegetables, meat, poultry and fish as they do elsewhere in the world, but Indian food has a distinct flavour, aroma and taste. Within the country, too, we find vegetables, pulses and non-vegetarian dishes taste different from region to region. It is the use of spices, herbs and condiments that make all the difference. While cooking food, we make an endless use of combination of flowers, leaves, seeds, roots, barks and bulbs to produce an infinite variety of flavours: spicy, hot, sour, sweet, pungent, mild, aromatic and fragrant. It is the art of using these spices that differentiates an expert cook from an ordinary one. Besides the taste, it is the preserving quality of some spices that gives them special significance. All kinds of meat and vegetables can be preserved with certain spices for fairly long periods. This gave way to the use of spices for making a variety of pickles.

It was the world of Indian spices that attracted the foreign invaders to India. In the past, large quantities of Indian spices were exported to the Middle East and the European nations.

How are Spices Obtained?

Spices are natural things like leaves, barks, buds, roots, fruits and berries. Their conversion to spices does not require special technology. Drying them in the sun, natural fermentation and grinding is all that may be required. For example, cinnamon and bay leaves (*tej patta*) are leaves; cloves are buds; *khus-khus* is obtained from poppy seed and saffron is derived from the flower. Aniseed, fennel and cardamom are fruits. Similarly, raw mango pulp and tamarind are used. Equally important are common everyday items such as onions, garlic and ginger. Turmeric, too, is a root. Asafoetida is obtained from an exudation by root incision.

What are Spices Made of?

Like all other food, spices are made up of varying quantities of carbohydrates, proteins, fats, vitamins and minerals along with a certain amount of water. Fresh herbs may have as much as 85 percent water, but the dried spices have 10 to 15 percent of water. Carbohydrates and proteins vary greatly with the type of spice. Whereas, in some products, the carbohydrates may be as high as 30 percent, in others proteins may be 15 to 20 percent. Seed based spices like mustard have a high fat content, but most of them are low in fat. The quantity of vitamins and minerals are equally variable.

What distinguishes spices, herbs and condiments from other food are their distinctive fragrant, aromatic and pungent characteristics. These are due to the presence of certain essential oils. Some spices have nonvolatile chemicals. Eg:- Red chillies – capsaicin, Pepper – piperine and charicine, Ginger – zinzerone. Some spices have a strong colour. Chillies have an orange colour due to the presence of carotene. Turmeric has curcuma which develops during the curing of the rhizome.

Saffron gets its colour from crocin, a bitter tasting sugar compound. Condiments such as tamarind, raw mango pulp and pomegranate seeds, used as souring agents, contain different acids such as tartaric acid, oxalic acid, malic acid, or hydroxy citric acid.

Nutritional value of spices

In comparison to other ingredients, spices are used in very small quantities. Therefore, their content of carbohydrates, proteins or fat has little meaning in everyday cooking. However, some of them are important, as they are rich in vitamins and minerals. Since the requirement of these is small, the role of spices is important in providing nutritional needs. The regular use of onion, garlic, ginger, turmeric, chilli powder, mustard, and curry leaves can greatly help in fulfilling this need.

Benefits of spices

Spices, herbs and condiments are useful to us in many ways:

- They improve the taste of the food.
- They make food easily digestible.
- They promote good health.
- They help preserve food.
- Many spices have medicinal qualities.

Taste of food: Ask any cooking expert if he can produce the best dishes without spices, herbs and condiments. The answer will be an emphatic 'no'. Take any food item such as rice, wheat, vegetables, non-vegetarian items, snacks or desserts, their distinctive taste can always be attributed to the use of spices, herbs and condiments.

Digestion of food: Spices promote greater flow of saliva in the mouth. This improves digestion. Many spices such as saffron and nutmeg have a distinct effect on digestion and they increase the flow of some enzymes in the small intestine. However, use of excessive chilli induces increased acidity. This can lead to gastritis and gastric ulceration.

Good health: Many spices have antiseptic qualities. They can kill bacteria and keep the mouth clean. Some of them have carminative action that helps in relieving flatulence. They mildly stimulate the heart and the lungs. Some spices such as garlic have anti-microbial and antiseptic qualities. Turmeric has anti-bacterial qualities, and promotes tissue healing. Others such as asafoetida, *ajwain*, aniseed, clove and cinnamon help reduce the flora in the large intestine.

Preservation of food: With spices, food of all descriptions can be preserved for longer periods without refrigeration. This quality of spices is responsible for the great variety of pickles that we now enjoy.

Medicinal qualities: Many spices have medicinal qualities. They are freely used in Ayurveda. They are used not only for simple ailments such as indigestion, cough and cold, but also for treatment of problems such as rheumatism, lungs and kidney ailment, and even in childbirth.

Spices in the Indian kitchen

There are more than fifty spices, herbs and condiments in common use. In any Indian kitchen, you will find about twenty-five spices on the shelf. Many of them would have come from the kitchen garden. With this huge treasure trove of flavours, one can create an infinite number of different dishes.

Spices can be used individually or in combination. They can be roasted and grounded to powder. With water, they can be made into a paste to produce a variety of flavours, from sweet to sour, fiery to bland and fragrant to pungent. Scientific research has proved that people, who enjoy a wide range of spicy food, tend to live longer than those who live on a milder diet. Spices protect against food poisoning and keep infections away. Spices such as garlic, onion, cinnamon and cumin are especially known for their antibacterial effects. Other spices with protective qualities are cloves (widely used in Chinese medicines).

Apart from their medicinal properties, spices and other condiments are useful to offset the harmful effect of extremes of temperature. In the North, warming spices take the bite out of the freezing winter days. In the South, bittersweet tamarind has a soothing effect in the airless midday heat. In everyday cooking, we use spices such as coriander, cumin, turmeric and chilli almost for every vegetarian and non-vegetarian dish. Salt and pepper are used as flavouring agents.

Homemade spices

There is nothing better than home-grounded spices. Although it increases one's work, yet the extra effort is worth, as you are sure of the quality of the spices in their pure form. No doubt, a large variety of spices are available in the market; they may look all right, but with time may lose their flavour. If you want to avoid the extra effort, and buy from the market, buy branded packaged spices. They are worth the extra cost. Check manufacturing date always. Some companies market special formulations for certain specific preparations. Try in small quantities.

Earlier, grinding of spices with a pestle and mortar was a very arduous task. With electric grinders in almost every home, it has become easier to grind your own spices and spice mixtures. Here are a few details about the popular spices, herbs and condiments:

Alkanet – the root is used for colouring

Alkanet (*Ratin jot*): Alkanet is used as food colouring agent in Kashmiri cooking. The unique feature of alkanet is that neither it dissolves in water, nor does it colour the water but once you fry it in hot oil for a while, at once it imparts its deep red colour to the oil.

Allspice

Allspice (*Kababchini*): This is a dark purple berry from a tree native to the West Indies. Once dried, it becomes brownish black, very much like black peppers, only bigger and smoother. The name is derived from its mixed flavour of cloves, cinnamon, nutmeg and black pepper. This spice is used in dishes such as biryani and kebabs.

Aniseed

Aniseed (*Vilayati saunf*): This is an oval, striped, greenish brown seed, about 2 mm long, with a tiny tail. It is used less in comparison to its cousin, the larger but less aromatic fennel seed with which it is frequently confused. Aniseed is an important ingredient in dishes requiring an aromatic flavour. It is also used in the *supari* (mouth freshner) mixture chewed after meals.

Asafoetida / Asafetida (*Hing*): It is a root exudate and has a strong pungent flavour. It is used in small quantities. It can be bought in small rock form (balls) or as ground powder. It is used in almost every South Indian dish, fish dishes, vegetables such as beans and for tempering dals and lentils. Asafoetida is said to combat flatulence and has digestive properties. A pinch of it can be fried in hot oil before the rest of the ingredients are cooked. Because of its strong scent, it is best stored in its original pack inside a second airtight container.

Asafoetida Powder

Bay Leaf (*Tej Patta*): Also known as laurel leaf, it is pointed and oval in shape. On an average, it is about 8 cm long. Both the fresh and the dried leaves are used. The dried leaves are pale and brittle. Ground bay leaf is used in *masalas*. Bay leaf is used in stocks for soups, in aromatic curries such as kormas, and in pulaos and biryanis.

Bay Leaf

Caraway (*Shahi Jeera*): The caraway seed is a tiny greyish-brown seed, one-eighth inch long. It is a biennial plant. It has medicinal properties. It is used for flavouring rice dishes and for breads.

Caraway Seeds

Cardamom (*Elaichi*): There are three main types of cardamoms – white and green ones are called *choti elaichi* and the blackish brown ones are known as *badi elaichi*. They are used whole or ground, with or without casing. *Badi elaichi* is commonly used in garam masala and we use them in kormas, *pulaos* and biryanis. *Choti elaichi* as a whole or in powder form is mostly used in

Choti Elaichi

Badi Elaichi

Indian sweets and desserts. It is also used in certain kormas and biryanis. It is best to grind them with a pestle and mortar, as and when required.

Cayenne Pepper (*Mirch* powder): Cayenne comes from the seeds of plants from the capsicum family. It is a blend of various types of chilli powder. It is believed that the smaller the chilli, the hotter it is. Cayenne pepper is not as hot as chilli powder, but should be used sparingly.

Green Chilli

Dried Red Chilli

Chilli Red

Chilli (*Mirch*): This is the hottest flavour on earth. It must be used with extreme care. The fresh chilli is green in colour. It becomes red as it ripens. Both the fresh green chilli and the dry red ones are used in cooking. While tempering, whole red chillies are dropped in hot oil to release their flavour. The chilli powder is achieved after grinding dry red chillies. Take care not to touch your eyes or any part of the face while handling chillies.

Cinnamon

Cinnamon (*Dalchini*): This is a bark with a sweetish aromatic flavour. It has been used in flavouring since times immemorial. Though available in powder form, it is prudent to buy it in stick form. It is used as tempering in *pulaos*, meat and poultry dishes and in garam masala.

Cloves

Cloves (*Lavang*): Dried clove is dark red-brown in colour. It is bulbous at one end and tapering at the other. It has essential oils that relieve pain and comforts toothache. Clove is the world's second most important spice. Grind them whenever required.

Whole Coconut

Coconut (*Narial*): This is a fruit seed commonly available along the seacoast. It is extensively used in many regions, particularly in South Indian cooking. Fresh coconut may be grated and frozen. If the fresh fruit is not available, you may use the desiccated variety found in most grocery shops. It is used in bakery extensively. Coconut milk is used in many soups and curries to give them a smooth consistency.

Cracked Coconut

Coriander (*Dhaniya*): This is one plant in which leaves, seeds and even roots are used in cooking. Apart from making chutneys and being used in curries, coriander leaves are used for garnishing cooked dishes. The seeds are small-ridged, light brown in colour and can be easily squashed under the thumb. The leaves are light green, flat with jagged edges and have a flavour totally different from the seed. The seed, whole or in powdered form, is used in most Indian dishes. Seeds form the bulk in readymade ground garam masala. The green coriander or *hara dhaniya* can be kept fresh in an airtight glass jar in the refrigerator. Dried coriander leaves can be used by immersing them in cold water for 15 minutes.

Coriander Seeds

Coriander Leaves

Cumin Seeds

Cumin (*Jeera*): The seeds are long and slim, similar to caraway seeds. They have a distinctive warm aroma. Cumin is an important ingredient in almost all *masalas* and curries. It is one of the five spices in *panch phoran*. It is used as a whole in tempering. It is also used in its roasted form in *masala* and for garnishing. To roast cumin, put as much as you need in a hot *kadhai* and stir till the seeds turn dark brown. Cool and grind coarsely in a mortar or in electric grinder. It is best bought whole. Grind in small quantities as and when required.

Curry leaves (*Curry patta, Meethi neem*): These leaves are similar to bay leaves, but much smaller.

Chopped Dill Leaves

They are greyish green or pale green in colour. The fresh leaves have a remarkable fragrance and flavour. No South Indian dish is complete without curry leaves. They can be used both fresh and dried. The dried ones can be crumbled over food.

Dill Seeds

Dill (*Sowa*): This is a herb which has hair-like leaves. Both the leaves and seeds are used in cooking. The seeds are oval, shaped like a rowing boat, and grey-brown in colour. It has a sweet aroma and a lemony taste. It is bitter if used in excess. In India, dill is used more for medicational purposes than as a spice. It improves the taste of naans and rice dishes.

Fennel Seeds

Fennel (*Saunf*): These are small plump oval seeds, greenish brown in colour and have an anise flavour. It has digestive properties; due to this quality its tea is given to small children when suffering from stomach ache. It is served along with *paan masala* at the end of the meal. Its aromatic flavour makes it ideal for certain dishes and pickles. It gives warmth and sweetness to curries if used sparingly.

Fenugreek Seeds

Fenugreek Leaves

Fenugreek *(Methi):* This is yet another plant whose seed and leaves are edible. The leaf, grey-green in colour grows on small clover-like plants. It is used to make parathas, dry vegetable in combination with potatoes and other vegetables; and in many other ways, it is used just as spinach. It has a strong bitter taste, which one begins to like gradually. The tawny coloured seeds are chunky and very hard. Use of fenugreek seeds is popular in North Indian cooking and Punjabi dishes. The seeds are main ingredients of many curry powders; otherwise they should be used sparingly. Dry *methi* leaves, rich in carotene, vitamin A, ascorbic acid, calcium and iron are used in some curries and non-vegetarian dishes.

Lemon Grass

Lemon grass (*Takrai*): It is not as widely used in Indian cooking as elsewhere. The bulbous lower end of the grass, which contains aromatic oil, is used for its distinctive fragrance. It is used to flavour herbal tea, pulses and Gujarati soups.

Lovage Seeds

Lovage (*Ajwain*): The seeds are tiny, round and striped, greyish-brown in colour, a little bitter, slightly musky but with a distinctive intense flavour. These seeds are used in parathas and breads. Due to their medicinal properties, these are used to cure digestive problems.

Molasses and palm sugar (*Gur* or jaggery): *Gur*/jaggery is a mound of coarse brown sugar. It is obtained by boiling sugarcane juice until all the water is dried. Palm sugar is obtained from the sap of tropical palm trees. Its colour varies from pale gold to dark brown. *Gur* or jaggery is used in Bengali and Gujarati cuisine. In Northern parts of India, it is eaten with *Makki* or *Bajra* rotis. It is mixed with hot clarified butter and eaten. It is also used to make *Chikki* (brittle) and flavour certain dishes in Western India.

Mango powder (*Amchur*): It is obtained by drying the pulp of raw mangoes and then grinding them to a powder form. It has a sour taste and is popular in North India and Punjab to add zing to paratha filling, curries and vegetables.

Black Mustard

Mustard seeds (*Sarson, Rai*): There are three varieties of mustard seeds – white, yellow and black. The black ones contain a higher proportion of the pungent and volatile mustard oil. The white and yellow varieties are milder. When dropped into hot oil; the mustard seeds pop and splutter, releasing their flavour. It is advisable to cover the pan while using them, otherwise they might harm your eyes. Mustard is very popular in Bengal, and is used as one of the five spices in *panch phoran*. In South India, no dish finishes without tempering with mustard seeds.

Javitri

Mace (*Javatri, Jaiphal*): Mace is one of the unique spices that grows inseparably with another popular spice, nutmeg. It is reddish-brown in colour and has a distinct flavour resembling that of nutmeg. It is not frequently used, but goes well with fish, vegetable and sweet dishes.

Pudina

Mint (*Pudina*): There are three main varieties of mint: spearmint, peppermint and apple mint, though experts believe there may be as many as forty varieties of it. Fresh mint grows in India. Its use is restricted to garnishing, flavouring tea and beverages, and making chutneys and sauces. Sometimes, it is used in some curries in its dried form.

Jaifal

Nutmeg (*Jaifal*): It is a large seed, little smaller than a hen's egg, greyish-brown in colour. It has an aromatic flavour. It is commonly used in Hyderabadi and Mughlai cuisine and some desserts, in grated form. It is an important ingredient in garam masala. It is best bought whole. It should be grated fresh when required. It has medicinal properties. Taken with honey, it is a good remedy for the common cold.

Pepper

Pepper (*Kali Mirch*): Pepper is a small round seed with a wrinkled skin. Being pungent, it should be used sparingly. It loses its flavour quickly. It is best to buy it whole, and grind it fresh when required. It is commonly used in egg and soup preparations. Many non-vegetarian dishes and *pulaos* are flavoured with it. It is also used in making herbal tea.

Pomegranate Seeds

Pomegranate Seeds (*Anardana*): The dried seeds of the pomegranate fruit are popular in almost every kitchen in North India. The seeds are used in coarsely powdered form. They are slightly sour in taste, and have a particular flavour of their own. They are used in specialised North Indian cuisine, contributing both colour and taste. They are used in paratha fillings, *chhole*, chutneys and in Mughlai curries. They are also a constituent of some *churans* and *chaat masalas* that have digestive qualities.

Poppy seeds (*Khus-khus*): The Bengalis call this *postu*. These are integral part of their cuisine. They are also used in other parts of India in various other Indian dishes. The poppy seed is the world's most minuscule seed and is a minor spice, used to thicken curries, or to decorate breads and sweets.

Saffron

Saffron (*Zafran, Kesar*): It is called *kesar* in Kashmir and *Zafran* in Iran. It is the most expensive spice in the world. Considering the cost, buy a reputed brand. Many fakes are available in the market. Saffron is the filament of the crops cultivated in Kashmir. It is used to give food a bright yellow colour and a distinctive aroma. The filament can be first roasted, crumbled in a little hot water or hot milk, and left to infuse to bring out the full strength.

Sesame

Sesame (*Til*): Sesame seeds are creamish yellow in colour and have a neutral nutty taste. They are used to texture delicate cooking. They are used in Indian breads such as naan, buns and confectionery. The sesame seeds, when roasted, are also used in salads, for garnishing and to improve the taste of stirfried vegetables. Mixed with jaggery, they are used to prepare excellent *Chikki* (brittle).

Tamarind

Tamarind *(Imli)*: It looks like a cinnamon-coloured pod of broad beans. It grows on tall trees, and peeled and seeded when ripe. The fruit is squashed into bricks and packed in cellophane paper for sale. It has an acidic taste, a tart flavour and is popularly used in South Indian dishes. It is an important constituent of chutneys and used for making *chaat.*

Turmeric Powder

Turmeric (*Haldi*): Bought as powder, it is used in most Indian curries to give them their characteristic golden yellow colour. It is mildly antiseptic, and relieves sprains when applied as a paste with oil. It has a delicate taste, which turns bitter if used in excess. It also has digestive properties.

Fresh Ginger

Ginger (*Adrak*): It is used both in the fresh state and also as dried powder called *sonth*. It is extensively used in Indian cooking. Ground ginger powder is used in baking and marinades. The fresh one is an important spice and is used chopped or ground along with other wet ingredients, cut into julienne or even grated. Ginger has a hot pungent flavour and must be used with care.

Salt

Salt: Pure salt is Sodium Chloride, a crystalline compound. It is the oldest and one of the most important seasonings in the world. It is derived from several sources – seawater, water from salt lakes and from underground deposits. Since the salt derived from these sources may not be pure, it is refined in special refining units. It is made free flowing through special treatment. Good quality salt is freely available in the market, and is reasonably priced. Salt is an essential nutrient in the human body. It controls the distribution of moisture in the cells. If the salt metabolism in the body gets deranged, it can cause serious problems affecting breathing, retention of fluids in the body, and kidney function. Increased intake of salt can cause high blood pressure and other problems. Doctors advise that reduced salt intake would reduce incidence of stroke and heart attacks. American experts advise that 2.4 grams (about one tsp of salt) per day is the ideal intake.

The black variety, the rock salt (*kala namak*) is found underground. It has a pretty pink, grey or even blue colour. It is an essential ingredient in *chaat masala* and is also used in raitas.

The Onion Family

The onion family plays an important role in lending taste, flavour and nutrition to our everyday food. Let us get to know the members of this family.

Onion

Onion (*Pyaz*): All varieties of onions – red or pink, white and yellow, and spring onions are indispensable to Indian cooking. One must be careful while sautéing onions in oil or butter. When soft and transparent, the flavour of the onions is sweet, and mild. They quickly turn brown if cooked on a very high temperature and get burnt and give a bitter taste to any dish. Small onions often called pickling onions are used for pickles, and also served raw after treating them with vinegar. Onion paste is also used to cook a variety of curries. The long slender spring onions are the immature bulb of the yellow onions and are used in salads, an accompaniment to many roasted dishes and for garnishing where a touch of green is required.

Shallot

Shallot: These are a variety of small onions, which taste like a combination of onion and garlic. They are ideal for dishes where the taste of onion predominates such as *dopiaza* curry, onion pakoras or onion *bhaji.* The South Indians use them in *sambhar* and other curries.

Garlic (*Lahsun*): Renowned for its strong odour and a peculiar flavour, garlic is an important

Garlic

ingredient in many dishes. A giant variety, the elephant garlic, is mildest of all. It enhances the flavour when used in moderation. Raw garlic is most effective in salad dressing, in marinades and in certain sauces. When frying garlic, care must be taken to cook it gently as it burns easily. It is used in both non-vegetarian and vegetarian dishes. Whole cloves of garlic can also be pickled. Garlic has medicinal properties. It helps relieve cold and build immunity for the body.

USING SPICES, HERBS AND CONDIMENTS

Spices should preferably be bought whole and grounded at home to convert into the powders. The loose spice powders available in the market are often mixed with many other items to increase the volume and weight. Moreover, whole spices have better shelf life than powders. It is advisable to buy them in small quantities and store them in airtight containers.

Sometimes, a recipe may specify spices to be roasted and ground. Roasting helps spices to release their flavour. To roast them, just heat a pan or a *kadhai* and place the spices in it and stir till they change colour and the aroma becomes pronounced. Grind them in a mortar/ a coffee grinder or in a dry grinder of electric mixer.

Sometimes, a recipe may suggest only pounded or crushed spices. This can easily be achieved in a mortar. You may crush cardamom for tea or *kheer*, or garlic for salad dressing.

When you buy airtight containers for whole spices, invest in a steel spice box. This is a round box with a tight lid. It has a number of small bowls or *katories* fitted inside to hold the daily requirement of spices. This is an ideal addition to a kitchen. Taking out spices from the jars for cooking everyday is inconvenient. The idea is to keep a small quantity of spices in the spice box to last you for 3 to 4 days.

In recipes you will often come across the term 'garam masala'. This is a combination of spices such as cardamoms of all varieties, cloves, mace, nutmeg, cinnamon, caraway seeds and allspice. This is used in veg and non-veg curries and in savoury rice dishes. Usually, the garam masala (roasted and ground) is added to a dish at the end of cooking but sometimes it is added when curries are simmering. The Punjabi version includes coriander, cumin and pepper along with the other spices. It is said that garam masala has a warming effect on the digestive system.

Practical things to be done

1. Garam Masala (Kashmiri)

To make cooking convenient, most cooks prepare *masalas* in advance. Whenever a particular combination is required, they take an appropriate quantity and make a paste. This paste is then used as required in the recipe.

Equipment used:

A large pan or a *kadhai*, a slotted ladle, a large plate.

Gadgets:

Mortar and pestle/ a food processor/electric grinder.

Ingredients: 60 gm coriander seeds; 50 gm cumin seeds; 40 gm fennel seeds; 25 gm black peppercorns; 15 gm black cardamom; 10 gm mace; 25 gm cinnamon; 4 bay leaves; 5 gm dry ginger powder.

To make garam masala, follow this simple procedure:

1. Put all the ingredients, except the ginger powder, in a large pan or *kadhai*. Roast them over low flame, stirring continuously as it heats up.
2. As soon as the mixture gives off steam, stir for a few seconds and then switch off the heat.
3. Transfer the spices to a plate and let them cool.
4. Now grind them to a fine powder in a food processor/electric grinder or in a mortar.
5. Combine the ginger powder with the spice mixture. Mix thoroughly. Store in an airtight container in a dry place. Use as much as required in curries to enhance the flavour.

Kashmiri *masala* is also available in the dry disc form known as *tikki* masala.

2. Curry Masala

This is a *masala* mix of thirteen spice powders. These should be ground at home for best results. The mixture can be used in all the curries. One tsp of *masala* will weigh 5 gm approximately.

Ingredients: 60 gm coriander powder; 20 gm garam masala powder; 30 gm cumin powder; 20 gm fenugreek powder; 25 gm gram flour (*besan*); 25 gm garlic powder; 20 gm paprika; 20 gm turmeric powder; 5 gm ginger powder; 5 gm chilli powder; 5 gm yellow mustard powder; 5 gm black pepper powder; 5 gm cinnamon powder.

Mix all the ingredients thoroughly and your curry powder is ready. This combination will yield about 250 gm of *masala*. Store it in an airtight container.

3. Tandoori Masala

Ingredients: 40 gm coriander powder; 20 gm mango powder; 30 gm cumin powder; 20 gm dried mint (*pudina*) powder; 40 gm garlic powder; 20 gm beetroot powder; 40 gm paprika; 10 gm chilli powder; 20 gm ginger powder; 5 gm red food colour.

Mix all the ingredients together. Store in an airtight container until you need it.

4. Ready-to-use Masala Paste

This is the onion *masala* paste, which can be used in combination with the curry *masala*. It makes cooking convenient.

Ingredients: 1 kg onions; 1 kg red tomatoes; 250 gm fresh ginger root; 250 gm garlic; 2 bay leaves; 1 tsp garam masala; 2 green chillies (opt).

To make *masala* paste, follow this simple procedure:

1. Peel and slice onions.
2. Wash, pat dry and remove the eye of the tomatoes and chop them roughly.
3. Separate the garlic cloves and peel them.
4. Peel, wash, pat dry and chop the ginger.
5. Grind all ingredients together in the wet-grinding jar of your electric mixer. If it can't be grounded at one time, grind a smaller quantity of mixture at a time. Store the mixture in a steel container.
6. Heat 4 tbsp cooking oil in a big *kadhai*. When the oil begins to smoke, drop in 2 bay leaves. When the bay leaves begin to change colour, slowly pour in the ground mixture. Cover and cook till the moisture has evaporated.
7. Uncover and stir fry over high heat till the oil separates and the mixture turns dark in colour.
8. Remove from heat and cool. Divide into required portions and store in airtight containers in the refrigerator. It will be fresh for a fortnight. Just 2 tbsp of this ready to use *masala* in combination with other dry spices will help you make most of your curries in a few minutes, as the onion-tomato *masala* has already been fried.

5. Ginger-Garlic Paste

Some recipes do not require onion *masala*, but need only ginger-garlic paste. Such pastes are available in the market. However, homemade ones are better and economical.

Combine peeled and chopped ginger and garlic in equal proportion and grind in your electric grinder.

Add 2 tsp vinegar to make the grinding smooth and easy. Store in clean, airtight jars in the refrigerator. It will be fresh for a fortnight. One tsp of this paste is all that you will require.

6. Vindaloo Paste

This is a very hot and spicy paste popular in Western India. It goes well with pork, beef, chicken, mutton and prawns.

Ingredients: 225 gm onions chopped; 200 gm tomatoes chopped; 10 red chillies broken; 1 tsp mustard seeds; 50 gm fresh root ginger; 1 tsp cumin seeds; 12 garlic cloves; 3 tbsp white vinegar; ½ tsp fenugreek seeds; 5-6 tbsp oil.

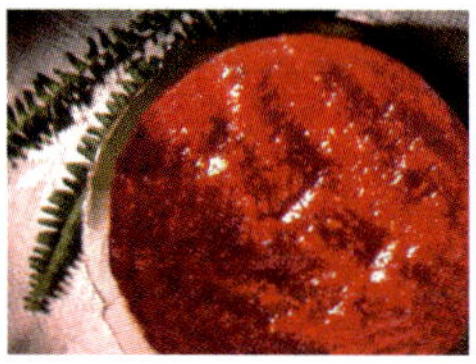

To make paste, follow this simple procedure:

1. Put together the red chillies, half ginger, peeled and chopped garlic, mustard, fenugreek and cumin seeds.
2. Mix them with vinegar and grind. Do not add any water.
3. Heat cooking oil in a *kadhai* and fry the finely chopped onions till golden brown. Add the chopped tomatoes and fry for some more time, squashing them to a paste.
4. Stir in the spice-vinegar mixture and the remaining ginger finely chopped.
5. Fry this *masala* till the oil separates. Cool and store in a clean jar in the refrigerator. It will last for at least ten days.

7. Traditional Indian Gravy

Utensils used: A *kadhai* or a nonstick pan; a long handled spoon; a tsp; a tbsp; a cup. We are cooking for two persons.

Ingredients: 2 tbsp onion-tomato *masala*; 1 tsp curry powder; salt to taste; 1 cup water; 1 tbsp cooking oil; ½ tsp cumin seeds.

To prepare the traditional Indian gravy, follow this simple procedure:

1. Heat oil in a *kadhai*; add cumin seeds and crackle.
2. Put in the onion-tomato paste and stir.
3. Mix the curry powder with a little water and add this paste to the mixture in the *kadhai*. Stir fry till the oil separates.
4. Add 1 cup water and salt to taste and simmer over low heat till the gravy thickens.

Once the basic gravy is ready, you can add boiled potatoes and peas to it, or add chunks of fried *paneer* (country cheese). Garnish with chopped fresh coriander leaves. Serve with rice, chapatti or paratha.

■■

Spice box with spices

COOKING METHOD # 3

Let us learn how to cut vegetables in different ways for various recipes.

Cut onions are used for cooking, grilling, baking, and garnishing or to eat raw in salads.

Cooking Method # 3.1

Slicing Onions

One can cut onions into thin or thick slices to use in a variety of dishes, salads or for garnishing.

1. Peel onion, trimming the top and the root; cut in half and place it cut side down on the chopping board.
2. Hold the onion firmly with one hand, holding the knife in the other, cut it in vertical slices (guiding the knife with your bent fingers).

Cooking Method # 3.2

Dicing and chopping Onions

You can slice the onion and then cut into even sized dices or chop them finely. The size of the dice depends on the thickness of the slices you made.

1. Peel onion, and cut it in two halves. Lay one half, cut side down, on a chopping board.
2. Using a chopping knife, make a series of horizontal cuts from the stalk towards the root. Cut the root but not through it.
3. Make a series of lengthwise vertical cuts, cutting almost but not quite through the root.
4. Cut the onion crosswise. You will get dices. Guide the blade of the knife with your bent fingers.
5. If you want to chop the onions into smaller pieces, continue chopping with an up and down motion of the knife, holding the point down with one hand.

Cooking Method # 3.3

Cutting Onion rings

To make onion rings, take a large onion. Peel and trim the stalk and the root. Turn the onion on its side, hold it firmly on the board with one hand and cut thick or thin slices in downward strokes. Leave the slices whole or push them apart into rings.

Cooking Method # 3.4

Peeling and Chopping Garlic

Chopped garlic is ideal when used in salad dressings and stews. In curries, it is used in a paste form.

1. Crush the garlic bulb with your hands to separate the garlic cloves. Or take cloves from the bulb with your fingers.
2. To crush a clove, set the flat side of a chef's knife on top and strike it with your fist.
3. Peel off the skin. Finely chop the clove with the knife, moving the blade to and fro.

Cooking Method # 3.5

Peeling and chopping Ginger

Ginger has to be peeled like a vegetable or a fruit before slicing, chopping or grinding it to a paste.

1. Using a sharp knife, cut the skin from the gingerroot.
2. Crush the ginger under the flat of a knife.
3. When the ginger is crushed and its fibres separated, it is easier to chop.

4. Chop the ginger as coarse or fine as per your wish. To extract juice from the ginger, squeeze the grated ginger in muslin.

Cooking Method # 3.6

Preparing fresh chillies

Break the stalk and wash the chillies under cold water. If you want a mild, spicy flavour, remove the seeds.

1. To remove the seeds, cut the chillies lengthwise with a small, sharp knife.
2. Scrape off the seeds and cut away the fleshy white ribs from each half. Chop the chillies or grind them to a paste, as the recipe specifies.

Cooking Method # 3.7

Chopping green coriander or mint

1. Strip the leaves from the stalks; wash under running water; put them in the food processor and run the machine on and off in short spurts chopping the leaves. Do not over chop them, as this will reduce the herbs to a puree.
2. Or pile the leaves on the chopping board. Holding the tip of the knife blade against the board and rocking the handle up and down chop the leaves coarsely or finely as desired.

Cooking Method # 3.8

Peeling, seeding and chopping tomatoes

Tomatoes are used in almost all curries, stews, sauces and soups. Sometimes a recipe suggests skinning or peeling of tomatoes; other recipes may just require them chopped. For baking and stuffing, the skin is left on. A slice is cut from the top of the tomato and the seeds gently removed with the help of a knife.

To peel tomatoes:

1. Boil water in a large pan. With paring knife, cut the core out of the tomato.
2. Lightly crosshatch the bottom with the knife.
3. Drop it into the boiling water. Leave it immersed for 10-15 seconds or until the skin curls away from the crosshatch.
4. Remove from water and let the tomatoes cool slightly. Peel off the skin.

To seed tomatoes: Cut the tomato crosswise into halves and squeeze. Use a knife to scrape away the interior.

To chop tomatoes:

Cut the tomato halves into slices with a serrated knife. Then roughly chop.

■ ■

DAY 05

Pulses and Legumes

Pulses and legumes take the place of meat in a vegetarian diet. They are the edible seeds of cultivated plants, and include lentils, beans, pulses and dried peas. There are over sixty varieties of pulses and beans available in our country. They are a primary source of protein to millions of vegetarians. When cooked, they can be used whole or pureed. They can be cooked in a variety of ways, and are important ingredients in curries. They can be used as stuffing for many dishes, and for making a variety of patties that can be roasted or deep-fried as snacks.

The most commonly used pulses in the form of dals are: *arhar* or *toor* dal, *masoor* or lentil, *sabut moong*, *chana* dal, *dhuli moong*, *katti moong*, *dhuli urad*, *katti urad*, *sabut masoor*, split chickpeas, *sabut urad*, etc.

Dried beans and peas also form an important part of our diet. The most commonly used ones are: *kala chana*, *kabuli chana* or chick peas, *raungi*, peas, green gram, black-eyed peas and soya beans. The following table should help you identify them easily:

Name	Colour of Seed Coat	Colour When Split
Toor dal	Dark brown	Yellow
Urad dal	Black	White
Moong dal	Green	Yellow
Masoor dal	Earthy brown	Pinkish red
Chana dal	Dark brown	Yellow
Maah dal	Earthy brown	Used whole
Kala chana	Dark brown	Used whole
Kabuli chana	Creamish white	Used whole
Raungi	Creamish yellow	Used whole
Rajmah	Dark red	Used whole
Dried peas	Green	Yellow, used whole
Dried green gram	Green	Used whole
Soya beans	Creamish yellow	Used whole

Pulses

They can easily be classified as convenient food. Split dals/pulses do not require much preparation, e.g., soaking. After cleaning and rinsing, they can be cooked within 15 to 20 minutes. They are truly wonderful as they are easy to cook for daily meals and blend well with many other items.

The yellow varieties are usually served with plain steamed rice. Others like *urad*, *saboot moong* (*moong* whole) or *saboot masoor* are served with parathas, *tandoori* roti, chapatti or naan, and sometimes with plain fried rice as well.

Dals in the Indian Kitchen (Lto R): 1st row: Dried Peas, *Dhuli Moong*, *Dhuli Masoor*, Split *Urad*, White *Chana*; 2nd row: *Chana* Dal, *Sabut Urad*, *Sabut Moong*, *Dhuli Urad*, Split *Moong*; 3rd row: Black *Chana*, *Toor* Dal, *Raungi*, *Sabut Masoor*, *Rajmah*

Most of the pulses are consumed after being cooked in water with salt and a pinch of turmeric. When it is done, the dal is mashed with a wooden ladle; blended with boiled water and then tempered with a little cumin or brown mustard seeds, spluttered in 1 tbsp hot oil to which either one whole red chilli or a pinch of red chilli powder and sometimes even asafoetida is added. This tempering (*tadka*) is poured over the cooked dal. Alternatively, an elaborate tempering can be prepared. Heat 2 tbsp oil in a small pan; crackle cumin in it; add 1 medium sized onion and tomato each and 2 green chillies finely chopped. Fry for a while and add a dash of red chilli powder and finally pour it over the dal. Simmer the dal covered for 10 minutes over low flame; garnish with finely chopped fresh coriander leaves and serve it hot. This dal should not be of thick consistency.

This method is usually used to cook dals of the yellow variety and red lentils. For other varieties, the cooking method is similar except that the consistency is thicker and the tempering requires more onions and tomatoes, ginger and garlic, some ghee and fresh cream with fresh coriander for garnishing. You will learn more about the procedures for cooking dals in the practical session.

Though dals of all varieties are usually served with rice preparations or a variety of breads but some dals are used to make certain other preparations as well. For example:

- ***Moong* dal:** *Halwa*, *khichdi* and fried snacks.
- ***Chana* dal:** *Halwa*, fried snacks, for tempering in South Indian dishes.
- ***Urad* dal:** *Dosa*, *idli*, *vada*, for tempering in South Indian dishes.
- ***Saboot* dal:** Fried snacks.

Normally, dals do not require to be soaked prior to cooking. However, whole dals, other than the yellow variety, are best cooked if soaked for 15 to 20 minutes before cooking. This way the cooking time is also reduced. A pan with a lid can be used for cooking dals. Ideally, one should use a pressure cooker, which fastens the cooking process.

Moong Dal Halwa

The yellow variety of dals and the pinkish red *masoor* dal is popular in Uttar Pradesh, Bihar, Madhya Pardesh, West Bengal and Orissa. *Toor* dal is the basic ingredient of *sambhar* and *rasam*, and is mainly used in Western and Southern India. *Urad*, both whole and split, whole *moong* and *masoor* are popular amongst the North Indians. These dals are a part of the renowned fried dal.

Urad Dal Vada

Purchasing Pulses

While purchasing pulses, ensure that their colour is bright and clear, and are plump to look at. Old pulses look faded and shrunk. The grains must be even sized, and must be from a single lot. That ensures uniform cooking. Reject the lot that has cracks or pinholes. These indicate insect damage. Avoid loose stocks that may have little stones and twigs. Clean stocks packed in polythene bags cost a little extra, but they are a good buy.

Nutritional value

Pulses are high in complex carbohydrates and fibres, low in fat, and are cholesterol free. They are rich in potassium, iron and foliate, and low in sodium. They are rich in vitamins and minerals.

Storing Dals

Once a packet of pulses is opened, the contents must be transferred to an airtight container. Store in a cool dry place at room temperature. It is best to buy a monthly or a bimonthly supply of dals. Once cooked, it can be stored covered in a refrigerator for up to five days. Dishes made with dals can be frozen.

Cooking Pulses

The best way to cook pulses is to simmer them in a covered pan or pressure cooker in water, stock, broth or any other liquid using three cups of liquid to every cup of dal. If desired, seasonings or flavoured ingredients such as cardamom can be added to the cooking water. Dals absorb

Dal

flavours well. Do not add acidic ingredients such as lemon juice or tomatoes until the dals are well done. They slow the cooking process. Salt should be added at the end of the cooking time for the same reason.

Sometimes dals are used to make *vadas* or dal cakes that are deep-fried. They also make excellent stuffing for parathas, puris and cutlets. A little cooked dal mashed and added to soups, broth or stews improves the flavour and the texture of the soups. They also act as a thickening agent.

Black Beans, Pinto Beans and Red Kidney Beans

Test if Sufficiently Cooked

For dals cooked whole, test one grain by mashing it between two fingers. The skin may be slightly chewy but the interior should be soft. For the split variety, the whole pulse should be soft and blended with the liquid it is cooked in.

Beans

Beans are amongst the oldest form of food. They are an important staple diet for millions of people all over the world. Before reaching the consumer, beans are cleaned to remove pods, stems, and other debris. Different varieties of beans are cultivated in almost every part of the world. Most of them have a mild flavour and slightly mealy texture. They have a tough skin and retain their shape when cooked. They serve as ideal side dishes with bread preparations or with steamed and fried rice. Boiled beans are used in salads with a light dressing of vinegar or lemon juice. Almost all variety of beans are popular in North India. The people in other parts of India too are accepting beans as a part of their diet.

White and Green Chickpeas

Purchasing Beans

A large variety of beans are available in the market. It is, therefore, essential to know about some of the most common ones.

Red kidney beans are kidney shaped and recognised by their rich red colour. On cooking, they look robust, and have a sweet flavour. At parties they are served as a traditional Punjabi dish, i.e., *rajmah*. They are also seen in stews, in the Mexican 'Chilli Con Carne' soups and salads, or as a baked dish. Baked beans in tomato sauce are sold packed in tins/cans. Just heat them and serve. Their best accompaniment is continental food.

Black beans have an oval shape and a tough, black skin. They are used in thick bean soups and in Oriental and Mediterranean dishes.

Black-eyed peas/cowpeas are small, oval-shaped, and creamish-white with a black spot on one side. They are commonly known as *raungi*. They are used as a vegetarian dish, served with a tempering of onion, tomatoes, ginger and garlic. They are served with steamed rice or bread.

Pinto beans are of the same species as the kidney beans. They are beige-coloured and speckled. They are also used as a main vegetarian dish, in salads and baked dishes.

Chickpeas or Garbanzo beans are wrinkled and irregular in shape, somewhat larger than a pea and coloured in shades from creamish-yellow, to dark reddish brown or dark green. The yellow ones are popularly known as *kabuli chana*. The brown ones are known as *kala chana* and the green ones as *hara chana*. All of them need soaking for 5 to 6 hours before cooking in a pressure cooker for almost 40 minutes or simmering for one and a half hour to 2 hours or until tender. They can be used as a main vegetarian dish served with steamed, boiled or fried rice, or with bread dishes. Boiled black or green *chana* can be used to make salads with a light dressing or excellent vegetarian *pulaos*.

Soybeans or Soya beans are small, almost round and yellow in colour. Though a few varieties are black, red and green, but the yellow variety is commonly used. They are one of the best sources of vegetable protein, oil and carbohydrates.

Soybeans

40 percent of the beans' dry weight comes from proteins. Since boiled soybeans have a strong metallic taste, they are converted into a wide variety of products such as soya flour, soya milk (made from cooked soybeans), tofu, (curdled soy milk), and tempeh (fermented soybeans). They are also used as bean sprouts and textured vegetable protein, made to look like meat, and formulated as chunks, flakes and granules. The chunks are used as a meat substitute. They are cooked as a main curry dish after being soaked in warm, salted water for ten minutes. The excess water is squeezed out and the chunks are added to a gravy to make curry, or to fried rice and *pulaos*. The flakes are used as meat extenders in hamburgers. The granules are added to other ingredients to make a variety of dishes including cutlets. Puffed soya beans can be eaten as a snack, or added to yogurt.

In general, when buying beans, ensure that they are of similar size and colour. When they get old, like pulses, they lose their texture and colour. Avoid defects such as cracks or pinholes that may indicate insect infestation. Make sure there are no debris like stones and twigs.

Nutritional Value of Beans

Dry beans are high in complex carbohydrates and fibre. They are low in fat, but a good source of protein. They are cholesterol free, rich in potassium, iron and foliate and a good source of vitamins and minerals as well. All beans are low in sodium.

Beans are comparatively expensive than other dals but are tasty and full of nutrients. Some people hesitate to eat them because of the intestinal gas and bloating they cause. Here are a few tips to avoid these problems:

- Discard the soaking water before cooking beans.
- Cook beans well. Slight over cooking breaks down the starch that causes intestinal gas and bloating.
- *Raungi*, split peas and other pulses are the most digestible. Start with them. Gradually move onto other beans.
- To begin with, consume small helpings of beans.
- Slowly chew them well.
- With the increase of fibre intake, you must drink at least 8 to 10 glasses of water each day.

Storing Beans

It is best to buy beans in small quantities (depending on the size of your family). In a small family of four persons, one could buy one kilogram of each variety. Store them in airtight containers in the kitchen cupboard. Cooked beans can be kept covered in the refrigerator for one or two days. Bean leftovers and mashed beans can be frozen for later use. Add a little water and seasoning after thawing, and heat through. Your bean dish will be ready again.

Cooking Beans

Dry beans increase in volume after cooking. The suggested quantity to cook would be a fistful per portion or 1 cup dry beans for four persons. Take the required quantity in a large plate or a tray. Carefully pick out any stones and twigs that may be present. Rinse well. Soak for 6 to 8 hours before cooking them. The detailed method is discussed later. The main dish, stews, baked dishes, casseroles, stuffing, sandwich spreads, soups and salads can be made with cooked beans. The cooked dishes are so tasty that no one will miss meat in the menu.

Test if Sufficiently Cooked

Take out one bean from the cooking liquid and press between two fingers, if it mashes easily, it is sufficiently cooked.

Peas

Dried peas are nutritious and versatile. They make a menu attractive. They may be green or yellow, split or whole. The split peas are cooked like dals. They are usually husked. They are used in soups, salads and pulao. They are also used in some continental dishes with tomatoes, mozzarella cheese and Italian dressing.

Peas

Green dry peas have a more distinctive flavour than the yellow ones. Split or whole, green and yellow peas are used interchangeably in many recipes. The decision to choose one or the other is a matter of choice.

Purchasing Peas

When peas get older, they loose their colour. When buying dried peas; ensure that they are of the same size and colour. Buy clean, insect free peas without any cracks or pinholes.

Nutritional Value

Dried peas contain less number of calories than meat, but are a good source of protein. They are high in complex carbohydrates and fibre, low in fat and sodium. They are cholesterol free and rich in potassium and other minerals and vitamins.

Storing Dried Peas

Like dals and beans, dried peas should be bought in smaller quantities and stored in airtight containers in the kitchen cupboard. Cooked peas can be covered and stored in the refrigerator safely for five days. Dishes made with dried peas can be frozen.

Cooking Peas

Peas are cooked after rinsing and soaking them like beans. Split peas do not need to be soaked. If you want to hasten the cooking process, you could soak them for 10 to 15 minutes. To cook split peas, add a pinch of turmeric and twice as much water as peas; bring to a boil and reduce heat; simmer in a covered pan over low heat till tender. This will take about 30 minutes or cook in a pressure cooker for 15 to 20 minutes. Temper the peas just like dals. Dry peas go well with vegetables, fish, meat, poultry and pasta. With peas you can make side dishes, dips, soups and salads, too.

Soaking and Cooking of Beans and Peas

The soaking process before cooking makes dry beans and whole peas easier to digest. Use 2½ cups water for 1cup of beans. Both beans and peas swell after soaking. Use a large utensil to hold the soaking water and the beans in their swollen form. Soak them for 6 to 8 hours or overnight. Drain and rinse before cooking.

To cook beans and peas, follow the same method as that of cooking peas described above. Beans

Sprouts of Various Pulses

may require about one hour of simmering over low heat. Cover the pan partially as they generally boil over.

TIPS: If you have forgotten to soak the beans or peas for the specified period, do not despair. Wash them, add to boiling water, boil for 5 to 6 minutes, switch off the heat, cover the pan and soak them for 1 to 2 hours. Drain, rinse and cook in the usual manner.

Sprouts

We can sprout almost any seed, grain or pulse. Sprouting means germinating so that it begins to grow like a plant. Sprouts are more nutritious than the whole dry seeds, because on germinating; the reserves of protein and starch are converted to more soluble products that are easily digested.

For sprouting; the grains, beans or seeds should be whole. The most popular sprouts are from whole *moong*. Wheat, soybeans, *kala chana* and other beans also sprout well, as seeds like fenugreek, pumpkin and mustard. Soybean sprouts turn mouldy and must be rinsed sufficiently and cooked before consumption.

Sprouts can be used in salads, as garnish, in sandwiches or mixed with cheese or eggs to make a filling for grilled sandwiches or patties. You could also stir fry sprouts lightly, in combination with other vegetables for a tasty side dish. Sprouts made from fenugreek seeds are good for people suffering from high blood pressure, high blood sugar and arthritis. Wheat sprouts make a good addition to bread. They are either left whole or converted into flour.

COOKING METHOD # 4

Cooking Method # 4.1

Sprouting pulses and beans

The procedure for sprouting the common pulse *'Moong'* is as follows:

1. Clean and wash the seeds, beans or pulses to be sprouted. Soak 1 tbsp of seeds or 60 gm of grain or beans in 2 cups of lukewarm water.

2. Some swell to about 5 to 6 times of their original size. Therefore, use a big utensil. Drain and place in a large, clean jar. Cover the jar with a clean, dampened piece of muslin. Secure the cloth with a rubber band around the rim of the jar. Place the jar in a warm place, away from direct sunlight. Keep rinsing the beans 2 to 3 times a day. Soybeans and chickpeas should be rinsed 4 to 5 times. Replace the muslin cover after each rinse.

3. Now sprout them in the sprout farm. After soaking, spread them in the farm containers and add water twice a day. The extra water will drain in the lowest container.

4. When the sprouts, with a white tail, grow to the size you desire, rinse them. Throw away seeds that have not germinated. You can store sprouts under refrigeration for 2 days.

On having the basic information about the various pulses, beans and peas that are a part of our everyday diet, you can revise the details at your convenience.

Cooking Method # 4.2

Using a Pressure Cooker

A pressure cooker is a cooking aid to use steam for cooking food. A variety of pressure cookers are available in the market and you decide which one can meet your requirements. After buying one, you must read the instruction manual provided with the pressure cooker. Whereas a pressure cooker is a great cooking aid, it can be equally dangerous if mishandled, as serious scalding injuries can be caused by steam.

While using a pressure cooker:

- Do remember that the temperature inside a pressure cooker is 121°C as compared to 100°C of boiling water.
- Do not touch hot surfaces. Use the handles.
- Do not use the pressure cooker for purposes other than those it is intended for.

- Do not fill the cooker more than two-thirds full. Many food such as rice expand on cooking.
- Do not pressure cook food such as oatmeal, split peas, barley, noodles, spaghetti and macaroni that produce foam on cooking. The foam may block the steam passages and the safety devices.
- Ensure that there is enough water in the pressure cooker. It uses 1 cup water for every ten minutes of cooking.
- Do check the vent tube if it is open and clear before you close the cooker.
- Do ensure that the cover is properly closed.
- Do not put the weight on the cover when you put the cooker on fire. Place the weight only when the steam begins to come out from the vent.
- Do not put additional weight on the vent weight when cooking.
- Do not lift the weight off the cooker when in use. This can cause serious burns.
- Do not force the cooker to open. Cool it under water before opening it.
- Do not use the cooker for pressure frying with oil.
- Do not use the cooker for shallow or deep-frying unless the model is capable of it. Otherwise you can damage your pressure cooker.
- Do change the rubber gasket whenever necessary.
- Do get the cooker repaired only by an authorised service representative.

Why is cooking in a pressure cooker beneficial?

1. It is faster and saves time. On an average, cooking in a pressure cooker takes almost 50 percent of the time as compared to conventional cooking.
2. It is economical. Saving time and cooking fuel makes it more economical.
3. Food cooked in a pressure cooker is healthier and the nutrients are well preserved due to faster cooking.
4. It ensures full retention of food flavours, so the food is tastier.
5. The food is sterilised at a higher temperature than is done by boiling water.

You can cook more than one item in a pressure cooker, simultaneously. For example, *Varan Bhaat* and Kidney Beans and Meat Soup. The only condition is that the items must be of similar type, requiring a similar cooking time. Pressure cookers come with steaming sections that can be placed together, or steaming containers are piled up on one over the other. It depends upon their shape. *Idli* moulds and *dhokla* trays available in the market can also be used in a pressure cooker without its weight on the vent.

TIPS: To clean the blackened inside of a pressure cooker, boil a mixture of 4 tbsp vinegar added to 250 ml water for 5 minutes. The cooker can be easily cleaned.

Expert cook suggests...

1. A few drops of oil added to the dal speeds up the cooking process in the pressure cooker.
2. Rubbing a little oil on rice/dals when storing protects them from insects.
3. Dried neem leaves when added to rice/dals when storing protects them from insects.
4. When making *'dahi vadas'* add a little curd to the ground 'dal' and mix well. The *vadas* will turn out softer, and absorb less oil.
5. If you have forgotten to soak pulses that needed to be soaked overnight, soak them in a thermos flask in boiling water. Allow to soak for an hour.

Dishes Cooked in Pressure Cooker

Khara Pongal

Kidney Beans and Meat Soup

Dal Makhani

Kabuli Chana Dry

Moon Dal Palak Saag

Boiled Black Eued Beans

Practical things to be done

1. Cooking Toor Dal

Equipment used: A pan with a lid, a large plate / *thali* or a tray, a cup, a small pan for tempering, a bowl for washing and a long-handled ladle.

Portion: ¼ cup dal per person. If you are cooking for two persons.

Ingredients: ½ cup *toor* dal; 1 medium onion finely chopped; 1 tomato finely chopped; ½ tsp ginger-garlic paste; ½ tsp cumin seeds; 1-2 dry red chillies, broken into pieces or ½ tsp red chilli powder; ¼ tsp turmeric powder; salt to taste and 1 tbsp oil or ghee.

Follow this simple procedure:

1. Clean and wash the *toor* dal. Add 2 cups of water and boil in a pan with a pinch of turmeric.
2. When the dal comes to a boil, reduce flame. Place the lid, half covering the pan. Simmer till well done. Stir briskly with the ladle to blend the dal well. Add salt. Remove from heat and set aside.
3. Place the small pan on gas and put in oil or ghee. For a simple tempering, when the oil is hot, put in the cumin seeds, broken pieces of red chillies or the red chilli powder and pour this mixture over the cooked dal. Serve with steamed or boiled rice.

   For an elaborate tempering, heat oil in the pan; add cumin seeds and crackle; add chopped onions and stir fry for a while; add chopped tomatoes and broken red chillies or red chilli powder and fry well; add the prepared tempering to cooked dal and stir well. By adding water, the consistency of the dal can be adjusted as per choice.

The South Indians use the *toor* dal to make *sambhar* and *rasam*. *Sambhar* has a thicker consistency in comparison to *rasam*. *Sambhar* is cooked with lots of vegetables and served with *idli*, *dosa* and *vada* as part of the main course. *Rasam* has a watery consistency, is cooked with tomatoes and spices and is served as an appetiser at the beginning of a meal with roasted *papads*.

TIPS Add one tbsp of oil to the cooking liquid of dals to reduce foaming. Salt and acidic food such as tomatoes, lemon juice or vinegar improve the taste of beans and peas. However, they slow the cooking process. Add them when the beans or peas are tender. After tempering, simmer the curried dish of beans and peas for 15 to 20 minutes to improve the taste and flavour. Garnish with chopped fresh coriander leaves before serving.

2. Rajmah Curry

Utensils used: A pan with a lid; a large plate/ *thali* or tray; a bowl for washing; a large vessel for soaking; a cup; a small pan for tempering and a long-handled ladle.

Portion: ½ cup per person. We are cooking for 2 persons.

Ingredients: 1 cup *rajmah* (red kidney beans); 2 medium onions, ground; 2 large tomatoes, pureed or blanched and chopped; 2 tbsp cooking oil; 1 tsp curry powder; 1 tsp ginger-garlic paste, ½ inch fresh root ginger cut into julienne; 1 large black cardamom with the pod split open; ½ tsp turmeric powder; salt to taste; 2 green chillies cut into two lengthwise (optional); a few sprigs of fresh coriander, chopped.

Follow this simple procedure:

1. Clean the beans in a plate or tray. Wash and soak them in plenty of water for 6 to 8 hours or overnight.
2. Drain the beans and put in the pan with 3 cups of water and split black cardamom. Bring to boil over high flame; reduce heat and simmer half covered for 1½ hour or till tender. Add salt. Remove from heat and keep aside. Or place *rajmah* in the pressure cooker with water and cardamom; cover with the lid and cook on high flame till steam starts coming out; put the weight and cook till the 1st whistle; then lower the flame and cook for 45 minutes. Switch off the heat; wait and let the pressure come down (approximately 10 minutes).

1. Soaked Rajmah
2. Rajmah getting Swollen
3. Cooked Rajmah

3. Heat oil in the small pan; put in onion paste and fry till light brown.
4. Add ginger-garlic paste and the curry powder. Fry till the colour begins to change. Sprinkle a little water over the *masala* to prevent it from sticking to the bottom of the pan.
5. Add tomato puree and stir fry till the oil separates. Add this mixture to cooked *rajmah*; add ½ cup to 1 cup water if *rajmah* is too thick and simmer over.

TIPS Simmering enhances the flavour and texture of all dals, beans and peas. The consistency of the dish can be adjusted by adding hot water if the water dries up during simmering. The cooking time can be reduced and cooking gas can be saved if you use a pressure cooker.

Day 06

Cooking Vegetables

With everyone convinced of the health benefits of vegetables, they have become a part of almost every meal. It was in the 50's that people began to appreciate the importance of fresh, high quality vegetables. Ever since, our fascination for them has steadily grown. Better farming methods have made it possible to have vegetables beyond their normal season. We can now pick and choose from a variety available to us all round the year.

Modern cultivation methods, genetic engineering and improved transportation have assured a constant supply. New varieties and hybrids are constantly being selected and developed. The consumer is offered good produce of a uniform size, colour and shelf life. Sometimes, the flavour may suffer because of these new techniques. Vegetables are rich in vitamins and minerals, contain little fat and no cholesterol. However, the nutritive value depends upon factors like weather, soil conditions and variety.

SELECTING VEGETABLES

There are specific indications of quality of each vegetable. However, in general, crispness and bright colour indicate freshness. Vegetables past their prime have wilted leaves, brown patches and soft flesh. Damaged and bruised vegetables should be avoided. Fresh vegetables are tender and sweet. Vegetables that are immature often lack juiciness, and may sometimes be bitter. Some recipes require baby corns or baby potatoes. These are the dwarf variety. If they are the normal variety picked at an early stage, they lack the flavour of the mature vegetable. However, small squashes are always sweet and have more flavour than the large ones. With practice you will begin to differentiate fresh vegetables from the stale ones.

STORING VEGETABLES

Root vegetables and hardy pumpkins keep well at normal room temperature. Green and soft vegetables such as cucumber should be stored in the refrigerator. Use the crisper compartment or the lower shelves. The vegetables could be loosely folded in a cling film or cloth. Airtight wrapping encourages bacteria. Vegetables should never be washed until just before use. Moisture causes the vegetables to rot, and there is loss of vitamins. Different vegetables should be stored separately. Onions cause potatoes to spoil more quickly. A variety of metal, wire and plastic storage racks are available in the market to store potatoes, onions and similar vegetables.

PEELING VEGETABLES

It is important to be aware that modern pesticides stick to the vegetable skin.

Simple washing may not be enough to remove them. It is best to peel vegetables to reduce the likelihood of contamination. Vegetables such as potatoes absorb water easily. They are best boiled or steamed with the skin. This helps retain their vitamins and absorb less moisture. Beetroots, when cooked with their skin, do not bleed.

Cutting Vegetables

There are several methods of cutting vegetables. Evenly cut vegetables cook uniformly. The dish also has an attractive appearance. You must use good sharp knives. Select a large or a small chopping knife, depending upon the vegetable. It is important to handle the knife correctly. Grasp it firmly with your fingers wrapped around the handle. Use the free hand to steady the vegetable on the chopping board. The fingertips should curl under and the knuckles should guide the knife.

A mechanical chopper can make chopping and cutting easier. Several manual gadgets for this purpose are also available in the market. A food processor with a variety of blades and discs can do cutting, chopping, grating and mincing easily. You have to be careful not to overwork the vegetables to a pulp. Let us now discuss the various ways of chopping vegetables that one needs to know in everyday cooking.

Dicing Vegetables

This is the most common cut used to prepare vegetables both for curries and dry preparations.

1. Peel and square off the sides of the vegetable. Slice vertically, cutting thick for large pieces, and thin for small ones.
2. Stack the slices together. Cut even strips of uniform thickness.
3. Arrange the strips together into a pile. Slice them evenly crosswise to make pieces of required size.

Cutting into Julienne

Julienne means to cut into thin strips, or small match-like pieces. This is a favourite cut for garnishing, for French fries and sometimes for special stir fried dishes.

1. Peel and cut a thin strip from one side so that the vegetable lies flat on the chopping board.
2. Chop the vegetable crosswise into 5 centimeter pieces. Then cut lengthwise into thin vertical slices.
3. Stack the slices together and cut into thin strips lengthwise. The trick is to keep the tip of the knife on the board while you cut.

Slicing into Chiffonade

This cut is used while preparing leafy vegetables like spinach, cabbage and lettuce. We chop them into coarse shreds.

1. Remove the stalk if tough. To do this, fold the leaf in half with the stalk upwards and the ridge outwards. With the other hand, tear the stalk from the leaf.
2. Stack the leaves together and roll the pile tightly.
3. Slice across the roll to make coarse strips.

Shredding Cabbage

We just discussed how to slice leafy vegetables into chiffonade. Cabbage is also shredded in the same manner.

However, the inner stem has to be removed before shredding the cabbage.

1. Set the cabbage; cut side down on the chopping board. Cut cross-wise into very fine slices. After shredding, throw away any thick ribs.
2. This can also be done in a manual shredder or a food processor. For this you must use quartered chunks of the cabbage.

Cutting Cauliflower

Cauliflower can be cooked whole, cut into florets or grated and used as paratha filling.

Above: Breaking Cauliflower
Below: Grating Cauliflower

1. Break off or cut the outer leaves and trim the stalk near the base of the head.
2. Using a paring knife, cut around the core to remove it.
3. Break the cauliflower into smaller pieces. Cut into pieces of desired size. You can use a metal or plastic grater to grate the florets. A food processor can do the work easily if worked carefully in short spurts.

When you wish to cook the cauliflower as a whole, the lower stem should be cut off. Then hold cauliflower in a muslin cloth and lower it into boiling water. The cauliflower is then partially cooked. The rest of the cooking is done after the spices are added, and served whole.

TIPS: Cauliflower can be washed and steamed whole in the steaming basket of microwave for 4 to 5 minutes on micro high (depending on the size).

Preparing Broccoli

Broccoli is a member of the cabbage family. It comes from Italy and looks like a small, green coloured cauliflower.

1. Trim the base of each stalk and throw away any tough leaves.
2. Using a paring knife, strip the tough outer skin from the base of the stalk up to the heads.
3. To divide the broccoli, split each stalk length wise 2-3 times.
4. If you want to separate the broccoli into florets, lay the stalks on a board and cut off the florets where they start to branch. Break apart any additional stalks.

Expert cook suggests...

1. Do not throw away the white stalks of the cauliflower. Chop them fine and use it instead of onion to make any onion-based curries. The curries will taste as good.
2. Adding a little milk while cooking cauliflower keeps it white.

Cutting and Preparing Jackfruit

Jackfruit is an exotic vegetable of India. It is eaten as a vegetable, pickle and as a fruit. Unlike other vegetables, it is tricky to cut and prepare jackfruit.

1. To cut it for cooking one should smear the palms with any cooking oil so that its sticky milk does not harm the skin.
2. Its tough skin is removed with a sharp knife and then it is cut into any desired size.
3. Some boil it first and then cook it, whereas others prefer to fry its pieces and then cook like mutton with vindaloo *masala*/punjabi gravy/coconut paste.
4. When ripe, its egg like seeds and flesh, are consumed as a fresh fruit.

Fruit Vegetables

Most cooks accept them as vegetables. However, tomatoes, aubergines and peppers of all varieties are fruits. All three have common cooking characters. They mix well with other vegetables. They are also ideal to be used as stuffing with a variety of ingredients.

The tomato is indispensable to cooking. In the market, we have a large variety ranging from round to long in shape, green or yellow to the common red in colour. Their size varies from tiny cherry tomatoes to that of an apple. Green tomatoes are not a separate variety. They are unripe tomatoes picked before time. They are good for making pickles. The yellow variety is popular for its colour, sweetness and lower acid content. They are good for salads and preserves. The ripe red tomato is easily perishable. Therefore, much of the supply that reaches us is picked when still green. Then they are ripened through special techniques though they suffer in flavour. Those that are allowed to ripen on the plant have a distinct flavour. Tomatoes are used both in cooking and in

Tomatoes, Brinjals, Green and Red Peppers

salads. You have already learnt how to blanche, peal, seed and chop tomatoes in the previous lesson.

The aubergine or the brinjal possibly originated in Asia. It belongs to the same family as the tomato. Most brinjals are deep purple in colour. Some varieties are green and white. They are both round and elongated in shape and differ in size. The round ones are best for *baingan bharta* as they yield more flesh. The tiny elongated ones are good for making stuffed brinjals. The brinjal is a popular vegetable because of its vibrant colour and the melting richness of its flesh. Though the traditional varieties are not likely to be bitter, some brinjals, particularly the over-matured ones with well-developed seeds, could be bitter. Salting helps draw out the bitter juices.

Peppers or capsicum are milder members of the chilli family. They are available in shades of green, red, yellow, orange and purple. They are good for cooked dishes, for stuffing with different ingredients as well as for eating raw in salads.

Scoring Brinjals

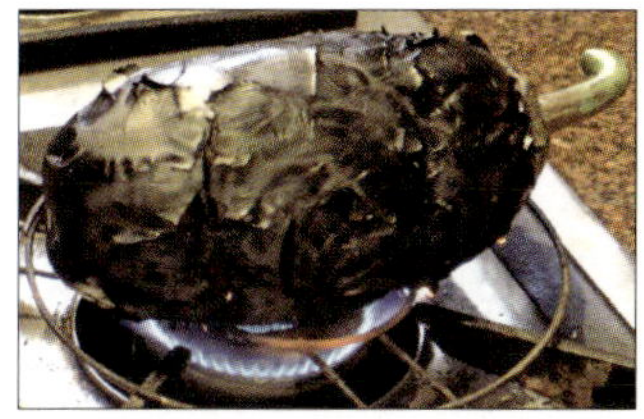

To make dishes such as *baingan ka bharta*, one needs to follow the simple procedure:

1. Take the whole brinjal. Rub it with a few drops of cooking oil.
2. Char-grill the brinjal on the gas stove. When done, remove from gas.
3. Wash and peel the charred skin right away.
4. Mash the cooked brinjal. Proceed with making the *bharta* as described in recipe.

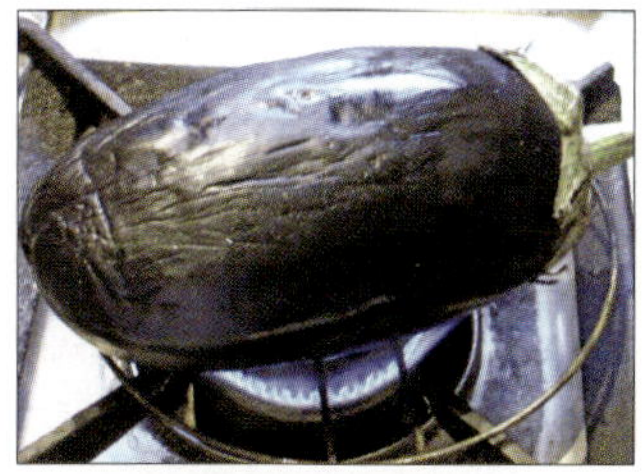

Brinjal being Scored

Coring, Seeding and Slicing Capsicums

A variety of cuts are used to slice or chop capsicum. The cut will depend upon the dish one wishes to prepare.

1. Using a sharp, pointed knife, cut around the core, twist and pull it out.
2. Cut the pepper in half and scrape out the seeds.
3. Cut away the raised ribs on the inside of the capsicum.
4. Place the halved capsicum cut side down on the chopping board. Press down with the reel of your hand to flatten it. Slice it or chop it with a large knife.
5. To prepare the capsicum for stuffing, cut off the core and scrape out seeds and the ribs. Wash well under running water and proceed as the recipe directs.
6. If you wish to cut the capsicum into rings, do not cut into half. After cutting away the core, remove the seeds and the ribs. Cut the pepper cross-wise with a large, sharp knife.

TIPS: For stuffing capsicums, after coring and deseeding, wash them; rub a little salt inside and invert them for 20 to 30 minutes before use.

Peas and Beans

All varieties of peas and beans belong to the legume family. Sweet corn, though treated like a legume, is not a member of this family. Around the world there are many varieties of peas and beans typical to individual regions. However, there are a few like the green peas that are common to all regions. Most of them are prepared in the same way for cooking.

There are three common types of peas and beans.

1. Those that are eaten young in the pod before the seed is ripe.
2. Those that are shelled to remove the mature seeds from the pods.
3. Those that are dried to be cooked later.

Dried peas and beans have been discussed earlier. Let us now discuss the fresh varieties. Snap beans, often called string beans, are tender and eaten with the pod.

Very often the strings need stripping and then the beans are chopped into small pieces to cook in dry preparations in combination with other vegetables like potatoes or onions. They are often cooked whole and made into curries as well.

Peas, Broad Beans, French Beans

The French beans, a part of the Chinese cuisine, are popular on account of their slender pods and taste. They are also known as haricot beans. You only need to trim the ends and chop them into the desired size. When the pods are over matured, you will need to strip the strings.

One of the common varieties is the broad bean, which is delicious steamed, sautéed, curried, stir fried and also pickled. Mature shelled beans are almost always dried. Fresh green peas herald the coming of winter. They are now available most of the time. Their sweetness diminishes when the climate turns warm. They can be cooked into a variety of dishes in combination with other vegetables: used in rice dishes, make an ideal ingredient for stuffing, and go well with meat and poultry, too. Steamed or boiled peas can be used in salads, or could be stir fried to make a side dish in a hurry. Unfortunately, most green peas lose flavour soon after picking. This explains the popularity of canned and frozen peas. Unlike beans, most fresh peas are eaten shelled.

Expert cook suggests...

1. To get thin and long pieces of French beans, cut them with scissors instead of a knife. It cuts the beans quickly and easily.
2. To preserve green peas without using any preservation, shell them and pack them in an airtight polythene bag. When frozen, they remain fresh for a very long time.

Slicing, Shelling and Skinning Beans and Peas

You must remove the tough strings of summer beans before chopping them. With French beans you need to only trim the ends.

1. Holding the bean between your forefinger and thumb, make a thin diagonal slice to cut off the string. Then chop into desired size.
2. To shell beans and peas, squeeze the pod between two fingers to split it open. Scoop out the contents with your thumb.
3. To skin broad beans, make a slit lengthwise in the skin of the bean. Pinch the opposite end of the skin to squeeze out the flesh inside the bean.

Corn

Corn

The bright yellow and creamy white varieties of sweet corn were cultivated in Mexico earlier. Now they are available all over the world. White corn came earlier, but the yellow corn with higher Vitamin A content is more popular. Like peas, corn contains sugar that begin to convert to starch as soon as the cob is picked. Therefore, freshness is important. Canned sweet corn is available in the market. Its use is restricted to making continental dishes or soups.

Baby-corn, a miniature variety, has become a favourite because of its use in Chinese and Continental cuisine.

Traditionally, corn is boiled or char-grilled over open fire, smeared with lime juice and *chaat masala* or butter and eaten from the cob itself. Alternatively, the kernels can be removed from the cob and cooked, steamed or boiled to make a variety of salads, curries, stir fries or stuffing. When the kernels are dried, they can be pounded to make porridge or dry snacks. They can be ground to flour to make the famous *Makki-ki-roti* from North India. The kernels can be specially treated to make popcorns, a favourite snack.

TIPS

Maize flour or *makki-ka-atta* is also used in Western cooking to make many breads and pies. It is also a base of famous Mexican dishes like Tortillas and Tacos. Delicious cakes and cookies are also prepared with maize flour and cornflakes.

Husking Corn and Removing Corn Kernels

1. To husk the corn, pull the papery husk down the ear of the corn to the base. Snap or trim off the husk and stalks. Strip away the silky golden threads known as corn silk.
2. To remove the kernels from the cob, hold the ear of the corn vertically and cut from the tip down. This way whole kernels will pop out leaving a thin layer of pulp on the cob.

The Gourd Family

Pumpkin, marrow and squashes are members of the gourd family. They come in various colours, shapes and sizes. The summer squashes, long gourd or *ghia* or *lauki* as we call it, is a summer vegetable. However, it is available throughout the year. It is soft-skinned and green or whitish green in colour. The small round *tinda* is yet another variety of this squash and is very popular in North India. The squash, gourd and pumpkin are also used in South India as one of the ingredients in *sambhar* or the traditional dal dish that accompanies most South Indian meals. The summer squash is pleasantly mild in taste and can be peeled and chopped to make a variety of dishes from dry-fry to curries, soups and stews, solo or in combination with other vegetables, dals and meats. You could grate and steam squash to mix with beaten curd to make a delicious raita. You could grate it to make koftas but it should be salted first to draw out moisture.

Pumpkins, Bitter Ridge, Bottle, Zucchini, *Parwal*

The winter squash or the white and yellow pumpkin and marrow have thick skin, large seeds and a slightly fibrous flesh. It is picked when fully matured. The skin is hard and often ridged. It has to be peeled and the seeds scooped out before the vegetable is chopped for cooking. The white pumpkin (*petha*) can be made into a number of sweet meats and the yellow pumpkin is made into side dishes, curries and also into a number of South Indian dishes such as *avial* and *sambhar*.

Nonstick cookware is ideal for healthy cooking. To get the best from your cookware:

1. Always cook on low or medium heat. This helps protect the coating, and also saves fuel.
2. Use only wooden or plastic spatulas to avoid damage to the coating.
3. Wash cookware with mild soap and water.

Roots and Tubers

These include turnips, carrots, radish, beetroot, parsnip, yam and the all-time favourite, potato. They grow underground and keep well without refrigeration.

Radish, Beetroot, Arum Table Radish, Potatoes, Carrots

The cooking of roots and tubers should begin in cold water. The cooking should continue at a gentle simmer till tender but not breaking up. Some roots and tubers get discoloured on being cut. To avoid this; they must be soaked in saline water. They can be cooked as dry dishes and also as curries.

Carrots are red, purple, black and even orange-yellow in colour. The size ranges from short, round and stubby to fairly long and pointed. The tender new carrots are sweeter than the mature ones. They are ideal for salads and garnishing and can be combined with other vegetables as they do not get mashed during long cooking. This makes the carrots ideal for soups and stews. Mixed with other vegetables; chopped carrots can be cooked as a side dish. Cut into julienne, it goes well into stir fried noodles. Grated carrots can be used to make *kheer* and *halwa*. Parsnips are closely related to the carrot family. They can be used to make excellent soups and stews. They are not used in Indian cooking.

The **radish (mooli)** can be small, bright red or white long ones, which are harvested young and eaten raw in salads. The long and thick ones are ideal for making a dry preparation popular in Bengali cuisine. They can be grated to make stuffing for parathas, or eaten raw in salads or used as garnishing. The leaves can be finely chopped along with a little radish tube and made into an excellent stir fried side dish.

Though there is no resemblance between the two, the turnips are a member of the cabbage family. They have a mild, bland taste and can make delicious soups and stews. They go well with meats and poultry.

Turnips are also cooked like *saags* with their own greens or mixed with other leafy vegetables like spinach, etc., or as a dry vegetable in the chopped form.

The **kohlrabi** looks and tastes very much like the turnip. It can be substituted for turnips in most dishes. The leaves can be finely chopped and cooked like spinach. In Kashmir it is eaten the most in many forms and is called *'kadam'*.

Beetroot is small and round with a thin reddish-brown skin and a dark pinkish-red flesh that has a notable sweet taste. Peeled and chopped or sliced beetroot is popularly used in salads. It has a tendency to bleed and stain other ingredients. It is considered ideal for making certain soups and stews in combination with meat. In India, it is also used to make delicious *halwa*.

POTATO

Potato is too well-known to be described. It forms an important part of the diet around the world. It is the tuber of the underground root of the potato plant. It contains a lot of starch. The starch converts to sugar at low temperature causing the potato to turn black. Do not refrigerate potatoes. The starch acts as a binder and a thickening agent holding together curries, koftas, stews and cutlets. For crisp fries, cut potatoes should be soaked in water to remove starch, and dried before frying.

Potatoes

With the onset of winter come the tiny baby potatoes, which taste excellent in dry as well as curried preparations like the *dum aloo*. New potatoes are expensive and easily perishable. As the potatoes mature, the skin thickens and the starch content increases. Potatoes can be boiled in their jackets, mashed to make a delicious filling for parathas, baked in their jackets in an oven or in hot ashes, quartered, chopped, or sliced to make dry or curried dishes. They can be peeled or cooked with the skin on for better flavour and nutrition. Boiled potatoes make crisp cutlets with exotic fillings. They can be mashed to make *aloo bharta*. Peeled, halved and deep or shallow fried, potatoes are used to garnish roasts and steaks. They can be combined with meat to make stews and soups. Everyone has tried the famous potato wafers, *papad*, and French fries. Potatoes are one of those indispensable vegetables that have numerous / endless uses.

The **Sweet potato/ *Shakarkandi*** belongs to a different family. It is not as extensively used as the potato. It is either white or maroon in colour with a mealy white flesh. The sweet flesh makes savoury pies and puddings. It is often boiled, mashed and combined with milk and sugar to make porridge for breakfast. Chopped into chunks and deep-fried, it makes a good *chaat*.

Sweet Potatoes

Yam

The **Yam** is another tuber, popularly known as *jimikand*. In size it is much larger than the sweet potato. It is peeled, cubed and made into curries. It is also used boiled or steamed and mashed to make a delectable *bharta*.

Clockwise: Matchsticks, Waffled, Diced, Chips

CUTTING AND COOKING POTATOES

Potato straw: These are very thin strips of potatoes served with sauce or with just a sprinkling of *chaat masala* to make it mouth-watering. To prepare them, trim the ends and sides of the potato. Cut into finest slices. Stack the slices and cut into fine strips. Fry in hot oil until golden brown. Drain on absorbent paper.

Potato matchsticks: These are thicker than straws and are also called French fries. The process of cutting is the same as above but the strips are thicker, about ¼ inch thick and 3 inch long julienne strips. Fry in hot oil till golden. Drain on absorbent paper.

Potato chips or fingers: These are as thick as the fingers. The strips are about ½ inch thick and 3 inch long. These are fried twice. First, fry in hot oil for 4-5 minutes till tender. Drain and cool. Fry again till golden and crisp. Drain on absorbent paper.

Potato *bhaji*: This is a common preparation. It is ideal as a side dish, or to be served at breakfast with plain parathas. It is ideal to go into the packed lunch. Trim the ends and sides of potatoes, and cut into ½ inch thick slices. Stack the slices together. Cut into ½ inch squares. Fry twice like potato fingers.

Potato crisps: These are paper thin, round slices of potatoes fried in hot oil until golden brown and drained on absorbent paper.

Waffled crisps: This is cut with a special blade or the mandolin. These are paper thin, round and fluted slices of potatoes to be fried till golden brown.

All the above preparations are deep-fried. Soak the cut potatoes in cold water with a pinch of salt. Drain and pat dry on a clean kitchen towel. Fry in small batches. If you put in too many potatoes in the oil, you will never get the desired crispness. Keep stirring. Potatoes tend to stick together. Always drain on absorbent paper. Sprinkle salt and any other seasoning just before serving. Salt makes them soggy. Serve immediately otherwise the crispness will be lost. Only the *bhaji* can be served cold as it is not served as a snack but as a side dish.

Expert cook suggests...

1. To bake potatoes quickly, boil them for 10 minutes and then bake them in the oven for 20 minutes at 350°F.
2. Potato skins will remain tender when potatoes are baked in aluminium foil.
3. A pinch of alum added to the water in which potatoes are boiled helps keep them white.

BULBS

The onion family that includes onions, leek, shallot, spring onions and garlic belong to this category. We have already discussed them earlier. These serve both as vegetables and seasoning. They are a part of most cuisines worldwide.

Leaves

All the hearty greens such as spinach, turnip greens, mustard greens and red/green *chaulai* come into this category. Most of them are cut into chiffonade style; stir fried or boiled; pureed and simmered over low heat and tempered with spices, tomatoes and onions. They are popular in India and especially in the northern part, where mustard greens or *sarson-ka-saag* is enjoyed thoroughly with *makki-ki-roti*.

Expert cook suggests...

1. Slice some onions and add salt to them; after half an hour squeeze out the excess water and dry the onions in the sun for two or three days till they are crisp. Powder in a mixer. Use this powder in curries or wherever you need to use onions. This powder has a long shelf life.
2. To prevent onions from burning and to retain their pink colour while frying, add a little milk when frying them.
3. Slice and fry onions in oil. Drain on absorbent paper and grind in a mixer. Store in a jar. Use whenever you need to make a curry.
4. To save on time and your tears while chopping onions, blend a kilo in a mixer and store the paste in an airtight container in the refrigerator.

Mushrooms

A mushroom is the fleshy fruiting body of a fungus. There are an estimated 40,000 species of mushrooms worldwide. Modern cultivation is of recent origin. Earlier, they were collected in the natural state.

Mushrooms contain high quality protein. Some varieties also boast of vitamin A or D. They have a chewy texture and an earthy flavour. The cultivated varieties are available almost all round the year. They are available in abundance during winter. Easily perishable, mushrooms are protected by strong pesticides. They must be washed well in cold water and pat dry before cooking.

Wild mushrooms are often poisonous. Since it is difficult to identify the edible ones, it is best to buy the cultivated variety.

Dicing, Chopping and Slicing Mushrooms

Mushrooms must be cut evenly so as to cook uniformly. They are delicate and bruise easily. Always use a sharp knife. A food processor can also be used. However, one has to be careful not to overwork them. Mushrooms are delicate! Give them special care.

1. To dice mushrooms, trim the stalk level with the cap. Placing the mushroom stalk side down on the board, cut the cap into thick (for large dice) or medium (for medium-sized dice) horizontal slices.
2. Stack the slices together and cut across to make dices of desired size.
3. To cut into julienne, hold the mushroom by the stalk and cut the cap into thin horizontal slices, discarding the bottom slice when the gills appear.
4. Stack the slices together and cut lengthwise into thin strips. These go well with mixed vegetables or mixed fried rice.
5. To chop mushrooms, hold the cap firmly and cut into slices.
6. Stack the slices one on top of the other and cut crosswise into sticks.
7. Chop the sticks fine by holding the point of the knife down with the flat of your hand and bouncing the blade up and down. Work to and fro across the board. This can also be done in a food processor.
8. To slice mushrooms, trim the stalk level with the cap. Place the mushroom stalk down on the board. Hold firmly. Slice vertically through the stalk and cap.

Cooking vegetables

Most vegetables are cooked in a *kadhai*. With people becoming health conscious, the conventional *kadhai* is giving way to a variety of nonstick cookware. A pressure cooker is often used for boiling vegetables, particularly the tough ones. It is also the utensil of choice for making most soups and stews.

Drawing out bitter juices

Through this method, salt is used to treat vegetables such as cucumber, aubergine (brinjal) or bitter gourd (*karela*) to remove the bitterness in them.

1. Cut the vegetables into slices or chunks. Sprinkle salt evenly.
2. After 30 minutes, wash well under running water. This not only draws up the bitter juices but also firms up the texture of the vegetable.
3. For cucumbers, cut the top off the cucumber from the root. Sprinkle salt on it. Rub with the cut piece. Soon you will see froth appearing on top. Discard the cut top. Cut off the slice with the froth. Discard that too. Wash well, peel and cut into desired size.

Practical things to be done

1. Dum Aloo

Utensils used: a *kadhai*, a frying pan, a spatula, a colander, a large plate.

Gadgets: chopping board; a sharp chopping knife; a food processor.

Portions: We are cooking for two persons.

Ingredients: 1 large onion, peeled and quartered; 1 inch piece of ginger, peeled and finely chopped; 2 garlic cloves, peeled; 2 tsp curry powder; 500 gms potatoes; 2 tbsp vegetable oil; ½ cup heavy cream; oil for deep frying; 1 tbsp chopped fresh mint; 1 spring onion, finely chopped with the greens for garnishing; salt and freshly ground pepper according to taste.

Dum Aloo

Follow the procedure given below.

1. Mix onion, ginger, garlic and curry powder. Grind to a smooth paste in the food processor. Add one tbsp water, if necessary.
2. Cut the potatoes into quarters about 1 inch in size. New potatoes do not need to be peeled. If the potatoes are old, remove their skin. Wash well under running water in a colander. Pat dry on a kitchen towel. Heat oil for deep-frying in a *kadhai*. Fry the potatoes in small batches till golden brown.
3. Heat 2 tbsp of oil in a frying pan. Add the *masala* paste. Fry gently, stirring with the spatula, for 2-3 minutes. Add the yogurt, cream and chopped mint. Mix well.
4. Add the fried potatoes. Stir. Lower the heat. Simmer for 5-7 minutes till the potatoes are tender, and the sauce has thickened. Season with salt and pepper. Taste the salt and flavour. Sprinkle the chopped spring onions. Serve hot. This dish goes well with puri, paratha or plain steamed rice.

2. Gobi Matar

Utensils used: a *kadhai*, a plate to cover, a ladle.

Portions: We are cooking for two persons.

Ingredients: ½ kg cauliflower, cut into medium size pieces; 250 gm fresh peas, shelled; one medium size onion, chopped fine; 1 inch ginger, chopped; 1 clove garlic, chopped; ¼ tsp turmeric powder; ¼ tsp chilli powder; ¼ tsp cumin seeds; 2 tbsp cooking oil; salt to taste; green coriander to garnish.

Gobi Matar

To cook the vegetable, follow this simple procedure:

1. Boil peas separately. Do not cover. They will turn yellow if you cover them.
2. Put the oil, onion, garlic and ginger in the *kadhai*. Fry over low heat, stirring constantly till the mixture turns light pink.

3. Add cauliflower, salt, cumin, turmeric powder and chilli powder. Cover. Cook for about 10 minutes over low heat.
4. Add boiled peas. Mix. Cook for a few minutes. Garnish with chopped coriander. Serve hot.

Expert cook suggests...

1. To increase the storage life of lemons, rub a little coconut oil on the skin before storing them in the refrigerator.
2. Peel and grind garlic. Add an equal quantity of salt and store. Use this salt instead of the normal salt. This way you can store garlic for long periods.
3. To peel tomatoes without effort, place them in the freezer overnight. The skins will crack and come off easily.
4. If carrots turn stale, dip them in cold water overnight. They will become fresh.
5. Coriander leaves will stay fresh if you remove their main stems, and store them in a steel box in the refrigerator.
6. Green chillies remain fresh in the refrigerator for a long time if you remove their stems before storing them.
7. Lemons can be made juicier by keeping them immersed in warm water for some time.
8. When cooking *'bhindi'* add a few drops of lemon juice for a crispy taste.
9. Add a little salt when frying or roasting red chillies. This prevents the burnt chilli smell and throat irritation caused by burning chillies.
10. Rub your hands with lemon peel to remove the smell of garlic and onions.
11. Place garlic cloves in the sun. They peel off easily.

Baby Carrots

Whole Cauliflower

Sarson Ka Saag

Mushrooms, Methi, Moong, Sprouts

PROGRESS CHECKLIST # 1

Do not skip this checklist. Answer all the questions. They are based on what you learnt in the last six days. Whenever in doubt, go back to the appropriate lesson and reread the relevant section. Your sincere efforts will make you a great cook.

1. Have you understood why it is important that one must eat a balanced diet?

   ☐ Yes ☐ No

2. Did you visit the market and looked around the vegetable and fruit shops?

   ☐ Yes ☐ No

3. Have you understood the concept of planning every meal?

   ☐ Yes ☐ No

4. Can you differentiate between different varieties of rice?

   ☐ Yes ☐ No

   If you cannot, visit a provision store, and ask the salesman to show you the different varieties available. Compare the prices of each variety.

5. Did the family enjoy the rice you cooked?

   ☐ Yes ☐ No

   If not, try again until you are satisfied.

6. Were you able to knead the flour for the rotis well? Did the rotis come out good?

   ☐ Yes ☐ No

   Keep trying. Practice makes one perfect.

7. Have you understood why the use of spices, herbs and condiments requires expert handling.

   ☐ Yes ☐ No

8. Can you recognise different pulses?

   ☐ Yes ☐ No

   If you cannot, go to a store and get to know all kind of pulses.

9. Were you able to peel and cut vegetables for the practical sessions neatly?

   ☐ Yes ☐ No

   Keep trying. Cutting vegetables is an important step towards becoming a great cook.

Day 07

Milk and Milk Products

Dairy products are amongst the most versatile food that are part of many recipes. Milk is a complete food. The newly born mammals live and grow only with milk as their diet. Besides being nutritive, dairy products are generally inexpensive. These products in the form of milk, curd or yogurt, butter cream, cheese of all variety, clarified butter or ghee and dried milk (*mawa* or *khoya*) are important in our everyday life. Milk is a basic necessity for all.

Milk

We drink milk, both hot and cold, with breakfast cereals, corn flakes or porridge, in soups and sauces, ice creams, puddings and other desserts, in cakes, breads and biscuits, in milkshakes and sometimes in curries too. The most popular of all milk is cow's milk. It contains 87 percent water, 3.5 percent protein (mostly casein) and 5 percent carbohydrates (lactose). The fat content varies from 3 percent to over 5 percent, depending on the breed of the cow and its feed.

Milk Products
Clockwise: Yellow Butter, Processed Cheese, Buttermilk, Curd, *Khoya, Malai,* White Butter, Milk, *Paneer*

The milk from goat and sheep is rich in fat and protein. It is used mostly for making processed cheese. It is also sold as health food, popular among the health-conscious people. Buffalo's milk has the highest fat content. It is commonly used in North India. It makes excellent *mawa* or *khoya*, sweetmeats and cheese.

Most countries do not encourage sale of raw milk straight from the dairy because it may contain dangerous organisms that cause tuberculosis. To destroy the bacteria, the milk is pasteurised by heating it to 144°F for 30 minutes. The milk may also be homogenised to evenly disperse the fat within the milk.

Purchasing Milk

Milk is available in many forms in the market. Everyone must know how each variety differs in use and form, from the other.

Whole milk: Whole milk is characterised by a smooth, rich flavour. It contains a fat content of at least 3.5 percent. It enjoys popularity both as a beverage and food for many decades.

Low-fat milk: Low-fat milk is very popular. There are two major types of low-fat milk available: 1 percent or 2 percent. The content of fat is marked on the packaging.

Skimmed milk: Skimmed milk has a fat content of less than 0.5 percent. It has a 'cloudy' appearance. It lacks the richness in taste of either whole or low-fat milk. Those accustomed to drinking whole or low-fat milk, find skimmed milk watery and without flavour.

Kesar Elaichi Milk

Flavoured milk: Flavoured milk is made by adding sugar and flavours to milk. The milk may be whole, low-fat, or skim. The flavouring could be chocolate, strawberry, almonds, and of other items.

Eggnog: It is a flavoured milk containing a mixture of dairy products like milk, cream, partially skimmed milk, eggs and sweeteners. It may be flavoured with nutmeg, vanilla, or other flavouring.

Lactose-treated milk: Milk that has been treated with the enzyme lactose is particularly helpful for individuals who have lactose intolerance. Lactose intolerance or lactose deficiency is a disease caused by a lack of enzyme lactose, which is needed by the intestine to split lactose into its two components for absorption. After drinking milk or eating a dairy product with lactose, the lactose-intolerant individuals experience symptoms that include abdominal cramps, bloating, and diarrhoea. Lactose-treated milk is ready to drink. It can be used in recipes as it has only 30 percent of the lactose found in regular milk. This variety of milk is available only in speciality stores in the metropolitan cities.

Certified milk: This is plain raw milk that has not been pasteurised. Private dairies sell this kind of milk.

Evaporated milk and evaporated skimmed milk: These products are made by heating milk to stabilise the milk protein, and then removing about 64 percent of the water. Both products are sold in tins and plastic bottles. Evaporated milk has 7.5 percent milk fat and evaporated skimmed milk has not more than 0.5 percent milk fat. One-half cup of either product can be mixed with one-half cup of water to make 1 cup of milk. Both are used for cooking, baking and making beverages.

Milkmaid

Sweetened condensed milk and skimmed milk: These products also have about 60 percent of their water removed. They are highly concentrated, extremely sweet, thick and syrupy, like with 8 percent milk fat. Sweetened condensed skimmed milk has not more than 0.5 percent milk fat. Both are used to whiten and sweeten both tea and coffee in the absence of fresh milk. They can also make some delicious desserts and *halwa*.

Powder milk or dry milk: This milk is totally free of moisture as its water content is completely evaporated. It may be low-fat or no-fat milk. It is convenient in hot climates When mixed with water, we have milk slightly thinner than fresh milk. It is used commercially in baking to give a brown crust to bread and its increased shelf life.

Cultured buttermilk: Adding a bacterial culture to fresh, pasteurised skimmed milk makes buttermilk. The bacteria convert the sugar in milk lactose into lactic acid, thereby giving buttermilk a thick consistency and tart and buttery taste. Buttermilk is enjoyed as a beverage. It is also used in baking when sour milk is needed. It is also used in making salad dressings and some cold soups.

Natural buttermilk: This is the liquid that is left behind after milk has been churned to extract the fat as butter. In India, yogurt is churned with water to make buttermilk. Its consistency varies with the amount of water added. It makes a refreshing drink, very popular in the rural areas.

Natural Flavoured Buttermilk

When purchasing fresh milk, make sure it is pasteurised and homogenised. Always store milk in a stainless steel container as certain nutrients in milk, such as riboflavin, are destroyed by light. Always store milk in a refrigerator.

Nutritional Value

Milk is a good source of:

- High-quality protein
- Carbohydrates
- Riboflavin
- Vitamins A and D
- Calcium and other minerals such as phosphorus, magnesium and zinc.

Buttermilk has about the same nutritional composition as the milk from which it is made. Evaporated milk, when mixed with an equal part of water, has about the same nutritional value as an equal amount of fresh milk. Condensed milk is much higher in calories than fresh milk due to the high fat content and the added sugar. Powdered skimmed milk, when mixed with water, has about the same nutritional value as an equal amount of skimmed milk.

Storing Milk

Fresh milk is perishable. It can be stored in the refrigerator for a maximum of 2 days. Whole milk stays fresh longer than either skimmed or low-fat milk. If the milk turns bad, it means that it has been mishandled. The milk has been subjected to warm up one or more times. Always keep the milk container closed. This ensures that the milk does not absorb other odours in the refrigerator. Do not let the container sit on the kitchen table during meals.

Food made with milk, such as pudding and custard, should be covered tightly in the refrigerator. They must be used within 2 to 3 days. Evaporated, condensed, and non-fat dry milk can all be stored unopened in a cool, dry place for nearly 6 months. Once opened, evaporated and condensed; milk should be poured into another container, refrigerated, and used within 5 days. Once reconstituted, non-fat dry milk should be refrigerated and used within 3 days.

Cooking with Milk

Saboodana Payasam

Milk products are an important part of many recipes. The addition of milk products gives a creamy consistency to many sauces and curries, helps dissolve dry ingredients in baked products, and adds good nutrition and flavour to food. Substituting low-fat or skimmed milk for whole milk works well in most cooking and baking recipes to reduce the fat content.

When cooking with milk, remember a very important rule. Use moderate heat. Heat the milk slowly to avoid 'curdling'. Milk 'curdles' when the casein, the protein in the milk, separates out of the milk. When this happens, the milk develops a grainy appearance with a lumpy texture. Once the milk has curdled, there is no way to bring it to its original form. However, soft cottage cheese or *paneer* can be made from curdled milk. Heat and squeeze the juice of half a lemon into the curdled milk. Soon you will find the soft white substance separating from water. Strain in a muslin cloth. Let it hang from a hook over the kitchen sink. All the water will drain away leaving the residue as soft *paneer*.

When mixing food and hot milk products, add the milk slowly with a spoon or using a wire whisk if preparing a sauce. This helps avoid formation of lumps. Be especially careful when adding milk to food high in acid as milk has a tendency to curdle very quickly if not beaten briskly.

Another problem with milk is the creation of a top layer or 'skin', a film that forms on top of the milk during cooking. Keeping the pot of milk covered can prevent this. Another problem with milk is scorching. Milk sticks to the bottom of the pot during cooking, and gradually begins to burn. This gives a bad taste to the food you are cooking. To avoid this, pour 2 tbsp of water in the vessel in which you are going to boil the milk. Then, pour in the milk and boil slowly.

Using a Milk Cooker

A milk cooker is a double boiler made of thick aluminium or stainless steel. You have to pour in half a cup of water into the outer container and the milk into the inner container. It has a lid with a whistle which goes off to inform you when the milk boils. This saves you from the headache of the milk boiling over, scorching or the 'skin' forming on top.

Calories Chart of Milk

PRODUCT	SERVING SIZE	CALORIES	FAT CONTENT (gms)
Skimmed milk	1 cup	86	0.5
1 percent milk	1 cup	102	3
2 percent milk	1 cup	121	5
Whole milk	1 cup	150	8
Half and half	1 tbsp	20	2
Light cream	1 tbsp	29	3
Light whipping **Cream, fluid**	1 tbsp	44	5
Heavy whipping **Cream, fluid**	1 tbsp	52	6
Sour cream	1 tbsp	26	3

Cheese

Cheese is a versatile food. It has many uses in cookery. Cheese is available in a variety of flavours ranging from mild to very sharp. It is an important ingredient in many recipes. It is also a great snack.

Purchasing cheese

Cheese is made from various types of milk. Milk from cows and goats is the most popular for making cheese. In many parts of the world, cheese is produced from various other sources of milk – sheep, reindeer, yak, buffalo, camel, mares, and donkeys. Cheese is produced when bacteria or rennet (or both) are added to milk, which then curdles. The liquid, known as whey, is separated from the solid, which is the cheese. It is believed that cheese was discovered by accident thousands of years ago in the ancient Far East.

Cheese can be divided into different categories depending on the texture or whether it has been ripened (also called cured). The texture of cheese varies from soft, semi-soft, firm to hard. Ripened cheese are those that have been fermented with bacteria and moulds. By contrast, unripened cheese is fresh and untreated. Unripened cheese is generally more perishable than the ripened cheese. The processing time is short since no time is spent in ripening it. When the cheese is manufactured, it is packaged and sold with a relatively short expiration date in comparison to the ripened cheese. Popular types of unripened cheese include ricotta cheese and cottage cheese.

Variety of Cheese

The ripened cheese needs several months to age and develop into a marketable cheese. Examples are Provolone and Parmesan cheese. For those who love blue cheese (and are willing to pay extra for the salad dressing when dining out), the blue vein in the cheese is a 'mould' that has been carefully controlled. It adds the characteristic flavour to the blue cheese. This cheese needs months of aging to create a ripening effect.

When a cheese or a combination of cheese is made into another type of cheese, it is referred to as 'processed cheese'. Whereas natural cheese is made directly from milk, processed cheese is a modified form of natural cheese that has been grounded or shredded from a variety of natural cheese. Processed cheese, which contains more sodium than natural cheese, takes many forms:

- Pasteurised processed cheese is a combination of cheddar and other cheese with emulsifiers to make it smooth (for this reason, this cheese melts better).
- Pasteurised processed cheese food and spreads are made like processed cheese except for the addition of optional ingredients such as cream, milk, buttermilk, non-fat dry solids, or whey. It contains more moisture and less fat than processed cheese.
- Mixing ripened cheese without the use of heat makes cold pack cheese.

When purchasing cheese, check for mould even when in airtight packaging. Mould commonly appear as white, blue, or green fuzzy spots. Also check for dryness. The cheese will have darker edges if this is the case. Many processed cheeses are marked with 'sell by' or 'use by' dates. Make sure the cheese has been kept cold. Only four type of cheese do not require refrigeration – cold-pack cheese, cold-pack cheese food, pasteurised processed cheese food, and pasteurised/processed cheese spread. When opened, they do need to be stored in a refrigerator.

Nutritional value

Cheese is an excellent source of nutrients such as protein and calcium. However, because most cheese is prepared from whole milk or cream, they are high in saturated fat and cholesterol. Cheese is rich in saturated fat. It is difficult to determine which cheese is high or low in saturated fat and cholesterol. There are different kinds of cheese available in the market – part-skim, low-fat, processed, and so on.

Storing cheese

Because of high fat content, several kinds of cheese readily absorb refrigerator odour, spoiling an otherwise good product. Therefore, store all cheese in plastic wrap or foil (except blue cheese, which must be wrapped loose). Cheese needs to be wrapped in airtight container to prevent it from drying. Hard and firm cheese keeps fine for a week to several months in the refrigerator, while semi-soft and soft cheese is more perishable. They stay fine for only one to two weeks. For unripened cheese, such as cottage cheese, check the 'sell by' or 'use by' date. These products should last at least for two days. In general, the home cheese does not last longer than the soft cheese.

Whenever you have to keep *paneer* in the refrigerator, immerse it in a bowl of water. Keep changing the water everyday. The *paneer* will keep fresh for at least 4-5 days.

Not all reduced fat or part-skimmed cheese is low on fat. They have a lower fat content as compared to similar natural cheese. For instance, one reduced-fat cheddar gets 56 percent of its calories from fat. This is considerably less than the 71 percent of regular cheddar cheese. To be sure, read the label. For less fat, saturated fat, cholesterol, and calories, choose a cheese made from skimmed milk or low-fat milk, with 4 grams of fat in 30 grams of cheese.

Besides cheese that contains less fat, there are also several varieties of cheese in the market with no fat. Examples include non-fat cream cheese and non-fat processed cheese. They are available only in selected cities of our country.

If conscious about sodium intake, cheese is high in sodium. Natural cheese, such as cheddar, has less sodium than processed cheese. Low-fat cheese often has more sodium than other kinds of cheese. Read the label carefully.

Cooking with Cheese

Cheese is rich in nutrients like proteins and fats. Many people avoid them for this reason. However, there are several ways to use cheese keeping the cooking light and healthy. Try some of these methods:

- Use less cheese than the recipe calls for.
- Substitute low-fat cheese for the regular one.
- Use a mixture of half of regular cheese and half of low-fat cheese.
- Use a regular cheese which is strong flavoured.

When cooking with cheese, observe these simple guidelines

1. Use low heat. It is best to use low heat, because cheese has a tendency to toughen when subjected to high heat, due to its high protein content. Avoid 'boiling' altogether.
2. Use shorter cooking time. Most recipes require the addition of cheese at the end of the recipe to avoid overcooking. Stir often to enhance the blend of flavours and ensure a good, smooth consistency.
3. Grate the cheese. The best way to add cheese to a recipe is to grate it. Grating breaks the cheese into small, thin pieces that melt and blend quickly and evenly in the dish.

Cream

Cream is used in many ways in the kitchen, such as in sauces, soups, hot and cold beverages, baked food, and when whipped, as a topping for desserts and hot beverages.

Purchasing cream

There are several types of cream. Most of them are pasteurised. Sometimes, ultra-pasteurised cream is available at the supermarket. As compared to pasteurised cream, ultra-pasteurised cream has a longer shelf life, but it does not whip as well.

Heavy whipping cream or heavy cream: Heavy cream is a very thick, semi-fluid liquid that has at least 36 percent fat (by weight). It is often used as a topping after a short period of whipping and can be used in sauces. Do not over-beat heavy cream. It will turn into butter!

Light whipping cream or whipping cream: Light-whipping cream contains 30-35 percent milk fat. Whipping cream marked as ultra-pasteurised does not whip as well as regular whipping cream. However, it has a longer shelf life.

Light cream: Light cream is also called table cream or coffee cream. It has a fat content of 18-30 percent (usually it is 18 percent). It has a strong, rich flavour. It is used as an ingredient in both sauces and baked products. It cannot be whipped well.

Half-and-half: Half-and-half (half milk, half cream) normally has a fat content of 10-12 percent. Its consistency is heavy and the flavour is rich. Like light cream, it cannot be whipped well.

Sour cream: Sour cream is made from pasteurised cream (with 18 percent fat content) to which a starter containing certain bacteria is added. The bacteria converts the milk sugar lactose into lactic acid, giving the product its thick consistency and tangy taste.

Prepared whipped cream: Whipped cream is available in aerosol cans. It also contains sweeteners and stabilisers.

Whichever type of cream you buy, ensure that the container is clean, tightly sealed, and cold. Check for the date code on it.

Though we use fresh cream for most of our cooking requirements, the consistency varies with the quality of milk used. The full-cream milk yields a double cream while the toned milk gives us the regular cream.

Nutritional Value

Although cream does contain some nutrients, it is mostly fat.

Storing Cream

Cream is easily perishable. It should be kept refrigerated in its carton. Do not leave cream out on the kitchen table while you are having your morning coffee – keep it cold! Observe the 'use by' date on the carton. If 'sell by' dates are used, allow 2 to 3 days beyond the date. For sour cream, allow about 5-6 days past the 'sell by' date. If sour cream gets mouldy, even if it is just a few dots, throw it out. Cream that has been ultra-pasteurised can be kept refrigerated (unopened) for up to 3 weeks. Once opened, it has to be used within a week.

Cooking with Cream

Those who are conscious that cream is rich in fat, and desire to use it as little as possible, in recipes, can substitute low-fat products for cream, such as:

Instead of:	Use:
1 cup heavy cream	1 cup evaporated skimmed milk
1 cup light cream	1 cup low-fat yogurt
1 cup sour cream	1 cup reduced fat sour cream, low-fat, or non-fat yogurt.

There are several substitutes for real whipped cream. You can whip light whipping cream instead of heavy whipping cream.

They will not always be acceptable. Some may work better for you on certain food than others. In any case, try them out and jot down those that work well.

- Whip ½ cup light whipping cream and fold into ½ cup plain or vanilla non-fat yogurt.
- Use low-fat plain vanilla yogurt.
- Blend low-fat cottage cheese and vanilla mix in sugar if desired.
- Whip well-chilled evaporated skimmed milk and fold in vanilla and cinnamon.

If you decide you must have real whipped cream (in moderation, anything is fine), use light whipping cream. Make sure the cream is cold, as cold cream whips better than warm cream. For best results, place the cream, bowl, and beaters into the freezer for about 10 minutes before whipping. Use a bowl that is deep enough for the beaters to fit and small enough for the beaters to maintain contact with the cream. Beat rapidly, scraping the bowl frequently for 2 to 3 minutes, until you get stiff peaks. Do not over-beat. The cream will become granular and turn into butter. If you wish to add sugar to the cream, do it after whipping. Sugar makes the cream harder to whip and less stable. Use confectioner's (powdered) sugar rather than granulated sugar for a smooth product. Whipping should increase the volume of cream by double. It is best to use whipped cream right away. However, it can be stored in the refrigerator, covered, for a few hours.

Ice Cream and Ice Milk

Ice cream is food produced by freezing while stirring a pasteurised mix composed primarily of milk, egg yolks, sweeteners, and flavouring. Ice cream is one of the most popular treats. You will learn more about ice creams in the lesson on **'Ice creams, Sherbets and Cold Desserts'**.

PURCHASING ICE CREAM

To be labelled as ice cream, a product must have at least 10 percent fat by weight. Premium ice creams have much more than the minimum required. They have about 16 percent fat. In comparison, ice milk, which is prepared from the same ingredients as ice cream, has 2-7 percent fat. Ice milk usually has more sugar. Ensure that the ice cream or ice milk you buy is well below the frost line of the freezer, or is preferably from a freezer with a door. The container must be rock solid and clean. If it feels sticky or looks frosty, it has probably thawed and refrozen.

NUTRITIONAL VALUE OF ICE CREAM AND ICE MILK

Ice cream and ice milk are a good source of calcium, riboflavin, and protein. Ice cream is also a good source of fat. Some brands of ice cream are made with fat substitutes. Ice milk has less fat.

STORING ICE CREAM AND ICE MILK

Ice cream and ice milk are best kept in a plastic container with a tightly fitting lid in the freezer. This helps prevent it from drying out and absorbing flavours from other food. If kept in the original carton, place plastic wrap over the top of the ice cream before putting the lid on. This gives some added protection from development of ice crystals. Ice cream and ice milk last for about 4 weeks in the freezer. For best quality, it is best to use within 2 weeks.

YOGURT

Yogurt is an ancient food and has a reputation for being a healthy food. It is nutritious, particularly in its low-fat and non-fat forms. In addition to the claim of promoting long life, yogurt is recommended by some researchers as a cure for digestive ills, high cholesterol levels, and even cancerous tumours in animals. The focus for these health claims is primarily on the bacteria added during yogurt production. The bacteria, Lactobacillus bulgaricus and Streptococcus thermophilus, ferment or culture ordinary milk into a tart, creamy gel. Is yogurt capable of all these things?

Scientific studies have not confirmed the claims about yogurt's healing properties. However, yogurt is definitely beneficial to individuals who cannot digest lactose, a sugar found in milk products. Many people in the world are lactose intolerant. The condition is fairly common. For the lactose intolerant, dairy products containing lactose cause diarrhea, abdominal cramps, and nausea. Yogurt is easier to digest because enzymes from the yogurt bacteria break down the lactose during the fermentation process. There is some evidence that after the yogurt is eaten, the bacteria continue to help break down lactose in the intestinal tract. Yogurt may also help manage diarrhoea caused by antibiotic therapy by reestablishing the 'good' bacteria killed along with the bad during treatment.

PURCHASING YOGURT

Yogurt has been made the same way for centuries. First, cow's milk (in many countries, it is goat's or sheep's milk) is pasteurised to kill unwanted bacteria. Then it's cooled to about 113°F, and the yogurt culture containing bacteria is added. The mixture is kept lukewarm for some time. It is then chilled allowing time for the bacteria to grow until the mixture becomes a tart, acidic gel.

To make their product last longer on store shelves, manufacturers may heat-treat the yogurt after fermentation. While this does not affect the calcium content of the yogurt, it kills the live culture, the ingredient most people expect in yogurt. If the manufacturer heat-treats the yogurt after fermentation, the label must say 'heat-treated after culturing'. If the yogurt contains living bacteria, the label may say 'active yogurt culture', 'living yogurt culture', or 'contains active cultures'. Do not be confused by a label that says, 'made with active cultures'. All yogurts are made this way. Only those brands that are not heat-treated after fermentation retain their living cultures.

There are three main types of yogurt to choose from:

1. Unflavoured, plain yogurt
2. Flavoured, but containing no fruit (such as vanilla, lemon, or coffee)
3. Flavoured and containing fruit. They may be of two styles:

a. **Sundae-style:** The fruit is at the bottom of the container with plain or flavoured yogurt on top. This product is normally stirred before eating.

b. **Blended-style** (also called Swiss-style): The fruit is blended throughout the plain or flavoured yogurt.

Whichever style you buy, ensure that the container is clean, tightly sealed, and cold.

Besides fresh yogurt, there is frozen yogurt. Frozen yogurt is available either soft-serve or hard. Like fresh yogurt, it must have the two types of bacteria added during processing. Other than that, frozen yogurt may bear little resemblance to the fresh counterparts. Frozen yogurts taste more like desserts because they are not fermented as long as non-frozen yogurt. Therefore, they are less acidic than non-frozen yogurt and taste sweeter. Frozen yogurt may not have the same amount of living bacteria as their non-frozen counterparts, if they are alive at all. Some manufacturers make frozen yogurt by fermenting milk the traditional way, then freezing the mixture. Others make a kind of ice milk mixture and add the bacteria later. As a result, the number of live culture organisms in frozen yogurt varies greatly in different brands.

Nutritional Value of Yogurt

Yogurt is a good source of:

- Protein
- Calcium, phosphorus, and potassium
- Riboflavin and Vitamin B12

Yogurt contains the same amount of fat that was present in the milk product it was made from. Whole milk yogurt contains at least 3.5 grams fat per half-cup, low-fat contains between 0.5 and 2 grams fat, and non-fat yogurt contains less than 0.5 grams fat.

Calories Fat Chart of Yogurt (1 Cup Portion):

Type of Yogurt	Calories	Fat (grams)
Whole milk, plain	139	7
Low-fat, plain	144	4
Low-fat, fruit flavoured	225	3
Non-fat, plain	127	0

The calorie content of fresh yogurt varies dramatically due to two major factors. They are: the fat content and the inclusion of sweeteners. Yogurts with fruit have a lot of sugar or sweetener added to help preserve the fruit. For fewer calories and sugar, one is better off buying plain yogurt and adding own fruit, fresh or canned, or fruit spread. For less fat, choose non-fat or low-fat yogurt.

Like fresh yogurt, frozen yogurt varies in the amount of fat it contains. On the high end are yogurts with as much fat as ice cream – about 14 grams/cup. On the low end are non-fat yogurts. With or without active cultures, frozen yogurt can be a healthier option than ice cream (that is, of course, without the chocolate chip topping). Try to choose a frozen yogurt with not more than 4 grams fat/cup.

Storing Yogurt

Store yogurt in the refrigerator up to the 'use by' date or 7 to 10 days past the 'sell by' date. If you open the container and find some liquid sitting on top of the yogurt, don't worry; it's still safe to eat. Just drain off the liquid or stir it into the yogurt. Mould and gas bubbles signal spoilage.

Cooking with Yogurt

Yogurt Mushroom Relish

Plain yogurt, either non-fat or low-fat, can be substituted for many ingredients higher in fat in salad, salad dressings, soups, sauces, and desserts. Here are some examples.

- Substitute plain yogurt for mayonnaise. In situations where the taste of mayonnaise is desired, use half calorie-reduced mayonnaise and half yogurt. This works well for dishes such as potato salad, coleslaw, tuna salad, cold pasta salads, and appetizers.
- Substitute plain yogurt for sour cream in dips and salad dressing recipes.
- In baking, substitute plain yogurt for sour cream in recipes for pancakes, waffles, loaf breads, and muffins.
- In baking, substitute 1 cup plain yogurt for 1 cup light cream.

- In cooking, substitute 1 cup plain yogurt for 1 cup sour cream.
- On baked potatoes, use plain yogurt instead of sour cream. Mix with fresh herbs.
- Mix plain yogurt with ricotta cheese (made from skimmed milk) and use as a spread on toast, bagels, and crackers.
- For whipped cream, whip 1/2 cup heavy cream and fold in 2/3 cup plain yogurt.

When a creamy texture is desired, drain the yogurt to remove some of the liquid. Because of yogurt's acidity content, you may want to decrease the amount of other acidic ingredients in your recipe, such as lemon juice.

When cooking with yogurt, use only low heat. High temperatures may cause separation, evaporation of liquid, and a curdled appearance. To help keep yogurt from separating during cooking, blend one tbsp of cornflour (unless the recipe calls for flour to be mixed with it) with a few tbsp of yogurt and stir the mixture into remaining yogurt to be used. Proceed according to the recipe. Yogurt may become thin if it is over-mixed. Do not stir excessively.

Yogurt can also be used to make tasty desserts. Make a yogurt parfait by alternating layers of yogurt and fruit or layers of a variety of yogurts. Make a pie by blending yogurt, fresh or frozen fruit, and 1 cup whipped cream. Pour into pie shell and freeze.

Some healthy toppings for frozen yogurt include the following:

- Pureed fruit sauce or fruit spread.
- Crushed oatmeal cookies.
- Wheat germ.
- Chopped dried fruit.
- Fresh fruits.

Butter

Butter is made from the milk of cow, buffalo, goat and sheep. One that is commonly used is from the milk of cows and buffaloes.

Salted Yellow Butter

Butter consists of 80 percent fat, water and whey, which is milk solid left from the separating process. The milk protein in the whey makes the butter spoil quickly and, with milk sugar, causes it to scorch when overheated.

Butter is available in many forms:

- **Salted** – salt adds flavour and helps preserve butter. The amount of salt varies by brand.
- **Unsalted or sweet** – made from fresh cream without added salt, the kind we make at home. This is frequently used for baking and cooking, and even for eating with parathas, which is a popular method of consuming fresh butter in North India.
- **Whipped** – contains fewer calories per tbsp because of the air whipped into it. It spreads better than thick butter.

The quality of butter depends upon the cream used. This in turn depends upon the season and the feed of the animal. The colour varies from pale to yellow. Commercial producers add colour to maintain uniformity. This is mostly in case of salted butter. The butter produced at home has a creamy white colour and a light texture. For health reasons, butter is pasteurised, which means the milk used to make it has been sterilised by briefly heating it to destroy any harmful bacteria. The butter that we make at home is made from the cream that collects after the milk has been slowly boiled and allowed to cool. This is unsalted, has a better taste, but does not keep well. It is best to refrigerate and consume it within 2 to 3 days.

Salted butter is made from fresh or soured cream. It has a salt content between 1.5 percent to 3 percent. Most cooks prepare the unsalted variety for delicate pastries, cakes and icings or even for cooking. The whipped variety spreads evenly and melts quickly, but it is so bland that people prefer not to use it.

Butter is the best fat for baking or stir frying some vegetables and as part of some sauces because of its rich flavour. Do take care when a recipe specifies whether hard, soft or melted butter is required. Sometimes, creamed butter can be mixed with various flavourings to form compound butters that go well with meat, fish and poultry dishes.

Purchasing Butter

When purchasing butter, ensure that it is cold and in clean, undamaged packaging. It should smell fresh and have a sweet aroma. Check for a dating code. Intensity of colour is no indication of quality but the colour should be uniform.

Storing of Butter

Butter can stay fresh for 2 to 3 weeks or even longer provided it is wrapped tightly in plastic, since it absorbs odours in the refrigerator. Butter can be frozen double wrapped for 6 to 8 months. If poorly stored, it can go rancid.

Nutritional Value

Butter contains 714 calories per 100 grams, no carbohydrates, no protein, 78 grams fat, 828 mg. sodium (if salted), 11 mg. sodium (if unsalted) and 221 mg. cholesterol.

Cooking with Butter

Though a variety of low-fat butters are available in the market, it is best to avoid butter as far as possible. Use fruit butter instead if you must. It does not contain any fat. Rather than using butter in sandwiches, try loading your sandwiches with fresh vegetables like lettuce, tomatoes, onions, peppers or cucumber. Instead of butter, try to flavour your food with herbs, spices, vinegar or lemon juice. Use a nonstick pan to cook or stir fry. This will cut down your use of butter or oil.

Clarified Butter or Ghee

Homemade Ghee

Butter is clarified by melting it slowly to separate the fat from the water and milk solids. It is simmered until the moisture evaporates totally. The butter caramelises, producing a strong, sweet flavour. If made from cow's or buffalo's milk, it can be heated to a much higher temperature. Ghee can be bought from the market in tins, packs and jars, or made at home.

Ghee has a high fat content. You can refrigerate it for about 2 months, freeze it for 3 months or keep in a cool, dark corner of your kitchen cupboard. Ghee is a popular cooking medium in India and in the Arab countries. It can also be used for sautéing, smearing on chapatti, frying parathas and puris, or even as a topping, in its melted form, for dals.

Khoya or Mawa

When milk is simmered over low heat continuously, all the moisture evaporates leaving a semi-solid crumbly residue. This is *khoya* or *mawa*. It has a light brownish colour and a milky-creamy taste. It is used to make sweetmeats, *halwas* and used as filling for savoury pancakes. It can be made at home or bought in the market. The one made at home is purer. Use cow or buffalo's milk to make *mawa*.

Practical things to be done

1. Making Yogurt

The yogurt that is made at home is healthier, fresher and has lesser tart to taste. The flavour and texture depends on the fat content of the milk, the quality of yogurt used as a starter and the time it takes to set. Pasteurised milk is best for making curd.

Utensils used: A heavy bottomed saucepan, a bowl with a lid, a spoon.

Ingredients: A tbsp of fresh yogurt, 500 ml. of pasteurised milk.

This is the procedure for making yogurt:

1. Bring the milk to boil. Let it cool till it is lukewarm.
2. Whisk in the yogurt. Pour the mixture into a glass bowl.
3. Cover and keep in a warm place. The yogurt will set in 6 to 8 hours.

During winters, you will find that the yogurt is difficult to set. To facilitate better setting, wrap an old towel or a woollen garment round the container to keep it warm. Alternatively, you can place the container in a large hot case and close the lid. A third method is to place the container in an oven with the pilot light on. Normally, it takes 6 to 8 hours to set. To prevent the curd from becoming sour, transfer it to the refrigerator as soon as it has set.

2. Preparing Clarified Butter (Ghee)

Utensils used: A heavy-bottomed saucepan, a strainer, a bowl, a ladle, muslin cloth.

Ingredients: 500 grams of unsalted butter.

To prepare clarified butter, follow this simple procedure:

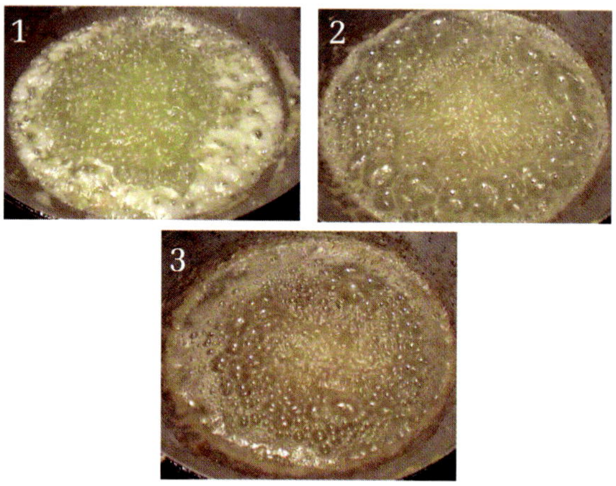

Process of Making Ghee

1. Melt the butter in a saucepan till it becomes liquid.
2. Cook on low heat till it starts getting clearer.
3. Keep cooking till the ghee separates completely from the residue and appears pinkish in colour. Strain through a fine sieve.

3. Making Mawa or Khoya

Utensils used: A heavy-bottomed pan, a ladle.

Ingredients: 2 litre pasteurised cow or buffalo's milk.

Follow this simple procedure to make *mawa / khoya*:

1. Bring the milk in the pan to a boil over low heat.
2. Simmer without increasing the heat, stirring constantly so that the milk does not scorch. Keep simmering and stirring till all the moisture evaporates leaving behind a crumbly mass. This is the *khoya*. Use as required.

Mawa / Khoya

4. Making Paneer

Utensils used: A saucepan, a ladle, a strainer, muslin cloth, a bowl.

Ingredients: 2 litre pasteurised milk, 250ml. yogurt or sour cream or the juice of one lemon.

Follow this simple procedure to make *paneer*:

1. Mix the milk and the yogurt/ sour cream/ lemon juice well. Bring to a boil.
2. Simmer until the milk curdles, stirring all the while for about 5 minutes.
3. Let it stand at least for 1 hour.
4. Line a strainer with the muslin cloth and place it over the bowl. Hang cloth over the sides of the strainer. Pour in the milk mixture and allow it to drain for 30 minutes. Collect the solids and refrigerate.

TIPS

- If the yogurt (curd) is sour, stir in half a cup of milk and mix well. This will lessen the sourness.
- To make sweet tasting curd, sweeten the milk before stirring in the yogurt starter.
- Sometimes a recipe specifies using hung curd to give a creamy consistency to curries, or to use in a salad dressing. To do this, hang the curd in a muslin cloth from a hook above your kitchen sink for 1 to 2 hours. The water will drain leaving behind the thick, creamier curd residue.

- Gather whey in a small bottle. Keep it in the refrigerator. This is a good substitute for the yogurt/ sour cream/ lemon juice for further use. Use it within 7 days.
- When using frozen *paneer*, take it out from its packaging and defrost on your kitchen counter. Never use frozen *paneer* without defrosting it.

Expert cook suggests...

1. To remove sourness from curd, tie it in a muslin cloth and wash it 3 or 4 times in plain water.
2. Put a lime-sized ball of jaggery in ghee to keep it fresh for a long time.
3. After making ghee from 'malai', do not throw away the leftover golden residue. Mix it with flour and knead it to make delicious 'puris'.
4. Wrap country cheese (*paneer*) in blotting paper before placing it in the refrigerator. It stays fresh for longer.
5. Immerse deep-fried *paneer* in water for a few seconds. Store it in a refrigerator. The *paneer* will remain soft.
6. If you feel milk is going stale and may curdle on boiling, add a pinch of baking soda and the milk will not curdle.
7. Holding the cheese container over boiling water can soften cheese that has gone hard.
8. If you are going out for a few days, keep a bowl of milk in the deep freeze. On returning home, keep the bowl of frozen milk in the hot water, and within a few minutes, you will have milk for tea or coffee.
9. To ensure that cheese does not dry in the refrigerator, pack it in aluminium foil before placing in the refrigerator.

Amba Paneer

Paneer Chettinad

Paneer Kofta

Paneer Phal Ungli Kebab

Paneer Squares with Hari Mirch Gravy

Paneer Veg Sizzler

DAY 08

Beverages

Beverages in the form of coffee, tea and chocolate are favourite the world over. The South Indians especially prefer drinking brewed coffee. Tea is preferred to coffee in other parts of the country. With several varieties available, most tea-drinking people prefer instant coffee. Only a few have mastered the art of brewing it.

The caffeine content of tea and coffee is a subject of concern for most people consuming these beverages. Tea contains less caffeine than coffee. Brewed coffee contains more caffeine than instant coffee. Regardless of caffeine content, coffee and tea are top rated beverages. They are taken first thing in the morning, with breakfast, in the afternoon, and in the evening.

Indians have never developed a taste for drinking chocolate, whether hot or cold. Only a small percentage of the population has picked up this habit. Chocolate is popular mostly among children. Drinking chocolate has the advantage of being free of caffeine. It is good for health due to its milk content. Taken just before going to bed, it promotes relaxation. It is said to have sleep inducing properties.

Tea

Tea is one of the most inexpensive and popular beverages in the world. It is easy to prepare. It comes in many different varieties. Tea is the dried leaf of an evergreen shrub, Camellia Sinensis, grows wild in places such as China, Japan, and Indonesia. Cultivated in China for over 4500 years, tea was brought to India by the British in the 19th century. Now India is the largest producer of tea in the world. Tea plants flourish in the shade of trees on sloping land where there is a good deal of rainfall. Assam tea plants are fast growing. They yield dark and light green leaves of excellent quality.

Purchasing Tea

There are three types of tea based on how long the tea leaves have been processed: black, green, and oolong.

Black tea is the most popular form of tea. It is made by fermenting the freshly harvested tea leaves until they turn black. The tea produced has a very deep flavour and dark colour.

Green tea leaves are dried without fermenting. They retain their original green colour. Green tea has a light colour and a weaker flavour than the black tea.

Oolong tea is produced from tea leaves that are partially fermented to a brownish-green colour. It is a combination of black and green tea.

There are over 3,000 varieties of tea, each with its own flavour, body, colour, and aroma. Like wine, they take their namesfrom the areas where they are grown.

Here are some popular regional tea varities:

Assam tea is bright and full-bodied. It has a rich, malty taste. It is grown in the north-eastern part of India.

Ceylon tea is a rich, pungent tea from Sri Lanka.

Keemun tea is smooth with a flowery aroma. It is the finest of China's black tea.

The terms 'orange pekoe' and 'pekoe' do not refer to a particular variety or flavour of tea. They refer to the size of the leaf. Small tea leaves brew faster than the large tea leaves. Tea is, therefore, sorted by size. 'Souchong' refers to large leaves, 'pekoe' refers to medium leaves, and 'orange pekoe' are the smallest leaves.

When people choose their favourite tea, their preference is based on its aroma, colour and flavour. This depends upon the quantity of tannins (tanicin), caffeine and pectin. The aroma in the tea is due to volatile constituents that are partly present in the leaf, and partly formed during oxidation and fermentation processes. Tea is a variable product. By blending tea, a company can protect the flavour of its brand from major changes in the quality. One variety can taste different from the other. However, by blending tea one can maintain a constant quality throughout the year. Tea packers sometimes add flowers, herbs, spices, and flavours to their blends.

Loose Tea

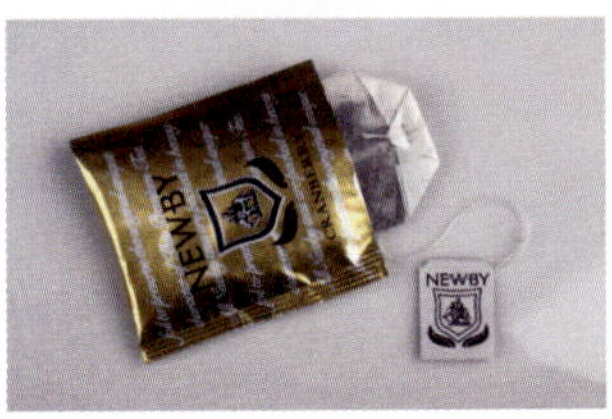

Tea Bag

Tea can be purchased as loose tea, in packets or as tea bags. It is brewed in boiling water. Tea dust that is grainy, black and free of fibre gives a rich brew quickly, but is rather acidic. In addition to the regular tea, there are decaffeinated tea and herbal tea. Decaffeinated tea contains a maximum of 5 to 9 milligram of caffeine per cup. Herbal tea is a misnomer because it does not contain any leaves from the tea plant. Herbal tea is made from dried buds, leaves, and flowers steeped in boiling water. They are caffeine free. Because some herbs have medicinal effects, they act like drugs in your body.

Nutritional Value

Tea does not have much nutritional value. It contributes no calories to the diet. The calories come from milk and sugar in the tea.

Storing Tea

Air and moisture hasten the deterioration of tea. Loose tea, tea bags, and herbal tea should be stored in airtight containers at room temperature. Tea can be stored for 6 to 9 months. Keep tea away from sunlight.

Coffee

Next to tea, coffee is one of the most popular drinks around the world. In India, one of every six people prefer coffee to tea. Coffee is obtained from beans of a tropical tree. Beans come from a variety of coffee trees found in tropical areas around the world. Coffee beans are often identified by where they come from, such as Java, an island in Indonesia. Coffee producers use several varieties of coffee beans to produce their own distinctive blends. The type of roasting technique they have undergone also identifies coffee beans. After being cleaned, skinned and dried, they are roasted to different degrees – dark, medium and light, to develop their flavour. The amount of roasting affects the colour and flavour of the coffee brewed from the beans. The more intense the roasting, the more darker and strongly flavoured it becomes. Most commercial blends of coffee are made from a light medium roast, also called American or full-city roast. A very dark roast is used to make beans for espresso, a strong dark coffee.

Purchasing Coffee

When buying coffee one can purchase whole beans (loose or in bags), ground coffee (in vacuum-packed cans, bags, or loose), or instant coffee (in vacuum-packed sachets, jars or cans). Whole beans can be ground at home using an electric coffee grinder, which has stainless steel blades to pulverise the beans, or in an electric coffee mill, which uses grinding disks to ensure a more precise, uniform grind. Most coffee grinders are small and easy to clean. Fresh ground coffee yields a fresh, fragrant and tasty product.

Instant coffee is brewed coffee that has been dried using the freeze-drying process. A very strong brew is first made, and then spray dried. The powder is hygroscopic, and must be stored in airtight containers. The flavour of instant coffee depends on the blending.

Whole Coffee Beans

Ground Coffee

Instant Coffee Granules

The grind of a coffee, such as coarse, medium, or fine, refers to the size of the granules produced from the coffee beans. Coffee beans must be ground so the water can extract the flavour. The names of some grinds are connected with the type of coffee maker in use. The finer the grind, the more conspicuous is the flavour. The size of the grind is also related to the method of making the coffee. For example, if granules are treated with hot water for a short time, a fine grind is recommended.

As a general guide to purchasing coffee, do the following:

1. When buying coffee beans, check that they are of uniform size and colour. The coffee aroma must be distinct, and there should be no trace of mustiness. Buy from a reputed retailer. Purchase in small quantity as they do not stay fresh for too long.
2. To buy ground coffee, select the proper grind for your coffee maker. Too fine a grind may produce bitter coffee. Too coarse a grind may produce a weak coffee lacking flavour.
3. When buying ground coffee, buy enough to last one week. Even in the refrigerator it has a short life. 750 gm makes about 40 cups. Unopened cans of coffee can stay on the shelf for one year.

Kinds of Coffee

Coffee is consumed in a variety of ways – plain black, brew and with milk and sugar. It is also prepared in several ways to please the individual taste. Here are a few common varieties.

Name	Description
Café au lait:	A combination of strong coffee mixed half with hot milk.
Espresso:	A strong dark coffee made from coffee beans that are roasted until almost black. Brewed in espresso machine that force water through the ground coffee under pressure. Served in small cups after dinner.
Cappuccino:	Equal parts of espresso coffee and steaming hot milk, topped with whipped cream and cinnamon. Served in tall cups.
Demitasse:	Demitasse means half cup. This strong coffee is made from a dark roast. Served in small cups.
Mocha java:	A mix of regular strength coffee and hot cocoa.
Irish coffee:	A mix of hot coffee and Irish whisky topped with whipped cream.
Viennese coffee:	Strong, hot coffee, steeped with cloves, cinnamon sticks, and allspice strained into cups. Served with whipped cream.

Decaffeinated Coffee

Decaffeinated coffee is the coffee from which caffeine has been removed. Caffeine can be removed by one of the two methods, by using water or using a solvent such as methylene chloride. The use of methylene chloride in decaffeinating coffee has been a matter of consumer concern. In response, many coffee producers are switching over to the water method. This is often stated on the label. Decaffeinated coffee may be purchased as whole beans, ground coffee, or instant coffee.

Coffee Makers

Those who like freshly brewed coffee use coffee makers to brew fresh ground coffee. Several types of coffee makers are in use.

Coffee Percolator: This is a popular coffee maker. It uses the regular coarse ground coffee. In this type, heated water forces up a tube in the middle of the percolator and sprays over the coffee granules held in a basket at the top of the pot. The water level in the percolator should be below the bottom of the basket holding the coffee granules.

Coffee Maker

Automatic Drip-filter Coffee Maker: This coffee maker uses the drip grind coffee granules especially made for the purpose. Sufficient cold water is filled in the reservoir to make the desired amount of coffee. Water in the reservoir heats instantly as it flows past the heating element. It is then sprayed over the finely ground coffee in a basket lined with filter paper.

Drip Coffee Maker: This coffee maker uses medium drip grind coffee granules. Boiling water poured into a filter cone above the coffeepot drips slowly through the granules held in a basket in the centre of the coffee maker. It drips slowly into the coffeepot.

CAFFEINE CHART IN BEVERAGES

The following table gives a good idea of how the content of caffeine varies in different beverages:

Item	Average	Range
Coffee – one cup – 150 ml.		
Brewed, drip method	115	60 to 180
Brewed, percolator	80	40 to 170
Instant	65	30 to 120
Decaffeinated, brewed	3	2 to 5
Decaffeinated, instant	2	1 to 5
Tea – one cup – 150 ml.		
Brewed	60	25 to 110
Instant	30	30 to 50
Iced – one glass – 300 ml.	50	30 to 75
Chocolate – one cup – 150 ml.		
Cocoa		4
Chocolate		3
Soft Drinks – 1 can – 300 ml.		
Cola drinks		30 to 46
Lemon drinks		0
Diet Cola		35 to 50

NUTRITIONAL VALUE

Coffee does not contain any significant amount of nutrients. It has no calories, and therefore no nutritive value. To avoid calories, skimmed milk could be used.

STORING COFFEE

Coffee beans have fairly high oil content. When the fat becomes stale or rancid, it produces undesirable flavour (and odour). Both air and moisture hasten rancidity. An airtight container is necessary. The oil in the beans has a tendency to pick up flavours of other food. That is another reason to keep it airtight. Store coffee beans at room temperature for 1 to 3 weeks or in the freezer for 3 to 4 months.

When storing ground coffee, store in airtight containers in the refrigerator or freezer. Once the coffee bean is ground, the quality of the coffee deteriorates quickly for two reasons. Firstly, most of the oil in the bean is exposed to the air. Secondly, the flavour of the coffee is volatile. It is easily lost within a short time at room temperature. Ground coffee can stay fine in the refrigerator for 7 to 10 days. It can last longer in the freezer.

STORAGE TIME FOR COFFEE

Instant Coffee	
Unopened	6 months
Opened	2 to 3 months
Ground Coffee	
Unopened	12 months
Opened	not recommended
Coffee beans	1 to 3 weeks

CHICORY

Chicory Roots

Chicory is the root of a plant that resembles beetroot. It grows in South India. Added 25 to 30 percent to coffee, it makes the coffee slightly bitter, and adds colour and body to the brew. As a part of instant coffee, it contributes to its brewed taste.

CHOCOLATE

Mixing chocolate or cocoa in water or milk makes for a cold or a hot drink. Chocolate was discovered in Mexico in the form of a drink. Later, the Spanish introduced it into Europe. The Jesuits were the first to improve this exotic product.

Cocoa Beans

Chocolate, at this time, was always prepared with water. It was very sweet and was flavoured with vanilla, and improved with ambergris and musk. Soon chocolate became fashionable amongst the high society of Spain. It was in Austria, Spain, and France where most chocolate was consumed as a drink. Chocolate powder began to be retailed during the 19th century.

Today, thanks to instant products, chocolate can be prepared quickly. However, true hot chocolate needs to be prepared the previous day. Keeping it overnight improves the flavour and makes it frothy. It also concentrates and gives it a special smoothness.

Here are a few methods of making chocolate.

Foamy Chocolate: For 1 lt (4¼ cups) milk, have 200-250 gm chocolate, 1 tbsp vanilla-flavoured sugar and a pinch of powdered cinnamon. Break the chocolate into small pieces in a saucepan. Heat gently. When the chocolate begins to soften, add the flavouring together with a small cup of boiling milk. Beat the chocolate thoroughly with a whisk. Gradually pour in the rest of the hot milk. Warm over a gentle heat, whisking all the time to make the chocolate foamy. 6 tbsp thin cream could also be added to it. Vanilla or cinnamon may be replaced by 1 tbsp instant coffee.

Iced Chocolate: Prepare a foamy chocolate as in the recipe earlier, but reduce the quantity of chocolate to 125-150 gm. Add 2-3 tbsp sugar or 3-4 tbsp castor (superfine) sugar. Allow the chocolate to cool completely. Put in a blender adding crushed ice. Serve immediately.

Milky Chocolate: Mix some cocoa powder and castor (superfine) sugar, using twice as much sugar as cocoa. Add some boiling milk and heat, stir with a wooden spoon, until the mixture is completely smooth. Alternatively, cocoa may be mixed with sweetened condensed milk and then diluted with boiling water. It could also be added to some boiling sweetened milk and then whisked.

Viennese chocolate: Melt 200 gm chocolate in a Bain-Marie with a cup of milk. Stir while letting it come to the boil for about 10 minutes. Heat ¾ litre milk with 1 tbsp sugar. Pour it into a saucepan and whisk for 5 minutes. Make chantilly cream by whisking 5 tbsp heavy cream with 15 gm icing sugar. Flavour with vanilla. Pour the chocolate into cups and top each with a dome of chantilly cream.

CHOCOLATE POT

A chocolate pot is a tall vessel for serving hot chocolate. It is shaped like a truncated cone or like a jug, with a spout and a horizontal wooden handle. The chocolate pot has a lid pierced with a hole for a beater to pass through. This is intended to make the chocolate foam when it is poured into the cups. The pot may be made of silver-plated metal, solid silver, porcelain, or earthenware.

Practical things to be done

1. Making Tea

Utensils used: a saucepan; a teapot; a spoon

Ingredients: Tea leaves (1 tsp per person), milk and sugar (as desired), water.

The procedure for making hot tea is given as follows:

1. Preheat the teapot by rinsing it with hot water. This keeps the tea hot during the brewing.
2. Bring fresh cold tap water to a full rolling boil. Water that has been reheated gives tea a flat taste. Only boiling water can extract the full flavour and benefit from the tea leaves.
3. Use 1 teaspoonful of tea or 1 tea bag per cup, and pour the boiling water over the tea in the teapot.
4. Brew for 3 to 5 minutes. Do not judge the strength of tea by its colour. It takes time for the leaves to unfold and release the flavour.
5. Add milk and sugar to taste.

2. Iced Tea

Iced Tea

To make iced tea, follow the same procedure as for making hot tea, but use 50 percent more tea to allow for melting ice. For example, you would use 4 tea bags to make 4 cups of hot tea, but to make 4 glasses of iced tea you need 6 tea bags.

To make 4 glasses of iced tea use this easy method:

1. Bring 2 glasses of fresh cold water to a full rolling boil in a saucepan.
2. Remove from the heat. Immediately add 12 tea bags or ¼ cup loose tea.
3. Stir, cover and let stand for 5 minutes.
4. Stir again and pour into a pitcher. Strain the brew if you are using loose tea. Hold an additional 1 ltr of fresh cold water to dilute the brew.

3. Instant Tea

Hot Tea: To make a cup of hot tea, use a level tsp instant tea to a teacup of boiling water. For a pot of tea use 2 level tbsp instant tea for each litre of boiling water.

Iced Tea: To make 1 glass of iced tea, use a rounded tsp instant tea for a glass of water. For a 1-litre jug, use 2 rounded tbsp of instant tea.

4. Making Coffee

Coffee Set and maker

To make good coffee, follow this simple procedure:

1. Use spotlessly clean equipment because the fat found in coffee readily adheres to coffee making equipment. This residue, if not cleaned, will lead to horrible-tasting coffee as the fat turns rancid.
2. Use fresh coffee.
3. Start with cold water. Never use hot tap water as it contains a build-up of minerals due to storage of the water in hot water tanks. This will have an adverse effect on the flavour of your coffee.
4. Measure accurately so that the coffee is neither weak nor strong. For drip coffee, use 2 tbsp or 1 coffee measure of ground coffee to each cup of water for a medium strong cup of coffee. Use fewer granules for weaker coffee and more for stronger coffee.
5. If using filters (paper or cloth), make sure they are clean.
6. For the best flavour, make at least three-quarters of the capacity of your coffee maker.
7. Coffee is best when served immediately. Do not hold for more than 60 minutes.
8. Remove the coffee granules as soon as brewing is completed. The granules absorb the aroma from the coffee.
9. Keep coffee warm. Never boil it, as it will turn bitter. There is only one way to reheat coffee and that is in a microwave.

5. Making Cold Coffee

Cold Coffee

Cold coffee is usually served in tall glasses with a topping of whipped cream. It is a summer favourite of many. If you are calorie conscious, avoid the cream topping.

To make a glass of cold coffee, follow this procedure:

1. Heat 1 tbsp of milk. Dissolve ½-1 tsp of coffee in the milk.
2. In a blender, mix the milk-coffee mixture, a cup of milk, sugar and a handful of crushed ice. Blend well and serve in a tall glass.
3. If you like, sprinkle malted chocolate or cinnamon powder over it.

Expert cook suggests...

1. To remove instant coffee powder, which has become damp and hard, pour some hot water into the jar, and let the coffee dissolve. Store the liquid in the refrigerator. Use when required.
2. To make aromatic tea, add a little orange peel to the boiling water.

Day 09

Eggs

Though eggs from a variety of birds are edible, yet the eggs from hens are the most popular. The eggs of ducks and geese are also used. Modern techniques have made mass production of eggs possible. Fresh eggs are now readily available.

The first thing a new cook learns is how to boil eggs. Learning to cook poached and scrambled eggs follow this. Shallow and deep-fried eggs are ideal for breakfast or a tasty snack. The age-old omelette has a number of variations. One can use the imagination to use interesting combinations and fillings. Eggs play a very important role in cookery, as they are the basis for custards, soufflés, batters, crepes, pies, breads, cakes, beverages, entrées and desserts.

Turkey, Duck and Goose Eggs

In many countries, egg cartons are dated at the time of packing. One can test for freshness at home by immersing an egg in water. If the egg sinks on its side, it is very fresh; if it sinks vertically, rounded end up, it is two or three weeks old; and the egg that floats on the surface of the water could be several months old. It should be thrown away.

A fresh egg is cloudy and clings closely to the yolk. It is best for poaching. When whisking egg whites, greater volume can be achieved with whites that are a few days old. Eggs that have deep yellow yolks are not necessarily superior in taste, though they add colour to sauces and cakes. The colour of the yolk depends on the diet of the chicken. The colour of the shell varies with the breed of the hen. Eggs are truly one of the unique food products. They provide versatility and can be used for any meal. Eggs are available throughout the year at reasonable prices.

Purchasing Eggs

Eggs are graded by size. Normally all the eggs in a carton would be of the same size. However, in lack of proper inspection, sometimes eggs of different sizes are mixed. Since they are sold loose, you can check before purchasing them. Weight to weight, eggs have the same nutritional value. If possible, buy eggs from refrigerated cases. Every grocer does not store eggs in the refrigerator. Check the carton to make sure it contains only clean eggs and that they are not cracked. Check the date on the carton. Unfortunately, it is not mandatory to sell by dates in all countries. There is no difference between brown and white-shelled eggs. The breed of the hen determines the shell colour. It does not affect the grade, nutritive value, flavour, or cooking quality of the egg. Brown egg is often more expensive because they come from larger hens that require more food. Egg substitutes are available that are low in cholesterol, but not

Hen Eggs

always low in fat. They are often made from egg whites and vegetable oil.

NUTRITIONAL VALUE OF EGGS

Eggs are nutritious. A fertile egg becomes a chick in 21 days. This shows that an egg has everything to sustain life. Eggs contain high quality protein and varying amounts of vitamins and minerals.

Most eggs weigh about 50 grams. Two eggs would yield 12 grams of shell, 30 grams of yolk and 58 grams of white. The egg yolk is half-water and the rest is fat and protein. The white is mostly water with some proteins. Two eggs would provide about 30 grams fat each and protein of high quality. The fat is unsaturated. Eggs may provide as many as 14 vitamins. Two eggs provide the daily requirement of vitamin A, B12 and folic acid, and one-fourth the requirement of other vitamins. Two eggs may contribute as much as 600 mg of cholesterol. However, this is not as harmful as it is normally made out to be.

STORING EGGS

Store eggs away from other food so that they do not absorb undesirable odours. Keep eggs in a refrigerator as they maintain freshness better this way. Eggs should be stored with the large end up to keep the yolk centred. As an egg ages, the yolk flattens. The thick section of white becomes watery. Stale eggs have a 'rotten egg' odour that smells like sulphur. Raw egg whites can be stored tightly covered in the refrigerator for 4 to 5 days. Yolks, if covered with water, can be refrigerated for 2 to 3 days. Hard-boiled eggs should be refrigerated in their shells. They can be stored for one week or so. Egg substitutes can last 1 year in the freezer. Once thawed, they can be stored for 7 days in a refrigerator.

THINGS TO BE KEPT IN MIND

Before learning to cook eggs, one must be aware of a problem with contaminated eggs, that received much media attention. A few years ago, a potentially contaminated egg could be recognised by its broken or dirty shell. Now a perfectly fine-looking egg may contain the disease-causing bacteria, *Salmonella enteritidis*. *Salmonella* enters the egg before an infected hen forms the shell. It is impossible to know by its appearance if an egg is contaminated. Perhaps *Salmonella* affects 1 in 200. It is advisable to take the following precautions to avoid food borne illnesses when using eggs and poultry. Here are a few tips to avoid the dangers from contaminated eggs:

- When buying eggs, ensure that they are fresh.
- Check the date if marked on the carton.
- The eggs must be clean.
- Prefer purchasing eggs from grocery stores that store eggs in refrigerators.
- Buy according to your need. As far as possible, store eggs in the refrigerator. Alternatively, store in a cool place.
- Cooked eggs can be stored up to a week. Fresh eggs stay longer.
- When you store eggs, place the new ones behind the old ones. Use old ones first.
- If the eggs are hard-boiled, store in a refrigerator.
- Do not use cracked eggs. Throw them away.
- Cook both yolk and white until firm. Avoid soft or medium cooked eggs, soft omelettes, and scrambled eggs.
- Do not use raw eggs in recipes that do not require further cooking, such as mayonnaise, Caesar salad, mousses, and homemade eggnog.
- Do not use a container that has had raw egg mixture in it until it is washed thoroughly.
- Use an egg separator instead of eggshells to separate the white from the yolk.
- If a recipe requires eggs at room temperature, take the eggs out of the refrigerator about 30 minutes before you need them.
- Eat all egg dishes fresh. Store leftovers only in a refrigerator.

If you find blood spot on opening an egg, do not be alarmed. It does not indicate a fertile egg (as some people believe). The blood is not due to bacterial problems either. Simply remove the blood spot with the tip of a knife or eggshell. It is perfectly safe to eat the egg.

Cooking Eggs

Eggs can be cooked in many ways: baked, cooked in the shell, poached, fried, and scrambled. The use of nonstick pans has become popular for cooking eggs. You can reduce the calorie content substantially by avoiding butter or margarine. At the same time one can enjoy a good product. When making fried eggs, scrambled eggs, and omelette, the use of nonstick pans with light greasing with vegetable oil keeps down the amount of fat. When cooking eggs, use low to medium temperatures to prevent overcooking. Overcooked eggs are tough and rubbery and can cause acidity.

A simple method of cooking eggs is by boiling them in their shells. Cooking eggs to various degrees of hardness can be accomplished by either placing the eggs directly into the boiling water and reducing the temperature to simmering, or by first placing them in cold water and bringing to a simmer. The following is a simple guide:

Soft-cooked eggs	3-5 minutes
Hard-cooked eggs	15-20 minutes

Hard-cooked eggs should be cooled down immediately with cold water in order to prevent the 'green ring' (it is harmless) that appears on the yolk. It is best to peel the eggs while still warm, especially if the eggs are very fresh. Fresh eggs are more difficult to peel.

To make poached eggs, simply break the egg onto a plate, and gently slide it into a pot of simmering water. Some chefs prefer to add a tsp of vinegar to help the white become solid. However, this method is not recommended because it has a tendency to make the white too tough. The eggs cook instantly. The white will congeal into rounded mass within a few minutes. The egg can be removed with a large slotted spoon or with a flat vegetable skimmer. The egg can be served on top of toast. There are devices that are specially designed to cook poached eggs, giving them a nice, rounded shape. It is a good investment if you cook poached eggs regularly.

Fried eggs can be easily made either 'sunny side up' (staring at you!) or turned over and cooked to the desired degree of completeness. Regardless of the type of dish prepared, use fresh eggs, which will ensure maximum flavour and appearance.

When cooking breakfast for many people, scrambled eggs are probably the easiest way of serving eggs. The egg mixture seasoned lightly with pepper and some milk can be prepared ahead of time. It can also be kept refrigerated. To make scrambled eggs, pour the egg mixture into a hot nonstick pan. Stir gently with a wooden spatula in a circular motion. Scrambled eggs are preferred to other forms of egg dishes at breakfast and sometimes for a buffet brunch. However, to be well appreciated, scrambled eggs must be prepared as close to serving time as possible. That ensures best in terms of product quality.

An omelette is a variation of scrambled eggs. The difference is that when the egg mixture is added to the pan, the mixture is spread out instead of stirring it. The mixture is allowed to cook. Variations of the plain omelette are endless; western style may include diced chicken, ham, peppers, and onions; Spanish style may include a tomato sauce with peppers and onions; low-fat cheeses may be added; jellies, potatoes, and similar stuffing can also be used. An omelette can be a personal creation. As the lower portion begins to turn brown, tip the pan and flip one half of the omelette over the other.

A very delicious variation of omelette is foamy omelette. It may even be served as dessert. To prepare the dessert, follow the given recipe:

When the lower portion is cooked, add fresh apple dice in the centre; fold one half over the other. Remove from pan and finish baking in the oven for a few minutes. Sprinkle with powdered sugar. Serve hot. Watch everyone enjoying it.

The main ingredients in custard are eggs and milk. To make it more easily digestible, use fewer eggs and skimmed milk. The product will taste just as good.

Cracking an Egg

- Tap the middle of the egg sharply against the rim of a small bowl.
- Holding the egg low over the bowl, insert the tips of your thumbs into the crack of the shell.
- Gently pair the egg apart. Tip the contents into the bowl and discard the shell.
- Remove any pieces of shell from the egg with the tip of a tsp. There is, however, no way to

prevent egg yolks from breaking when you crack open the eggs.

Special note: If you have to separate eggs without an egg separator, after inserting your thumbs into the crack of the shell, pull the shell apart and take the yolk on your fingers. The white will automatically slide into the bowl.

Frying Egg

FRYING AN EGG

Heat 1 tbsp each of vegetable oil and butter in a sauté pan until foaming. Break the egg into a plate and gently slide it into the hot pan. Fry over medium heat for 3-4 minutes until the white is set. Keep spooning the hot fat over the yolk to help cook it. Lift the egg with a slotted spatula. Drain the fat into the pan itself. Sprinkle salt and freshly ground pepper, and serve. Single fry egg is also called sunny side up.

POACHING AN EGG

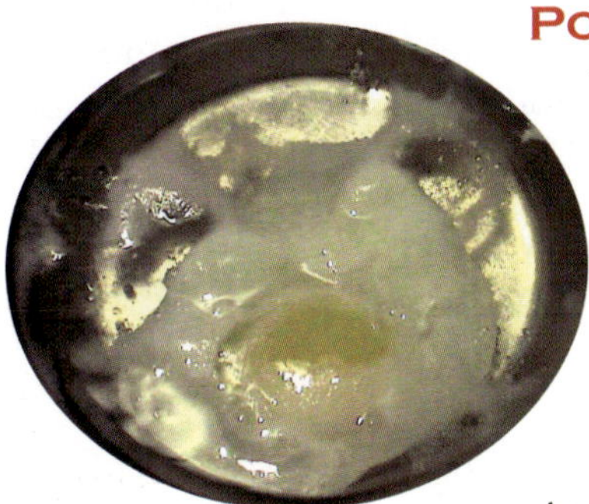

Use a nonstick milk pan or a sauté pan. Fill it two-thirds full with water and bring to a boil. Add a pinch of salt. You could also add 1 tbsp white vinegar to help set the egg white. This is optional. Lower heat till the water is simmering gently. Break the egg into a plate and gently slide it into the water. Rapidly boiling water will break the egg whites. Be careful to add the eggs only when the water is simmering. Poach uncovered over low heat for about 3 minutes for a runny yolk and 6 minutes for fully cooked yolk. Lift the egg out with a slotted spoon. Drain excess water. Place on a serving dish. Sprinkle some salt and pepper if you like. The poached egg is ready.

SEPARATING EGGS

Many times you come across a recipe that requires only egg whites or only yolks. To separate them, use two bowls, one for the yolk and the other for the whites. Tap the middle of the egg sharply against the rim of a bowl. Holding the egg low

1. Cracking an Egg; 2. Separating Egg; 3. Egg being separated;
4. Fully separated Eggs

over the bowl, pair the shell apart. Tilt gently to pour the white into the bowl while retaining the yolk. Tip the yolk into another bowl. Here, eggs are being separated with an egg separator.

SCRAMBLING EGGS

Scrambled Eggs

It is best to use nonstick frying pan for making scrambled eggs. For creamy scrambled eggs, the best procedure is to cook the eggs very slowly and gently, stirring all the while. Serve plain or with chopped fresh herbs or even with chopped spring onions and tomatoes. For each serving use 2 eggs and 1 tbsp milk. Break the eggs in a bowl; put in the milk and a pinch of salt and pepper each. Whisk well. If you prefer herbs or onions and tomatoes, add them. Whisk once again. Meanwhile, heat 1 tbsp butter in the pan until foaming, then pour in the egg mixture. Cook over low heat stirring gently with a wooden spatula. When set, remove from heat, stir once again and serve with buttered toast or parathas.

BOILING AN EGG

Remove eggs from the refrigerator 30 minutes before cooking. Otherwise they will crack in hot water.

Soft-Boiled Eggs

Soft-boiled eggs:

Place a small pan two-thirds full of water to heat. When it begins to simmer, lower the eggs into the water gently, with the help of a ladle. Bring to a boil. Lower the heat and simmer for 4 minutes. Remove the egg with the help of a ladle. Slice across the top with a knife. Serve in an eggcup. The yolk will be runny. A pinch of salt and pepper could be added as per taste.

Hard-Boiled Eggs

Hard-boiled eggs:

Follow the same procedure as above, but simmer the eggs for 10 minutes. If you boil longer, a greyish black ring will appear around the yolk. Lift the eggs out and plunge into a bowl of cold water. Crack the shell with a spoon and peel it off. Immerse in cold water for at least 5 minutes. Slice lengthwise in halves, sprinkle salt and pepper. Serve hot or use as desired. Hard-boiled eggs can be refrigerated too.

After cooking eggs, take care to wash all the utensils, the pans, the bowls, the spoon, the slotted spoon and the spatula with warm soapy water. Rinse with a little vinegar and wash with cold water. This will take away the smell of eggs. Never wash the utensils that you have used for cooking eggs with other utensils. The egg odour will get transferred to all of them.

TIPS: To remove the egg smell from the utensils, use tea decoction to rinse the used pans and plates after being washed.

Practical things to be done

1. Plain Omelette (French)

Ingredients: 1 tsp oil; 2 eggs, shelled (or use 1 egg and 2 eggs whites for less cholesterol and fat); 1 tsp water; 1/4 tsp salt; 1/4 tsp white pepper.

Portion: To serve one.

Use the following procedure:

1. Heat oil in a frying pan.

2. Combine eggs, water, salt, and pepper in a bowl. Whisk the mixer with a fork or an egg-beater.
3. Pour the mixture into the pan while stirring in circular motion with fork and moving the pan back and forth at the same time to spread out the mixture uniformly.
4. Let the egg set for a few seconds. Lift the pan at a 45-degree angle. Fold the omelette 1/3 from one side and1/3 from the other.
5. Place on a plate and serve immediately.

The omelette can be stuffed with a variety of stuffing like onions and tomatoes, onions and mushrooms, and cheese and mixed vegetables. Fill before folding sides.

2. Foamy Omelette

Ingredients: 1 tsp oil and vegetable cooking spray; 2 eggs, separated; 1 tsp milk; 1/8 tsp salt.

Portion: To serve one.

Use the following procedure:

1. Beat egg whites with whip until foamy. Heat oil in nonstick pan.
2. Beat yolks; add milk and salt and mix together.
3. Gently fold egg whites into the yolk mixture.
4. Pour into heated frying pan and cook until brown on lower side.
5. Fold into half and finish cooking in an oven at 350°F or on low flame.

Make the omelette special. Fill any one of these before folding:

- Chopped onions, mushrooms, tomatoes and fresh herbs.
- 2 tbsp grated cheese.
- Grated cheese with finely diced ham or boiled chicken.
- Any other stuffing of your choice.

There are several ways to make your egg supply stretch. Here are a few simple methods:

- To make scrambled eggs and omelette, use one whole egg and extra egg whites to make larger servings.
- When baking, replace one whole egg with 2 egg whites; two whole.
- Use cup egg substitute to equal one whole egg.
- Make French toast with bananas and skimmed milk instead of eggs and regular milk.

Expert cook suggests...

1. To prevent discolouration of egg yolks in boiled eggs, immerse eggs in cold water immediately after removing them from hot water.
2. To preserve eggs for a longer time, coat the eggshells with a few drops of ghee or oil, and place in the refrigerator.
3. To make a fluffy omelette, add a pinch of powdered sugar or cornflour to the egg mix.
4. To shell hard-boiled eggs, crack the shell all over and roll the egg between the palms of the hands to loosen the shell. Begin shelling from the air pocket, the whole shell will come off in one piece.
5. Chill egg whites for quicker and easier beating.

Dates Pudding

Kheema (keema) Anda masala

Things You Must Keep in Mind

Using Motion in Cooking

Few of us think about it, but movement in food is important in cooking. We do not just add all the ingredients and expose them to heat to cook. Besides being mixed, they need movement. When toasting spices, they need to be moved. When stir frying a dish, the ingredients need to be moved quickly. The basic purpose of this movement is to expose the ingredients uniformly to heat. All parts get cooked evenly.

Movement has yet another important role to play. It incorporates air into the product. When an egg is whisked, the white and the yolk are whisked to incorporate air into little droplets of the egg. This helps make the egg fluffy. In the same way, when bread dough is kneaded or a cake mix whisked, the purpose is to incorporate air into the mixture. This ensures soft bread and a spongy cake. Grinding and whisking dal for making *vadas* has a similar purpose.

When flavoured milk is shaken in a glass or mixer, we get a frothy milkshake due to the air incorporated in the milk. When the ice cream mixture is whisked, it is not only to mix the ingredients uniformly, but again the purpose is to incorporate air into the mixture. This ensures a smooth ice cream.

While movement is useful as a cooking procedure, it has its own risks. Overworked dough or an over mixed cake batter may not result in a quality product. If yogurt is excessively beaten, the butter may surface leaving behind the whey. Similarly, if a non-veg dish is overdone, the meat may come off the bone.

In cooking, understand why one needs to do something. Follow instructions precisely to achieve the best results.

■ ■

Day 10 Snacks and Savouries

All kinds of snacks and savouries are prepared in the Indian kitchen. There are more tid-bits prepared in Indian cookery than in any other cuisine all over the world. The social cup of tea or coffee is always accompanied with a variety of snacks to nibble, and the Indian housewife can always produce '*chevda*', '*sev*' and various '*namkeens*' without hesitation from her larder. The 'samosa' – spiced minced meat or vegetables wrapped in thin pastry and crisply fried in hot fat, and the 'bhajia' and 'pakoras' are all-time favourites.

Variety of Dry Indian Snacks

Indians are fond of meeting each other. On these occasions, besides offering beverages such as tea and coffee, it is customary to offer snacks. Even on festive occasions when people meet, it is not without offering snacks. With much festivity in the country, the opportunity for in-between meals is vast. The recipes we will discuss can be served at variety of occasions.

Serving snacks

Snacks are served in Indian homes at all times. In the morning between breakfast and lunch and in the evening at teatime and then between tea and dinner. Almost always the snacks are accompanied with a selection of homemade chutneys, pickles or tomato ketchup and chilli sauce. This is followed by tea or coffee in winters, and cold drinks in summer. The ardent fans of tea and coffee prefer them in all seasons.

Types of snacks

Snacks can be deep-fried, roasted, baked or served cold like sandwiches. The common favourites in the deep-fried variety which include fritters or pakoras, *vadas*, samosas, cutlets, chops and a variety of other ready-to-fry snacks available in the market. The finger chips made from potatoes or the French fries are well liked by both children and adults.

The baked variety includes items such as bread pizza, which is buttered bread slices baked with a topping of mashed potatoes, *paneer* or cooked mince meat and scrambled eggs, with a sprinkling of grated cheese on top. Cakes, cookies and patties, another variety that can be served both as snacks and desserts. Tiny pizzas using the same pizza dough as the normal one is another baked snack.

Cold snacks include sandwiches made from fresh bread slices. The sides are trimmed and the slices are lightly buttered with butter or cheese spread, which is easily available in the market in a variety of flavours. Thinly sliced cucumber and tomatoes topped by a lettuce leaf or a cabbage leaf, with a sprinkling of salt, *chaat masala* and English mustard make the sandwich complete. You could top the filling with a cheese single available in

Stuffed Baked Potato Balls

Paneer Kachori

Bread Pakoras

packets. Cut the sandwich diagonally to make triangles and serve with ketchup.

For variety, you could spread butter or cheese spread on one bread slice, put in the filling and cover with another bread slice on which a little green chutney has been spread. Ham, cold slices of roast meat and poultry make a tasty filling as does an omelette cut to size. For another variation, you could mash hard-boiled eggs with a tsp of butter, a pinch of salt and pepper and use this as a sandwich filling. These sandwiches can be dipped in a batter of gram flour and deep-fried to make bread pakoras.

Many vegetables thinly sliced or diced can be dipped into batter and deep-fried to make pakoras. Chunks of *paneer* on which a little salt, chilli powder and cumin powder has been sprinkled, can also be dipped in batter to make pakoras.

Pakora Batter

Gram flour is used to make batter for pakoras. Add 1 tsp of cornflour, ¼ tsp of baking powder, a pinch of salt and chilli powder with ½ tsp of *ajwain* to a cup of gram flour. Pour in a little water at a time. Mix well to make the batter thick enough to coat and stay on the food item. A thin batter

L to R: Pakora Batter and *Moong* Dal Batter for Pancakes

slips away. This batter can also be used to coat fish fillets, balls of spicy boiled potato mixture or cooked minced meat balls and even thickly sliced hard-boiled eggs. However, all frying should be done in small batches to prevent the food from sticking. The fried food should be removed on to absorbent paper to soak up the excess oil. Pakoras are served with green chutney or tomato ketchup.

Vegetables such as carrots, beans, beetroot, potatoes and cabbage are boiled, shallow fried in a little oil, lightly spiced and then coarsely mashed to form balls or thick fingers. These are then dipped in a thin batter of cornflour, rolled in breadcrumbs and deep-fried. The excess oil is removed by placing on absorbent paper; and finally served on a platter spread with lettuce or cabbage leaves, accompanied by tomato ketchup. The same method of coating is used for cutlets, fish fillets, chicken legs and breasts.

Refined Flour Batter

Banana Fritters

This batter is used mainly to coat sweet fritters made from bananas, apples or apricots. To make this, sieve 200 gm refined flour into a bowl; add 2 tsp baking powder, Add 2-3 tbsp of vegetable oil, a pinch of salt and 1 cup warm water. Mix the ingredients thoroughly. Leave batter in a cool place to rest for one hour at least. Just before using you could add two stiffly beaten egg whites with a pinch of salt. Cut the banana into two, slice lengthwise again into two. You will get four pieces from one banana. Dip each into the batter and carefully drop them into the hot oil in a *kadhai*. Fry till golden brown on all sides and remove on absorbent paper. For apples and apricots, peel, stone and core the fruit, cut into an inch thick slices, dip in batter and deep fry.

Hamburgers are an all-time favourite, particularly with the younger people. All fried food look and taste appetising, but they are not advisable in excess, especially if you are health conscious, a weight-watcher or anyone suffering from high blood pressure, diabetes and acidity or ulcer. Fruits and sandwiches are the best snacks for all occasions.

Using Leftovers

Pakora

Leftover boiled rice could be mixed with curd and left to stand overnight, or at least for 2 hours. Mix finely chopped onions, green chillies, ginger and fresh coriander. Put in enough gram flour and salt to make a very thick batter, which can be shaped into balls. Drop spoonfuls of this into hot oil and fry till golden brown. Serve with chutney or ketchup. The rice makes the pakoras crisp. The curd gives it a tangy taste, which is very pleasing.

Leftover mixed vegetables make an ideal filling for shells made from boiled potatoes mashed fine with a little cornflour mixed with it. Make this into cups, fill with the vegetables and close. Dip into thin cornflour batter, roll into breadcrumbs and deep-fry.

To test if the oil is hot enough while deep-frying, drop a tiny bit of the ingredient into the oil, if it begins to sizzle and turns brown, the oil is ready.

Snacks and savouries depend much upon how imaginative you can be. You can combine almost any ingredient to make a tasty treat. The recipes discussed earlier will help you in creating newer items.

Expert cook suggests...

1. Sandwiches stay fresh if placed on lettuce leaves.
2. To add crispness to '*vadas*' and 'pakoras', add two tbsp of rice flour to the *vada* / pakora batter / mixture.
3. To make breadcrumbs cut 2 or 3 slices of bread into small pieces. Add 2 tsps flour and churn in a mixer.
4. Do not discard biscuit or snack crumbs. The salted ones can be used to bind cutlets and the sweet ones can be used as a pudding base.

Aloo Pakora

Paneer Pakora

Steamed *Vadi*

Day 11

Chaats

The Indian palate, so used to spicy treats, is always in quest of something tasty. *Chaats* of all varieties have been titillating the taste buds of Indians for ages and are still a hot favourite. Go to any market place, including your colony's small cluster of shops, in the evening, and you will encounter a horde of venders selling a variety of *chaats* ranging from the Bombay *Bhel Puri* and Bengal's *Jhal Muri* to *Gol Gappas* or *Pani Puris*, and even fruit *chaat*.

The basic ingredients can be anything from dry roasted puffed rice mixed with finely chopped onion, ginger, green chillies, cucumber, tomatoes, fresh coriander, topped with *sev* or *bhel*, which is a thin hairlike ingredient made from gram flour deep-fried in oil. This mixture is tossed with a little *chaat masala* and salt and served.

Tikki Chole/Ragda Pattice

Bhel Puri

The Bombay *Bhel Puri* is *sev* and puffed rice mixed with chopped vegetables and fresh coriander leaves, and topped with a homemade tomato sauce.

The Bengali *Jhal Muri* uses lots of puffed rice, a little *dalmoth*, which is a *namkeen* made from soaked *chana* dal deep-fried in oil, a few roasted peanuts, chunks of boiled potatoes, onion, tomatoes, green chillies and fresh coriander. Everything is tossed with just a little mustard oil and a squeeze of lemon, garnished with coarsely ground roasted cumin seeds.

Jhal Muri

Boiled potatoes and sweet potatoes, peeled and chopped into chunks, shallow-fried on a skillet and topped with green chutney and *chaat masala* is another variety of *chaat* popular in North India.

Chunks of pineapple, apple and bananas liberally sprinkled with *chaat masala* and lemon juice, garnished with roasted cumin seeds, is a hot favourite, too. The *gol gappa* or *pani puri* is small puri made of wheat flour or a mixture of wheat flour and *rawa* mixed in a ratio of 2:1. It is kneaded into stiff dough, rolled out into a big disc and cut with a biscuit cutter into rounds of 1 inch diameter. These puris are deep-fried till they puff up like balloons. While serving, a small hole is made into the top layer and a mixture of boiled *kabuli chana* or chickpeas and boiled potatoes are used as filling. These *gol gappas* are then filled with tangy, spicy water made with a mixture of tamarind water, green chutney, chilli powder and *chaat masala*. This is a highly spicy tangy *chaat* but a great crowd puller.

The *gol gappas*, that do not puff up, can be used to make *papri chaat*. Place a slightly crumbled *dahi vada* on a plate, top with some boiled chick peas and the flat puris. Smother with well-beaten curd. Top with a little green chutney, sprinkle a little chilli powder and coarsely ground roasted cumin seeds. Garnish with a little fine *sev* and fresh coriander.

Chaat is the Indian fast food, which is considered a treat on the days when the family goes out. You could just as easily make it at home. Let us learn about a few popular items.

Sev

Ingredients: 8 tbsp gram flour, a pinch of soda bicarbonate, ¼ cup water, oil, salt to taste.

Method: Make a batter with the gram flour and water, adding salt to taste. To prepare the *sev*, the dough must be reasonably stiff. Knead the batter with warm water, soda bicarbonate and 1 tsp ghee. When smooth, fill into the *sevanazhi*. This is a hollow, barrel-shaped equipment with perforated discs. These discs fit inside the equipment and the perforations are of varying sizes. The batter or dough is filled into this hollow barrel. When a handle is turned at the top or a pressure applied at the top, the batter gets pushed out in strands of desired thickness. Heat oil in a *kadhai*. Hold the gadget above the oil and let the batter fall in long strips. Deep-fry till brown. Cool. When they are crisp, place in an airtight container. A number of variations are possible when making this dish. For example, the batter can be made spicy with chilli powder.

Bhel

Ingredients: 2 cups puffed rice (*murmura*), hot chutney, 1½ cups *sev*, sweet chutney, 12 crushed crisp puris, green mango, 1 onion, coriander, 3 boiled potatoes, 1 tomato.

Bhel Ingredients

Method: In a large bowl, mix puffed rice, *sev* and crushed puris. Add finely chopped onion, peeled, chopped potatoes, chopped mango and chutneys to taste. Mix well and garnish with chopped coriander leaves and chopped tomato. Serve immediately.

Puris

Ingredients: 1½ kg refined flour (*maida*), oil, ghee, salt to taste.

Method: Knead the flour and the other ingredients to make stiff dough. Roll out thinly on a large board, with the help of a little dry flour to avoid sticking. Cut out small round shapes about the size of a lemon with a biscuit-cutter or a small *katori*. Deep-fry in hot oil till they rise like little balloons. When brown, drain and remove on absorbent paper. These puris should remain crisp when cooled. For the crisp but flat puris used in bhel and *sev* puri, roll the dough out much thinner so that they do not puff up.

Sev Puri

Ingredients: 2 dozen flat; crisp puris; 1 chopped green mango; 1 cup *sev*; hot chutney; 1 large onion; sweet chutney; 4 boiled potatoes; coriander leaves.

Method: Chop the onion fine. Peel and chop potatoes. Chop coriander leaves. Arrange the puris on a plate and add a layer of chopped potatoes. Now top generously with crisp *sev*. Add the chutneys to taste. Garnish with finely chopped green mango and coriander leaves. Serve immediately.

Batata Puri

Ingredients: 2 dozen puris, a pinch of roasted, ground cumin seed, 6 boiled potatoes, ¼ cup curd or yoghurt, chilli powder, sweet chutney, green gram sprouts (*moong*), hot chutney, salt to taste, chopped coriander leaves, 1/2 cup *sev* (optional).

Method: Peel and chop the potatoes into small cubes. Beat curd. Arrange the puris on a flat plate. Make a hole in the centre of each puri and stuff with potato cubes. Sprinkle salt and chilli powder to taste. Spread the hot chutney. Pour a little curd on each puri and add sweet chutney. Garnish with *moong* sprouts, *sev*, chopped coriander and a dash of the cumin seed powder. Serve immediately before the puris turn soggy.

PANI PURI OR GOL GAPPAS

Ingredients: Puffed puris as required, ½ tsp black pepper, 4 tbsp tamarind, ½ cup sprouted green gram (*moong*), 2 cups water, 1 small bunch coriander leaves, jaggery or sugar to taste, 1 tsp chilli powder, salt to taste, ½ tsp roasted ground cumin seeds.

Method: Boil the tamarind in water till soft. Strain. Add the ground spices, salt and chopped coriander leaves. If the mixture is too thick, dilute with a little water. Make a small hole in each puri and stuff with some *moong* sprouts. Serve the *pani* and puris separately so that each guest can serve himself by dipping the puri into the *pani*. Chutneys may also be served with this *pani* and puris, if preferred.

FRIED ALOO CHAT

Ingredients: Medium sized potatoes – 750 gm, red chilli powder – 2 to 3 tsp, mango powder – 2 tsp, chopped coriander – ¼ cup, chaat masala and oil for frying.

Preparation and Cooking:

1. Peel and halve potatoes; soak them in salt water for 30 minutes. Place them in a steaming basket and micro cook on high for 5 minutes. Remove from the basket.
2. Heat oil for deep-frying.
3. Deep fry potatoes on high fire till golden and remove with perforated spoon on kitchen paper. Wait for 15 minutes to cool.
4. Press each potato on a rolling board with a rolling pin and deep fry on high fire till crisp. Remove and sprinkle chaat masala, mango powder, chilli powder and chopped coriander over them. Toss well.

Practical things to be done

1. Hot Chutney

Ingredients: 1 bunch coriander leaves; 1 pinch asafoetida; 1 bunch mint leaves (*pudina*); 2 tsp *amchur* powder; 6-7 green chillies; 1 lemon; 1 tsp chilli powder; salt to taste; ½ tsp roasted cumin seeds.

To make hot chutney, grind together all the ingredients except lemon. Lastly, squeeze in lemon. Mix everything thoroughly and serve.

2. Sweet Chutney

Ingredients: 4 tbsp tamarind; 1 tsp aniseed; 4 tbsp jaggery; 1 tsp roasted cumin seeds; coriander leaves; salt to taste; 1 tsp chilli powder; 1 tsp coriander seeds.

To make sweet chutney, follow this simple procedure:

1. Soak tamarind in ½ cup hot water. Strain out its pulp.
2. Grind jaggery with all other ingredients.
3. Mix tamarind pulp with other ingredients.
4. Add water according to consistency required. Garnish with chopped coriander leaves when serving.

DAY 12

Salads

Salad is a dish of raw or cold cooked food, usually dressed and seasoned, served as an appetiser, a side dish or at times, as a main dish as well. Salads add freshness to a meal and combine the goodness of the ingredients used in them. Apart from this, they are a healthy addition to any meal because they contain a lot of fibre, which helps cleanse the digestive system of toxic substances, fights constipation and keeps the body fit.

Because of its fibre content, and the ability to fill up the stomach and satiate hunger without additives such as oil or fat, salads are God's answer to a dieter's woes. All dieticians recommend a bowl of salad with each meal. You can make salads with a variety of raw vegetables cut into tiny bits or sticks, fashioned from fresh, peeled seasonal vegetables and served with a red chilli pepper sauce, a dash of olive oil and vinegar or ripe tomatoes moistened with olive oil and lemon. Cooked vegetables are more versatile, tossed in vinaigrette dressing or mixed with mayonnaise. They are also the basis of hearty salads such as French salad with tuna and olives.

Paneer and Fruit Salad

When choosing vegetables for salads, the deciding factor should be the texture. Uncooked vegetables should be crunchy. If they seem tough, they should be blanched. Vegetables should be cooked until tender but firm. They should be refreshed by washing them with cold water, or by immersing them in a bowl of chilled water, and then drained thoroughly. Whether raw or cooked, marinating robust vegetables such as onions, for an hour, makes them better for salads. However, they may lose flavour and become acidic after 12 hours.

Mixing a Salad

Dressings and mayonnaise should be added just before serving, except for potato vinaigrette, where the dressing is added to warm vegetables. Vegetable salads should be stored covered in the refrigerator or they lose their crispness. However, most salads taste better at room temperature. Take them out of the refrigerator 15-20 minutes before serving.

Green Salad

The art of balancing colour, texture and taste is most important for green salads. Whether made of lettuce alone or a mixture of greens, it should be dressed suitably and never smothered by other ingredients. Each salad combination provides its own taste and texture. Mild herbs like parsley, basil or chives contribute their own perfume, which is ideal for a green salad.

The dressing gives salad an individuality. For green salad, light vinaigrette is the best choice. Variations may be made with flavoured mustard, a little of finely chopped shallot or spring onion and your choice of vinegar or oil. Green salad should always be tossed together at the last minute so that there is no time for the dressing to wilt the leaves, especially if you are using a hot dressing. If you like a garlic flavour, rub a salad bowl with a cut garlic clove, or add a piece of crushed garlic to the dressing. The French love garlic. They rub garlic over a crust of bread and bury it in the lettuce. The crust is kept in the bowl when tossing the salad, but discarded before serving it.

Mixed Green Salad

Tossed Green Salad

Tossing a Salad

The French serve fresh green salads after the main course, to clear the palate for cheese and dessert. In the United States, green salad usually opens the meal, or may be eaten between the appetiser and the main course. In Britain, it often appears in the company of a cold main dish, while Italians may serve it with fish or meat. Green salads that contain other vegetables or sea food, are usually served as a first course. Indians do not have the concept of a course meal. All the dishes are served at the same time. Hence, the salads become a side dish to be eaten during the meal itself. A typical Indian green salad may have onion, cucumber, lettuce, cabbage, radish, carrots, tomatoes and beetroot, either finely chopped or cut in various shapes like slices or sticks.

TIPS Indians add revived dry fruits (chopped) to their salads. They soak food items such as cashew nuts, walnuts, almonds, raisins, dates and peanuts, etc., for a few hours, then add to the fresh vegetables and finally season them. In fact, salad making is an art; you may add 2 to 3 ingredients or numberless, so that the salad looks appetising the way it is presented. Now even in India, health conscious people who consume salad as a main dish add the greens like spinach and fenugreek, radish and turnip greens along with fresh grated coconut, spring onions, cottage cheese or tofu, cooked eggs, chicken and fish pieces to their salads. Some combinations include even fresh fruits in the chopped form.

Outside India, an array of exotic vegetables are available in the market. One can choose from a selection of

Apple, Carrot and Nuts Salad with Chicken Balls

Shrimp Salad

lettuce. Dandelion greens, watercress, endive and chicory are a few other exotic greens available in the market. You can add a number of variations to the simple green salad. The American chef's salad could include julienne of ham, turkey and cheese, dandelion greens in hot bacon dressing, toasted goat cheese on a bed of curly endive, salad greens with fresh foil grass, sweetbreads, or thinly sliced smoked duck breast tossed with walnut oil and raspberry vinegar with peas and walnuts.

Herbs are liberally used with salads everywhere in the world. In India, we hardly ever use them. Parsley, basil and chive are popular herbs used with salads. They are mild and do not detract from the taste of the salad. It is only recently that people in India have developed a taste for herbs. That, too, is limited to a small group of exotic cooks found in the metropolitan cities. For the rest of the Indians, fresh coriander and mint leaves are the only garnishing added to almost every dish including salads.

Plain Salads

These consist a basic ingredient, either raw or cooked, but always served cold with a cold dressing such as mayonnaise, vinaigrette, mustard and soft cheese dressing. The basic ingredients could be beans, meat or shellfish, and the range is fairly wide to include French beans, carrots, celery, cauliflower, lentils, red or white cabbage, potatoes, rice, cheese, crab, crayfish, cold chicken or ham. The beans and lentils are boiled before being added to the salad. Sprouted beans, most popularly called *moong* sprouts, could be added to the salad to make it richer, heavier and more nutritive.

Mixed Salads

These are more elaborate dishes combining various ingredients of contrasting but complementary flavours, textures, and colours. They can include hard-boiled eggs, some fruits, exotic ingredients such as truffles, foe grass or lobster medallions, or simple ingredients. Mixed salads must always be decorative. The dressing should blend with the flavour of the ingredients and not mask it. These salads are served as starters, but can also accompany hot or cold roast meats and hot or cold meals. Most often, an adventurous cook creates his own salad, producing an immensely wide range.

Chicken and Pineapple Salad

Salad dressings

Clockwise: Mayonnaise, French Dressing, Vinaigrette

Dressing is an integral part of a salad. We often feel that a squeeze of lemon, a dash of vinegar or a pinch of *chaat masala* and pepper is all that a salad requires. Cooking has become an art. There is stress on food that pleases the eye and satisfies the soul as well as the stomach. Indian cooks too have learnt the art of using varied and exotic dressings for salads.

French Dressing

A basic vinaigrette can be prepared with ¼ cup wine vinegar, 1 tsp oil, salt, pepper, sugar and mustard powder if you like to lend pungency to your salad. This vinaigrette could have other embellishments like:

- For a typically Indian edition of cooked vegetables salad, add to the vinaigrette 1 small crushed clove of garlic and 1 tbsp finely chopped onion, fried until soft, in 1 tbsp oil with a tsp of curry powder.
- For all raw salads or cooked vegetables, replace the vinaigrette with mayonnaise, plain or flavoured with herbs or garlic.
- For western style raw salads other than green ones, thoroughly soak 4 anchovies to remove the salt and fillet them; puree them with 1 tsp of capers; add this mixture to the vinaigrette.
- For curly endives, red cabbage or dandelion greens, put the salad in a bowl and season with salt and pepper. Instead of using vinaigrette, fry 100 gms diced fat streaks of bacon, add 1-2 tbsp vinegar to the bacon in the pan, then pour over the salad while still hot, and toss.
- For lettuce, replace the oil of the vinaigrette with 4 tbsp of whipped cream.
- For beetroot, celery, potato and chicory, instead of using vinaigrette, blend 1 tbsp of French mustard with 2-3 tbsp cream, add 1 tsp or more of vinegar and season with salt and pepper.

Salad bowl

Serving the salad appropriately is as important as the dressing and garnishing. Salads are usually served in bowls. Sometimes a shallow dish or a platter is used when serving more elaborate mixed salads.

A salad bowl is a deep bowl, which traditionally comes with matching servers in wood, horn, glass or silver. A salad bowl should be chosen to match the salad. In Western countries olive-wood salad bowls are often reserved for highly seasoned green salads, which need to be tossed easily. Mixed salads, with ingredients of different colours, are best served in a shallow transparent bowl. You could also use individual salad bowls for serving portions of salad at the side of the plate.

These are a few of the popular ingredients for salads:

Green Salads: Lettuce, chicory, cabbage, cucumber, spinach, dandelion greens, watercress, etc.

Plain Salads: Radish, carrots, cauliflower, peas, French beans, potatoes, cabbage, rice, meats, fish, eggs, etc.

Salad Bowl

Mixed Salads: Fruits such as papaya, grapes, oranges, watermelon, muskmelon, avocado, apricots, rice, lentils and beans, meats, poultry, fish, eggs and the ingredients of both green salads and plain salad, almost anything can go into a mixed salad as they are elaborate. They bear testimony to a cook's culinary and imaginative skills.

GARNISHING SALADS

Just as a dressing lends flavour to a salad, garnishing gives perfection to its presentation. The look of a dish tempts the palate much before you taste it. Here are a few garnishes to go with your salad:

Herbs: Chop a bunch of chives, chervil and parsley with a few tarragon and mint leaves; make some vinaigrette and mix in the chopped herbs.

Nuts: Chop 50 gms walnuts, peanuts, and hazelnuts; prepare a salad, season it with vinaigrette, and sprinkle with the chopped nuts, tossed just before serving.

Cheese: Mash 50 gms cheese and 2 tbsp cream; add a few drops of Tabasco sauce and 1 teaspoon brandy, season with a little salt and pepper, if desired; and mix well.

Pour this mixture over the salad. Toss just before serving. Add salt sparingly just before serving your salad. It makes the salad grow limp. It also dilutes the dressing as it makes the vegetables shed water. Serving salad appropriately is as important as the dressing and garnishing.

Practical things to be done

Today we shall learn how to make a salad dressing, prepare a simple vegetable salad and how to serve it. Many kinds of salad dressings are available in the market, but homemade ones taste better.

1. Commonly used Salad Dressings

For a light **French Dressing**, whisk 1 cup wine vinegar, 3-4 tbsp olive oil, a pinch each of salt and pepper, mix using a wire whisk. Store in the refrigerator in a glass bottle. Keep it for a fortnight.

For **Mayonnaise**, whip 2 eggs, 2-3 tbsps of sunflower oil, a pinch of salt and pepper in a food processor. Store in a glass bottle in refrigerator. Keep it for 2-3 days.

For **Cheese Cream Dressing**, mix together 1 cup hung curd, 1 tsp salad oil, 1 tsp mustard powder, 1 tsp white pepper powder, 1 tsp sugar, 1 tsp salt. Chill before use.

2. Cutting Cucumber Sticks and Crescents

Follow this simple procedure to cut cucumber sticks and crescents.

Cucumber Sticks

1. Peel the cucumber. Cut it into half lengthwise. If you like, scoop out the seeds with a tsp. Cut halves in several lengthwise strips, and then cut across in desired length for sticks.
2. Peel the cucumber in strips, leaving a thin line of skin alternating with an expanse of peeled flesh. Halve it. If you like, scoop out the seeds. Cut the cucumber in thin crosswise slices. Your crescents are ready.
3. For a decorative garnish, fan out the cucumber crescents with your hand. This could be the centrepiece for your salad, surrounded by other ingredients to complement the colour and texture.

Expert cook suggests...

1. To remove the fibres of an orange easily, soak the orange in warm water for 5 minutes.
2. If tomatoes are soft for salad, put them in the refrigerator for some time before cutting.
3. Cut tomatoes vertically rather than horizontally for salad. They cut better.
4. To increase shelf life of fruits, refrigerate them in open containers instead of polythene bags.

COOKING METHOD # 5 – FRYING

Using Oil, Butter or Ghee

Except for contributing by way of softening food or lending its own taste, fats like cooking oil, butter and ghee do not do much on their own. However, when heat is applied, they do wonders in cooking food. Fats are essential for human nutrition. Since it is easy to exceed the daily requirement, one has to be careful to keep their use within reasonable limits to avoid health problems. Nonstick cookwares have made it possible to use the least amount of fat when cooking.

Sautéing means to cook food quickly over high heat in a small amount of fat. For example, sautéed chicken and sautéed vegetables. Here are a few tips:

Sautéing Chicken

Stir frying Vegetables

Sautéing Vegetables

Deep-Frying Puri

- Use just enough fat to prevent sticking. A nonstick pan is ideal.
- Cut meat into pieces before sautéing to prevent sticking to the pan and to get evenly cooked.
- The pan must be preheated before adding the food so that the food does not simmer.
- Do not overfill the pan. This lowers the temperature.
- Flip the food while cooking so that it gets evenly cooked.

Stir frying is to cook small-sized food over high flame in a small amount of oil. The high flame and the constant movement of the food keeps it from sticking and burning. This method preserves the crisp texture and bright colour of vegetables and cooks food quickly. Chicken and vegetables are often stir fried. Here are a few tips:

- Cut meat, poultry, fish, vegetables, or any combination into thin strips or dice them.
- Avoid watery ingredients because they make the fat splatter.
- Coat the cooking surface with a thin layer of oil.
- Preheat the equipment to high temperature.
- Stir food rapidly during cooking. Do not overfill the pan or *kadhai*.
- When the meat is done, add small pieces of vegetables such as broccoli, cauliflower, sprouts, carrots, mushrooms, tomatoes, or green onions, as they cook quickly.

Deep-frying means to cook food completely covered in hot fat. Fried food cook quickly and small-sized tender food are best to ensure that they are well cooked. The goals of deep-frying are a crisp surface, golden colour, good flavour, and a minimum of fat absorption by the food. For example, deep-fried items are French fries, fish, fried chicken, puris, *bhaturas* and pakora, etc. Here are a few tips:

- Ensure that the oil is well heated before putting in the product to be fried. This is important to make sure that the food is uniformly cooked both inside and outside. If the temperature is too low, the food will absorb more oil.
- Fry just before serving the food as fried food gets soggy quickly.
- Slide in the food carefully into oil so that you do not burn your fingers.

- When frying fish or another strong-flavoured food, do not fry anything else in the same fat. The food will absorb the strong flavour. For instance, French fries will taste like fish.
- Stir with a perforated, long-handled spoon to prevent the food from sticking together.
- Keep the frying equipment clean.

Pan-Frying Chicken

Pan-frying is cooking food in a pan over moderate heat in a small to moderate amount of fat. It is different to sautéing because it uses less heat and requires more fat. Fish fillet chops and chicken pieces can be pan-fried.

Here are a few simple tips to follow:

- Use enough fat to cover about one-half of the thickness of the food.
- Turn the food at least once for it to get evenly cooked.

TIPS

- Frying becomes better if a few drops of vinegar are added to the hot oil or ghee.
- Use a plastic spray bottle to spray a little oil on nonstick cookware. It makes work easier.

Expert cook suggests...

1. Use a little toothpaste and an old toothbrush to clean your mixer grinder to get a sparkling shine.
2. To keep your mixer blades sharp, put some salt in the mixer and run for a few seconds. Do this once a month.

Progress Checklist # 2

Do not skip this checklist. Answer all the questions. They are based on what you have learnt in the last six days. Whenever in doubt, go back to the appropriate lesson and reread the relevant section. Your sincere efforts will make you a great cook.

1. Were you able to make good yogurt and *paneer*?

☐ Yes ☐ No

Keep trying. Milk products are important in cooking.

2. Does everybody look forward to a good cup of tea or coffee made by you?

☐ Yes ☐ No

3. Can you fry an egg, or make a good omelette?

☐ Yes ☐ No

4. Did you make the snacks in the practical session?

☐ Yes ☐ No

5. Did you try making snacks other than those suggested in the practical session of the lesson?

☐ Yes ☐ No

6. Did you try making *Aloo Chaat* and *Bhel Puri*?

☐ Yes ☐ No

7. Were the *chutneys* made by you in the practical session appreciated?

☐ Yes ☐ No

Keep trying. Chutneys are easy to make. They attract immediate attention in a meal.

8. Are you serving green salads with every meal?

☐ Yes ☐ No

Salads offer an easy and tasty way of eating vegetables. Make it a part of every meal.

If the answers to all the questions are not 'yes', go back to the relevant lesson. Reread it. Understand the concept that is being taught. Do the practical exercises. You will be well on your way to become a great cook.

Day 13

Stuffed Puris and Parathas

In Punjab, North India, climatic conditions favour the growth of the best quality wheat. The chapatti, *phulka*, paratha, tandoori roti, naan and *bhatura* are varieties of bread or *roti,* all of which originate from Punjab. Stuffed paratha (fried roti stuffed with chopped vegetables or meat) is a great favourite. Served with lassi or buttermilk, it is the midday meal of a Punjabi farmer.

The chapatti looks much like the Mexican tortilla. It is a flat, round, pan-roasted pancake made of whole-wheat flour. The paratha uses the same ingredients but is flaky and fried. Puris are deep-fried discs in oil. They swell into round hollow balloons.

Indian breads can also be made from rice flour, maize, millet or lentils. The breads made from wheat flour are by far the best.

Paratha

Parathas can be plain with some spices, or stuffed with a special filling. The filling is sandwiched between two separately rolled rotis. Alternatively, the ingredients can be kneaded into the dough with a little oil or ghee, a pinch of salt, cumin powder and coriander powder. The dough is kneaded in the same manner as that for *chapatti*. The dough should be soft and pliable. The filling can consist vegetables, minced meat and poultry. Eggs or pureed lentils cooked with spices also make good fillings.

Top to Bottom:
Dal Dough, Leftovers Dough,
Spinach and Fenugreek Dough

The following can serve as a guide:

Grated: Cabbage, cauliflower, radish, beetroot, carrots, cheese, cottage cheese (*paneer*).

Shredded: Greens such as cabbage, spinach.

Chopped: Onion, coriander leaves, mint leaves, fenugreek leaves (*methi*), green chillies.

Pureed: Spinach, green *methi*, lentils.

Minced: Cooked potatoes, meats, *paneer*.

If you are making a plain paratha, then the dough is kneaded with a pinch of salt and a tsp of oil. A big round chapatti is rolled out. Its surface is smeared with ghee or vegetable oil. The top is folded over one-third and the bottom is folded over to overlay the first fold so that sort of a rectangle is formed with tapering ends. Some ghee is smeared over the surface again. The tapering ends are folded to overlap each other till a square is formed. This square is lightly dusted with dry flour and rolled out into ½ cm thick square.

This is placed on a hot *tawa* or griddle. Soon the paratha begins to change colour and swell in spots indicating that one side is done. Turn over and cook the other side. Keep the heat medium or the paratha will scorch. With a spoon, drop some ghee around the edges and the top. Press the paratha lightly with a spatula, on both sides for a golden finish.

The **shredded and grated vegetables** are mostly kneaded with the dough along with finely chopped green chillies, coriander or mint leaves, onion and grated ginger. Salt, oil and *ajwain* are added. You could add a little *masala* powder if you wish. The dough is kneaded with all the ingredients, rolled into ½ cm thick rounds and cooked like the plain parathas.

Mooli Stuffing

Mooli Paratha

They are not folded like plain paratha because the ingredients break out.

Pureed spinach and fenugreek leaves are kneaded with the dough, with the seasoning and round parathas are cooked with ghee.

The lentils commonly used are *chana* dal, *masoor* dal, *dhuli moong* dal and *dhuli urad* dal. They are cooked till soft, removed from water and fried in a little oil with salt, *masala* and cumin seeds. While cooking, the lentils are coarsely mashed with a wooden spoon or a ladle. Some finely chopped fresh coriander leaves are sprinkled and the mixture is used as filling.

Maize flour is also used to make parathas. However, it seldom has smooth edges as the maize flour is grainy in texture. Adding 2-3 tbsp of wheat flour helps in making the dough smooth. The dough is kneaded with a little oil and hot water. It requires prolonged kneading. These parathas are thicker, about ½ cm thick.

Paneer Paratha

Plain Layered Paratha

Tandoori Paratha

Paneer is crumbled, seasoned well and used as a filling. *Paneer*, whether used in the dough or as a filling, should be seasoned with *amchur* and spices. Without them, it has a bland taste. *Paneer*, used as a filling, is mixed with very finely chopped onion, green chillies, green coriander leaves, a little *ajwain*, salt and *amchur*. This mixture is filled in the paratha.

Innovative cooks prefer to add any chopped, shredded or mashed vegetables like methi and spinach leaves, grated carrot, radish or cauliflower, or mashed potatoes and paneer to the maize flour dough. If maize flour is kneaded with buttermilk or whey, it yields tasty and soft parathas.

Parathas using rice flour are also kneaded with hot water but require no oil. No other ingredient is added. These, too, have uneven and broken edges and are as thick as the maize flour parathas. Rice flour roti or paratha are fondly eaten in Western India. Both require slow, low heat cooking. They are heavier to digest and must be eaten sparingly. Unlike other parathas that are consumed with *dahi*, raita, or butter and chutney, plain rice flour paratha and maize flour paratha are served with curried vegetables and green *saags*. The maize flour paratha is ideally served with *sarson-ka-saag* (mustard greens) or spinach.

For *aloo* paratha, the potatoes are boiled, peeled and mashed, mixed with salt, *amchur* or *anardana*, chopped coriander and green chillies. This is used as a filling. Or cook the mashed potatoes with chopped onions, ginger, green chillies, salt and turmeric, red chilli and garam masala. When cooked, let it cool. Add freshly chopped coriander. Mix well, and use as a filling.

For meat minces, the mince is cooked with chopped onions, ginger and green chillies and *masala* till it is dry and is used to fill parathas.

PURIS

These are small rounds of dough, 3-4 inches in diameter, deep-fried in hot vegetable oil or ghee. The dough is stiffer than the paratha dough. The oil that is added to the flour before kneading is a little more than that for parathas. Wheat flour, rice flour and even maize flour can be kneaded to make puris. However, wheat flour is most commonly used. The Bengali *luchi* is made from refined flour (*maida*). Puris can be made plain or with stuffing. Puris made with rice flour and maize flour are never stuffed.

Here are a few ideas that you can use.

Matar Kachori

- For plain puris the flour is mixed with a little oil, salt, *masala* powder and *ajwain* or cumin seeds. It is kneaded into stiff dough. Small balls of the dough are rolled out into small rounds and then one by one dropped in hot oil. When it puffs up, the side is changed and gently pressed down with slotted spoon to immerse it into the oil. At once it puffs up again.

- You could mix some gram flour, finely chopped green chillies, coriander leaves along with salt and *masala* in the wheat flour before kneading.
- The stuffing is usually boiled and pureed lentils as coarse stuffing may cause the *puri* to disintegrate. These puris need softer dough than the normal puris.

FILLING PARATHAS AND PURIS

A bigger ball of dough for a paratha and a smaller one for puri is rolled into a ball. Then, using both hands, form a cup with the dough. Lightly grease the inside of the cup, stuff a little filling and close the ball by folding the edges from all sides. It is again rolled into a ball and flattened with the hand on the rolling board. Thereafter, the paratha or puri is rolled out using a light hand so as not to cause the filling to break out. Alternatively, you could roll out the dough into small rounds, place little filling in the centre, fold from all sides to make a ball, and proceed as before.

GOBHI PARATHA

Ingredients: 700 gms whole-wheat flour, 1½ inch piece ginger, 700 gms cauliflower, 2 tbsp chopped coriander, 1 onion and 2 green chillies, ½ tsp *garam masala*, 1 tbsp dried pomegranate seeds (*anardana*), ghee, salt to taste.

Method: Grate cauliflower coarsely. Do not use the stalks. Heat 1 tbsp oil and put grated cauliflower in it; stir fry on high fire for 2 minutes; and mix with finely chopped onions, grated ginger, chopped coriander leaves, chillies, crushed pomegranate seeds and seasonings; cook for 2 minutes more and remove. Transfer in a bigger plate and cool. Sieve flour, add 1 tbsp ghee, a pinch of salt and enough water to knead to a stiff dough. Cover and keep aside for 10 minutes and divide into 6 portions. Roll out one portion into a thick roundel, spread a little ghee all over it and place the mixture in the centre. Fold the sides up carefully. Roll into a ball and roll out into a 7 to 8 inch disc, without letting the stuffing break through. Cook on heated *tawa* and smear with fat and fry on both sides till nicely brown. Serve hot with plain curds.

Step by step procedure of stuffing *Gobhi* Paratha:

1. Placing *Gobhi* stuffing on the rolled disc.
2. Fold the disc.
3. Reshaped into a stuffed disc.
4. Rolled Paratha.
5. Cooked Paratha.

MAKING PARATHAS AND PURIS

Here are a few recipes to make parathas and puris.

BESAN KI ROTI (gram flour roti)

Ingredients: 700 gms flour, 2 green chillies, ½ cup warm water, ½ tsp pomegranate seeds, ghee, 1 small-sized onion.

Method: Finely chop the onion and the chillies. Mix the flour, a little ghee, chopped onion and chillies and pomegranate seeds. Knead with warm water into stiff dough. Divide the dough into equal portions. Roll out as thicker chapattis. Cook on both sides, adding a little oil/ butter or ghee to the edges. Remove when brown on both sides.

SWEET ROTIS

Ingredients: 8 tbsp *toor* dal / channa dal, 1 tsp powdered cardamom, 8 tbsp sugar, 500 gm whole-wheat flour (*atta*), 1 tbsp ghee.

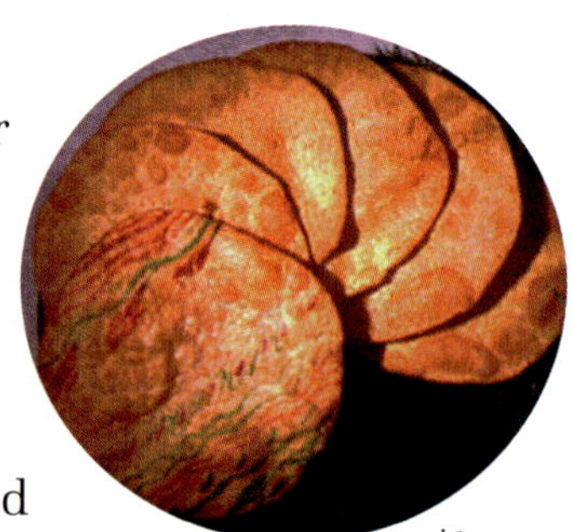

Sweet Crisp Fried Rotis

Method: Soak dal in cold water overnight, wash well and remove all the coarse skins. Boil in enough water till well cooked and very tender. Drain off water. Mash the grain with a wooden spoon. Add sugar and ghee and cook on a medium heat till dry, stirring constantly. Add cardamom and divide into 10 to 12 portions; keep aside. Knead wheat flour into dough and divide into 10 to 12 portions. Roll out one portion and place 1 ball of the dal filling in the centre. Fold up the roti and seal well. Roll out roti taking care not to let the stuffing break through. Heat *tawa* and cook the roti with little ghee, like a paratha or deep-fry. To make them special for children, paint them with food colours.

LAYERED MEAT PARATHAS

Ingredients: 700 gm whole-wheat flour, ½ tsp chilli powder, 300 gm ground minced meat, 1 tsp garam masala, 1 onion, salt to taste, 1 tsp coriander powder, ghee or butter.

Keema Paratha

Method: Mince onion, heat 2 tbsp ghee or butter and sauté onion till golden brown. Add coriander, chilli powder, garam masala and salt. Fry till nicely brown. Add 3 tbsp water and simmer till tender. If necessary, add more water and fry till dry. Meanwhile, sieve flour. Add salt. Rub in a little butter, add water and knead well into stiff soft dough. Break off small portions and roll into 8 paper-thin, round, even chapattis. Smear one chapatti with ghee and place another one on it. Smear again and place another one until you have layer of four. Sprinkle the surface with a little water and spread a thin layer of meat. Cover with four more chapattis with a smear of ghee between each layer. Make 3 such parathas. Roast on a *tawa* till light golden. Add a little ghee on the sides and fry on both sides till nicely brown and crisp.

SWEET CHANA-DAL PARATHA

Ingredients: 700 gms flour, 3 cloves, 700 gms gram dal (*chana*), 2 tsp *til* oil (sesame oil) or vegetable oil, 700 gms sugar, ½ tsp ground cardamoms.

Method: Sieve the flour, add oil and enough water gradually and knead to thick dough. Roll lemon-sized balls from the dough and keep aside. Meanwhile, boil the dal in water for about an hour till tender. Drain off the water, add sugar, cardamoms and cloves and stir till thread-like syrup is formed. Grind or mash the mixture to a paste. Roll into balls of the same number about double the size of the flour balls. Flatten out the flour balls. Place a ball of the gram mixture in the centre and cover completely with the flour dough. Roll into a smooth, large ball in the palm of your hand. Place on a rolling-board and roll out with a rolling pin into a round disc about one-sixth inches thick. Bake on a *tawa* till both sides are crisp golden brown. Spread with butter or ghee and serve hot. In western India this dish is called '*Puran Poli*.' '*Puran*' means sweet stuffing and '*poli*' means roti.

Puran Poli

SAVOURY PURIS

Ingredients: 8 tbsp refined flour (*maida*), 2 tbsp gram flour, 2 tbsp *kasoori methi*, 5 green chillies, 1 tsp cumin seeds, ghee as required, 1 tsp coarsely-ground black pepper, 1 clove garlic, 1/4 tsp turmeric, salt to taste, 1 tbsp coriander leaves.

Methi Puri

Method: Sieve flours, turmeric and salt together; add cumin seeds and pepper; grind garlic and add along with coriander leaves, *kasoori methi* and chillies to flour. Rub a little ghee into the flour. Adding warm water gradually, knead the flour into stiff dough. Make small balls of the dough and roll out into puris. Fry in hot ghee until golden brown. Do not roll out too many puris at a time. They will not puff up.

DALBHARI PURIS

Ingredients: 4 tbsp *moong* dal, 4 tbsp gram dal (*chana*), 3 cardamoms, ½ tsp cumin seeds, 4 cloves, 8 peppercorns, 1 kg whole-wheat flour (*atta*), 1½ tsp salt, or to taste, 3 tbsp ghee.

Dalbhari Puri

Method: Soak both the dals overnight, drain off the water and grind dals to a fine paste. Grind the cloves, peppercorns, cardamoms and cumin seeds. Heat 1 tbsp ghee in a pan. Fry the dal paste with ground *masala* and salt. Knead the wheat flour to stiff dough with 2 tsp ghee, water and salt. Divide the dough into small portions. Roll each portion into a ball. Flatten it in the palm of your hand and put in a little fried dal. Close up the dough and roll out into a thick puri. Deep-fry in ghee till golden. Remove on oil absorbent paper.

Practical things to be done

1. Aloo Paratha

Aloo Paratha

Equipment used: A shallow plate with a raised edge; a *tawa*; a rolling board and a rolling pin; a separate bowl of ghee or oil; a tsp; a spatula; a large flat plate.

Gadgets: A pressure cooker.

Ingredients: 3 large potatoes; 3 cups wheat flour; 1 cup water or more; oil or ghee for frying; dry flour; 2 tbsp finely chopped fresh coriander; 2 green chillies, deseeded and finely chopped; ½ inch piece ginger, peeled and grated; 1 tsp *amchur* (mango powder); a pinch of sugar; salt to taste; ¼ tsp coriander powder.

Follow this procedure to make the parathas.

1. In a pressure cooker, place the potatoes and cover with water. Put on fire and cook to 3 whistles.
2. Cool and peel the cooked potatoes. Mash and mix chopped coriander, ginger, chillies, salt, sugar, coriander powder and *amchur*. Mix well and divide into 8 to 10 portions.
3. In the shallow plate, knead the flour into soft dough as you did for chapattis and divide into 8 to 10 portions.
4. Put the *tawa* on the fire.
5. Take 1 portion dough and roll it into a ball. Flatten slightly with your palms and dust both sides with dry flour.
6. Make a cup or start rolling on the rolling board with the rolling pin, making a circle approximately 4 inches in diameter. Pick it off the board and cup it in your left hand. Place 1 portion of the stuffing into the centre of the dough. With your right hand, pull the edges of the circle closed over the stuffing to cover it completely. Form a ball and flatten it with your fingers.
7. Dust on both sides with dry flour and roll out a paratha gently, keeping the pressure light so that the stuffing does not come out. Sprinkle a little more dry flour if the paratha tends to stick to the board.
8. Place the paratha on the hot *tawa*. Let it cook on medium heat. When it begins to swell up in spots, turn over.
9. With a spoon, pour in a little ghee round the edges and on top of the paratha. Turn over and cook till light brown. Serve with curd/raita, pickles and green chutney.

As you have mastered the art of making stuffed parathas, it's a good idea to learn making plain paratha.

The step by step procedure is illustrated below:

1. Knead 2 cups wheat flour with 1/2 tsp salt and 1 tsp oil.

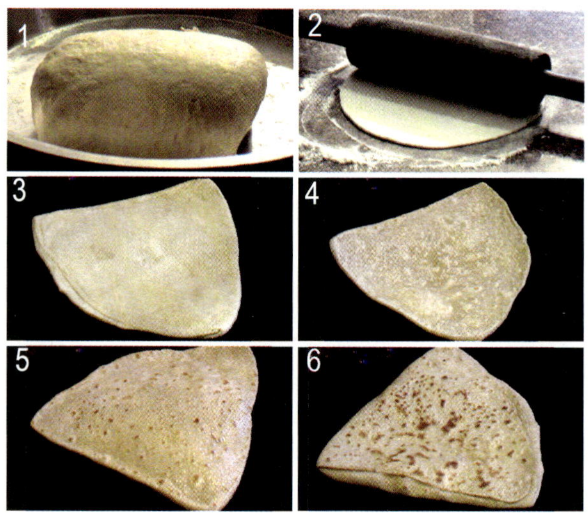

2. Roll a lemon-sized ball of dough into a disc; apply 1 tsp oil; fold it into half; apply a little more oil and fold into a triangle.
3. Roll and place paratha on a hot *tawa.*
4. Cook till it changes colour and change side.
5. Apply 1 tsp oil when brown mark starts appearing on the surface.
6. Cook till it turns brown on both sides.

TIPS Though it is a common practice to boil and peel potatoes for any kind of preparation, but for nice and dry stuffing it is advisable to first peel potatoes, wash and then boil either in a pressure cooker or in a microwave oven, so that they can be handled (mashed) properly with a potato masher when still hot. Experts say, "handle the potatoes when hot, but use them when cold". So follow the advice for better results.

Using Leftovers

Several leftovers can be used as filling. Here are a few suggestions.

- By mixing leftover dals during the kneading process with flour, salt and chopped coriander leaves, you can make tasty parathas or puris with this dough.
- Left over mixed vegetables can also be mixed into flour and kneaded into dough to make parathas.

Expert cook suggests...

1. Dry leftover slices of bread, powder them in a mixer, and add them to the flour while mixing dough for 'puris' and 'parathas'. They will be soft and tasty.
2. Add 2 tbsp semolina (*rawa*) and a cup of milk to the dough for puris. They will come out fluffier.
3. Adding a few drops of vinegar to the puri dough will ensure that the puris do not soak cooking oil.
4. Crumble one slice of bread into '*bhatura* batter' for quick fermentation.
5. Instead of reheating 'puris', take two 'puris', sandwich a filling of your choice between them, and place them in a sandwich toaster. Excess oil will ooze out. You will get a crisp 'puri-*sabzi*' snack. Serve with sauce or chutney.
6. To make 'puris' fluffy, use bottled soda to knead the dough.
7. When the *tawa* is too greasy, put some sour curd on it, leave it for thirty minutes and then rinse it.
8. When making dough for puris add 1 tsp of semolina for every 100 gms of flour. The puris will come out fluffy and crisp.

Sada Paratha

Things You Must Keep in Mind

Health Hazards

Good food provides nutrition to the family. However, we cannot overlook that it is also good nutrition for bacteria that cause sickness and ill health. These bacteria abound all over, and whenever they find food coupled with a warm and humid environment peculiar of most kitchens, they grow rapidly. Such health hazards exist in every kitchen. It is for you to keep the risks from such hazards low. Here are a few things you must remember.

- Wash your hands thoroughly with soap and water before you start cooking. Rewash them each time your hands get contaminated due to one reason or another.

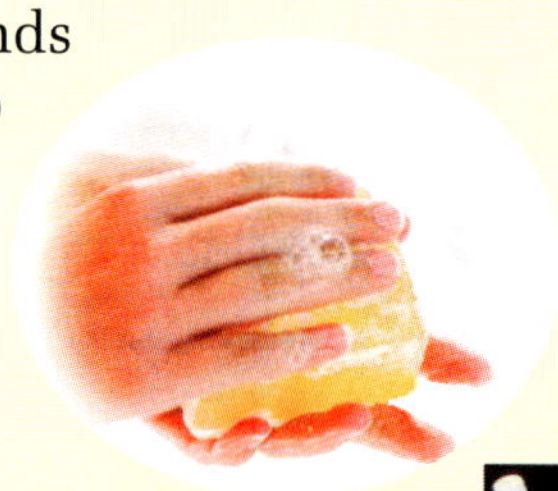

- Wash vegetables and other food items to ensure perfect cleanliness.
- Prefer granite, marble or acrylic surfaces for the kitchen. They are easier to keep clean.
- If you use a chopping board, clean it every time after use. It is not enough to just wipe it with a cloth.
- Cooking utensils must be spotlessly clean and hygienic.
- Napkins or towels used in the kitchen must be washed with detergent everyday.
- Do not leave cooked or semi-cooked food on the kitchen counter. Store all the food in the refrigerator.
- Non-vegetarian food items like meat, fish and poultry must not be handled more than necessary. Store them in the coolest part of the refrigerator.
- When preparing food items for cooking, for example, marinating meat, return the items to the refrigerator as a warm environment promotes bacterial growth.
- Thaw meat items in the microwave oven only if you want to cook them immediately.
- When reheating cooked food stored in a refrigerator, do not reheat the whole lot. Heat only as much as you want to use. Reheating food frequently increases the chances of food contamination.

- Always remember that reheating food does not always kill the contaminating bacteria. Even when they do, the toxins left behind by them may be hazardous.
- As a cook, your family's health is in your hand. Make cleanliness your watchword.

■ ■

COOKING METHOD # 6 – MICROWAVE COOKING

Microwave is a form of electromagnetic energy. Microwaves cause water molecules in food to vibrate thus generating heat. Microwave cooking is fast and uses less water for cooking. Therefore, there is less loss of nutrients. Contrary to what many believe, it is absolutely a safe method of cooking food.

However, to get the best from your microwave oven, you need to remember that the distribution of heat in microwave cooking is not uniform. Oven temperatures cannot be controlled. Different food require different timing. One cannot shallow or deep-fry using a microwave oven. Smaller pieces of food cook better than larger pieces. Stirring or rearranging food midway helps cook food uniformly. It is alright to open the oven door to check the progress of the cooking. When you close the door, do not forget to start the oven again.

The five main uses of the microwave oven are:

1. Reheating
2. Warming
3. Defrosting
4. Making popcorns
5. Heating frozen food

Demerits of Microwave Cooking

In spite of its many uses and apart from cooking, microware has in no way replaced the cooking range and oven as the primary cooking equipment. This is mainly because the microwave does not brown food and cooks unevenly, leaving cold spots and hot spots in food. If you have ever eaten pizza warmed up in a microwave, you will understand about cold spots and hot spots. Your pizza may have been tough, overcooked, and too hot to eat in one area, while still cold in other.

This problem can be solved to a certain extent by stirring and rotating food while cooking. New microwaves have turntables that almost completely solve this problem.

Though microwaves produce heat directly in the food, they really don't cook food inside out. With thick food like a roast, the microwave cooks about an inch of the outer layer. This heat is then slowly conducted inward, cooking along the way. Microwave food continue to be cooked even after they are removed from the oven because the food molecules are still vibrating. This is why 'standing time' is included in microwave recipes.

To understand more about microwave cooking, you need to know in detail what a microwave does or does not do well.

There are several factors that influence microwave cooking. These include:

- **Size** (larger food take longer time)
- **Shape** (thin food cooks quicker)
- **Density** (porous food cooks quicker)
- **Type of ingredients** (water and fat cook quicker)
- **Volume** (increasing volume means increased cooking time)
- **The starting temperature of food** (warmer food heats up quicker)

Food that have increased moisture, will heat more quickly. You don't need to add fat to meat, poultry or fish, and you can use little water for vegetables.

Does well

- Very less fat is needed in microwave cooking because food does not stick to the dishes in which it is cooked. So, microwave cooking is healthy cooking.
- Microwave is ideal for cooking fish as the fish stays moist and cooks through absolutely evenly.
- You can cook delicious chicken, mutton, pork or meat steaks in a microwave.
- Fruit desserts, chutneys, relishes and preserves cook well in a microwave, as they do not stick to the bottom. Since there is no fear of scorching, you could bake caramel puddings and it turns out really well.
- Vegetables cooked in a microwave are quickly and evenly done with brilliant colour and enhanced flavour, and retain, maximum vitamins.
- Microwave cooking is good from the point of view of health, efficiency and economy.
- Ovens come with a user's manual that tells you all that you need to know about its use as well as a selection of recipes. So, if you can afford it, buy a microwave but let it be an addition to your ordinary oven/grill, for what you can achieve with one, can never be done with the other.

Does not do well

- A microwave oven does not roast well. The trick is to roast in an ordinary oven, grill or over charcoal. You could speed up the cooking process by blanching or defrosting in the microwave.
- The microwave does not grill or sauté.
- Any baking with flour does not come off in the microwave. If you are using cornflour or rice flour, then, by all means, use the microwave oven.
- Soufflés and custards baked in a microwave are not passable good. An ordinary oven gives you the best results.
- Food cannot be browned in a microwave. To weight against the balance of all that a microwave does not do well, we have a whole range of things that actually turn out much better in a microwave.

A few myths related with microwave cooking are with the attachment of the grill and the combination modes (when micro and grill work simultaneously) food gets nicely browned. If you understand your microwave properly and perfect your cooking timings, even the soufflés, custards/ egg custards for the sweets and savouries and basic white sauce, etc., not only come out better but also save your valuable time. In fact, if more than specified time is given to cook a recipe, it spoils the dish.

Cooking in a microwave oven

- When you cook food on a stove, the centre of the pan is the hottest place, but, in a microwave, food cooks from the outside of the dish and proceeds to the centre. This is very much like the way it cooks in a conventional oven.
- When you are cooking food of the same kind and uniform size, it is best to arrange them in a circle, without touching, towards the edge of the cooking dish.
- If you are cooking different food at the same time in the same dish, place the slower cooking food, such as shellfish or carrots and some other vegetables, towards the edge of the dish and the quicker cooking food, such as chicken, fish, mushrooms, peppers, etc., towards the centre of the dish. This will cook food evenly.
- If you are making a soup or a stew or sauce, remember to cook solid ingredients separately with little or no liquid. When the solids are almost entirely cooked, add the rest of the liquid. This is done because microwave energy acts on food in liquid as if it were one mass. Water and thin liquids heat rather slowly and vegetables cook better with little liquid.

- If you are cooking a whole chicken or duck, it is best to cut it into serving portions before cooking.
- If a breast of chicken is to be cooked, divide it into half along the breast bone and place the two pieces so that the thin, rib edges are facing each other and the thicker breast bone edges are towards the side of the plate. Similarly, when cooking fish fillets, arrange them with the thin tips towards the centre of the plate.
- Keep these directions in mind and enjoy cooking the healthy way.

Cookware for Microwave

- Buy circular or oval-shaped dishes as those with corners can create pockets of microwave energy and your food may get burnt.
- Buy containers that mention 'Microwave Safe' on the label.

- It is not good to use metal pans made for conventional ovens or aluminium foil because the microwaves will be reflected and could damage the oven.
- Also avoid metal trimmed cookware or dishes.
- Don't use margarine or cheese spread tubs in the microwave. When food gets hot, it may melt the plastic, causing migration of the plastic into your food.
- Not all glass and ceramic is microwave safe. Here is a quick test for glass. Microwave the empty container for one minute. If it is warm, it is unsafe for microwave cooking; if it is lukewarm, it is all right for reheating food and if it is cool, it is good for actual cooking.
- Don't use plastic foam containers or any plastic disposable container. They may melt in the microwave.
- Melamine dinnerware may burn and turn brittle.
- You should never thaw frozen meats in the plastic wrap or foam tray in which it is packaged. It should always be transferred to a microwave safe dish to prevent harmful chemical from getting into the food.

Points to Remember

- When you defrost food in the microwave, cook it immediately as defrosting food in the microwave often starts the process of cooking.
- Uneven distribution of microwaves in the oven can cause 'hot spots' or overcooking of food in certain areas. This also occurs on thin edges of food. Frequent stirring or rotation of dish or a microwave with a turntable can minimise this problem.
- Debone large pieces of meat before cooking because the bone shields the meat around it from thorough cooking.
- Do not cook whole, stuffed poultry in the microwave. Cook bird and stuffing separately for even cooking and then combine.
- Arrange smaller items of mixed food uniformly in a covered dish, so that they cook evenly. Add a bit of liquid, so that the food does not dry out.
- If your recipe specifies a certain size of cooking container, use the exact one recommended. The size and shape of the container is important. Cooking the food in a container different from the one recommended could cause the cooking time to vary.
- When cooking in a covered dish, make sure there is some room for excess steam to escape either by lifting corner or piercing holes in a plastic wrap. Do not let plastic wrap touch the food because dangerous chemicals may get into the food.
- Take care to use the exact cooking time recommended. Microwave cooks quickly and 15 seconds more can mean the difference between having dinner and not having dinner.

- While increasing the size of the recipe, increase the cooking time, too. Follow this general rule while increasing the size of the recipe.
- When doubling a recipe, increase the cooking time to slightly less than double and change the dish size accordingly.
- When cutting a recipe in half, decrease cooking time to slightly more than half and change the dish size accordingly.

Microwave Safe Crockery

- Take care to observe the standing time given in the recipe for all food, usually about one-third of the cooking time. Food completes cooking during the standing time.
- While cooking meat, check for completeness by poking in a fork in several places, avoiding fat and bones, as these will never give you the correct message. Fish should flake if cooked.
- Never cook hard-boiled eggs in a microwave, as they will burst. Do not try cooking even single fries (sunny side up) in microwave without pricking the yolk with a fork or toothpick.
- Sealed containers must not be heated in the oven. The food or liquid could expand quickly and explode.
- To prevent a steam burn when removing lids or wraps from the cooking dish, lift the cover slowly, tilting it so that the steam is released away from you.
- Use potholders or kitchen gloves/mittens to remove heated food from the oven.
- Never turn on an empty oven without keeping a glass of water in it. This can cause the oven to break.
- Read package directions carefully. Make sure you know how to set the microwave oven controls.

You are advised to read the instruction manual provided with your microwave carefully before operating this hi-tech gadget.

MAINTAINING YOUR MICROWAVE

- Don't use an oven if the door does not close firmly or is otherwise damaged.
- Always check the interior and the exterior for any sign of deterioration.

Microwave Material Foil, Cling Wrap, Kitchen Paper Roll, Butter Paper

- If there are signs of rusting inside the oven, have it attended to immediately.
- Clean the door and oven cavity — the outer edge too — with water and mild detergent. Do not use abrasives such as scouring pads or steel wool.
- Do not allow oil or cleanser reside to accumulate on sealing surfaces.
- Follow the manufacturer's instruction manual for maintaining procedures.
- The oven should not be adjusted or repaired by anyone except properly qualified resource person.
- Take care to use the tips on maintaining your microware properly to avoid radiation problems.

To remove food odour from the oven, put a piece of lemon in 1 cup water and microwave for 1 minute. Remove and discard the water with lemon.

DAY 14

South Indian Dishes

South Indian dishes are relished all over the country. Irrespective of the size of the town, there are South Indian restaurants selling all that their cuisine has to offer. If not a restaurant, then a kiosk selling *dosa*, *idli* and *vadas* with which *sambhar* and coconut chutney come free in unlimited quantities. The food is tasty, spicy, less oily and of course different. It is an all-time favourite among families. There is a choice for weight-watchers, too.

Indians are conscious of the medicinal properties of spices and herbs they use. The crops that grow in the region and also the climatic conditions govern their choice of food. Rice, coconut and tamarind are most commonly grown in South India, therefore, the food of the region is based on these ingredients. Here, the people are basically rice eaters and the addition of tamarind in the vegetarian and non-vegetarian dishes is soothing in the airless midday heat of south. Though the food here tends to be fiery, yet, paradoxically more refreshing.

Some Ingredients used in South Indian cooking

In Kerala, in particular, there are coconut palms, tamarind and jackfruit trees. Spice gardens make Cochin (Kochi) rich and famous. The tropical heat is put to good use to mature pickles. It also helps overnight fermentation of batter for *idlis*, *dosa*, and *vadas* without the addition of yeast. South Indians steam their food as the accompaniments are tangy, hot and spicy.

The most common food items on a typical South Indian menu comprises the *dosa*, which is a plain pancake with or without stuffing of one's choice; the *idli*, which is a round rice or *rawa* cake, steamed in a steamer, with or without other vegetables mixed in it; *vada*, which is a ground *urad* dal dumpling deep-fried in hot oil; *upma*, which is a salted semolina *halwa*, with or without vegetables; *uttapam*, which is a thick pancake with lots of onions and chopped vegetables, if preferred; and these are served with *sambhar* made from *tuar* dal and vegetables, and coconut chutney. The menu may include a couple of other chutneys, too. *Rasam* and dry roasted *papadums* (*papad*) precede the meal. *Rasam* is a highly spiced tart appetizer made with tomatoes and specially ground *rasam* powder. It is of watery consistency and often served with plain rice.

The main ingredients for South Indian cooking include parboiled rice, ordinary raw rice, *rawa* or *suji*, *dhuli urad* dal, tamarind, fenugreek and mustard seeds, whole red chillies, onions, asafoetida, curry leaves and fresh coconut. You could use potatoes and other seasonal vegetables as the recipe specifies. Let us learn about each item, and get to know them better.

Dosa

Sela or parboiled rice is the best for preparing the *dosa* batter. It lends crispness to the *dosa*. The ideal ratio is 2 parts parboiled rice, one part ordinary rice and one part *dhuli urad* dal and 1 tsp of fenugreek seeds. Both qualities of rice and the dal should be picked clean of stones and debris, washed in two or three changes of water and soaked separately for 6 to 8 hours. They should be grounded in a mixer-grinder.

Indian grinding is done on a huge block of stone, which has a round depression in the centre. The ingredient to be ground is placed into this depression little at a time, and ground with a big oval-shaped stone. You have to use a circular motion to move the stone with both hands. This is the traditional grinding stone. These days a motorised version is available. However, a mixer-grinder is the most convenient.

Once the ingredients are grounded, they are mixed together in a large vessel, covered and left in a warm place to ferment. The fenugreek seeds soaked with the rice give the batter a unique flavour and aids fermentation. During summer the batter will ferment within 12 hours. You may need to leave the batter overnight to ferment in winters. After the batter has fermented, it must be mixed well once again before use. Let us now learn how to make a plain *dosa*.

PLAIN DOSA (SADA DOSA)

Ingredients: 2 cups *Sela* or *usna chawal* (boiled) rice of ordinary quality; 1 cup *permal chawal* (ordinary quality rice); 1 cup *dhuli urad* dal (split black gram dal); 2 tsp *methi dana* (fenugreek seeds); 2 tsp salt (to taste); oil for making *dosa*.

Portions: For 20-25 pieces

Soak rice, dal and fenugreek seeds together in a pan for at least 6 hours. Grind to a fine paste, using some of the water in which it was soaked. If required add more water to get a batter of medium pouring consistency. Mix everything together and add salt. Mix well. Keep aside for 12 hours or overnight in a warm place to get fermented. After fermentation, the batter rises a little and smells sour. Mix the batter uniformly with a ladle or a long-handled spoon, before preparing the *dosa*. Heat a nonstick *dosa tawa* or a well seasoned griddle on medium flame. Pour ½ tsp oil on the *tawa*. Rub the *tawa* with an onion, cut into half, or with a piece of old cloth. Remove the *tawa* from fire and pour 1 heaped ladle of batter. Spread quickly starting from the centre. Return to fire. Cook on a high flame. Pour 2 tsp oil upon the *dosa* and on the sides. When it turns golden brown, gently loosen the sides with a spatula and fold over. Remove from the *tawa*. Serve hot with coconut chutney and *sambhar*.

MASALA DOSA

Ingredients: For the batter: Follow the same recipe as for plain *dosa*. Potato *masala* (stuffing) for filling: 8 medium-sized potatoes, boiled; ½ cup boiled peas; 2 tbsp oil; 1 tsp mustard seed; 1 tbsp *chane ki* dal (roasted gram dal); 1 dry red chilli, broken into pieces; 5-6 curry leaves; 2 green chillies, chopped; ¼ inch piece ginger, grated; 2 small-sized onions chopped; 1 tbsp cashew nuts, broken into bits; ¼ tsp *haldi* (turmeric powder); ¼ tsp chilli powder; salt to taste.

Portions: To make 20-25 pieces

Peel and boil potatoes and mash them roughly. Heat 2 tbsp oil in a *kadhai* and add crackle ¾ tsp mustard seeds; add 1 tsp *chane ki* dal and dry red chilli; when dal changes colour, add curry leaves, ginger and green chillies. Stir fry for 2 minutes on low flame. Add onion. Cook until transparent. Add cashew nuts, salt, *haldi* and red chilli powder. Fry for 1 minute. Add 1 cup water. Boil and keep covered on low flame for 5-7 minutes or till the dal turns soft. Add mashed potatoes and peas.

Cook for 5 minutes. Mix well. Remove from fire and keep *masala* aside.

To prepare masala dosa: Mix the batter uniformly with a ladle. Heat a nonstick *tawa* on medium flame and prepare it for *dosa*. Remove the pan from fire and pour 1 heaped ladle of batter. Spread quickly, but lightly. Return to fire and cook dosa

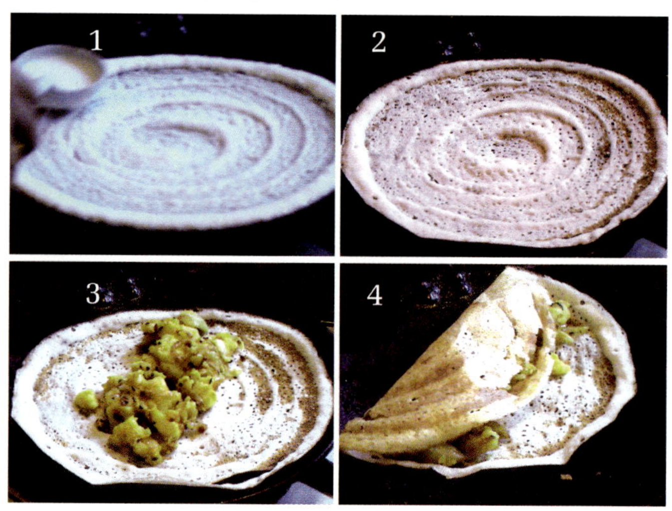

on high flame. Pour oil on the dosa and on the sides. After golden brown spots appear, gently loosen the sides and the bottom with a spatula. Put 2 tbsp of *masala* in the centre and spread a little. Fold over both sides. Remove from *tawa*. Place a blob of white butter (optional) on the *dosa*. Serve hot with coconut chutney and *sambhar*. You may serve mint and tomato chutney, too.

Note: The potato *masala* may be used as a filling for *rawa dosa* too, and it can also be served with plain *dosa*.

These days readymade *dosa* and *idli* batter is available in almost all the cities and towns of India; it is sold by weight; you just buy it and leave for fermentation in the warmer corner of your kitchen and follow the same instructions to cook as discussed in the dosa recipes.

RAWA DOSA

Ingredients: 1 cup semolina *rawa* (*moti suji*); 1 cup rice flour, ½ cup refined flour (maida), 1 onion (chopped), 3 cups water, 2 green chillies (chopped), 10-12 curry leaves (chopped), 8-10 cashew nuts, a pinch of asafoetida (hing), 2 pinches of cooking soda.

Filling (optional):

Potato *Masala*: Follow the same recipe as for *masala dosa*. You can make a filling with ½ fresh coconut, grated without brown skin (for *rawa* coconut *dosa*).

Portions: To make 8 pieces.

Mix semolina, rice flour, refined flour, green chillies, onion, curry leaves, a pinch of hing, cooking soda and salt in a vessel. Add 3 cups water and make a batter of pouring consistency. Now add cashew nut to the batter. Leave the batter for atleast ½ an hour.

Grease a non-stick tawa with oil. Pour a large spoon of batter over it. Spread the batter by swirling the tawa. Pour 1 tbsp of oil on and around the dosa. Cook till it gets crisp and golden in colour.

INSTANT COCONUT *DOSA*

Ingredients: ½ cup *maida* (plain flour); ½ cup *rawa* (semolina); 1 cup sour curd; ¾ tsp salt; 2 pinches cooking soda (soda-bicarbonate); 1½ cup water (enough to get a pouring consistency); 10-15 curry leaves or coriander leaves, chopped; ½ cup freshly grated coconut.

Portions: To make 4-6 pieces.

Mix *suji*, curd, *maida* and salt. Add *meetha* soda and curry leaves. Mix well to make a smooth batter without lumps. Add enough water to get a pouring consistency. Remove *tawa* from fire and pour 1 ladle of batter. Put 1 tsp oil or ghee on the *dosa*. Turn when the underside is brown. Let both the sides turn brown and then remove from the *tawa*. Serve hot with coconut chutney.

You can use a variety of ingredients to make the filling for your *dosa*. Here are a few variations:

- Chop a large-sized onion into fine pieces; crush or finely chop 6 cloves of garlic, 1 inch piece of ginger and 2 green chillies deseeded; crumble 150 gm of *paneer*; heat 2 tbsp oil in a *kadhai* and crackle cumin seeds; add onion, garlic, ginger and green chillies and fry for a minute. Add the crumbled *paneer* with a pinch of salt and turmeric and fry for 2-3 minutes. Add finely chopped fresh coriander and mix well. Use the mixture as a *dosa* filling.
- Dice equal parts of mushrooms, capsicum and onions. Fry in a little butter. Add salt and pepper to taste. Use as *dosa* filling.
- Cook minced meat with chopped onion, ginger, garlic and green chillies; add a pinch each of turmeric, coriander powder and cumin powder; fry well and garnish with chopped coriander leaves. Fill the *dosa* with this.
- You could cook finely diced prawns with onion, ginger, garlic and a little curry powder. Season to taste and use as *dosa* filling.

IDLI

Idli can be made both with rice and *rawa*. If you are making rice *idlis*, choose *sela* or parboiled rice. Do not add raw rice. The ratio of rice and *dhuli urad* dal is 2:1. The rice and the dal are picked clean, washed thoroughly under running water and soaked separately for 6-8 hours or overnight. Grind them separately. The rice should be a little coarse with a grainy consistency. The dal should be ground very smooth. Both are then mixed together, salt is added and the batter is left covered to ferment for 8-10 hours in summer, but during winter it would require overnight fermentation. When it has fermented it rises up, almost double its original quantity, and smells sour.

Idli

To steam the *idlis* you need an *idli* steamer that comes fitted with trays of moulds, which fit one on top of the other. These moulds are also available separately, without the steamer and can easily fit into a pressure cooker. If you are steaming the *idlis* in a pressure cooker, do not put the weight on the lid otherwise the *idlis* will spread into cooked batter.

Before pouring the *idli* batter into the moulds, lightly grease them with a little oil. Now, ladle in the batter, sprinkle a little chilli powder and chopped coriander leaves on each *idli* if you like. Steam each batch for 8 to 10 minutes. Before removing the moulds from the steamer or the cooker, insert a knife through one *idli*. If the knife comes out clean your *idlis* are done and if it sticks, steam them for another 4-5 minutes. Once done, let the *idlis* cool slightly. Then, taking a butter or palate knife, gently remove each *idli* from the mould. For variations you could add finely chopped carrots, beans, green chillies and ginger. The *idlis* can be topped with a variety of toppings or served plain with *sambhar* and chutney.

TIPS It is important to leave the *idli* batter for fermentation in a bigger vessel (than the one in which rice and dal were soaked) as after fermentation the batter rises almost to double its size.

Toppings

Try some of these toppings over *idlis*.

- Finely mash 100 gms *paneer*, add a pinch each of salt, roasted and ground cumin seeds, *chaat masala* and chopped fresh coriander. Mix well. Top each *idli* with this.
- Chop a small-sized onion very finely. Deseed and finely chop one green chilli. Cut ½ inch piece of ginger into tiny bits after peeling it. Heat 1 tbsp oil in a *kadhai*; add the chopped ingredients and stir fry for 2 minutes on medium heat; add 1 cup *moong* sprouts and stir fry on low heat for 3-4 minutes; sprinkle some *chaat masala* over this mixture and mix well. With a sharp knife, cut out a deep depression in the centre of the *idli*. Spoon the sprout mixture into this depression. Decorate with a thin slice of tomato and serve.

Stuffed Idli

- Grate some processed cheese over each *idli*, sprinkle a little pepper powder and serve.
- Using the same technique as with the *moong* sprout mixture, try a topping of baked beans, which is readily available in cans.
- Slice the *idli* horizontally and sandwich it with a layer of fresh coriander chutney. Another chutney that could be used is made by grinding together 10 whole red chillies presoaked in water for 20 minutes, 6 cloves of garlic and 1 inch slice of raw mango with a pinch of salt. This could be used as a sandwich spread for the *idlis*.
- Melt some jam in a small saucepan and coat the *idlis* with this as a sweet variation for children. Let your imagination run riot to innovate toppings for *idlis*.
- Before pouring the batter into the mould, place a thin slice of tomato and a cashew nut half. Pour the batter over this and steam the *idlis*.
- When you have ground the batter, add whole peppercorns, roasted cumin seeds, a pinch of asafoetida and crackled mustard seeds and curry leaves in it. Mix well and make the *idlis* with this batter.

Let us now learn about different varieties of *idlis*.

Rice Idli

Ingredients: 2 cups *sela* or *usna chawal* (parboiled rice); 1 cup *dhuli urad* dal (split black gram); salt to taste.

Portions: To make 24-30 pieces.

Soak the rice for 6 hours or overnight. Soak dal separately for 6 hours. Grind the rice coarsely by adding water. It should be like semolina/*suji*. Do not make it very fine. Grind dal by adding small quantities of water to the mixer to a very fine paste. Even after you feel that the dal is ready, grind it for some more time, adding a little water, till the dal turns absolutely smooth and fluffy and a few bubbles are seen.

Mix rice and dal batters together and add salt. The batter is of thick pouring consistency. Mix well. Keep aside for 8 hours or overnight in a warm place to get fermented. The batter should rise and smell sour. Keep for a longer period if it does not get fermented properly. To make *idlis*, mix the batter very gently. Wash the *idli* mould. Do not wipe. Grease the mould with oil. Fill with batter. Put 1 inch water in a big cooker or a big pan with a well fitting lid and place on the fire. Place the *idli* mould inside the cooker and put the lid on without the weight/the whistle. Keep the gas on full flame. After the water boils and the steam begins to come out of the cooker, keep on high flame for 2 minutes, then reduce the flame to medium. Steam for 14-15 minutes. Insert a clean knife to see if the *idli* is done. If it sticks to the knife, steam for another 3-4 minutes. Switch off the gas. Remove *idlis* from the moulds with a clean knife after 5 minutes. Serve hot with coconut chutney and *sambhar*.

Rawa Idli

Ingredients: 1 cup *dhuli urad* dal; 2 cups semolina *suji rawa* (*moti suji*); ½ cup sour curd; salt to taste.

Soak the dal for at least 2 hours. Soak *rawa* in curd adding enough water to cover it. Keep aside for 1 hour. Grind dal to a very fine paste with a little water. It should be absolutely smooth. Add *rawa* and salt to the dal batter and mix well. The batter should be of

pouring consistency. Keep the batter covered in a warm place for 8-10 hours to ferment. In winters you may have to leave it overnight. Or you can cover the batter with a piece of blanket or an old shawl. The batter will ferment in about 10 to 12 hours. Mix the batter gently and follow the same process as for rice *idlis*.

Uttapam

An *uttapam* is a thick rice pancake that is thicker than *dosa* in appearance. The basic ingredients to make it are the same as for *dosa* and rice *idli*. However, the proportions of the ingredients are slightly different. You take 2 parts of parboiled rice and ¼ part of *dhuli urad* dal. Both are picked clean carefully for stones or any other debris, washed in 2-3 changes of water and soaked separately for 6-8 hours. The key to making a light and spongy *uttapam* is the grinding of the rice and dal. The *dosa* and the rice *idli* require the rice to be ground a little coarsely, to have a grainy texture to give the *dosa* crispness and to make the *idlis* a little crumbly and light. But for the *uttapam* you should grind both the rice and the dal into a fine paste. The rice paste will not be as smooth as the dal paste but it should not have a grainy texture.

The rice and the dal pastes are mixed together and left in a warm place to ferment for 10-12 hours in summer and overnight in winter. Once the batter has fermented, a variety of finely chopped ingredients are folded into the batter, the most common being onion, green chillies, ginger and curry leaves. A ladle full of batter is poured onto a greased *tawa* to make a little thicker layer than the *dosa*. There is another basic difference between the two, while the *dosa* is cooked uncovered to crispness, the *uttapam* is covered with a lid and cooked on low heat for 3-4 minutes. Then it is turned over and cooked on the other side without a cover. When both sides are cooked evenly, the *uttapam* is removed to a plate and served with chutney and *sambhar*.

Some variations

Here are a few variations that can be tried while making *uttapam*.

Uttapam cooked in Microwave

- Chop some French beans and carrots finely; fold into the *uttapam* batter along with finely chopped onion, ginger, green chillies and curry leaves.
- Finely chop tender spinach and fold into the batter.
- Grate cauliflower or finely chop a few leaves of cabbage and mix with the batter.
- Finely diced mushrooms, spring onions and fresh coriander leaves make a good variation.
- To make an instant *uttapam*, mix together 1½ cups *rawa*, 1½ cups sour curd, ¾ cup water, ¼ tsp sodium-bicarbonate, 1 teaspoon salt and a pinch of asafoetida. Add enough water to make the batter of pouring consistency. Keep aside for half an hour. In another bowl, mix together 1-2 chopped green chillies, 2 finely chopped onions, 2 finely chopped tomatoes, a few curry leaves and salt to taste. Combine this with the batter and make the *uttapams*.
- You could use a mixture of chopped onion, tomatoes and cashew nuts as topping. Spread the batter for *uttapam* on greased nonstick pan, then sprinkle topping and press with the back of the ladle; add a few drops of oil; cover and cook for 2 to 3 minutes; change the side and cook a little more and serve.

Serve *uttapam* with a dollop of butter on top to make it more nutritious and tasty for children. Just like the fillings for *dosa* and *idli*, you can be innovative about using different ingredients to prepare special variations of *uttapam*. Avoid ingredients that turn pulpy on being cooked.

Vadas

Vadas are one of the ideal snacks, served once again with the ever-present *sambhar* and coconut chutney. *Vadas* are like the *dahi bhallas*. They are fried dumplings of *dhuli urad* dal paste beaten till fluffy and light. Grinding the dal in a mixer-grinder helps to cut down on the beating time as the churning machine traps enough air into the paste to make it light.

For perfect *vadas*, do not soak the *dhuli urad* dal for more than 1-2 hours. Drain and ground to a thick rough paste with a minimum amount of water (do not grind the dal very fine) and mix in finely chopped green chillies, ginger and fresh coriander leaves. A pinch of cumin seeds, salt and pepper complete the seasonings. Fill a *kadhai* with oil half of its capacity and heat it till smoking point; lower the heat to medium; moisten your palms with water; take a tbsp full of the dal paste onto your left palm and flatten it with the fingers of your right hand. Make a depression in the centre using a finger of your right hand. Then, gently slide the *vada* into the hot oil, taking care not to splash any oil on your hands. Deep-fry on medium heat from both sides till golden and remove it on absorbent paper to absorb extra oil. Take a soup plate or a small wide bowl and pour some *sambhar* into it. Immerse the *vadas* in the *sambhar*. Serve with chutney on the side.

Vadas should be fried in small batches of 3-4 numbers at a time as they tend to stick together. When the *vadas* are put into the hot oil, they should immediately float to the surface of the oil. This is a proof that the batter has been beaten well and enough air incorporated to make the *vadas* light. Immersing the *vadas* in hot *sambhar* is just one way of serving them. You could serve the dry *vadas* in a plate, *sambhar* separately in a bowl and the chutney on the side of the plate. The shaping of *vadas* on your palm and sliding them into hot oil is an art that can be perfected only with practice.

Variations of Vada

- For *masala vada*, soak ½ cup *dhuli urad* dal and 1 cup *chana* dal. Grind the dals with 4 dry red chillies, 4 cloves garlic (optional), and 1 teaspoon aniseed. Add 2 green chillies, fincly chopped, ½ tsp asafoetida, ½ inch piece ginger, finely chopped, a few chopped curry leaves, 1 large-sized onion, finely chopped, and salt to taste. Make the *vadas* with this mixture.
- To make *masala vada*, soak ¼ cup ordinary rice and 1 cup *dhuli urad* dal separately for ½ an hour. Grind them with as little water as possible. The batter will be a little coarse like *suji*. Into this, mix ½ cup finely chopped cabbage or spinach, 4 finely chopped green chillies, 1 large-sized chopped onion and a few curry leaves, a pinch of asafoetida and salt to taste. Make the *vadas* with this mixture.

Upma

A light, salted *halwa* made from semolina (*suji*) – *upma* – makes a refreshing breakfast dish. It takes little time and is easy to cook. Dry fry 1 cup semolina with 1 tbsp ghee or oil in a *kadhai*, taking care to keep the heat low (the *suji* scorches easily). Remove it from the *kadhai*. In the same *kadhai* heat 1 tbsp oil and crackle ½ tsp musturd seeds in it and temper 1 tsp *chana* dal, 1 tsp *urad* dal and 2 whole red chillies; put 1 thinly sliced onion and 2 chopped green chillies, too; fry till onions turn soft; add 2 cups of water and salt and simmer the mixture till the dals are soft. At this point add roasted *suji* gradually to the *kadhai* and stir so that no lumps are formed. Mix in some lemon juice and cover it for 2 to 3 minutes. Sprinkle some fresh chopped coriander leaves and serve it hot. Here, the only technique involved is to dry fry the *suji* on low flame to avoid burning. If the *suji* is underfried, the *upma* will be sticky. The right texture for *upma* is to be a little crumbly, just held together with only a trace of stickiness.

TIPS

Water added to *upma* can be half water and half buttermilk. 1 cup finely chopped vegetables or sprouted dals can also be added and cooked to it before adding water. 2 tbsp fried cashew nuts and 2 tbsp washed and soaked raisins can also be added to *upma* while garnishing it.

Variations of Upma

To cook ***matar upma***, you must follow this procedure specifically. However, when you have fried the dals, curry leaves and onion, add ½ cup tender shelled peas for 1 cup of *suji*. Fry for a minute, pour in the water and cover. Cook until the peas and dals turn soft. Add the semolina gradually and follow the usual method.

For *sewiyan upma*, use **Vermicelli** instead of semolina. The rest of the procedure is the same as for *suji upma*.

To make a tasty ***suji*-coconut *upma***, you could add ½ cup fresh, grated coconut for each 1 cup of *suji* at the end of cooking process.

For ***poha upma***, wash *poha* (*chiwda*) and set aside in a strainer. Soak a small ball of tamarind in ¼ cup of water for 15 minutes and extract the pulp. Put a pinch of sugar, salt and turmeric powder in it. Heat 2 tbsp oil in a *kadhai* and throw in 1 tsp *dhuli urad* dal, 1 tsp mustard seeds, a few curry leaves and chopped dry red chilli. When this begins to splutter, add 3-4 chopped green chillies. Fry for a minute and add the *poha*. Pour in the tamarind pulp and fry till the liquid dries up. Add ½ cup grated fresh coconut. Mix well.

Accompaniments

All South Indian dishes, ranging from the *dosa* to the lemon rice and tomato rice, are accompanied by *sambhar*, *rasam*, coconut chutney and a variety of other chutneys. We will now take up a variety of these accompaniments to give you a wide choice to choose from. Each one of them is easy to make and definitely very tasty.

Chutneys

Fresh coconut, mint leaves and tomatoes are the basic ingredients for most of the chutneys. They add a special flavour to the meals. They are distinctively different from the North Indian chutneys, and contain special ingredients to lend a unique flavour to them. You could try any of these with your meals.

Coconut chutney: Grind together 1 cup freshly grated coconut without the brown skin, 2-3 green chillies, ½ inch piece of peeled ginger, and salt to taste. The chutney should be like a thick paste. You could add a little water if necessary. Heat 2 tbsp oil in a pan; add ½ tsp mustard seeds, 1 teaspoon *dhuli urad* dal, 1 whole red chilli broken into tiny pieces, and a few curry leaves; crackle and pour over the chutney. Mix well and serve.

Coconut brown chutney: Fry 3 tsp *dhuli urad* dal and 2-3 whole red chillies in 1 tsp oil on low flame, till it changes colour. When cool, grind with 1 cup freshly grated coconut, a small ball of seedless tamarind, a pinch of salt and asafoetida. Keep aside in a bowl. Heat 2 tsp oil and crackle 1 tsp mustard seeds in it, add a few curry leaves and pour over the *chutney*. Mix well and serve.

Tomato chutney: Chop 4 large red tomatoes very finely. Heat 1 tbsp oil in a *kadhai*, reduce heat and add ½ tsp mustard seeds, a few curry leaves, a pinch of asafoetida and ½ tsp red chilli powder. Add chopped tomatoes and salt to taste; cover and cook over low heat till the tomatoes turn soft. Mash with the back of a ladle. Add ¼ cup water and simmer, covered, for 10 minutes. Keep mashing the tomatoes till thick and pulpy. Add 1 teaspoon *sambhar* powder and a tiny piece of jaggery. Mix well. Cook for a few more minutes and remove from the fire.

Sambhar and *Rasam*

Sambhar is cooked with *tuar* dal and specially prepared *sambhar* powder. You can add tomatoes, onions and other seasonal vegetables also. The dish is tempered with mustard seeds, whole red chillies and asafoetida. Garnish it with fresh coriander leaves before serving. It is served with every South Indian meal.

Vegetable Sambhar

Rasam is prepared with *tuar* dal, tomatoes and a specially prepared *rasam* powder. It is of watery consistency and is served with plain rice. You could serve *rasam* as an appetizer too, with dry roasted *papad* as a starter. It is served piping hot.

Tomato Rasam

South Indian cuisine

Here are a few tips for cooking South Indian food successfully.

- Use a nonstick *tawa* for the *dosa* and *uttapam*. This needs very little greasing and there is no fear of the *dosa* sticking to the *tawa*.
- If you are using a plain *tawa*, prepare it well before use. Ensure that it is spotlessly clean. Heat it and rub with an onion cut into half all over the *tawa*. Sprinkle some water over the hot *tawa* and wipe with a clean cloth. Repeat the process 2-3 times. The *dosa* and *uttapam* will never stick to the *tawa*.
- While making *sambhar*, take care not to overcook the dal, otherwise, the *sambhar* will be thick and mar the flavour of the dish.
- If you are making your own *sambhar* and *rasam* powder, be patient enough to fry the ingredients on very low heat. This improves the flavour.
- If you are using asafoetida grains instead of the powdered variety, dissolve the grains in a little water. Use only 1 or 2 grains as asafoetida has a very strong flavour.
- To prepare good *rasam*, never blend the tomatoes in a blender. This will thicken the

rasam. A really tasty *rasam* is always watery. Simply pass the cooked tomatoes through a strainer, pressing with a spoon to extract the juice.

- A tsp of melted ghee or butter added to hot *sambhar* and *rasam* at the time of serving, improves the taste.
- If you feel that the *dosa* batter will run short, mix in some *suji* and let it be soaked for 20 minutes. This will increase the volume of the batter.
- You can store twigs of curry leaves in a brown paper bag in the refrigerator. The leaves may dry up, but retain the flavour.

In the practical session you will learn how to make and store *sambhar* and *rasam* powders as the *masala* powders are best prepared at home to prevent adulteration.

Practical things to be done

1. Sambhar Powder

Utensils: A *kadhai*; spatula; a plate.

Gadgets: A mixer-grinder, mortar and pestle.

Portions: To make 200 gm powder.

Ingredients: 1 cup whole dry red chillies; 1 cup coriander seeds; ½ cup *chana* dal; 2 tsp whole peppercorns; 2 tsp cumin seeds; ½ tsp asafoetida grains (do not soak in water); 1 tsp fenugreek seeds; 1 tsp poppy seeds; ½ dry coconut grated; 1 inch long stick cinnamon; 1 tsp mustard seeds; a few curry leaves.

Follow this simple procedure:

1. Heat 1 tsp oil in a *kadhai*. Add red chillies and fry on low heat for 1 minute. Remove and keep aside.
2. Put 1 tsp oil in the same *kadhai* and fry the coriander seeds till they change colour. Remove from heat and keep aside.
3. Similarly fry each ingredient separately, on very low heat, using as little oil as possible.
4. Cool all the ingredients and grind to a fine powder. Store in an airtight bottle.

2. Rasam Powder

Utensils and gadgets: Same.

Portions: To make 100 gms powder.

Ingredients: 20 dry, whole red chillies; 12 tbsp whole coriander seeds; 2 tsp cumin seeds; 1 tsp mustard seeds; a few curry leaves; 2 tsp oil.

Follow this simple procedure:

1. Heat the oil in a *kadhai*.
2. Fry all the ingredients in the oil on very low heat. This will take 3-4 minutes. Remove and cool.
3. Powder in a mixer-grinder. Store in an airtight jar.

Expert cook suggests...

1. To avoid your '*dosa*' sticking to the *tawa*, cut a potato or onion in half; add 2 or 3 drops of oil on the hot *tawa*, and spread it all over with cut onion or potato.
2. To make instant *dosa*, mix 2 cups *rawa*, 1 cup flour, 1 tsp Eno, a little salt and water; mix well and make crisp thin *dosas* immediately.
3. Adding a pinch of soda bicarb to the *idli* batter will help make soft *idlis*.
4. When the '*idli* batter' turns sour, do not panic. Add 2 glasses of water and keep aside. Before using, strain off the clear liquid on the top. The sourness will go off with it.
5. Rubbing a little salt on the coconut kernels helps keep them fresh.
6. To store coconut for longer periods, cut into big pieces, immerse in water and store in a refrigerator.

DAY 15

Stocks and Soups

Stock is a clear liquid flavoured with substances extracted from meat, poultry, fish, vegetables, and seasonings. To make stock, these ingredients are simmered in water to extract the desired flavour and then discarded leaving behind a clear flavoured liquid that is made the base of most of good soups and sauces.

Many years ago, a common practice for restaurants was to make their own stock from leftover bones and fresh vegetables.The stock would simmer for many hours, sometimes left on a stove for 24 hours. The chefs would continuously add fresh bones and vegetables. In today's food services, few operators make their own stock. Many use an alternative. They use condensed soup cubes available in chicken, fish, brown stock, white stock and vegetable flavours.

Mutton Stock

The main problem with these bases/cubes is that they contain a high amount of salt. The basic prepared base needs the addition of equal quantities of carrots, onions, and celery to enhance the flavour.

Homemade stock can be prepared easily. The quality of the stock depends on many factors and the most important one is that the ingredients should be fresh.

Ingredients for Making Stock

Bones: Bones for the stock will need to be purchased. The type of bones will depend upon what type of stock you want to make. Stocks are categorised according to the kind of bones used and their colour.

- White stock is made from beef or veal bones or both.
- Brown stock is made from the same bones as white stock; only the bones are browned in an oven before making the stock.
- Chicken stock is made from chicken bones.
- Fish stock is made from bones and fish trimmings.
- Vegetable stock does not contain any meat products. It derives its flavour from the vegetables.

Vegetable Stock

Before the bones are placed into the stockpot, remember to 'blanch' them in boiling water for a few seconds to clean any residue and harmful bacteria off the bones. This will help to reduce the scum formation that naturally occurs during the preparation of a stock.

Vegetables: Fresh vegetables should be neatly trimmed and cut in as large as 1 inch cubes. The combination of vegetables consists of celery, carrots, and onions (usually $\frac{1}{2}$ kg onions to $\frac{1}{4}$ kg celery and $\frac{1}{4}$ kg carrots). You may wish to substitute some leeks for part of the onions. Leeks add a milder onion flavour than onions.

Seasonings: Prepare a **'bouquet garni'** with a combination of spices and herbs consisting of bay leaf, thyme, and other favourite herbs. The term 'bouquet' originated because the fresh spices would be tied together in a bouquet and allowed to float in the stock. They are removed prior to use. Another method is tying the spices in cheesecloth with a string and removing it before use. You can also add the spices into the stock, and later use a very fine strainer to filter out all the ingredients before use. Salt is not added to stock because it is used as an ingredient in other dishes.

In India a common practice is to add carrots, onions, cabbage, gourd pieces and thicker parts of cauliflower, etc., in boiling water along with 'bouquet garni' of bay leaf and whole condiments like peppercorns, cloves, cardamom and cinnamon stick, etc; simmer the ingredients for 40 to 45 minutes; discard the vegetables, squeeze the bag of bouquet garni and strain; cool and store to be used as vegetable stock as and when required. To the same combination, the bones are also added, and ingredients are simmered for longer period.

The procedure for making stock is as follows:

1. Cut the bones into 4 inch pieces to expose areas from which flavours can be extracted.
2. Rinse the bones in cold water, and blanch in boiling water.
3. Place the bones in a pot and cover with cold water.
4. Bring water to a boil. Reduce heat to simmer.
5. Add the vegetables and bouquet garni.
6. Ensure that the stock does not boil over. Skim off the fat as it comes to the surface. Make sure the bones stay under water.
7. Simmer for 6 hours for white and brown stock, 1 and ½ hours for mutton or chicken stock, 45 minutes for vegetable stock, and ½ an hour for fish stock.
8. When the stock is done, it can be drained through a fine sieve or strainer. If somehow the stock is cloudy, strain it once again through a cheese/muslin cloth.
9. Cool the stock and store under refrigeration.

A stock does not have to be watched constantly during cooking. Just peek at it from time to time. The final stock should have a deep flavour and good colour. While a stock is simmering, the pot should not be moved or stirred. For making clear soup some chefs/experts prefer to add some egg whites to stock in order to filter out the impurities and improve the taste and colour. It is recommended that you either freeze the stock immediately in small quantities, or keep it under refrigeration for a few days only. When stock that is refrigerated or frozen is to be used, heat it to boiling, and reduce to simmer for a few minutes before use.

Making Soup and Stew

One satisfying food we consume is soup. Its flavour and texture can be varied. Soup is a food that is primarily liquid. It is composed of several ingredients, either vegetable and/or of animal origin. Soup can be served either hot or cold at any time of the year. You must remember that the preparation of soup requires the same care and quality of ingredients as any other food. Ingredients used must be fresh and of a high quality.

Mutton Stew

Soup is an excellent appetiser. It can be served at the beginning of the meal as an appetiser to help take the 'edge of the appetite.' In winter, soups provide the effect of a warming sensation when consumed hot after coming in from the cold. Cold soup in the summer is refreshing prior to a meal. Soups and stews that are served as a main course generally are thick and contain protein. The food service industry finds the use of soups on the menu to be one of economic advantage, because of ease in preparation, versatility within the menu, and relatively inexpensive to prepare with good markup.

Consommé

Soups are categorised according to their consistency, their use, and even their ethnic heritage. Soups range in consistency from being thin to thick with many degrees of consistency.

Thin soups, also called clear soups, include broths (also referred to as bouillons), vegetable soup, and consommé.

Cold Cucumber Soup

Minstrone Soup

Mushrooms Chowder

French Onion Soup

A broth or bouillon is clear soup without any solid ingredients. Vegetable soup is a clear, seasoned stock or broth with vegetables and possible meats, poultry, or starches added (such as in chicken noodle soup). A consommé is basically the same as a broth except that it is prepared to the point of being very clear or transparent. The key to preparing a clear consommé is the use of egg whites, not stirring the pot once residue floats to the top of the pot, and straining the soup through several layers of good quality cheesecloth.

As its name implies, **thick soup** is classified according to its consistency. Thick soup differs from the thin soup not only in consistency, but also in terms of colour, being non-transparent. Also, thick soups are thickened either naturally or with the use of different thickeners.

Cream soups are thickened with flour and fat (called roux) or other thickeners, and usually contain milk and/or cream. They are often named according to the primary food that makes up the soup, such as broccoli. Care must be taken when combining the base (cream or sauce) with the desired stock. Always use a wire whisk to add the stock to the base in small amounts, beating slowly, but constantly. This will ensure that the ingredients blend uniformly and avoid curdling or breaking down of the soup. Favourite cream soups include those made from tomatoes, mushrooms, broccoli, and chicken, among others.

Pureed soups differ from cream soups in two basic ways. Pureed soups are thickened naturally due to the starchy nature of the vegetable or beans used. They can be pureed with a food processor. The pureed soup does not have the smooth consistency of the cream soup. The contents are also less identifiable. Split pea or potato soup are common examples.

Although the traditional **chowder** is made from shellfish (clams) and vegetables, chowders such as corn or potato are very popular. Chowders that have a heavy consistency are generally thickened with the use of a thin white sauce or light cream. Chowders made with clams generally contain a variety of vegetables.

Bisque differs from chowder in a sense that it has a smooth consistency, contains a variety of shellfish (lobster, crabs, etc.) or of mushrooms, usually does not contain pieces of distinct vegetables, and is thickened with the use of cream and eggs. Bisques are very similar to basic cream soups.

Some soups are categorised according to their possible origin. **The Minestrone Soup is an Italian favourite**. It is a combination of many flavours, both meat and vegetable. It contains a combination of beef and chicken stock, pasta, tomatoes, carrots, celery, legumes, and peas. It is a very heavy soup that can be given a thicker than normal consistency, if desired. **The French Onion Soup is a French favourite** characterised by being served hot. Other types of soups that are unusual include oxtail soup, turtle soup, the cold fruit soup, to name a few.

Serving Soup

- Soup is generally served in 1 cup measure.
- Or in small soup bowls if served as an appetiser.
- Or in large soup bowls if served as an entrée or main course.
- If serving soup hot, you may heat the cups slightly.
- If serving soup cold, you may place the cups under refrigeration prior to use.

Cold soups are potentially more hazardous in terms of spoilage than hot soups. During preparation some cold soups are subjected to heat as part of the cooking process. Upon completion of the cooking, the object should be to chill the soup as quickly as possible in order to preserve its flavour.

The following are the best ways to chill creamed soup that will be served cold.

Ice/Water Bath: Place the pot of creamed soup (or divide the soup into smaller pots) in a clean bigger vessel like a *'parat'*. Place as much ice as is available around the pot of soup. If the level of ice is not at the same level as the soup, add water until the water and ice are at the level of the soup. Stir frequently. Cover and refrigerate the soup when it is at approximately 45°F. Add more ice during the chilling process, if necessary. Do not place the pot of hot soup directly into the refrigerator.

Shallow Pans: Pour the soup into a shallow pan. The soup should be no deeper than one inch thick. Place uncovered in the refrigerator on the uppermost rack until it has reached an internal temperature of 45°F. Cover the soup immediately upon being chilled.

Making Quick and Healthy Stocks and Soups

Making your own stocks and soups does not mean slaving in the kitchen on a lovely Saturday afternoon while everyone is out having fun. With good planning, you can make healthy and tasty soups without spending hours in the kitchen. Here are some ideas.

Stock

Make 2 litres of stock each time. Have lots of small containers that can be put into the freezer. Plan to start making stock at a time when you are going to be in the kitchen for some time anyway, such as when preparing dinner. This way, the stock can continue to cook while you are eating and cleaning up. If time is really short, try vegetable stock – it cooks in just 1 hour. Chicken stock takes about twice as long.

Skimming Stocks and Broth When Simmering

Using a long-handled ladle, remove as much scum as possible and discard it. Do not worry about removing some of the liquid, as you would be adding water to the stock in any case. Add cold water to the pot from time to time as the stock or broth is simmering. When the liquid returns to the boil, more scum will rise to the surface and should be removed with a ladle.

Removing Fat

For cold stocks/broth/soups, you could allow the stock/broth/soup to cool, and then refrigerate it. As the liquid cools, the fat will form a crust on the surface. Remove this with a large spoon or ladle.

If you have a pet dog, this fat can be mixed with his food. Dogs love it.

How to Use Stock to Make Healthy Soups?

For a quick homemade vegetable soup, thaw frozen stock in the refrigerator. Add vegetables – fresh, frozen, or canned – simmer until they are tender.

- For a quick cream-style soup, puree a lightly cooked (or sautéed – it brings out the flavour) vegetable (such as broccoli, cauliflower, spinach or boiled mixed vegetables) in the blender or food processor. This pureed vegetable will act as the base and thickener. Next add 1 percent milk or evaporated skimmed milk with stock/water, and some herbs and spices for added flavour (see the list for matching vegetables and seasonings, page 128). Simmer for about 30 minutes. These soups taste better when refrigerated and warmed up a day later.
- **For quick soup, you may use a canned soup product.** Extend it with liquid and solid ingredients. This way, you can decrease the amount of fat and sodium per serving. For example, use a can of chicken rice soup; add water (or homemade stock), leftover chicken or turkey, and leftover vegetables and starches.
- **Vegetable purees** can be used to thicken many kinds of soup because they are bulky. Examples include pureed beans (lentils and split peas are excellent), potato, carrot, spinach and tomato. The amount needed to thicken soup varies depending on which one you use. See the list of soup cooking tips for more ideas.

Matching Vegetables and Seasoning

Match vegetables and seasonings as stated in this chart.

Vegetables	Seasonings
Carrots, yams, winter squash	Allspice, cinnamon, cardamom, nutmeg
Beans, cauliflower, greens (such as kale and spinach), onions, potatoes	Chilli powder, coriander, cumin, garlic, pepper
Cabbage, tomatoes, onions, peppers	Basil, bay leaf, oregano, thyme

Sweet Corn Chicken soup

TIPS Here are a few tips on cooking soups.

- Do not overcook soups. Flavour is lost through evaporation. Vegetables may curdle or break.
- Always simmer and not boil soup. This ensures the best flavour, texture of ingredients, and consistency.
- Just prior to serving, check soups for flavour, texture of ingredients, and consistency, adjusting as necessary.
- When using vegetables and beans in soup, ensure that all the ingredients are sufficiently cooked at the same time. This way none of the ingredients are overcooked.
- Cut vegetables into uniform pieces that can be readily identified for even cooking and visual appeal.
- Canned vegetables that are already cooked should be added towards the end of cooking.
- Starchy ingredients, such as rice or pasta, should be cooked separately and added at the end because they will cloud clear soup.
- Do not boil soups after milk or cream has been added. The soup will curdle.
- Do not add cold milk or cream to simmering soup. Heat the milk or cream first to prevent curdling.

Garnishing Soups

Soups can be served in soup cups or soup bowls or even soup plates. The soup cups, sometimes, have two handles and are placed in a quarter plate when served. The most important factor when serving soup is garnishing, done just before service. Here are few popular garnishes for soups:

Cream: (for cream soups and bisques) Stir double cream into the soup just before serving. An alternative could be cream whipped with some herbs.

Egg yolk and cream: (for broth and thick soups) Combine egg yolks with double cream. Stir in a large ladle full of soup and then stir in the remaining soup. Heat gently, stirring, until the soup thickens. Do not allow soup to boil.

Whole eggs: (for broth) Whisk the eggs well. Stir into simmering soup from a height so that it forms strings.

Butter herb and shellfish butters: (for pureed soups and bisques) Add small pieces of firm butter at the last minute. It should melt but not separate.

Accompaniments to Soups

The simplest and perhaps the most common accompaniment to soups is the croûton. When properly made, it is a very delicious and satisfying addition to a whole variety of soups. Croûtons are fried cubes of bread, or simply cubes of toast. Alternatively, whole slices of French bread or rolls can be dried or toasted in the oven to make croûtons. These can be rubbed with a clove of garlic, for fish soups. Tiny cocktail biscuits, bread sticks and cheese straw, served separately are excellent companions to soups. Crusty bread, too, is enjoyed with the soups.

Practical things to be done

1. Meat Stock

Ingredients: 1 kg mutton bones; 1 litre cold water; 1 large onion, coarsely chopped; 1 large carrot, quartered; 1 bay leaf; 3 whole cloves; ½ tsp dried thyme; 5 or 6 peppercorns; a few sprigs fresh parsley or coriander.

Portions: To make 800 ml.

To make meat stock, follow this procedure:

Mutton Mulligatawny Soup

1. Preheat oven to 400°F.
2. Place bones in a roasting pan and bake for 10 to 15 minutes, turning bones once. Pour off fat.
3. Transfer bones and remaining ingredients to a large stockpot. Simmer for 2 hours. Watch that it doesn't boil. Regularly skim the fat off the top.
4. Strain through a strainer lined with cheesecloth.
5. Refrigerate until the fat hardens on the surface and can be removed.
6. Store in the freezer for up to 3 months.

TIPS If for some occasion, you want to make more stock to serve soup to more number of people, just double the quantity of the ingredients used for the stock and give half time more for cooking it. Rest follow the same procedure.

2. White Vegetable Stock

Dumpling Soup

Ingredients: ¼ kg leeks (white only), rough-cut; ¼ kg onions, rough-cut; 2 sticks celeriac (or hearts of celery only), rough-cut; ¼ kg white turnips, rough-cut; 2 bay leaves; 1 tbsp garlic, chopped; 2 tbsp white peppercorns, cracked; 2 and ½ lt of water.

Portions: To make about 2 litres.

To make white vegetable stock, follow this simple procedure:

1. Place all the ingredients in a large pot and simmer for 1 hour.
2. Strain. The stock is ready.

The ingredient proportions in this recipe are only guidelines. Vegetable stock can be made from any kitchen vegetables. However, some vegetables, especially of the cruciferous family (cabbage, broccoli, cauliflower, etc.), may create a bitter taste if cooked too long, and should be avoided in reduced stocks. Those vegetables can be used in stocks that are made quickly and used right away. This white vegetable stock has a wider range of applications than red or darker stocks because it adds very little colour to the final product.

Almond Soup

Tomato Soup with Crotons

Whey Tomato Celery Soup

Tomato and Chowder

Things You Must Keep in Mind

Adding Special Ingredients

To help cook the main dish many times, special ingredients are added to facilitate the cooking process. For example, many food items are marinated with spices mixed with vinegar, lemon juice or yogurt. The marinade helps in developing the flavour in the food and also helps make cooking easier.

A pinch of soda bicarbonate may be added to help soften legumes and pulses.

The addition of milk, butter, yogurt and yeast is important in many baking recipes.

L to R: Cream of Tartar, Sodium Benzoate, White Vinegar, Dry Yeast, Cooking Soda

Baking soda is especially important for this cooking procedure.

Adding vinegar, sugar and oil are important in preserving many popular food. Vinegar and oil prevent pickles from spoiling. In the same way, sugar protects jams and acts as a preservative.

Several food require additional protection from spoilage if they are to be stored for some length of time. For this purpose several food preservatives such as potassium metabisulphide and sodium benzoate are used. A good rule is to use these as sparingly as possible.

■■

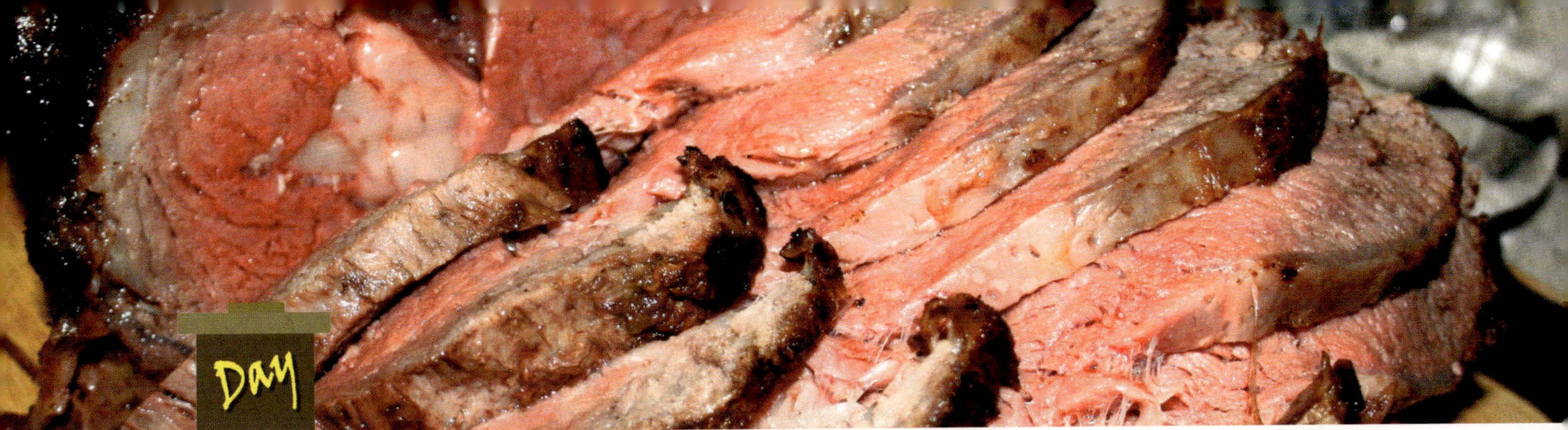

DAY 16

Cooking Meat

Meat is the flesh of domestic animals – beef and veal from cattle, pork and ham from hogs, and lamb from sheeps or goats. Meat is divided into two groups: red and white (based on the colour of the flesh). Red meat includes beef and lamb. White meat includes veal and pork. Another group includes variety of meat, which includes liver, kidneys, heart, tongue, etc.

Purchasing Meat

When purchasing meat, avoid meat with a sour smell, slimy touch, or odd colour such as brown or green. These indicate presence of bacteria or mould. The colour should be as follows:

- **Beef:** bright cherry red
- **Pork:** pale pink
- **Lamb:** pink
- **Veal:** pinkish white

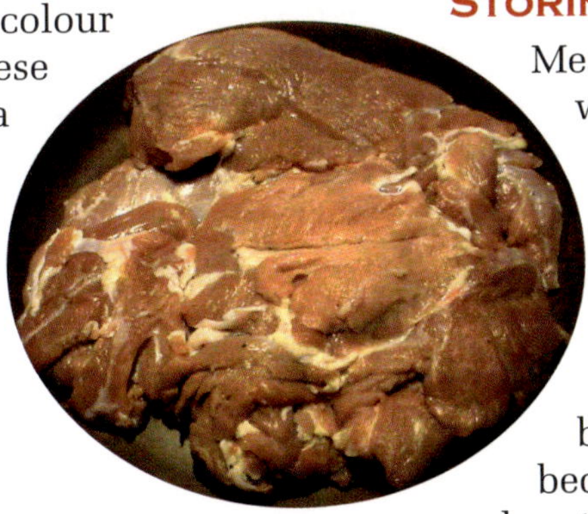

Raw Lamb Meat

Nutritional Value of Meat

Meat is a good source of several nutrients, including protein, iron, copper, phosphorus, zinc, and B-vitamins – thiamin, riboflavin, niacin, B6, and B12. Meat is also a good source of fat, saturated fat, and cholesterol. Meat can be intelligently planned as a part of the diet when lean cuts are chosen. They do not add fat when roasted or broiled. The serving sizes must be moderate.

The lean cuts of meat include:

- **Beef:** Cuts from the round, eye of round, top round, bottom round, round tip; sirloin, top and bottom sirloin steak, top sirloin roast; extra lean ground beef, usually 15 to 18 percent fat.
- **Pork:** Cuts from the tenderloin, leg, fresh boneless ham.
- **Veal:** All trimmed except commercially ground and veal patties. Some good choices include loin chop, rib chop, top round steak, or arm steak.
- **Lamb:** Legs of the lamb and loin chops.

Storing Meat

Meat should always be stored, loosely wrapped in plastic, in the coldest part of the refrigerator. Minced meat should be consumed within a day. Chops, steak and small cuts can last two or three days. Large roasts can be used within five days. Red meat keeps longer and better than white meat. Lean cuts stay better than fat ones because fat tends to become rancid. When thawing frozen meat place the wrapped product in the refrigerator a day or two before use. Allow it to thaw completely, or put it in the microwave oven set on defrost or thaw cycle.

Meat Storage Time

The quality of meat declines with time so it has to be stored properly. Amongst fresh meat, roasts (beef and lamb) or (pork and veal), steaks (beef), and chops (lamb or pork) store well for 3 to 5 days under refrigeration. Ground, stew and variety of meat have a storage life of only 1 to 2 days. Processed meats like bacon, frankfurters and ham (whole) can be stored for up to 7 days. Ham (slices) are all right for 3 days, and ham (half) for up to

5 days. Sausages (pork) stay fresh for 1 or 2 days. Smoked sausages have a storage life of 5 to 7 days, but dry or semi-dry sausages can be stored from 14 to 21 days. Cooked meat has a short storage life. Gravy and meat broth are stored well for 1 to 2 days, and cooked meat dishes for 3 to 4 days.

Bhuna Gosht

COOKING MEAT

To cook meat in a light and healthy manner, there are six simple steps to follow:

1. Start with lean meat.
2. Trim visible fat before cooking.
3. If using dry heat cooking method, allow the fat to pour off as the meat cooks.
4. If using a moist heat cooking method, chill the meat juices after cooking, or use a fat separator cup to remove the fat.
5. If stir frying, use a nonstick pan and a small amount of oil.
6. Trim off the remaining visible fat before eating.

When cooking tender cuts of meat you will want to utilise the dry heat cooking method. These include roasting, broiling, pan-broiling, grilling, stir frying, and sautéing. When cooking less tender cuts of meat, you will want to choose a moist heat method such as braising. Some not-so-tender meat can be cooked with dry heat if they are marinated before cooking. Marinating can be used successfully to tenderise small pieces of meat such as flank steak.

ROASTING MEAT

Roasting is a simple method of cooking but requires a relatively long cooking time. Red meat, that is roasted, usually pertain to meat items that are large in size, thawed if previously frozen, and cooked in an oven. The meat item may be seasoned, if desired. The meat should be placed on a rack in an open pan, fat side up without the addition of water or any other liquid. The meat should not come in contact with its drippings or else it will simmer. A general oven temperature for roasting meat is 275°F to 350°F. Lower temperatures usually mean less shrinkage, extended cooking time, and ultimately a more juicy roast.

To carve the roasted meat, follow these directions.

Roasted Lamb

1. Remove the meat from the oven. Let it stand 15 to 30 minutes before carving. This will allow the juices to settle evenly throughout the meat, and will provide very juicy pieces of meat.
2. When using a carving knife, be sure that it is very sharp. When you 'hack away' at a roast with a dull knife, you ruin its appearance. You will also end up with less meat. Use a proper carving knife having straight or serrated edges.
3. If you want very thin slices, use a sharp knife.
4. Always cut across the natural grain when carving. This helps tenderise the meat even more.

TESTING IF MEAT IS SUFFICIENTLY COOKED

Here are two popular methods to check if the meat is sufficiently cooked.

When broiling, many prefer to use the touch-testing method. Rare meat is soft, medium meat is medium firm, and well-done meat is firm to the touch.

TIPS

Roasting tips

Here are a few roasting tips:

- Put meat, fat side up, on a rack in a roasting pan so the fat can baste the meat and the rack holds the roast out of the drippings.
- Do not season before cooking because the seasoning will not penetrate. Also, salt interferes with the meat browning.
- Use moderate heat. 275°-350° F is best. A moderate temperature is important for the best flavour and taste, as well as yield. Cooking meat at higher temperatures significantly reduces the number of servings you will get out of it.
- Turn the roasting pan around during cooking to make up for the uneven temperatures in the oven.

- Put a pointed knife through the roast to check for doneness. If the knife passes through clean, your roast is done.
- Let the roast sit for at least 20-30 minutes before carving because the juices in the roast are still flowing and if cut too soon, the juices will flow from the meat.

BARBEQUES

Mutton Barbeque

Open-air broiling or grilling of meat or seafood over burning charcoal is known as barbeque. This method of cooking is gaining popularity these days for picnic and cocktail parties. Specially designed grills are available for this purpose. Before broiling, you can season meats with your favourite seasoning. It is suggested that you do not salt the steaks. The juices will drain out from the meat, making it dry and hard. Place thicker cuts of meat farther from the heat. When using thinner cuts of meat (less than ½ inch) for broiling, you may place the meat on a rack while still frozen. You will find that frozen meat holds its shape better than fresh ones.

These guidelines will be helpful for outdoor grilling.

- Use pyramid method to start charcoal fire, 20 to 30 minutes before cooking.
- Meat cuts can be cooked using either direct or indirect heat. Tender cuts such as steaks, chops and ground patties are perfect for the faster cooking using direct heat method. Medium tender cuts, large/thick cuts, and roasts are better suited for indirect heat.
- Use meat thermometer to determine doneness.
- Allow large cuts to 'set' for 15 minutes before carving.
- Use a marinade to add flavour and/or tenderise meat cuts.
- Total cooking time varies with the cut, temperature of meat (refrigerator or room temperature), temperature of the coal, outdoor temperature, and desired degree of doneness of the meat.

Expert cook suggests...

Reports link outdoor grilling to a possible increased risk of cancer. Whether this risk is of concern to most people or not, it may be advisable to follow these tips during outdoor grilling:

1. Choose leaner cuts of meat. Trim meat of outside fat to reduce the fat that drips on the coal.
2. Precook meat like spare ribs or ground beef containing excessive fat. This helps remove some of the fat before grilling.
3. Raise the level of the grill, so that meat is farther away from the coal.
4. Grill meat in aluminium foil until the last few minutes of cooking.
5. Clean grill after every use.

Broiling and grilling tips

A few tips to follow while broiling and grilling:

- These methods are not a good choice for pork or veal. These kinds of meat are cooked well. Broiling or grilling will dry them too much.
- Do not season meat before broiling or grilling. Salt interferes with browning.
- The more well done you want a piece of meat to be, or the thicker it is, the longer the cooking time, and the further from the heat source. Otherwise, the outside of the meat will be cooked, but the inside will not be done.
- To make crisscross grid marks when grilling meat, put meat diagonally on the grill. When the side is half done, rotate the meat to 90°.
- Turn meat on broiler when the top is browned.
- Turn meat on grill when the juices begin to flow on the top and the bottom is browned. Touch-test meat frequently, using the following guidelines:
  - Rare – soft
  - Medium – medium firmness, some resistance when pressed
  - Well-done – firm, resists pressing with finger

Stir Frying

For stir frying, use a large, heavy skillet or, preferably, a wok. Either put a small amount of oil in the wok or use a nonstick wok. The wok should be heated until very hot before you begin cooking. Because stir frying is a quick cooking process using high heat, it is a good idea to line up the ingredients by the wok before cooking. Use these simple tips to prepare your ingredients.

- Partially freeze the meat so that it can be easily sliced against the grain into thin strips. This way it cooks faster.
- Slice vegetables in the same size and thickness as the meat so that they cook uniformly. Diagonal slicing of vegetables exposes more surface area. This helps cook them faster.
- Ensure that the ingredients are not watery. Water makes the fat splatter.

Stir frying tips

A few tips to follow while stir frying:

- Cut thin strips or diced portions of meat, poultry, fish, vegetables, or any combination.
- Coat the cooking surface with a thin layer of oil.
- Preheat equipment to high temperature.
- Do not overload the pan. The food will not cook evenly or quickly.
- Stir food rapidly during cooking.
- When meat is almost done, add small pieces of vegetables such as broccoli, cauliflower, zucchini, sprouts, carrots, mushrooms, tomatoes, or green onions, as they cook quickly.

Braising

Braising is one of the most popular methods of moist heat cooking for meat. Both large pieces of meat, such as pot roast, are braised, as well as small pieces such as cubed or stew meat. The meat is lightly browned in hot oil to provide colour for the meat and to seal in the juices. A small amount of liquid, such as water, stock, or fruit/vegetable juice, is added, and the meat is cooked until tender. If cooking cubed or stew meat, the meat is generally covered with liquid. If cooking a roast, the liquid should cover from one-third to two-thirds of the roast.

Braising tips

A few tips to follow while braising:

- Before browning, make sure that the meat is dry. Coat small pieces of meat with flour. Shake off the excess flour. Do not season meat before cooking. Season only during the last 30 to 45 minutes of cooking.
- Brown meat over high heat. Then add the liquid. Reduce heat, and cover the pot.
- Cover the meat from one to two-thirds with liquid unless it is a stew. In that case the meat is completely covered.
- Cook meat until fork tender.

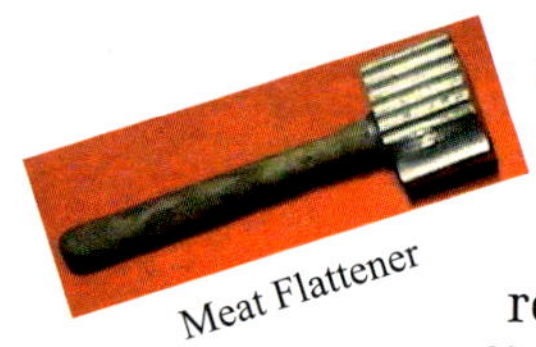

Cooking for Meat Dishes

When cooking meat dishes remember these simple tips for efficient work.

- Use dry heat cooking methods (roasting, broiling, grilling, stir frying) for tender pieces and moist heat (braising) for not-so-tender (or tender) meat.
- Using dry heat on a not-so-tender piece of meat will result in dryness and toughness.
- Use tongs, not a fork, to handle meat. This way you do not lose any juices that keep the meat moist and tasty.
- The larger the meat, the lower the heat. The thinner the meat, the higher the heat. This is important for even cooking.
- Always cut meat across the grain to make it more tender.

Marinating Meat

Marinating improves the flavour of meat. Marinades may be wine-based, or simply a mixture of oil, herbs and vinegar, or even curd with ginger-garlic and curry powder. You could also use a few pieces of raw papaya ground to a paste mixed with curry powder to marinate the meat. This acts as a tenderiser. This is usually done when cooking roasts, steaks or kebabs. During long marination, juice is drawn from the meat. This may be used in the cooking.

Beef meat is one of the darkest and toughest meat. It should be soaked in a robust marinade for one to three days. Tender lamb should be marinated with light herbs and curd. Mutton can be marinated in strongly flavoured curd-*masala* mixture also. Pork responds well to more exotic, sweet, sour and spicy flavourings.

Making Meat Tender

Larger pieces of meat are made tender so that on cooking, they turn out to be succulent. In roasts and steaks, this method makes cooking easier. It also ensures lesser cooking time, and a tastier dish. Marinating, pounding or scoring are the most common methods of making the meat tender.

To pound meat, lay the piece between two sheets of cling film or greaseproof paper and pound with a mallet or a rolling pin or the flat of a heavy knife.

The Process of Making Mutton Olives

Anti Clockwise: 1. Marinated Meat ; 2. Stuffing for Meat, Tender Meat, Meat Stuffed and rolled for Mutton Olives ; 3. Pour Brown gravy and bake in the oven

To score meat, place it on the chopping board. Using a sharp butcher's knife, make light slits in a lattice pattern on both sides of the meat.

Stuffing Meat

There are many meat preparations that call for stuffing, such as a roasted leg of lamb or a steak. The stuffing is often meat based; minced pork or sausage meat adds richness, while veal makes delicate stuffing. When preparing the stuffing, use plenty of pepper and spices, as well as flavourings such as onion, garlic and ginger, aromatic herbs like thyme or sage. You could also use chopped vegetables such as red peppers or carrots for colour, breadcrumbs for lightness and cooked rice for substance. Dried fruits and nuts go well with veal, pork and lamb. Even chopped seafood is excellent stuffing.

Unusual Preparations

Unusual preparations of all kinds of meat are common during the festive season in most countries. Roast suckling pig is one of world's most favourite dishes; the succulent flesh has a crisp coating of crackling and fat. It may be roasted on a spit or in a large roasting pan in the oven with stuffing of your choice. Suckling lambs are a favourite in Italy, Greece and the Middle East, where they are spit roasted with garlic, cumin, cardamom and black pepper or mint and tomatoes, or stewed with sauces of rosemary and vinegar. Chops can be breaded and deep-fried. In the Middle East, this roast is served with perfumed rice and hard-boiled eggs.

Variety of Unusual Indian Mutton Delicacies

Mutton Korma

Meatballs

Mutton *Kolhapuri*

Shami Kebab

In India, the commonest meat to be consumed are mutton, lamb, beef and pork (ham), but furred animals such as rabbits and deer, too, used to be a part of the menu not so long ago. With wildlife preservation coming into force, this game has been banned. We have, therefore, confined the study to the meat commonly eaten. Liver, kidneys and brain of lamb as well as of other animals are also consumed. Most of the preparations are either curried, stir fried or chargrilled.

Preparing Meat

It is best to buy meat from a good butcher. He can cut the meat to your specification. There is always something extra that you need to do to these cuts. Trim off the extra fat, but keep a thin layer as this keeps the meat moist and improves flavour.

Lamb chops: Using a chef's knife, trim off the extra fat. Cut around the contours of the chop, leaving about 2 mm fat on the meat.

Different Joints and Cuts

Pork chops

Here are a few of the common joints and cuts available in the market.

Leg of lamb: It is sold whole or halved; on the bone; weight 1.5 to 2.5 kgs (whole) and serves 6-8 people; 1-1.5 kgs shank (knuckles) half or fillet end, serves 4-6 people.

Chops: Chops cook easily and quickly, can be grilled or pan-fried or even stir fried with lots of onions, ginger and garlic. Lamb loin chops are succulent pieces of meat while pork loin chops are larger. In India, both types of chops are commonly consumed.

Minced meat: It is sold as fine mince or ground beef or mutton and lamb. It is suitable for burgers, *shami* kebabs, *seekh* kebabs, meat balls, meat loaf for stuffing and even for curries. It is easiest to cook.

Loin of pork: This is bored and rolled with or without skin. If the skin is scored, it makes crisp crackling; 2-2.5 kgs joint serves 8-10 persons, 1-1.5 kgs serves 4-6 people.

Rib of beef: This is a traditional cut for roast beef. Sirloin is another traditional favourite. A 2-rib, 2.5 kgs joint serves 6 people; a 4.5 kgs joint with 3 ribs serves 8-10 people.

Steak: These are slabs of meat about 1 to 1½ inches thick, can be chargrilled, grilled or pan-fried, served with roast potatoes and boiled vegetables or a salad.

Process of *Seekh* Kebabs being made in a Production Unit

1. Partially cooked and seasoned minced meat being put on metal skewers/*seekh*.
2. *Seekhs* being roasted on charcoal grill.
3. *Seekhs* ready to be consumed.

Rump steak: Using a pair of scissors, cut off the edging fat at 2 cms intervals, snipping through membrane and the fat.

Braising steak: With a chef's knife, trim off the fat around the edges. Then cut it into cubes of desired size.

Kidneys and liver: They are rich in iron and proteins, and cook very easily. They, however, become tough if overcooked. Ideal for curries, pan-fries and stir fries. Peel the fine membrane that covers the kidney. Slice the kidneys lengthwise into half, cut out pieces of fat and tubes at the core of the kidney. The liver can be sliced or cubed after any unsightly ragged edges are snipped off with a pair of scissors, and the ducts, if any, removed with a paring knife.

TIPS

In India, different communities consume different kind of meat. If some prefer mutton, the others prefer beef and pork products. Therefore, everyone buys the cuts and packed products according to their needs and choices and follow their own ways to cook the dishes. Out of ready to eat meat products sold in the market, steaks, chops, sausages, salamis, *seekh* kebabs, *shami* kebabs, slabs of ham, luncheon meat and bacon are most popular. Many big and small companies make these products and market all over the country.

Practical things to be done

1. Raan Musallam

This is a mutton leg with bone roasted whole. You could stuff in peeled garlic, cloves and sprigs of fresh rosemary, or marinate it with a curd-based marinade for 2-3 hours before roasting it. We will discuss both the variations.

Utensils used: A large dish; a chef's knife; a chopping board; a bowl; a meat thermometer.

Ingredients: A small leg of lamb (1.5 kgs); 2 tbsp olive oil or any vegetable oil; salt and pepper; 20 cloves; 10 garlic cloves, peeled and halved; a few sprigs of rosemary.

To make *raan musallam*, follow this simple procedure:

1. Take out the meat from the refrigerator. Let it stand covered on the kitchen counter.

Place the joint on the chopping board and using a chef's knife, score a diamond pattern in the fat. Insert a piece of garlic, 2 cloves and a sprig of rosemary in each of the cuts.

Roasted Leg of Lamb

2. Rub the joint well on both sides with a mixture of olive oil, a pinch of freshly ground pepper and a pinch of salt. Insert a meat thermometer into the thickest part of the joint away from the bone.
3. Roast the joint on a rack in a roasting tin. Halfway through, baste by spooning over the juices. At the end of roasting, insert the point of a knife into a thick part of the meat.
4. If the meat is well done, the juices will run clear. Check temperature and remove the joint from the oven. Let it cool. If a thermometer is not available, inserting the sharp point of a knife into the thickest part of the roast is the best test for doneness.

2. Using a Marinade

To use a marinade follow this simple procedure:

1. Mix together 200 gm curd, 2 tbsp curry powder, 1 tsp each of ginger and garlic paste, ½ tsp salt, 1/3 tsp of freshly ground pepper.

Carved leg of Lamb

2. Place the joint on a chopping board. Using a sharp chef's knife, cut 1½ inches slits at an interval of 2 inches all over the leg of lamb.
3. Rub the marinade well into the slits as well as all over the joint, taking care to coat it properly. Keep it in the refrigerator for 2-3 hours.
4. Place the joint on a roasting rack. Proceed as you did in the first roast. Alternatively, you could spit roast the joint on a wire grill placed over a charcoal fire. Remember to keep basting with the juices. If you are spit roasting it, then the leftover marinade could be used for basting. A little vegetable oil could also do the trick.

3. Carving the leg

The roast should always be left to rest for at least 10-15 minutes after roasting. This allows the juices to settle, making the meat easy to carve, besides keeping it succulent. You must use a carving fork and knife to carve the meat.

To carve the leg, follow this simple procedure:

1. Spread aluminium foil on the chopping board. With the help of two large spoons, transfer the roast from the oven or the spit onto the foil. Wrap it loosely in the foil. Let it rest in a warm place for about 15 minutes.
2. Place the joint meat side up on the chopping board. Cut a V-shaped wedge at the knuckle end. Cut slices away from this wedge till you reach the fillet end.
3. Turn the joint over. Cut horizontally into slices, parallel to the bone. Arrange the slices on a platter, decorate with lemon wedges and serve.

TIPS

This chapter gives you a lot of theoretical information on meats and meat products, their names and cooking styles, but for more information on cooking simple meat dishes, refer to the recipes.

MICROWAVE COOKING

With the growing popularity of the microwave oven, many meat dishes can be prepared in 20 minutes or less. Because microwave ovens vary from model to model, check your instruction booklet for actual cooking time and temperatures. As a general rule, most cuts should be cooked at a lower power setting, such as medium-low. Ground meat or reheated products may be cooked on higher power settings. An important factor in cooking meat in the microwave is the selection of the proper cut, in the appropriate size and shape. As a general rule, boneless cuts in uniform shapes and ground meats can be cooked successfully.

When cooking in a microwave oven, remember these simple hints.

- Roasts should not exceed 2 kgs. They should have a uniform shape for best results.

- Shape 1 kg of ground meat into 4½ inch thick patties. Form a ¾ inch hole in the centre of each.

Top with seasoning. Mix well for evenly cooked, well-browned burgers.

- Arrange uniform meat, such as patties or meatballs, in a circle, leaving a gap in the centre of the circle.
- Small portions cook faster than large portions. Thin portions cook faster than thick portions.
- Stir dishes with a high liquid content, like soups and stews, to distribute the heat from the outside to the inside.
- Use a rotating device to help facilitate uniform cooking, if possible.

Meat Cooked in Microwave

Meat Roasted in Microwave

Expert cook suggests...

1. To skim fat from the top of soup or stew, use a sheet of paper towel. The paper will absorb the fat immediately.
2. Use pieces of raw papaya to marinate meats. It will help make them tender.
3. If the curry turns out oily and pungent, coarsely grind 2 slices of bread and add them to the curry. Bread absorbs the extra oil and spice.
4. When the quantity of marinade is not enough for the meat to be marinated, put the meat pieces and the marinade into a strong polythene bag, and keep turning the bag to marinate the meat. It is more convenient to turn the bag than turn meat pieces.

■ ■

Burger Pattice

Meatballs Pulao

Tandoori Seekh Kebab

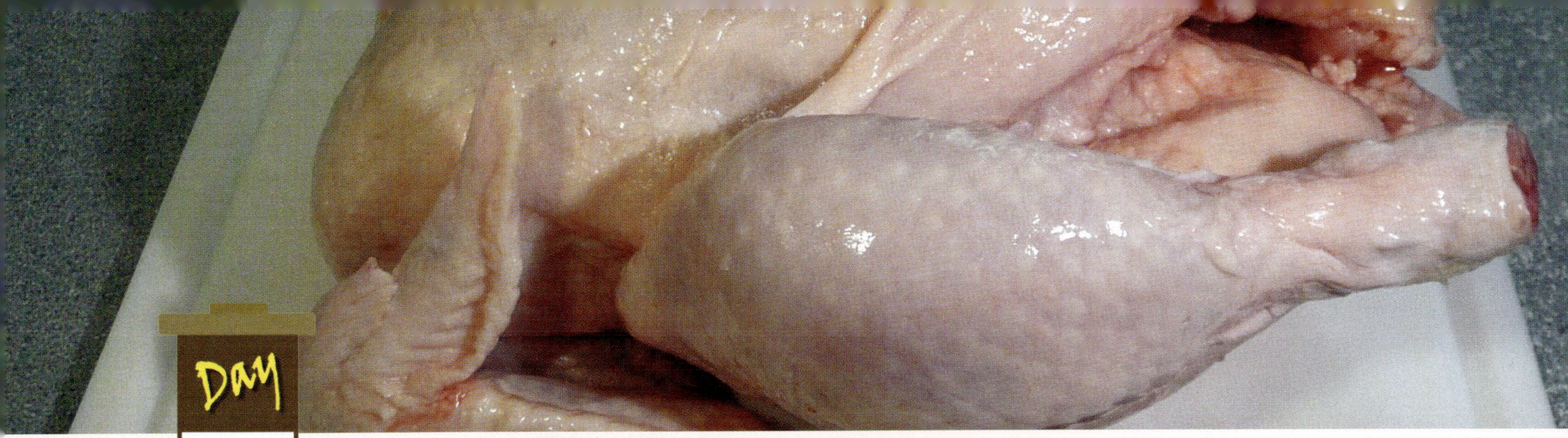

Day 17

Cooking Poultry

Purchasing Poultry

There are different kinds of poultry, including chicken, turkey, duck, geese, guinea, and squab pigeon. Each kind of poultry is divided into categories based on age. Age affects the tenderness of the bird. The cooking method also needs to be adjusted to obtain an ideal flavour and tenderness.

The following birds when mature need moist heat cooking such as simmering, steaming, braising, or pressure-cooking to make them tender and extract their full flavour.

- **Chicken:** Mature chicken, hen, or fowl (sometimes called stewing chicken)
- **Turkey:** Mature turkey, old turkey
- **Duck:** Mature duck, old duck
- **Goose:** Mature goose, old goose
- **Guinea:** Mature guinea
- **Pigeon:** Pigeon

Younger birds, which are available in the market, are naturally tender and can be cooked using almost any style. Older birds are less tender and must be cooked using moist heat, as in stews. In addition to purchasing whole birds, parts of poultry are also available.

Fresh poultry should have unblemished skin without feathers or bruises. The skin should be smooth, soft, and moist without any indication of slime. The colour of the skin, which ranges from white to deep yellow, is not a measure of nutritional value, flavour, tenderness, or fat content. The colour is determined by the breed of bird and its diet.

Chicken are generally fed corn and soybean meal, animal protein, and supplemental vitamins and minerals. Chicken with bright yellow skin may feed food containing marigold petals, alfalfa meal, or corn gluten meal. Choose fresh poultry that is tightly wrapped in packaging. Check the label for any 'sell by' or 'best if used by' dates.

When buying frozen poultry, make sure the package is intact, rock hard, and stored below the frost line in the freezer. If you see much frozen moisture inside the package, the product has most likely thawed and refrozen. Discoloured patches on the skin indicate freezer burn. Due to concern about the antibiotics given to chicken, what they are fed, and so on, some individuals choose to purchase organically grown chicken. This type of chicken is different than mass-produced chicken. It has more flavour, but also tends to be tougher and more expensive. Organically grown chicken is commonly available at health food or natural food stores. These birds have been raised outside the cramped cages. They have more flavour, too.

Duck

Guinea

Hen

Geese

Turkey

Cutting chicken into pieces

- Begin by removing the leg and thigh by cutting between thigh and breast.
- Divide the chicken into two by cutting along the backbone and tail.
- Remove wings and separate drumsticks from thighs at the joints.
- Divide wings into two pieces at the joints. Chop drumsticks and thighs into three pieces each. Slice the breast into three or four pieces depending upon the size of the chicken and the kind of pieces you require.

Pieces of Chicken

Nutritional value of chicken

As compared to red meat, skinless white chicken and turkey meat have similar cholesterol levels but have lesser total fat and saturated fat. Chicken and turkey skin contains much of the bird's fat. It should be removed before eating. When we compare the amount of fat in chicken to that found in turkey, one is surprised to note that chicken has almost 50 percent more fat than turkey. Chicken and turkey are rich in protein, niacin, and vitamin B6. They are also good sources of vitamin B12, riboflavin, iron, zinc, and magnesium. Chicken and turkey are low in sodium. Duck and goose are rich in fat when compared to chicken and turkey, as they contain all dark meat.

Storing poultry

When storing fresh poultry remove the packaging. Also separate any giblets (neck, liver, gizzard, heart). They spoil faster than the poultry. Rinse the poultry under cold water to remove the bacteria or other contaminants, pat dry with a paper towel, and store immediately wrapped loosely. Always wash your hands and work area thoroughly after handling raw poultry. Store it in the coldest part of your refrigerator where it will not drip onto any other food. Use it within 1 to 2 days. Whole poultry and poultry portions should be repackaged in moisture-resistant and airtight wrap such as freezer paper or heavy-duty aluminium foil. This helps prevent freezer burn and development of an unpleasant flavour.

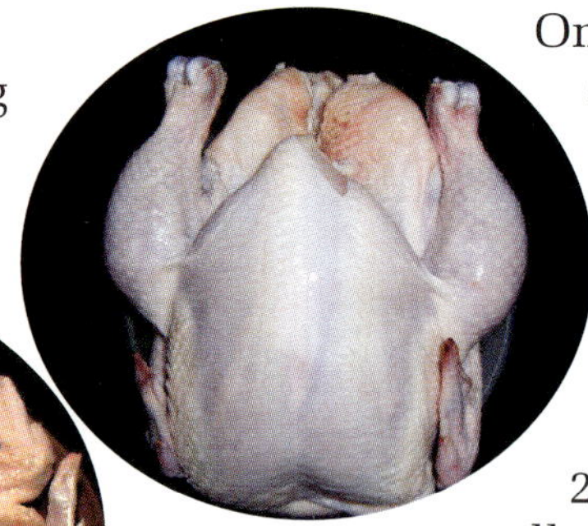

Whole Raw Chicken

Once cooked, poultry should not be held at room temperature. It should be put into the refrigerator right away. It can be held there for 3 to 4 days. Stuffing and gravy are good for only 2 days. It is best to remove all the meat from the bones of a whole bird before you put it in the refrigerator. Wrap it loosely until completely cool, then wrap tightly in plastic or foil.

Cooking poultry

- When roasting, broiling or grilling poultry, allow the fat to drip away during cooking.
- When braising, chill the meat juices after cooking, or use a fat separator cup to remove the fat.
- When stir frying, use a nonstick pan and a small amount of oil.
- Remove the skin before eating.

When you need to thaw the poultry before cooking, shift it from the freezer to the refrigerator ahead of time.

Unless you are stewing or boiling poultry, you will need to thaw it. Thawing helps birds cook more evenly. You can also thaw poultry in the microwave. Follow the manufacturer's instructions.

Before cooking, some basic preparation must be done. **The following rules should be followed to ensure delicious food that is safe to eat:**

- When handling raw poultry, be sure to select an area that is separate from the rest of the cooking area. Place the cutting board and knife at the farthest end of your counter.

Spit Roasting

- Wash your hands thoroughly before, during, and after handling the poultry. Do not touch any other utensil, apron, or food. A good method is to use plastic, disposable gloves.

- Wash the poultry thoroughly under cold, running water. Run the water inside the cavity as well as on the outside to remove any blood stains that may be there.

Tandoori Tikka

- After placing the bird into its cooking pan, thoroughly clean the work area with soap and water. Dry off with a paper towel.

Poultry should always be cooked until it is well done, is juicy, and not dry. Here are a few simple suggestions for roasts:

- Always follow a cooking time guide.
- To ensure that it is cooked well, insert a meat thermometer in the thickest part of the thigh (not touching the bone). The internal temperature should be at least 180°F. The breast should cook to 170°F, and stuffing to 165°F. Do not overcook, as it will dry out.
- The internal juices should be clear, and not red.
- The skin should be golden brown. The joints should be easily removable.
- If you have stuffed the bird, be sure that the internal temperature of the stuffing is a minimum of 165°F. When birds are stuffed before cooking, it is best to cook at a lower temperature and extend the cooking time to avoid overcooking the bird.

Age affects the tenderness of the bird. The cooking method to use for maximum flavour and tenderness depends upon it.

Roasting

All young poultry can be roasted. The type of meat is tender. Poultry is usually oven-roasted. However, it may also be spit-roasted or barbequed. Poultry cooks well because the skin (and the fat in it) keeps the bird moist during cooking. A common practice in cooking large birds is to initially truss the bird. This is done by tying the legs and wings together to make a compact unit. Trussing helps the bird cook evenly. Otherwise the extended legs and wings cook faster than the breast, and have a more attractive appearance. To truss a bird, follow these guidelines:

- Stand the bird on its end, breast towards you, and grab the neck bone. Wrap the centre of a clean string, about 4 to 5 times the length of the bird, around the neck bone. The string is now in back of the chicken.
- Lay the chicken on its back. Bring the string towards the tail end of the bird. Bringing it forward, cross over the ankles, pulling the string tight.
- Bring string up towards wing joint and flip the bird over.
- Cross the string over the wings, pull tight, and tie securely. Cut off excess string.
- Tuck the wings under the string to secure them.

If you want to stuff poultry, do it just before you begin cooking. It may seem like a good idea to stuff the poultry in advance. That is inviting trouble. Harmful bacteria can multiply in the stuffing and cause food poisoning. The cavity of the bird should be stuffed lightly. Stuffing expands as it cooks. Allow 1½ cups of stuffing for each kilogram of ready-to-cook poultry. Extra stuffing may be baked separately. To keep the stuffing in a whole bird, you need to close the neck and body cavities. Fold the neck skin over the back and fasten with a skewer, trussing pins, or toothpicks. Twist the wingtips under the back of the poultry to rest against the neck skin. To close the body cavity, use skewers, or tuck ends of legs under a band of skin at the tail, or into metal 'hock-locks', if provided, or tie legs together with clean string.

Roasted Chicken

To roast, place the bird backside down on a rack in a roasting pan. This way the breast develops a crisp, golden colour. Rub the skin with oil to prevent cracking and blistering, although it is not absolutely necessary. Start roasting at high temperature of 425° to 450°F to sear the surface of the bird and retain its natural juices. The oven can then be lowered to 325° to 350°F for the rest of the cooking. Whole birds and larger roasts should be allowed to stand 10-20 minutes before carving to avoid losing the juices when you slice the meat.

Broiling and Grilling

Grilled Chicken Kebabs

Halves of tender young birds and fryer parts are ideal for broiling or grilling. Smaller portions ensure that the product is thoroughly cooked. Poultry is broiled or grilled slowly as compared to fish. This is to prevent drying when ensuring that the centre is sufficiently cooked. Whether broiling or grilling, always season before cooking. Preheat the broiler or grill to moderately hot. Use tongs for turning to avoid piercing the poultry and losing valuable juices. When broiling, place the chicken on a nonstick broiling pan. Place about 3 inches from the heat. Cook until the outside is brown and the inside is cooked, but still moist and juicy. It should take about 8 to 15 minutes per side. The actual cooking time will depend on the size of the poultry and intensity of the heat. When grilling, place bone-in chicken pieces skin side down on a covered grill. Cook for 20 minutes. Then turn and cook until the juices run clear in about 15 minutes more. Bone pieces will cook in about 8 to 12 minutes.

Braised Chicken

Braising

This is a two-step process. First, the cut-up poultry, such as chicken, is sautéed or browned quickly. Second, the liquid is added and the pot is covered. Cooking may be done on top of the stove or in a slow oven. Cooking time will vary from 40 minutes to 1-1½ hours. The poultry is done when it is fork tender and firm to the touch. A favourite braised chicken dish is chicken hunter's style. The chicken is lightly browned and seasonings, tomatoes, and other vegetables are added. It is simmered until the chicken is cooked.

Poaching

Poaching is cooking in a gently simmering liquid such as water, chicken stock, or white wine. This method is usually used to cook older birds, as it tenderises them. Poaching is also used to cook whole birds for salad or cooked-chicken dishes. To poach, bring the liquid to a boil. Gently put the poultry in. The liquid must cover the poultry completely. Reduce heat to simmer. The liquid should barely bubble. The chicken is done when it is fork tender, the flesh changes colour, and feels firm, but not hard. Poaching takes about 35 minutes per kilogram for whole birds, or about 12 minutes for chicken breasts. Do not overcook. This is a common problem with poaching. The poultry will feel dry even though cooked in a liquid.

Chicken Stew

Pot-roasting

This is done with whole birds or with birds cut into pieces. The cooking is done in a covered casserole in the oven, or cooked over the fire with vegetables like potatoes, onions and carrots. The pieces are first browned in butter and then transferred to a covered casserole with tiny potatoes, onions and carrots, to cook in its own juice in a preheated oven. You could also cook it in a large covered pot over very low fire. Simple seasoning such as herbs, lemon and olive oil is added to mingle with the bird's juices.

Poached Turkey

Stewing

For stewing, the bird is cut into small pieces so that the liquid covers it completely. Slow cooking vegetables like carrots and turnips may be added along with the poultry pieces and mushrooms and pepper midway through cooking. You could add whipped cream at the end. This dish is simmered over low heat for a long time and seasoned with crushed garlic and finely chopped ginger. A pinch of salt and freshly ground pepper would complete the dish.

Deep-frying Poultry

Deep-Fried Chicken Wings

Chicken is the only bird that is commonly deep-fried. The pieces should be small and of equal size. Use a batter of refined flour or a coating of egg and breadcrumbs. The frying medium could be any vegetable oil. Creamed corn and grill tomatoes are ideal companions.

Stuffing Poultry

A good, seasoned stuffing adds flavour to the poultry. It also makes it possible to display the birds attractively. For stuffed roast, birds with white meat are preferred. The basic ingredient for stuffing is often a carbohydrate or a grain, for instance bread or rice. With turkey and wild birds chestnut stuffing is popular. Little birds such as pigeon and quail require a veal or pork-based mixture. Sometimes an oyster stuffing is used for goose and turkey. Flavouring the birds is important for roasting as stuffed roasts are a popular delicacy during the festive season. Apple, dried prunes or apricots are best flavouring for duck and goose; lemon and herbs for birds with white flesh; onion enhances most mixtures, and nuts add texture.

Stuffed Turkey

You must keep 175 gms stuffing for a 500 gms bird. Take care to fill the tail cavity loosely. The stuffing swells during cooking. While stuffing large birds, you could experiment and use a second variety of stuffing for the neck cavity. Use contrasting mixtures such as a sage and onion stuffing with pork and chestnut one, or rice stuffing with another one of celery, walnut and apricot. Breadcrumbs provide a versatile base for stuffing, binding lightly but firmly, and blending with almost any ingredient.

Here are a few bread stuffing recipes for you to experiment with:

Sage and Onions:

Gently fry 4 chopped, medium-sized onions with salt and pepper in 45 gms butter until soft but not browned. Let it cool. Stir in 100 gms fresh white breadcrumbs, 3 tbsp coarsely chopped fresh sage or 1½ tbsp dried sage. Mix well. Stir in 1 beaten egg and 125 ml water. Season to taste. Goes well with goose. Makes 750 ml.

Apples and Onions:

Gently fry 2 chopped onions and 2 peeled, cored and coarsely chopped cooking apples (green). Stir in 2 tbsp of chopped parsley and 100 gms fresh white breadcrumbs. Mix well. Makes 750 gms and is good for duck and goose.

Sausage and Chestnuts:

Peel 500 gms fresh chestnuts or drain 250 gms canned chestnuts. Coarsely crumble them. Fry 1 chopped onion in 2 gms butter till soft but not brown. Stir in 250 gms sausage meat and fry, stirring constantly until brown. Mix with chestnuts. Stir in 50 gms fresh white breadcrumbs and ½ tsp each of garam masala powder and nutmeg powder. Season to taste. Makes 750 gms and is good for chicken, turkey and goose.

Brinjal, Spinach and Roasted Pepper:

Cut one brinjal into ½ inch cubes, sprinkle with salt and keep aside for 15 minutes. Rinse and drain thoroughly. Sauté in 2 tbsp of vegetable oil until lightly browned. Stir in 250 gms (for 250 gms of brinjal) cooked spinach, squeezed dry and chopped, and 2 peeled, cored and seeded green or red peppers, cut into ½ inch cubes. In a frying pan, fry 2 chopped medium-sized onions in 2 tbsp oil until brown. Mix with the vegetable mixture with 125 gms fresh white breadcrumbs, 2 chopped cloves of garlic and the grated rind of 1 lemon. Season to taste. This makes about 500 gms of stuffing and is good for any bird.

These stuffings could also be used to stuff lamb, veal, pork or some vegetables as well.

Marinating Poultry

Poultry is tender meat. Many think it requires no marinating. Marinating not only tenderises meat,

Chicken in Curd Marinade

it also adds flavour to a dish. Light marinades, based on white wine with plenty of spices are perfect for white meats. More traditional red wine marinades can be used for duck and goose. Barbeque sauces are sometimes used to marinate poultry. You could also use the time-tested marinade of curd, ginger-garlic paste and curry powder, or even one made from olive oil, lemon juice and herbs. The birds should be sufficiently immersed in marinade to cover the poultry pieces or the whole bird. The bird or pieces are lifted out of the marinade for roasting. The marinade is used to baste the bird during cooking, or for making a sauce.

CUTS OF POULTRY

Before one can get down to cooking poultry, one must understand the various cuts of poultry, and how they are used.

Raw Chicken Wings

- Chicken wings with breast are mostly used for pan-frying, grilling and casserole. You could remove the skin before cooking or pull it off with your finger after cooking to keep the meat moist and succulent.
- Whole chicken legs are used for roasting, pan-frying, grilling or casserole. The skin can be treated as explained earlier.
- Boneless chicken breasts with and without chicken skin are used for deep-frying, grilling, pan-frying or stir frying.
- Chicken livers are used for grilling, pan-frying or stir frying.
- Turkey breast steaks are used for pan-frying and stir frying.
- Chicken drumsticks are used for deep-frying, grilling and barbequing.
- Minced turkey burgers are lower in fat than minced beef or lamb.
- Chicken thighs with and without skin are used for casseroles, barbeque, for biryanis or even curries.

Practical things to be done

Today we are going to prepare a whole chicken for roasting and chicken breasts for grilling and chicken stalk and a sauce to serve with any roast.

1. Preparing Whole Chicken

To prepare the whole chicken, follow this simple procedure.

1. Using your fingers, pull off the excess white fat on both sides of the opening at the tail end of the bird.
2. Carefully wipe the cavity with a kitchen paper towel. Use a fresh towel to wipe the skin. The skin crisps better if dry. You could also skin the bird. We will show you how to do it.
3. Cut out and discard the wishbone. Pull back the neck skin and mould the stuffing of your choice inside.
4. Turn the bird onto its breast and pull the neck skin over the stuffing before trussing. You have already learnt how to truss up a bird for roasting.

2. Skinning a Bird

To skin a bird, follow this simple procedure.

1. Cut off the wing pinions and trim the drumsticks. Slit the skin along the backbone from head to tail.
2. Using short sharp strokes of the knife cut and peel the skin from one side of the bird.
3. Turn the leg and wing skin inside out as you reach it.

3. Preparing Chicken Breasts

To prepare chicken breasts, follow this simple procedure.

1. Pull the small strip of tender fillet away from the underside. This ensures lesser time to cook.

2. Remove the white tendon away from the underside of the breast using a paring knife. Discard the tendon, as it is chewy.
3. To keep the skinless breasts moist, score the top diagonally with a chef's knife. Marinate or insert herbs or garlic butter into the slits.
4. If using breasts with skin, push your fingers between the skin and the flesh to make a packet. Insert garlic, herbs, soft cheese or butter.

4. Making Chicken Stock

Chicken stock can be used to make soups, stews or even to cook the chicken in instead of water. Keep it covered in the refrigerator for up to 3 days.

Utensils Used: A large stewing pot; a colander; a ladle; a large bowl.

Ingredients: 1 leftover roast chicken carcass or 1 kg chicken bones available in the market; 1 medium-sized onion, in halves; 1 medium celery stick, chopped; 1 medium carrot, chopped; dried herbs or cinnamon, cloves, cardamom tied in a small piece of muslin to make a bouquet garni to flavour the stock.

Follow this procedure to make the chicken stock:

1. Break up the carcass and put it into the stewing pan. Add the vegetables and the bouquet garni. Stir and add cold water to cover the ingredients well.
2 Bring to a boil over high heat. Skim off any scum that rises to the top. Lower heat, cover and simmer for 1½ hours to 2 hours.
3. Ladle the pan contents into a colander set over a large bowl. Strain, cool, cover and keep. This makes 1 litre stock.

5. Making a Gravy

This gravy is used with roasts. It is made with the juices that drip in the roasting tin while cooking. Follow this procedure to make it.

1. Fill the roasting tin so the juices settle in one corner. Spoon off most of the fat, leaving the dark juices in the tin. Discard the surplus fat. Put the roasting on medium heat gas burner.
2. Sprinkle 2 tsp plain flour over the juices in the tin. Whisk with a coil, whisk over medium heat or 2-3 minutes until the flour browns a little.
3. Pour in 300 ml hot stock or water. Bring to a boil, whisking all the time. If you like, add 4 tbsp white or red wine and whisk to mix. Simmer for 2 minutes and check seasonings. Serve with any roast. Makes about 300 ml gravy.

Potli Chicken

Baked Almond Chicken

Expert cook suggests...

1. While making barbeque, sprinkle some lemon juice over the hot coals just before the grilling is complete. It will add flavour to the chicken or mutton.
2. To cut chicken easily, freeze the uncooked chicken for an hour in the refrigerator before cutting it.

DAY 18

Fish and Seafood

Fish is the healthiest of all non-vegetarian food. It is nutritious and low in fat. Different types of fish can be used for every imaginable method of cooking. However, cooking it is the most challenging and rewarding of all food. The care with which it has to be cooked provides the challenge, and the ease with which it cooks is the reward.

Fish

Improved techniques of refrigerated transport have created a world market for seafood. All kinds of seafood are available everywhere in the world. Although freezing does affect the texture of fish, it does less damage than would occur through natural bacterial growth.

Seafood includes both finfish (usually called 'fish'), such as flounder and tuna, and shellfish, such as shrimp and scallops. There are two types of shellfish: molluscs (which are the true shellfish with hard shells) and crustaceans (which have segmented shells and jointed legs). Examples of molluscs include abalone, clams, oysters, and scallops. Examples of crustaceans include crabs, crayfish, lobsters, and shrimp. Octopus and squid, even though they lack shells, are also considered shellfish.

Nutritional Value of Fish

Fresh and frozen seafood are excellent sources of protein. They are:

- Relatively low in calories, fat, and saturated fat as compared to meat.
- A good source of omega-3 fatty acids.
- Low to moderate in cholesterol content.
- Low in sodium.
- A good source of certain vitamins such as vitamins E and K and niacin, and minerals like iodine and potassium.

The fat content varies from one kind of fish to another. Although they contain fat, it is less than the fat contained in equivalent servings of most meats. More important, the type of fat found in fish is rich in health promoting fatty acids (key components of fats) known as Omega-3. Omega-3 is polyunsaturated fatty acids found almost exclusively in fish and shellfish. They have several health benefits, as follows:

- Reduce the chance of developing heart disease. It may also reduce damage from heart disease.
- Usually lower blood triglyceride (fat) levels.
- May improve heart functioning.
- Can modestly lower blood pressure, thereby, reducing the chances of heart attack and stroke.
- May improve symptoms of arthritis and psoriasis.

Seafood Market

Shellfish, as well as fatty fish, are higher in Omega-3 than lean fish. Certain shellfish – shrimp and crayfish – are higher in cholesterol than other seafood. However, a 100 grams portion of either, still has less cholesterol than one egg. Shellfish is also very low in saturated fat. The effect of eating shellfish is that it is no worse than eating chicken without the skin. Eminent heart experts no longer see reasons to place limitations on specific shellfish for their patients with high blood cholesterol, provided the quantity is not excessive and there is moderate intake of saturated fats.

Canned seafood has much higher levels of sodium. By rinsing canned seafood, you can remove some of the sodium. Many canned seafood products are packed in oil or water. The water packed is a better choice to reduce total fat.

Preparing Fish for Cooking

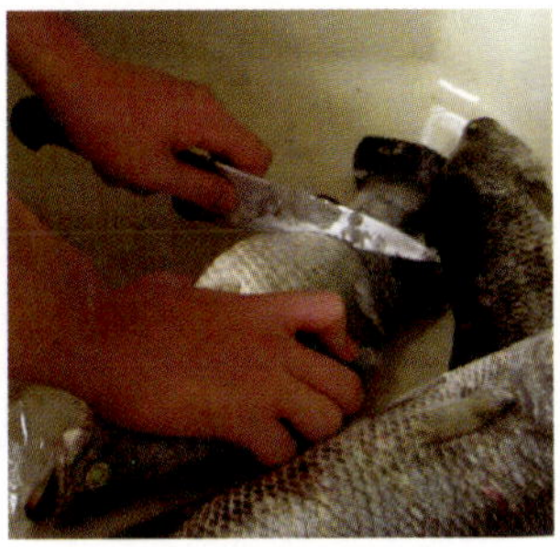
Scaling

Most people get the fish cleaned and cut into pieces by the butcher, but many prefer to do it personally. The procedure is described below:

To prepare fish for cooking, follow these simple steps:

- Cut the head off with a sharp knife.
- Cut deeply into the back of the fish. Make a smaller cut along the edge of the flesh. Avoid the bones.
- Inserting the knife into the flesh, gradually separate the flesh from the backbone. Do this slowly to avoid wastage of flesh.
- After completing one side, move to the other. Remove flesh in the same way. Turn the fish, and similarly remove the flesh on the other side. Use a sharp knife. Move it carefully.

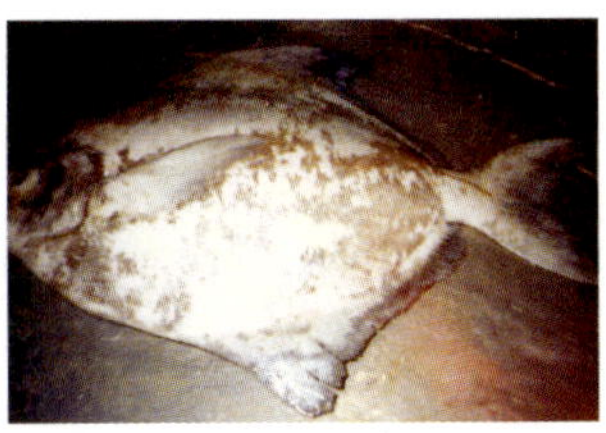
Large Pomphret

Purchasing Fish

When purchasing fish, you need to consider several things.

- What kind to buy?
- What form it should be in – whole, drawn, dressed, fillets, steaks, stick, and portions?
- Whether you want it fresh, frozen, or processed (such as canned)?
- How to choose high-quality fresh and frozen fish?

When buying fresh fish, first look over the way it is displayed. Fish should not be lying in water or juices. Seafood that does not have any skin or shell to protect it should not be in direct contact with the ice. Also, only buy fish that does not smell fishy. A fishy odour indicates high level of bacteria. A slightly sea-weedy or cucumber-like odour is all right.

Fresh fillets and steaks should have firm, elastic flesh and retain true colour; pearly white for flounder, sole, and haddock; reddish for tuna (except albacore, which ranges from light beige to rosy beige); grayish for bluefish, and pink to red and orange-red for trout and salmon. They should have a fresh-cut appearance with no drying or browning or curling up around the edges. If cut fish is left too long in a display case, the flesh begins to separate and may get slimy.

Whole fish, whatever the variety, has certain characteristics that indicate freshness. Fresh fish should never have a sour or ammonia like odour. Here is what to look for when buying whole fish.

- Bright, clear, full (sometimes protruding) eyes. As a fish ages, the eyes become cloudy and sunken.
- Bright red or pink gills. Gray, brown, or green gills are a sign of age.
- Moist, shiny skin with scales that adhere tightly and with distinct colour and markings.
- Firm, elastic flesh that springs back when pressed gently with the finger. With time, the flesh becomes soft and separates from the bones.

Fish Steak

When buying frozen fish, check that the package was stacked below the frost line of the freezer case. Look for packages that still have their original shape with the wrapping intact and no visible ice or blood. Fish that has thawed and refrozen may have a sour smell, a brown colour at the edges of the fillet, a dried-out appearance, or excessive frost or ice in the packaging. Be sure the fish is solidly frozen with no discolouration, freezer burn, or bad odour.

Storing fish

Fresh fish should be stored at 30°– 32°F, about 10 degrees cooler than most refrigerators. Place seafood in the coolest part of the refrigerator. Do not worry about it getting frozen. It does not freeze until the temperature gets below 28°F. When storing fresh fish, make sure it is wrapped well in moisture-proof paper or in an airtight plastic bag or container. Rewrap fish if it was not properly wrapped in the store. Fresh fish should be used 1 to 2 days from purchase, preferably within one day. Fleshy fish is more delicate than lean fish, such as tuna and mackerel, and should be used within a day.

Cooked fish should be sealed tightly, promptly refrigerated, and consumed within 3-4 days. Fish cannot be frozen as long as red meat and poultry because it has a high content of polyunsaturated fats, which are more prone to oxidation than saturated fats. Changes in texture also occur after some time. It is important to label all frozen fish clearly with the date. Use within a day after it is thawed.

If you want to freeze fresh fish that you have purchased, ensure that it is of high quality. Wrap it tightly in plastic bags, or in a wrap designed for freezing. Make sure all the air is pressed out before sealing.

Cooking fish

Fried Fish

Fish can be prepared in countless delicious ways. Because it is naturally tender, it lends itself to every kind of cooking method. Any cooking method (except frying of course) makes fish a light and healthy dish as long as minimal amounts of oil or margarine, if any, are used.

The following are some general pointers for successful seafood preparation:

- Cook fresh fish soon after purchase, the same day, if possible.
- Cook frozen fish that has been thawed within a day. Fillets, steaks, and portions up to 250 grams can be cooked directly from the frozen state to prevent excessive drip loss during cooking, and for convenience. Just double the cooking time. However, if you plan to bread the fish first, partially thaw the fish (you can microwave it for a few seconds) so it can be breaded successfully. Never thaw frozen breaded or battered fish sticks or portions before cooking, because the breading will become soggy.
- Do not overcook fish. It is tender as it comes from water. Very little cooking is necessary to develop flavour or soften connective tissue. Cook only until the product becomes firm and opaque, but is still moist and juicy. When fish cooks, it lightens in colour and turns opaque white or light gray. To test for doneness, slide a knife tip into the thickest part of the fish and check the colour. If it is still dark and translucent, it needs more cooking. If it is solid white, the fish is done. Do not cook fish until it flakes or separates. By this time, it has shrunk, toughened, and dried out.
- Do not over-season fish. Fish and shellfish generally have a delicate flavour that is easily overwhelmed. Seafood and its sauce should complement each other.
- Fish adapt well to almost all cooking methods, but because of a tendency to dry out during cooking using dry heat (baking, grilling, and broiling), lean or low-fat fish is better when cooked using moist heat. Dry heat methods are fine if lean fish is basted with a sauce before baking, broiling, or grilling or brushed lightly with a minimal amount of oil.

Marinades, sauces, condiments, herbs and spices for seafood

MARINADES

These combine ingredients such as wine, vinegar, lemon, or any citrus juice along with a mild-flavoured cooking oil and your choice of other flavouring agents to create tangy marinades for seafood. A basic oil-based marinade uses 1 cup vegetable oil, ½ cup lemon juice or vinegar, ½ tsp each of salt and pepper, 1 clove minced garlic, 3 tbsp freshly chopped or 2 tbsp dried herbs such as tarragon, basil, parsley, thyme, or oregano, alone or in combination.

Seafood Marinade

Marinated Fish

For less fat and convenience, use bottled salad dressing (low-fat products work fine) like Italian, vinaigrette, or Dijon flavour. For a summery taste, you can marinate fillets of fish with a higher fat content in lemon juice (3 tbsp juice per ½ kg of fish) for 1 hour.

To make a marinade, blend all ingredients thoroughly. If marinating whole fish, make 3 to 4 slits into the flesh down to the bone on each side so that the marinade penetrates. Marinate 1 to 4 hours in the refrigerator, turning fish or shellfish about every hour. The longer the fish marinates, more of the flavour will be absorbed. Do not marinate fish overnight like beef or poultry. It will turn mushy. Always drain the marinade from the fish before cooking and discard it. It could contain harmful bacteria or other substances. Use reserved fresh marinade during cooking for basting. Baste at least once during cooking.

Tomato-orange marinade

200 ml no-salt tomato juice.

¼ cup frozen orange juice concentrate.

¼ cup minced onions.

1 small clove garlic, minced.

Sauces and Condiments

Soy sauce (try low-sodium) and teriyaki sauce, which contain no fat, can be used in marinades. They can be brushed on fish and shellfish before grilling, broiling, baking, steaming, or cooking in a microwave. Tomato sauces and jarred salsas are also low fat and can be poured over fish before baking, or heated and added after poaching and sautéing. Cocktail sauce and tartar sauce (make your own with reduced-calorie mayonnaise and relish) are traditional condiments for fish and seafood. You can make your own sauce by combining fresh tomatoes with herbs as suggested below.

Tomato basil sauce

2 large ripe tomatoes, diced.

3 tbsp fresh basil, chopped.

2 tbsp olive oil.

1 tbsp balsamic or other vinegar.

Juice of 1 lemon (about 3 tbsp).

1 small clove of garlic, minced.

***Pour over fish before baking.**

Lemon sauce

3 tbsp lemon juice.

1 tbsp Dijon mustard.

1 tbsp melted margarine.

¼ tsp freshly ground pepper.

***Brush fish with it.**

Teriyaki sauce

½ cup low-sodium soy sauce.

2 tbsp dry sherry.

½ tbsp sugar.

1 clove garlic, finely minced.

½ tbsp finely grated fresh gingerroot or ½ tsp dried ground ginger.

***Use for marinade.**

Herbs and Spices

Basil, bay leaf, dill, oregano, paprika, pepper, seasoned peppers, tarragon, thyme, rosemary, sage, marjoram, chervil, chives, fennel, ginger, and garlic enhance the flavour of seafood.

Baking Fish

Baked Fish

Baking is a particularly easy way to prepare fish. Whole fish, whole stuffed fish fillets, stuffed fillets, steaks, and chunks of fish may all be baked. Use pieces of fish of similar size for even cooking. To bake, preheat the oven to 425°F. Rinse the fish under cold water and pat dry with paper towels. If baking a whole fish, pat the inside dry. Lightly oil a shallow baking dish (or use a nonstick pan) and place fish in it, skin side down if baking fillets.

To prevent the fish from drying out (this applies particularly to leaner fish), you can do a number of things besides adding oil.

- Wrap the fish in aluminium foil or parchment paper.
- Cover the fish with chopped vegetables, which will help flavour the fish and at the same time keep it moist. Use a combination of onions, celery, and carrots; or mushrooms and onions; or onions, tomatoes, and red and green peppers.
- Use a breadcrumb topping or other coating. First dip the fish in 1 egg white combined with ¼ cup skimmed milk, or dip in ½ cup buttermilk. Then coat with breadcrumbs.
- Brush on a minimal amount of low-fat Italian salad dressing or a thin layer of vegetable oil.

To enjoy the taste of 'fried' fish without excessive fat, bake fish fillets, dredging them in seasoned flour, dipping them in an egg white beaten with a little water, and coating them with breadcrumbs. Place fish in a shallow, lightly oiled (or nonstick) baking pan and dot with margarine or oil. Bake for 6 to 12 minutes per inch of thickness until fish is just opaque throughout. To bake prepared breaded frozen fish products, follow the directions on the package.

Broiling Fish

Steaks, whole fish, split whole fish, and fillets can all be broiled. To broil fish, preheat broiler pan. Rinse fish under cold water and pat dry with paper towels. Season it on all sides if desired with pepper, herbs, and lemon juice.

Lightly oil the broiler pan or use a nonstick pan. If broiling a small whole fish, slash the skin on both sides and turn it over halfway through broiling. Arrange fish fillets, skin side down in a single layer. Place fish, 1 inch thick or less, and 3 to 4 inches from the heat source; place thicker pieces 5 to 6 inches away. Fillets less than 1 inch thick do not need to be turned over. Baste with a marinade, such as low-fat salad dressing, during cooking. To broil frozen fish, double the cooking time and turn the fish over halfway through broiling.

Broiled Salmon

Grilling

Grilling is well suited for thick cuts of fish, such as whole fish, steaks, and kebabs. Fillets may also be grilled. Nonstick grills are ideal for cooking fish without having to oil the grill. It is helpful to use a hinged grilling basket or aluminium foil that has been punctured to allow airflow, particularly with more delicately textured fish. Prior to placing on the heat, lightly grease the basket with vegetable cooking oil (unless the basket is nonstick). When using a grill rack instead of the basket or foil method, pre-oil the unheated grill rack. Always use super clean grill racks and baskets.

Rinse the fish under cold water and pat dry with paper towels. For fish that is 1 inch thick or less, place the grill 2 to 4 inches above the coals or heat source; for thicker pieces, 5 to 6 inches away. Cook fish and shellfish over a medium-hot fire. Cook on one side for half the cooking time, basting frequently. Turn over and continue grilling and basting until done. Marinades and sauces add flavour and keep the fish moist when grilled.

The exact cooking time will depend on the thickness of the fish, the type of fire (wood, charcoal, gas, or electricity), the distance of the fish from the heat source, and whether you use a covered or an open grill. Watch carefully. Do what the professionals do – peek inside to check for completeness. Grill until the fish is just opaque throughout. Generally, shellfish cooks faster than finfish.

Microwave Grilled Fish

Sautéing

Sautéing is ideal for thinner fish fillets. Shucked oysters, shrimp, scallops, and squid respond well to this cooking method. To sauté, first rinse the fish under cold water and pat dry with paper towels. If desired, lightly flour the fish to help seal in the juices. Using a heavy skillet, heat 1 tbsp vegetable oil. Add fish to the pan being careful not to crowd, otherwise the fish will become soggy. Cook about 6 to 12 minutes per inch thickness until fish is just opaque throughout. Turn fish over halfway through cooking. For thicker fish, reduce heat to medium. Drain fish on paper towels and season.

Stir Frying

Stir frying small pieces of fish (or shellfish) together with an assortment of colourful vegetables is a quick, easy way to make a healthy, tasty entrée. Shrimp and scallops are very easy to cook this way. If using fish, be sure it is a firm fleshed fish like halibut, tuna, shark, or grouper. Stir frying is a very fast technique. Keep everything ready before heating the oil. Using a wok or large skillet, lightly coat the bottom and sides with vegetable oil. Add raw seafood and stir fry, tossing gently to coat on all sides, until about three quarters done, anywhere from 2 to 4 minutes. Shrimp will turn pink, scallops and fish opaque or white. Remove to a warm platter. Continue by stir frying the vegetables and making a light sauce, if desired. Return the seafood to the wok or skillet and cook 1 to 2 minutes longer. Serve at once.

Poaching

Poaching is cooking in a gently simmering liquid such as lightly seasoned lemon water, fish or vegetable stock. Poaching works well for fish in any form. To prepare a whole, dressed fish for poaching, rinse it under cold water. Bring liquid to a boil in a large skillet or sauté pan and add the fish or shellfish. Reduce to a simmer; the water should barely bubble. Gently cook 6 to 12 minutes per inch thickness of fish until it is just opaque throughout. It is not necessary to turn fish when poaching. Check before the time is up – poaching usually cooks seafood a little quicker. Remove when the fish turns from translucent to opaque or white and is firm but still moist. Reserve the liquid to make a sauce for the fish.

Pan Steamed Fish

Steaming

Whole fish chunks, steaks, and thick or rolled up fillets are all suitable for steaming. Shellfish tastes excellent when steamed. Steaming, like poaching, is ideal for those who want to avoid adding extra fat. To steam fish, fill a steamer or large saucepan fitted with a steaming rack and a tight cover with about 1 inch of plain or seasoned water, such as fish stock. Just make sure that it is a mild liquid, one that will not overpower the flavour of the fish. The water should not rise above the rack. Bring liquid to a boil. Reduce to a simmer. Wash the fish, place on the rack, and place the rack in the pot. Cover tightly. Steam until done – steam cooks quickly so check frequently for opaque flesh. Be careful to open the lid away from you to let the steam out of the pot.

Microwave Cooking

Almost all kinds of fish can be prepared in the microwave oven. Watch closely when you try a new seafood recipe for the first time using the microwave. If a range of times is given, start with the shortest one. You can always put the dish back in the oven and cook it a little longer, but you cannot turn the clock back if it has cooked too long. Write the correct time down on the recipe for future reference.

Split-second timing is the secret to cooking seafood in the microwave. Fish cooked in the microwave is done when the flesh has just begun to change from translucent to opaque or white and when it is firm but still moist. Fish will continue to cook after it has been removed from the microwave. Take the dish out before it looks done – when the outer edges are opaque with the centre still slightly translucent. Allow the fish to stand covered, for a few minutes before serving to let the heat distribute evenly and the fish to finish cooking. Here are some additional tips for cooking in the microwave.

Cooking Finfish in the Microwave Oven

- Defrost frozen fish before cooking.
- Use a shallow microwave-proof dish to hold the fish.
- Make several diagonal slashes through the skin of whole fish to prevent it from bursting.

- Arrange fillets in a dish with the thicker parts pointing outward and the thinner parts towards the centre of the dish. Rolled fillets cook more evenly by microwave than flat fillets.
- Cover the dish and vent by turning back a corner.
- Allow 3½ to 6 minutes per kilogram of boneless fish cooked on high (100 percent power) as a guide. Rotate the dish halfway through the cooking time.
- Cook side dishes first and keep them covered while cooking the fish. They will retain heat longer than fish.
- Brush fish with stock or juice before cooking in a microwave oven.

Cooking Shellfish in the Microwave

- Arrange a single layer of shellfish in a shallow dish and cover with plastic wrap turned back at one corner for venting.
- Allow 2 to 3 minutes per kilogram thawed shucked shellfish cooked on high (100 percent power). Stir and rotate halfway through the cooking time. Allow to stand for one-third of the cooking time after removing from the oven. Be careful not to overcook.
- Place clams, mussels, or oysters in the shell in a single layer in a shallow dish. Cover with plastic wrap, venting at one corner. Cook for 2 to 3 minutes on high flame (100 percent power). Check and remove pieces as they open. Continue until all have opened. 1 kg will take 12 to15 minutes.

Shrimps, Mushrooms and Bean Sprouts
(Cooked in Microwave)

Shellfish

This section will give useful information on the following forms of shellfish: clams, crabs, lobsters, oysters, scallops and shrimp. The flavour of shellfish ranges from mild to full. Scallops, lobsters, crawfish and squid have a mild flavour. Octopus has a moderate flavour and mussels, oysters and clams have a full flavour.

Crabs

Purchasing crabs:

Crabs are available live (they taste best this way) and cooked frozen meat or cooked frozen in the shell. When bought live, make sure there is some leg movement. Frozen crab is available all the year round. Fresh ones are available during warm months in the producing areas.

Storing crabs:

Live crabs should be kept in the refrigerator for only one to two days in moist packaging (seaweed or damp paper strips). Cooked crabmeat can be placed in freezer bags and wrapped tightly. The meat will be better protected if frozen in a prepared dish, such as a casserole.

Raw Crab

Handling and cooking crabs:

Crabs should be alive before cooking. To clean a soft-shell crab, do the following before they are cooked.

- Place the crab topside up on the work surface. With a pair of kitchen scissors, cut off the head about ¼ inch behind the eyes. Be sure the yellowish sandbag (stomach) is removed and discarded. Rinse well under cold running water and pat dry.
- Turn the crab on its back and cut off the tail flap, or apron, which is triangular in females and T-shaped in males. First, pry the apron up with your fingers, and then pull it down and

away. Discard the apron and the intestinal tract, which is attached to it.

- Peel back the pointed shell and scrape away the gills on each side. Rinse the crab with cold water and pat dry.

Do not clean soft-shell crabs until you are ready to cook them. The crab may then be dredged in flour for sautéing or breaded or battered for deep-frying. Sautéed or deep-fried soft-shell crabs take about 3 minutes each. Hard-shell crabs do not need to be prepared before cooking. They are usually simmered for 10 to 15 minutes in salted water and then cooled rapidly in ice water. They can also be steamed. To pick the meat out of a Dungeness or other hard-shell crab, do the following (a nutcracker comes in handy to break claws and legs).

- Grasp a front claw and twist it, breaking it off where it meets the body. Repeat with other claw and legs. Crack each piece and remove the meat.
- Break off the pointed shell on the underside.
- Pry off broad top shell. Discard the gills, spongy parts, and stomach (behind eyes) under shell.
- Place knife blade down the centre of crab's body; tap the knife with a mallet to cut in half. Repeat to cut each half into chunks, placing knife blade between leg joints. Pry out meat.

Frozen crabmeat is already cooked – just heat through before serving.

Lobsters

Purchasing lobsters:

Lobsters are available year-round. The most popular lobster has a large tail, four pair of legs, and two large front claws. Its shell is dark green, or blue-green. It turns red when cooked. Lobsters can be purchased live or frozen (whole or the tail only). Cooked meat (either fresh or frozen) is also available. Lobster is normally sold live by the kilo: a jumbo lobster is over one kilogram, a large lobster is ¾ to over a kilogram, a quarter lobster is ½ to ¾ kilogram, and a chicken lobster is under ½ kilogram. The spiny or rock lobster is not a true lobster, but a type of crayfish. The only usable meat of the spiny lobster is found in the tail, and it is less sweet than lobster. When buying live lobster, make sure there is some leg movement and that the lobster's tail curls under when picked up.

Raw Lobsters

Storing lobsters:

Store lobsters in the refrigerator in ventilated containers. Keep moist with seaweed, lettuce leaves, or damp paper towels or cloth. Never store in airtight container as they will suffocate and die. Live lobsters and cooked lobster meat should be used within 1 to 2 days. Cooked lobster meat can be placed in freezer bags and wrapped tightly. The meat will be better protected frozen in a prepared dish, such as a casserole.

Handling and cooking lobsters:

Live lobster (make sure there is movement of the legs and claws) are often cooked live by throwing them into boiling water (this kills them instantly) and simmering for 12 minutes for the ½ kilogram, and 6 for each additional ½ kilogram. When boiling lobsters, the shells turn red quickly, but that is no indication of completeness. Do not boil lobster – it toughens the meat. Lobsters can also be split and cut up in preparation of broiling. To split a lobster for baking or broiling, do the following:

- To kill the lobster instantly, place it on a cutting board on its back and insert the tip of a large knife between the eyes.
- Continue cutting back to the end of the tail. Work the knife down to the back shell to split the lobster.
- With your hands, crack the back of the shell by spreading the lobster open.
- With a paring knife, remove the intestinal tract, which resembles the long thin vein running the length of the lobster. Remove the sandy sack (stomach) beneath the eyes.
- With a sharp blow of the back of the knife, crack the claws to expose the meat.
- Whole or cut-up lobster can also be cooked by baking, sautéing, or simmering in sauce or soup.

Shrimp

Purchasing shrimps:

Raw Shrimp

Shrimp is a small crustacean that looks somewhat like a small lobster without claws. Generally, the larger the shrimp, the higher the price. There are many varieties of shrimp, such as brown, pink, and white. After cooking, all shrimp turn into the same colour. The term 'prawn' is sometimes used to mean large shrimp. The term 'green shrimp' refers to the raw shrimp in the shell.

Shrimp can be purchased in several forms.

- Green shrimp – raw in the shell.
- Peeled and deveined – raw with the shell and vein removed.
- Peeled, deveined, and cooked.

These three forms are usually sold frozen (unless it is locally produced) because shrimp is highly perishable. Shrimp is also available frozen and breaded (raw or cooked), canned, and butter flied (split in the shell). Raw and cooked shrimp have the following characteristics:

Raw shrimp:

- Firm meat.
- Translucent shells with greyish green, pinkish tan, or light pink tint and a minimum of black spots or edges.
- Moist but not displayed in liquid.

Cooked shrimp in the shell:

- Firm white meat with pink or reddish shells.
- Moist but not in direct contact with ice.

Shrimp are available throughout the year.

Storing shrimp:

Fresh shrimp should be stored in the refrigerator and used within 1 to 2 days. Frozen shrimp should be kept at temperatures below 0°F.

Handling and cooking shrimp:

Shrimp that is to be served hot must be peeled and deveined before cooking. If shrimp is to be served cold, it is usually peeled and deveined after cooking to maintain flavour.

To peel and devein shrimp, follow this procedure:

- Break off the head and discard. Starting at the head end, grasp the legs on one side and peel the shell around and off the body. Several segments may be done at once. The tail section may be left on for appearance.
- Make a shallow cut down the outer curve of the shrimp with a paring knife and remove the vein found just below the surface.

Shrimp can be cooked by baking, broiling, simmering, sautéing and deep-frying. Raw shrimp turn pink and firm when cooked. Cooking time depends on the size. It takes from 3 to 5 minutes to boil, steam, or sauté ½ kilogram of medium size shrimp in the shell. If overcooked, the meat will be tough and rubbery.

Boiling is a quick, convenient way to cook shrimp. You do not have to boil shrimp in plain cold water. Instead, to 2 cups of water or stock, add 3 tbsp of lemon or lime juice, and a tbsp of pickling spice, two bay leaves, thyme, garlic powder, paprika, or ground white or black pepper. These different combinations will impart some flavour to the dish.

Different Market forms of Fish

Whole or round: This, as the term suggests, means that the fish is whole, just as it is pulling out of the water. Nothing has been removed.

Drawn: The fish has been butted (the inside portion has been removed). The fins and scales have also been removed.

Dressed: The fish has been gutted and scaled, the fins removed, and usually the head and tail are cut off as well.

Steaks: These are cross-section slices, from ¼ to 1½ inches thick, of larger dressed fish. Steaks usually have a piece of the backbone in the centre.

Chunks: These are cross-section pieces cut thicker than steaks. They may have a piece of the backbone.

Butterfly Fillet: This is not a common market form. These are two fillets of a fish held together by the uncut flesh and skin of the belly.

Fillets: Fillets are the sides of the fish cut away from the backbone. They are often boneless and

skinless, though the skin of fatty fish is usually left attached to the fillets. That way it holds together better during cooking. Sometimes small bones called pins are present. They can be easily removed.

Stick and Portions: Sometimes blocks of fish are cut into sticks and portions. These are available breaded or not breaded, precooked or uncooked, usually in the frozen form.

Practical things to be done

Today, you are going to learn the different ways of cutting and preparing a fish for cooking. We will also cook a simple recipe.

You will need a chopping board; a set of knives; washing bowl; a tray; a pair of kitchen scissors; a pair of tweezers.

1. Preparing a whole fish

To prepare a whole fish for grilling or baking, follow this simple procedure.

1. Using kitchen scissors, cut off all the fins from the back and the stomach of the fish.
2. Trim the tail in a neat 'V' shape. Rinse the fish under cold running water, pat dry thoroughly.
3. Using a chef's knife, make several diagonal slashes in each side of the fish, cutting to the bone.
4. Insert thin lemon slices with sprigs of parsley in each slash. Sprinkle salt and pepper over the fish. Now, grill it or bake it. Check for completeness by piercing the fish with a fork. If it goes through easily, your fish is done.

Note: The trimmed fins and tails give the fish a neat, attractive appearance. The lemon slices and herbs give a flavour to the fish. A *masala* paste of ginger, garlic and curry *masala* is also appreciated for its flavour. For extra moisture, brush both sides of the fish with any vegetable oil before cooking.

2. Preparing Fish Fillets

Raw Fish Fillets

Fish fillets cook very quickly. One of the tastiest ways to cook fish fillets is by chargrilling. A large portion of big size fish is ideal for preparing fish fillets. You can cut them into the desired size. Follow this simple procedure.

1. Run your fingertips along the flesh to look for the tiny bones. Then, carefully pull them out with a pair of tweezers.
2. With chef's knife, trim the fat or any ragged skin from the edges to make the fillets neat looking.
3. Thoroughly rinse the fillets under cold running water, rubbing with your fingers to dislodge any scales.
4. Pat dry the fillets with a paper towel before cooking.

3. Skinning and Coating Fillets

Cooked Fish Fillets

When you need to coat the fillets to deep-fry, skinning them is a must. Skinned and coated fish fillets are also available in the frozen food section of grocery stores. A fishmonger will do it for you if you ask him to do so. If you want to do it yourself, follow the simple procedure.

1. Place the fillet, skin side down on the chopping board. Grip the tail end of the fish between the index finger and the thumb.
2. Working away from you, with a sawing action, cut between the flesh and the skin.
3. Beat an egg in a shallow dish. Dip the fillet in the egg to coat on both sides by turn. Lift it up to drain the excess egg.

4. Transfer the fillet to a plate of breadcrumbs. Using your fingers or a spoon, coat the fish thoroughly with the breadcrumbs on both sides. Then, deep-fry it in hot oil or chargrill it.

Note: Readymade breadcrumbs are available in packets. If you want to make fresh ones, toast a few slices of bread till light brown. Pound these in a mortar, or crush fine with a rolling pin, or grind in your food processor. Alternatively, buy a packet of rusks. Crush a few to get ideal breadcrumbs.

4. Preparing Prawns

Prawns

Whether raw or cooked, the shell of the prawn is removed in the same way. The dark vein that runs through a prawn is edible but looks ugly. In large prawns it can be gritty. Follow this procedure to prepare prawns.

1. Pinch the head between your fingers and pull it from the body to leave just the fleshy tail end intact.
2. Peel the shell from the body with your fingers, working down from the head. On reaching the tail, pull the meat out of the shell.
3. If you are using large tiger prawns, make a shallow cut along the back of the prawn with a paring knife to reveal the vein.
4. With the end of the knife, pick out the end of the vein and gently pull it out. Discard it.

5. Grilled Fish Fillets

Grilled Fish Fillets

Utensils used: A sauté pan or a nonstick frying pan; a small bowl; a large brush; a longhandled slotted spoon.

Portions: We are cooking for two persons.

Ingredients: 2 thick pieces of any fish fillet, skin on, 150-175 gms each; 2 tbsp sunflower oil; salt and pepper to taste.

To grill fish fillets, follow this procedure:

1. Remove the tiny bones; trim, wash well and pat dry the fish fillets with a paper towel.
2. Preheat the pan over high heat. Sprinkle water to test whether it is hot or not. The water droplets should dance and quickly disappear.
3. While the pan is heating, brush both sides of the fillets with sunflower oil. Sprinkle salt and pepper.
4. Reduce heat to low. Place the fillets, skin-side up, in the hot pan. Cook for 2 to 3 minutes. Turn the fillets over and cook the other side. Check to see whether the fish is opaque all along the cut edges. If not, cook for another few seconds. Serve hot with boiled potatoes and peas, or even with an Indian menu.

TIPS

- To get rid of bad food odour in the refrigerator, pour 2 or 3 drops of rose essence on a cotton pad, place it in a saucer and leave it in the refrigerator.
- To keep your fridge smelling fresh, fill a small bowl with soda bicarbonate and keep in the fridge.
- A drop of vanilla essence is an excellent deodorant when wiping the inside of the refrigerator.
- If you do not have an exhaust fan in your kitchen, hang a wet towel high above the stove. It will absorb the smoke and food odour.
- To keep the nonstick tawa sparkling, apply a coat of buttermilk or lemon juice.
- Clean the nonstick toaster by sprinkling salt on it. Follow by cleaning with a ball of newspaper or a soft cloth. The salt effectively absorbs the grease.
- Rinsing cooking utensils with hot water to which some salt has been added keeps them free from food odours.

Expert cook suggests...

1. Adding a few mint leaves when cooking fish ensures that the 'fishy' smell does not pervade the house.
2. After scaling, the fish should be rubbed with gram flour and washed to clean it properly.

PROGRESS CHECKLIST # 3

Do not skip this checklist. Answer all the questions. They are based on what you learnt in the last six days. Whenever in doubt, go back to the appropriate lesson and reread the relevant section. Your sincere efforts will make you a great cook.

1. Did you try frying puris and parathas?

   ☐ Yes ☐ No

Keep trying. Perfection comes only with practice.

2. Did you make *idlis*? And *dosa*?

   ☐ Yes ☐ No

Try them. Both of them are all-time favourites.

3. Did everyone appreciate the vegetable soup cooked by you?

   ☐ Yes ☐ No

Soups offer an infinite variety. Try them whenever you can.

4. Have you understood the different ways of cooking meat, poultry and fish?

   ☐ Yes ☐ No

Try them one by one over a period.

5. Have you understood why marinating meat, poultry and fish makes them tastier?

   ☐ Yes ☐ No

6. Can you cut a chicken into pieces?

   ☐ Yes ☐ No

7. Did you enjoy cooking the meat, poultry and fish dishes?

   ☐ Yes ☐ No

If your family is fond of eating non-vegetarian dishes, you will do well to get to know your butcher. This will ensure that you get the best raw material. Store all meat items in a refrigerator only. Store them in a deep freezer preferably.

8. Did you cook all the fish dishes in the practical session?

   ☐ Yes ☐ No

If your family is fond of fish and seafood, try cooking the dishes one by one.

Day 19

Exotic Sauces

Sauces add zest or piquancy to food. Hot or cold; seasoned liquid either are served with or used in the cooking of a dish. Our Indian gravies and curries, too, belong to this genre as do a variety of others ranging from the table variety. The hot and sour-sweet sauces, the light sauces and the dessert sauces are extensively used in many Western dishes and desserts.

In our country, the most popular sauces are the table variety like the tomato sauce or ketchup, soy sauce, chilli sauce, mustard sauce, Worcestershire sauce, the Tabasco and a few others, that have entered our cooking arena due to the outside cultural influences on our eating habits, otherwise, since time immemorial, Indians rely on aromatic *masala* curries and unique rich gravies to flavour the vast varieties of their dishes.

Table Sauces

But when you wish to acquire culinary expertise, the objective should be to know about food worldwide. Today's cuisine offers a combination of menus from all parts of the world. Western and continental dishes have found as much flavour with us as our curries have in the West. Food has attracted a lot of people to their brethren all over the world.

Here we will go through a short historical journey of sauce making in France, as France was and is still known for its delicate cuisine, etiquettes, manners and fashion, etc.

The word 'sauce' comes from the Latin word 'salsas' which means salted. Salt has always been the basic ingredient in most sauces. The function of a sauce is to add flavour to a dish that is compatible with the ingredients. The credit for inventing sauces goes to the French. There is a famous saying that 'England has three sauces, and 360 religions, while France has three religions and 360 sauces'. The French have contributed to the superiority of sauces, which is a claim disputed by none.

The early 18th century was evolutionary in sauce making as refined and aromatic preparations replaced the earlier heavy, hot or sweet-sour sauces. The hot sauces, which are more in number than others, are subdivided into brown sauces and white sauces. The basic brown sauce from which many others are derived include espagnole, demi-glace, and tomato sauces. The basic white sauces are béchamel and veloute. Cold sauces are usually based on mayonnaise or vinaigrette. The French chefs gradually widened their repertoire and adapted sauces from other countries, too. The diversity contributed to a variety of recipes based on a particular ingredient: fresh cream, garlic, fresh butter, mustard, shallots, red or white wine, onion, etc. Many chefs use mixtures based on curd, cheese and yogurt.

Essential Qualities of a Sauce

A sauce may be thick or thin, it may be strained or may contain visible ingredients, however, there are certain characteristics that are common to all varieties.

- A sauce should have a distinctive texture. A little creamy as for mayonnaise, frothy for sabayon, and glossy for brown demi-glace sauce.
- The sauce should have body.
- It should be flavoured subtly to the right degree, mild or pungent, to complement the dish. The colour of the sauce should set off the dish.
- Another important characteristic of the sauce is its consistency.
- Brown sauces should be translucent, while white butter based sauces should be semi-transparent.
- Some sauces may be light without any thickener added at all. Only white sauces and some sweet sauces are thick enough that they can coat the ingredients. A well-made sauce is never glutinous. Sauces that are served cold need to be thicker than hot ones.

Seasoning

The most important characteristic of a sauce is the right seasoning. A well-balanced sauce should have the right blend of ingredients without any single flavour dominating. Always take into account the food with which the sauce has to be served. It should never overwhelm the dish. It should highlight the flavour of the dish not mar it.

Equipment for Sauce Making

The right equipment to cook sauce is of utmost importance. You must always use a deep thick-bottomed saucepan to ensure proper distribution of heat to prevent the sauce from burning or curdling. The bain-marie is an essential accessory, as are a metal whisk and a spatula for scraping the residue from the base of the pan. To obtain a fine, smooth, and glossy sauce, you must work it through a fine sieve.

Cooking Techniques

Sauce making is an art. Its preparation requires a certain amount of skill. Techniques such as deglazing, reducing, thickening, preventing, skin, formation, emulsfying, thinning with milk, stock, or alcohol, enriching with cream and/or egg yolks, and the careful use of flavourings must be learnt.

There are four basic methods for making sauces:

- You can make them by mixing together cold ingredients. This is used for vinaigrettes. It is a simple method.
- **Emulsification:** This aims to disperse an insoluble solid in a liquid so that the mixture will remain stable for a certain period of time. This is used for cold sauces like the mayonnaise and tartar sauces, and hot ones like hollandaise or mousseline.
- Preparing a roux by heating butter and flour together and then adding milk or stock. This method is employed to make béchamel sauce.
- Cooking a stock of weal, chicken or fish, and adding a white or brown roux or some other mixture like a mirepoix, marinade, mushrooms, etc. These sauces may be thickened with butter, cornflour, or egg yolk, or flavoured with meat, chicken, or fish glazes.

Ingredients for Sauces

The choice of ingredients depends on the type of dish for which the sauce is intended. Most varied ingredients like herbs and spices are used. Particular sauces accompany some dishes. Mutton or fish with curry sauce, salt cod with garlic sauce, duck with orange sauce, beef with piquant sauce, etc. Ingredients that are commonly used are grated cheese, crushed tomatoes, anchovies, chopped ham, foie-gras, chopped truffles (a variety of mushrooms), shellfish, vinegar, fresh cream, red or white wine, alcohol, etc. The name of a sauce usually reveals its ingredients. Sometimes it is also named after its creator.

Whisking

To obtain a smooth consistency, it is necessary to whisk the sauce rapidly. This also makes it possible to cook the sauce over high heat without formation of lumps. It also prevents the sauce from burning at the bottom of the pan. Whisk the sauce in a figure of eight motion, working round the sides of the pan and across the middle. Pass the whisk in a circular motion around the base of the pan to ensure that the whisking is thorough.

REDUCING

This technique is important to make a good sauce. It cooks the sauce over high heat to evaporate the liquid to highlight the flavour and obtain the right consistency. This is essential for many of the classic French sauces, particularly those such as veloute, which is stock based. The longer a sauce is simmered, more subtle and mellow it tastes. You must leave the pan uncovered while cooking. This speeds evaporation and concentration of the sauce. The simmering should be done on gentle heat or the sauce may cloud. The time needed for simmering depends on the ingredients used. A veloute basic white sauce is simmered for 15-20 minutes. A good brown sauce requires an hour or more.

STRAINING

The mesh sieve is best for straining sauces to remove solid ingredients and to help emulsify liquid ingredients. The finer the mesh, the smoother and more glossy the sauce obtained. However, when a sauce is pureed, all the ingredients are left in the finished sauce. Set the sieve over a saucepan and ladle some sauce into the sieve. Pushing the ladle downward against the mesh in short strokes, press the solid ingredients to extract maximum liquid and flavour.

MOUNTING WITH BUTTER

Adding bits of unsalted butter to the sauce in the final stage of preparation gives it gloss and the fresh flavour of butter. This is known as mounting. For veloute and brown sauce, you need to remove the saucepan from the heat, add the cold, unsalted butter, shaking and swirling the pan to help the butter melt and mix well with the sauce. For a glaze base butter sauce, you need to remove the pan from heat and let it cool till it is just hot to touch. Then, add the butter, a little at a time, whisking thoroughly. Shift the pan on and off the heat so that the butter thickens and emulsifies making the sauce creamy.

THICKENING THE SAUCES

A variety of ingredients are added to thicken sauces. These are usually added in the final stages of cooking. Let us learn about some of them.

Arrowroot or potato starch: These are used to thicken the basic brown sauce and also sauces that are made from liquid in which food has been cooked. For every 500 ml of liquid, mix 2-3 tsp of arrowroot or potato starch with 2-3 tbsp of cold water or stock, whisk to mix and slowly pour the mixture into the cooking sauce, whisking the sauce all the while. Pour only as much of the starch mixture as is needed to make the sauce slightly thick. The sauce should be light and syrupy.

Cornflour: This is a popular thickening agent, especially in Chinese cuisine. It is also used for binding sweet sauces. It is added the same way as arrowroot or potato starch. It enables a sauce, which is stickier, to be cooked for a longer period without becoming thin.

Butter: Butter and flour are kneaded together to form a paste, which are added in small quantities to the sauce at the final stage of cooking. It improves the texture and flavour of the sauce making even a bland one rich. Add 30 gm kneaded butter-flour mixture to thicken 250 ml of sauce. Cream equal quantity of butter and flour with a fork or a whisk. Drop bits of this mixture into the boiling sauce, whisking rapidly. The butter melts uniformly mixing the flour throughout the liquid, thickening it at once. Continue adding the kneaded butter till you obtain the desired consistency.

Egg yolks and cream: Both of these ingredients enrich and thicken veloute and béchamel sauces. They are added just before serving as the sauce may curdle if heated for too long, or reheated. To thicken 500 ml sauce, use one egg yolk with one to two tbsp of cream. Whisk the egg yolk with cream in a bowl. Stir in a little hot sauce to cook this mixture partially. Bring the sauce to a boil and remove from heat. Whisk in the egg-cream mixture, return to heat to cook the sauce, whisking all the while till the sauce thickens slightly. If the sauce does not contain any flour, do not boil it. It will curdle. Serve immediately.

Coating Food with Sauce

To coat food, the sauce must be sufficiently thick to stay on the food but not so thick as to smother the colour of the food. To test the thickness of the sauce, dip a wooden spoon into the sauce and lift it out. If the sauce clings tightly to the spoon, it is thick enough. To coat food, fill a small ladle with sauce and gently pour it all over the food, repeat the action as often as you need to coat all the food completely.

Brown Sauces

The original version of Espagnole, or brown sauce, required two to three days to cook. At one time, it was the glory of the French kitchen. In the first stage, the roux was slowly browned to develop the flavour. To this was added brown stock, which requires a full day to prepare. Small pieces of veal, ham or fowl were added into the mixture. It was an elaborate affair. With constraints of time, modern cooks have substituted arrowroot or potato starch for the roux thickening to prepare. This makes a lighter sauce and the process is faster. Mounting with butter and adding flavourings like wine, onion, mustard or herbs develops the Espagnole and the basic brown sauce. Both are relatively easy to make. Let us learn about them.

Brown Sauce

Basic Brown Sauce:

Ingredients: 250 ml veal or beef stock; 2 tbsp arrowroot or potato starch; 2 tbsp cold water or Madeira; 1-2 tsp tomato puree (optional); salt and pepper.

Portions: To make 250 ml of sauce.

Method: To make brown sauce, follow this procedure:

1. Pour the stock in a saucepan and bring it to boil. Taste the stock to see if it lacks body. If it does, reduce it until concentrated.
2. Mix the arrowroot or potato starch with cold water or Madeira to make a paste.
3. Pour this paste slowly into the boiling stock, whisking rapidly. Add only enough paste to thicken the sauce to the desired consistency. If you are using tomato puree, whisk it into the stock mixture at this point. Add enough to colour the sauce.
4. Add salt and pepper to taste.
5. Strain the sauce. Check seasoning.

White Sauce

Gravy:

- Gravy is usually served with roasts. It is made from the meat juices, which congeal and caramelise in the bottom of the roasting pan.
  - Always serve dark brown gravy with red meats.
  - For white meat, use a golden colour sauce.
  - If you wish to add extra flavour to gravy from roasts, cook a quartered onion and carrot along with the bones, in the pan in which the meat has been roasted. Add a little stock or water. If the liquid is not dark enough, simmer it to reduce beyond a glaze till caramelised. This will add both colour and flavour.
- You can make the gravy thin or thick depending on the dish and your preference.
- For thin gravy, discard all the fat from the pan. Add stock, wine or water and boil, stirring to de-glaze the juices. Simmer the gravy to reduce it. Strain. Adjust seasoning.
- When making a thick gravy, leave about 30 gm of fat in the pan and stir in one to two tbsp of flour. Brown the flour, stirring it constantly so that it does not burn. Add stock, wine or water and simmer till the gravy thickens. You may add whipped cream or sour cream as a garnish.

White Sauces

These sauces are the most versatile. They can be used in a variety of ways. They can be used not only to coat food, but also to bind soufflés and fritters, and to thicken soups. They offer a neutral background to a wide range of flavourings, from wine to herbs and curry powder. White sauces are either milk-based, often called béchamel, or stock-based called veloute. Both use butter and flour roux. Fish, poultry or veal stock is a basic ingredient for veloute.

Béchamel:

Salt, pepper and nutmeg are flavourings of choice for a plain béchamel. However, the flavour can be greatly improved if the milk is first infused with onion, bay leaf and peppercorns. The most critical factor is the cooking of this sauce. The sauce should not taste of uncooked flour. When cooking, ensure that the milk does not scorch. The consistency depends on the dish it is intended for. You can make the sauce as thick or thin as you want to by varying the proportion of flour and butter to milk.

- Thin béchamel is used as a base for soups and some sauces.
- Thick béchamel is used for binding purposes.
- Medium béchamel is used for coating eggs, chicken, fish and vegetables.

Outlined below is the procedure to make béchamel.

Ingredients: 250 ml milk; 20 gms butter; 20 gms flour; a pinch of nutmeg powder; salt and white pepper.

Portions: To make 250 ml sauce.

Optional: A small onion, sliced; a small bay leaf; ½ tsp peppercorns.

Method:

1. Take a saucepan and pour the milk into it. Add the onion, bay leaf and peppercorns, if you are using them. Bring to a boil, switch off heat, and cover the pan and leave to infuse for 10 minutes.
2. Melt butter in a heavy saucepan. Put in the flour, whisking with a balloon whisk. Cook for 1 minute till the mixture is foamy. Strain the hot milk into this mixture, whisking constantly.
3. Return the saucepan to heat and bring the sauce to boil. Keep whisking constantly till the sauce begins to thicken. Add salt, pepper, nutmeg powder and simmer for 2 minutes. If you want to thin béchamel, use 15 gms each of butter and flour instead of the specified 20 gms. If a thicker sauce is desired, use 30 gms each of butter and flour.

Veloute

Veloute is a rich, creamy sauce. The quality of the stock used to make it must be good. Usually the stock is obtained when you poach fish or chicken for the main dish. If you are cooking a dish that does not require poaching, make the sauce separately.

Veloute, like béchamel, is based on a roux. They differ in their cooking method. You need a lot of liquid at the beginning of cooking so that the sauce is very thin to begin with. A gradual, gentle simmering for over an hour helps concentrate the flavour, break down starch grains in the flour, and give the sauce a creamy, velvety consistency.

You need to keep stirring the sauce to prevent it from sticking to the pan bottom. Add more stock and skim off the scum to clarify the sauce. Never hurry up the cooking of veloute. If not properly cooked, it will have a grainy texture. At the end of the cooking, if you find the sauce too thin, simmer it for a little longer to thicken it. To give a final touch, cream and few drops of lemon juice are added to enrich and improve the taste. Some cooks add egg yolks and cream too, to thicken the sauce. Veloute is a favourite choice when serving eggs, fish, poultry, veal and vegetables.

To make veloute, follow this procedure outlined below.

Ingredients: 375 ml chicken or fish stock; 20 gms butter; 20 gms flour; salt and white pepper.

Optional: 60 ml double cream; a few drops of lemon juice.

Method:

1. Pour the stock in a heavy-bottomed saucepan and let it boil. Take another heavy saucepan and melt butter in it. Put in the flour, whisk and cook for 1-2 minutes till the roux becomes creamy brown.
2. Remove the pan from heat and allow to cool slightly. Mix in three-quarters of the stock and whisk rapidly, but gently. Put back on heat and bring to boil. Keep whisking so that lumps do not form. Lower heat, add seasoning and simmer till the sauce begins to thicken. This simmering can take from 15 minutes to an hour.
3. While simmering, clarify the sauce after brief intervals. If you want a very fine veloute, simmer the sauce for several hours. At the

end of cooking, if the sauce is too thin, boil it over high flame to reduce the sauce to desired consistency.

4. If you are using cream to enrich the sauce, add it and boil the sauce again. Strain and add the lemon juice if you like it. Adjust seasoning.

CLARIFYING SAUCE

All stock based sauces need to be clarified. To do this, you need to gently simmer them for long. This brings the impurities to the top. They can be skimmed off with the ladle. The texture of the finished sauce should be almost translucent. To do a good clarifying job, it is necessary to remove the pan from heat at short intervals, add three or four tbsp of cold stock or water and put back on heat to simmer. The impurities will come to the surface. These must be skimmed off. Take care to remove as little of the sauce as possible with the impurities or else you will be wasting some of the sauce.

MAYONNAISE

Mayonnaise

This is the most popular sauce to serve with fried or grilled fish, chicken or hard-boiled eggs, fritters, salads, and even with French fries. It is a cold emulsified sauce based on egg yolks. Careful handling is recommended or the sauce will separate. Keep the ingredients at room temperature or slightly warm. A cold bowl or cold eggs straight from the refrigerator will prevent the sauce from thickening. The emulsion is prepared by adding the oil, drop by drop, to the egg yolk mixture. Once the emulsion has been prepared, the rest of the oil can be added in a stream.

Mayonnaise should be thick enough to form peaks so that it can be used to bind salads such as potatoes, or vegetables, and to serve with cold food. If you want to coat food with mayonnaise, add one or two tbsp of warm water to make it thinner. Flavours depend on the oil used. It is delicate if made with vegetable oil, nutty with walnut or hazelnut oil, and rich if made with virgin olive oil. Vinegar is the common flavouring, the quantity depending on choice. Lemon juice is a popular alternative. To make mayonnaise, follow this simple procedure.

Ingredients: 2 egg yolks; salt and white pepper; 4 tbsp white wine vinegar or 1 to 1½ tbsp lemon juice; 1 tsp Dijon mustard (optional, though it aids the emulsion and enrich the flavour); 300 ml cooking refined oil or olive oil.

Portions: To make 375 ml mayonnaise.

Method:

1. Take a small mixing bowl. Put in the egg yolks, salt and pepper, half the vinegar or lemon juice, the mustard, if you are using it. Set the bowl on a piece of cloth to prevent it shifting on the slippery kitchen counter. Using a balloon whisk, beat the ingredients until thick.
2. Add the oil, drop by drop, whisking constantly. After adding 2 tbsp oil, the mixture should be quite thick. Add rest of the oil in a slow stream. Keep whisking constantly. Mix in the remaining vinegar or lemon juice, some more mustard, salt and pepper. Whisk and taste for seasoning.

Note: If you are using a food processor, follow the original recipe. Process the egg yolks, salt and pepper, vinegar or lemon juice, mustard and 3 tbsp of oil in a blender for 10 seconds at a low speed. With the machine running, pour the remaining oil into the blender in a slow stream till the mixture emulsifies.

TIPS

If ever your mayonnaise sauce curdles and oil separates, do not get panicky, instead beat one additional yolk and slowly beat in the spoilt mayonnaise till creamy once again. Store under refrigeration and use it as and when required. Mayonnaise can be stored for more than a month.

TOMATO SAUCE

Tomato Sauce

Tomato sauce is the most versatile and widely used sauce. It is a perfect companion to several snacks, starters and main dishes. The quality of the sauce depends on the ripeness of the fruit. Deep red, vine-ripened tomatoes give the best results. If the tomatoes are pallid, you could add one or two tbsp of tomato puree to add colour and flavour, or use canned tomatoes. The flavour of the sauce depends on the length of cooking. Light cooking will give you a fragrant sauce. Prolonged simmering gives it a dark, full-bodied flavour. Cooked sauces can be stored in the refrigerator up to 3 days. Fresh ones, in which the fruit has been left raw, should be served at once. The commercial variety available in bottles is good, but the flavour of the homemade one is unique.

Uncooked tomato sauce: These are best served at once because tomatoes, like all other fruits, are most fragrant when freshly cut. These are served with the Italian pasta, soups, Mexican dishes, fish and vegetable dishes.

Cooked tomato sauces: The universal flavouring is onion and herbs though you may use a little of ginger and garlic along with a few chillies if you want the sauce to be a little spicy and pungent. The fat used depends on the country of origin, though olive oil and butter are fairly common. The liquid may be stock or wine. They are used to enrich other sauces and soups, served with all kinds of dishes ranging from snacks and starters to main dishes and pasta and pizza.

Barbeque sauce

A barbeque sauce is primarily intended for brushing meats, poultry and fish to flavour and moisten them during dry cooking. The commercial variety is tomato based, highly spiced and comes in bottles. The homemade one is more versatile.

- A soy sauce based mixture with a pinch of sugar is served with ham and pork.
- Yogurt is the natural partner for mutton and lamb.
- Olive oil and lemon enhance the taste of a fish dish.
- Strong and pungent flavours like mustard, chilli and lemon are the right ingredients for barbeque sauce.
- Sweet-sour mixtures are popular because the sugar helps crust formation on the cooking food.
- The sauce should be thick enough to stay on the food and not drip away.
- While barbequing food, take care to control the heat or the sauce will scorch. This sauce can be refrigerated for a week.

Nut sauces

Fruits and nuts are either used directly as thickeners or by infusing them to make nut milk. No matter how finely nuts are chopped, they always lend a grainy texture to the sauce. The best way is to puree them in a food processor, or pound them in a mortar with a pestle.

- Almond and coconut sauces are popular in our country.
- Walnut sauces are a favourite in South-east Asia, parts of the United States and Africa. You can refrigerate these for a week.

Savoury sauce

For a savoury sauce, the main ingredients are fruit pulps and sweeteners. The fruits add a distinctive character to the sauce. It is more of a condiment than a sauce. It is usually thicker than coating consistency. It is served cold.

Table sauces

Most of the table sauces are commercially manufactured sauces, since these are unique preparations, almost impossible to imitate at home except tomato sauce or chilli garlic, etc. The Worcestershire sauce, ketchup, soy sauce and other hot sauces and relishes belong to this genre.

Worcestershire Sauce:

Having originated in England, it is now manufactured in the United States, too. The traditional Worcestershire sauce is dark brown in colour, thin and pungent, with visible sediment. It is soy and vinegar based but also contains mushroom ketchup, walnut ketchup, tamarind, sherry, brandy, vinegar, pork liver, cayenne pepper, black pepper, mace, coriander, anchovies, garlic, shallot and caramel. It is used as a condiment and also in cooking to add piquancy to meat, fish, sauces and soups.

Ketchup:

We commonly associate the name with any tomato sauce made with vinegar. The word may actually have a Malay origin – Ketjap, the brine in which fish is pickled. In China, Japan and the countries of the Far East, ketchups based on fish or shellfish are still popular. The rest of the world has taken to using fruits, vegetables, nuts and mushrooms. All ketchups contain salt, vinegar, sugar and spices. Tomato ketchup is quite simple to make at home. The commercial variety has a better flavour. It resembles tomato sauce but is highly seasoned and often spicy with a touch of clove, cinnamon, allspice and cayenne pepper.

Soy Sauce:

It is the most popular ingredient for Chinese cuisine and food of the Far East. Soy sauce is deeply dark brown, thin and salty. It is widely used all over the world. It is made from fermented cooked soybeans and wheat and is best bought in a bottle. The taste depends on the quality of soybeans and wheat. Different varieties of Chinese, Japanese and Indonesian soy sauces have subtly different effects. The light Japanese soy is saltier than the dark. Being thin and clear, it does not darken marinades. Soy sauce can be used as a marinade, in soups and in some cooked dishes as garnishing.

Hot sauces:

The principle ingredient is chilli or red hot pepper. Some hot sauces are made from a thick puree of chillies, while others are thinner, the result of long fermentation. The best-known thin chilli sauce is the American Tabasco available in small, thin bottles. To make it, fresh ground chillies are salted and left to mature for as long as three years. The liquid is then extracted and mixed with distilled vinegar. They are used for seasoning cooked dishes, soups and stews, as well as in dips. The thick variety, which often includes garlic, is used in cooking curries and stews.

Vinaigrette Dressing

The principle ingredients of vinaigrette dressing are oil, vinegar, Dijon mustard, salt and pepper. The flavour depends on the careful balance of its ingredients. The best proportion is three parts of oil to one part vinegar. If you use lemon juice instead of vinegar, use one part lemon to four or five parts of oil. The amount of mustard depends on its piquancy. One tsp for every four tbsp of dressing is recommended. Chopped herbs mixed at the end of the preparation improve vinaigrette, adding flavour to the salad. Chopped shallots are suitable for vinaigrette served with meat and root vegetables. Garlic should be used sparingly. A cut clove rubbed on the inside of the mixing bowl adds enough flavour. You can store it for a week at room temperature. Just whisk it before use.

To make vinaigrette dressing, follow this simple procedure.

Ingredients: 2 tbsp vinegar or 1½ tbsp lemon juice; salt and pepper; 2 tsp Dijon mustard (optional); 6 tbsp oil.

Portions: To make 125 ml dressing.

Method:

1. Whisk the vinegar or lemon juice, salt, pepper and mustard if you are using it, in a mixing bowl.
2. Gradually pour in the oil in a steady stream, whisking all the while till the vinaigrette is blended and thickened. Adjust seasoning.

TIPS

Health conscious people can reduce the quantity of oil to half, while adding this dressing to the salads. Another way of making this dressing is to add all the ingredients in a bottle with a cap and shake it vigorously. Chill it before use. It can be stored under refrigeration for almost a fortnight.

Dessert Sauces

Dessert sauces may be hot or cold, are served separately or poured over the desserts. Many of these sauces are based on fruits in the form of a puree or jelly, and may be flavoured with vanilla or alcohol. Custard, flavoured or not, is a popular dessert sauce, usually served with puddings, cakes and fruit pies, etc. Chocolate sauces are favourite with ice creams.

Sweet Fruit Sauces:

These are generally thin and used to coat as well as accompany desserts. Many are based on jam or jelly, while others are made from simple fruit puree, strained and sweetened to taste. A little lemon juice or fruit liqueur improves the flavour. Soft fruits like berries and kiwi make good sauces. Peach sauce discolours quickly and should be served at once.

Custard:

Custard Sauce

Custard is a combination of egg yolks and milk. Sometimes a little cornflour / custard powder is also added to thicken consistency of custard sauce. The ideal proportion is 5 egg yolks for 500 ml milk. More yolks may be added for richness. When you use cornflour, you will need fewer egg yolks. This way the milk is less likely to curdle. Citrus fruits like oranges will curdle the milk. The egg yolks and sugar are whisked till thick, then mixed with milk and stirred over low heat with a wooden spoon or spatula, to cook to a creamy consistency. The secret is gentle cooking over low flame.

TIPS

In this chapter though you have been introduced to a number of popular sauces used in continental food, yet practically, white sauce / béchamel sauce or brown sauce / brown gravy are most commonly used to cook good day-to-day or party meals. Mayonnaise and Vinaigrette dressings can again be used in daily cooking and for other social get-togethers. Dessert sauces, no doubt lend a special treat to the puddings and pies, etc.

Practical things to do

1. Vanilla Custard

Utensils Used: A heavy-bottomed saucepan; a balloon whisk; a wooden spatula or spoon; a mixing bowl.

Portion: To make 500 ml sauce.

Ingredients: 500 ml milk, a few drops vanilla essence, 5 egg yolks, 60 gms sugar.

Follow this procedure to make custard:

1. Heat milk in the saucepan.
2. In a mixing bowl, whisk together the egg yolks and sugar till thick and light. Stir in the hot milk.
3. Return the pan with the custard to heat. Cook gently on low heat, stirring constantly, till the custard thickens slightly and starts coating back of the wooden spoon. Add vanilla essence and mix well. Do not overcook or boil the custard. It will curdle.

Note: A variety of ready-to-cook custard powders are available in the market. However, the homemade one is creamier.

TIPS

- If you run out of tomatoes when cooking, add tomato soup powder to the curry. It will taste just as good.
- Roast groundnuts and sesame seeds together and powder them. The more powder helps thicken gravies.

Expert cook suggests ...

1. When making mayonnaise, add vinegar before adding oil to the egg yolks. This ensures better mixing. It will also require less beating.
2. To peel tomatoes easily, roll them on a hot 'tawa' for 3 to 4 minutes instead of dipping them in hot water. This method of peeling tomatoes is ideal if you want to make tomato sauce.
3. When making mint sauce, chop the mint along with the sugar. It helps bring out the flavour.
4. Add leftover canned pineapple syrup to the custard. It will taste great.

COOKING METHOD # 7

COOKING THE NATURAL WAY

One may wonder what we mean by cooking the natural way. Much of the cooking depends upon use of water, steam, heat, fats and other additives. However, there are times when all we need to prepare a food item is by exposing it to the goodness of bright sunshine. Many items are made this way. Vegetables and food products are dried; *papad, vadis,* dried fruits and other products are exposed to sunshine. Many preserves and pickles do not mature well unless exposed to bright sunshine. It is God's / nature's way to help you become a good cook. Use it to the best advantage.

Lemon Squash   Dry raw Mango   Pickle being matured under sun

Given the basis, cooking in the Hindu concept can occur even without the use of fire. Indian example of this is the pickling of vegetables or unripe fruit using the heat of the sun, or the dehydration of vegetables for preservation by sun-drying.

Sun-dried *Sabudana Papad*

Mirch

According to Hindu food taxonomy, the purpose of all cooking is to convert potentially edible material into palatable form, '*ahara*'. In the Hindu ethos there is the added requirement that it should be both auspicious and ritually pure for those who are to eat it.

The legendary king, Nala, is believed to have excelled in cooking without fire and water. This is termed as *Nala-paka*. It is still cooked in the Jagannath temple in Puri, district of Orissa, writes Dr. K. T. Achaya in his book '*Indian Food – A Historical Companion*'.

■ ■

DAY 20

Pickles, Chutneys and Raitas

In an Indian menu, accompaniments are served with every meal; they not only provide pungent taste but also provide additional nutrients and make the meal attractive. A variety of pickles, chutneys and raitas are a part of our main meals. Some chutneys are also served with teatime snacks. For example, samosas, pakoras and other fried snacks are never served without fresh green chutney or sweet-n-sour tamarind chutney. Mostly *mathies* are enjoyed with mango *masala* pickle.

Fresh Lemon Pickle

Pickles and chutneys can be spicy, sweet, tart, hot, mild or aromatic. They are best served with plain food such as rice and bread, or with lightly spiced dishes to balance the taste. They do not compete with the flavour of the dish they accompany. There is a great variety of ingredients which are used to make these accompaniments. Some last for months and get better after maturing, while others have a shelf life of several days if stored in a cool place; and some are eaten straightaway. For example, chutneys are made from fresh herbs such as coriander and mint leaves, fresh coconut and green chillies, etc., and are eaten immediately. Those cooked with oil, vinegar, sugar and spices can be kept longer.

Pickles are marinated, rather than cooked, though there are a few that are cooked as well. Fruit, vegetables, partially cooked fish and even meats are marinated and left to mature for long periods in spiced oils. In Indian homes, dozens of different pickles are made. Traditionally they are left outside in the sun in earthenwares or glass jars covered with a muslin cloth to mature by day and stored in a cool place at night. Both pickles and chutneys are made and available commercially. However, they lack the taste and flavour of the homemade ones.

Raitas are yogurt based and provide a cooling contrast to a hot spicy meal, especially during the summer months. Raitas can be made from a variety of vegetables, fruits and even gram flour droplets called *boondi* (deep-fried in oil). Cucumber, tomatoes, carrots, onions; grated and steamed bottle-gourd, boiled potatoes, bananas, grapes and pineapples are commonly used to make raitas. A garnish of coarsely ground roasted cumin seeds, a pinch of red chilli powder, *chaat masala*, rock black salt and fresh coriander and mint leaves add flavour to the raitas. They are a favourite accompaniment to parathas, *pulaos* and biryanis, etc.

Stuffed Red Chillies

Mangoes and oranges also make excellent raitas. Deep-fried brinjal and ladyfinger pieces are also added to beaten and seasoned curds and finally raita is tempered with cumin and asafoetida just before serving.

PICKLES (*ACHAAR*)

A strongly spiced pickle is usually saffron coloured and relished throughout India, Indonesia and West Indies. The pickles were taken to Europe by the English people in the 18th century, but with a difference, whereas in India, both oil and vinegar are used as the pickling medium, the Western pickles are mostly vinegar-based.

In India, popularly pickles or *'achaar'* are made from unripe green mangoes, lemons, jackfruit, green and red chillies, cauliflower, potatoes, carrots, turnips, radish, brinjal, gourds, cucumber or a mixture of fruits and vegetables. Almost anything, including meats, fish and eggs can be pickled. Meats and seafood pickles are also commonly made here.

Onion Pickle

Exotic pickles may be made from palm hearts, olives, limes, dates, rose petals, ginger, garlic, and bamboo sprouts. Onions, gourds, cauliflower and capers too can be used in the same way.

Some pickles are very sharp flavoured and piquant; others are milder and even sweet. The summer season in India is quite unbearable, but it has a saving grace – the mango is in season. Everyone looks forward to the yearly mango crop. Housewives get busy blending the myriad spices needed for a whole year's supply of mango pickles, as well as pickles and preserves made from other fruits and vegetables.

In India, the spices commonly used for pickling are commercially available mixed in the right proportion and packed in small packets. Many prefer to make their own mixture. Fennel seeds, mustard, fenugreek, ajwain, carom seeds, sesame seeds and salt are the basic spices. There are variations in recipes of different regions. The oil of choice is mustard oil, sesame oil, cooking oil and olive oil. This again is a matter of preference.

The pickles are often made with the spices toasted and coarsely ground. Sweet pickles are made with jaggery as it gives a mild sweetness, a dark colour and good texture.

The pickles of Western variety use vinegar as a pickling medium. They are served with cold meats, cheese, curries, etc., with drinks, and in mixed appetizers. The vegetables used for pickling include cauliflower, cucumber, cabbage, marrow and courgettes, mushrooms, small onions, unripe tomatoes, etc. They are sliced if necessary and soaked in brine (salt and water mixture) or in cold water. They are then rinsed, put into glass jars, and covered with spiced vinegar. They can also be coated in vinegar with spices. Fruits like plums, cherries, apples, pears, peaches, etc., are cut into small pieces and usually cooked for a short time so that they will soak up the vinegar. Eggs and walnuts can also be pickled. The best salt to use is coarse sea salt. This gives the best flavour.

The Western people use malt, wine, cider, or spirit vinegars. Spices enhance the flavour and also act as preservatives. The classic formula is as follows:

To 1 litre vinegar, add a 2 inch stick of cinnamon, 1 tsp cloves, 2 tbsp fennel seeds, 1 tsp black pepper, 1 tsp mustard seeds, and 2 or 3 bay leaves. Bring the mixture to boil and then steep for 3 days. The vinegar is then strained and used either cold (for vegetables, which should remain crisp) or hot (for fruit, which should be a little softer).

Mixed pickles may combine a number of vegetables, such as onions, cabbage, cucumber, green beans, carrots, and green peppers. Some vegetables and fruits are pickled on their own; for example, beetroot with dill, red cabbage with white wine vinegar, peppers with thyme and bay leaf, lime with pepper, and peaches with spices and lemon rind. Indian pickles use almost the same spices. The process of heating the vinegar with aromatic spices is also a common feature in Gujarati pickles except that it is not vinegar but oil, which is heated with bay leaves and aromatic spices.

There are varieties of pickles, which cannot be preserved, but are mixed with spices, left to marinate for a day or two and consumed within a few days. Such pickles are made with potatoes, cauliflower, turnips and carrots. Small onions and green chillies are often immersed in vinegar and served as ready-to-eat pickles, as do medium thick, long strips of radish soaked in vinegar.

Pickles add special flavour to any meal. They are easy to make if you know how. A mixed vegetable pickle made from turnips, carrots, peas and cauliflower is popular in North India, especially during winters. Let us see how it is prepared.

Mixed Vegetable Pickle

Ingredients:

500 gms each of turnips, cauliflower and young carrots; 250 gms shelled peas; 2 pods garlic; 2 inch piece ginger; 200 gms onions; 2 tbsp chilli powder, 1½ tsp ground mustard seeds;

1½ tsp garam masala; ¾ tsp turmeric powder, salt to taste; 500 ml mustard oil, 250 ml vinegar; 1½ kg jaggery.

Method:

Mixed Pickle

1. Slice turnips into ¼ inch discs. Quarter carrots lengthwise and cut cauliflower into 2 inch pieces. Boil water in a large saucepan, add all the vegetables and cook for 5 minutes to soften.
2. Drain off the water and spread the vegetables on a clean towel to dry. Wipe off excess water.
3. Grind ginger, garlic and onions together to a paste. Heat the oil and fry the paste. Add the remaining spices and fry till the oil floats to the top.
4. Cool the fried *masala* and add the vegetables. Shake vessel to mix well. Put in a large jar and keep in the sun for 2-3 days till vegetables turn a little sour. Shake the jar well everyday.
5. After 2-3 days, heat vinegar with jaggery and boil. Cool and add to the vegetables. Place jar in the sun for another 2 days till well blended and tender. Preserve in airtight jars.

Chilli Pickle

Ingredients:

250 gms green chillies; 1 tsp turmeric powder; 1 tsp fenugreek powder; 2 tsp mustard seeds; 2 tsp cumin seeds; 6 garlic cloves; 1 small piece ginger; 2 cups vinegar; 1½ cup mustard or sesame oil; 3 tsp sugar; 60 gms salt.

Method:

Spicy Green Chillies

1. Wash and slit the chillies. Add salt and place in a covered jar for an hour.
2. Grind all the spices with a little vinegar.
3. Fry the ground spices in oil till the oil surfaces. Remove the chillies from the salt water. Add to the fried spices and fry for a few minutes.
4. Add the remaining vinegar, sugar and salt to taste. Simmer for 5-10 minutes.
5. Cool and store in sterilised bottles.

Pickles in different regions of the country have different flavours, unique to their food habits. This is largely governed by the kind of crops grown. Though most of the spices used for pickling are universally common, pickles from different regions may have a variation in the method of pickling. There may be a few spices added or substituted for others. We are now going to show you how to make mango pickles in the South Indian and the North Indian way.

South Indian Mango Pickle

Ingredients:

6 green mangoes; ½ cup oil; ½ cup salt; 12 green chillies; ½ tsp chilli powder, 1 tbsp sugar (optional).

South Indian mango Pickle

Dry roast and powder:

1 tbsp sesame seeds; a pinch of asafoetida; ½ tsp fenugreek seeds.

Seasoning:

½ tsp turmeric powder; ½ tsp mustard seeds; 1 sprig curry leaves.

Method:

1. Clean, wash and peel the mangoes. Cut into thin slices.
2. Chop the chillies.
3. Season the mustard and curry leaves in hot oil. Add the chopped chillies and mango slices, and fry on low heat until the mangoes turn soft. Add chilli powder, turmeric and salt, and continue to fry until the oil surfaces. At this stage, you may add a tbsp of sugar if the mangoes are too sour. Remove from heat.
4. Add the mustard and powdered spices, and mix well. Cool and bottle.

North Indian Mango Pickle

Ingredients:

1 kg green mangoes; 2 tsp turmeric powder; 60 gms salt; 2 cups mustard oil; 1/2 cup *kabuli chana*.

Roast separately and grind:

½ tbsp fenugreek seeds; 1 tbsp onion seeds; 2 tbsp mustard seeds; 2 tbsp aniseed; a pinch of asafoetida; 30 dried red chillies.

North Indian Mango Pickle

Method:

1. Wash, wipe and dry the mangoes. Cut into eight pieces each. Ask the green-grocer to cut it for you. They have sharp knives/cutters for this purpose. Apply salt and turmeric powder to the mango pieces. Add *chanas*. Put in a jar and leave in the sun for a couple of hours each day for 2-3 days, or until pieces look quite dry. Always cover the jar with a muslin cloth. Remove the pieces and throw away the salt water.
2. Powder the lightly roasted and pounded spices coarsely. Add this coarse powder to the mangoes. Add a little more salt and mix well.
3. In a *kadhai*, bring the oil to a boil, cool and pour over the mango mixture. Mix well and store in clean sterilised bottles. If you are using jaggery, add it to the oil when it is boiling.

South Indian Lemon Pickle

Ingredients:

6 large lemons; 6 tsp chilli powder; ½ tsp turmeric powder; 2 tsp salt; 1 tsp fenugreek seeds; a pinch of asafoetida; 2 tbsp oil; 1 tsp mustard seeds.

South Indian Lemon Pickle

Method:

1. Boil enough water to cover the lemons when immersed. When the water is boiling, add the turmeric powder and the lemons. Boil for two minutes. Remove from fire, cover vessel, and set aside for a few minutes.
2. When the lemons have cooled, remove from water and pat dry with a cloth. Cut each into 8 pieces. Add the salt and mix.
3. Fry the fenugreek and asafoetida in one tsp of oil in a *kadhai*. Remove, powder and set aside.
4. Cover the lemon pieces with the chilli powder. Season the mustard seeds in oil, cool and pour this over the lemon pieces. Add the powdered fenugreek and asafoetida and mix thoroughly. Bottle it.

North Indian Lemon Pickle

Ingredients:

25 lemons (*nimbu*); 10 cloves garlic (optional); 25 dried red chillies; 1 tbsp onion seeds; 1 tbsp cumin seeds; 2 tbsp mustard seeds; 1 tsp fenugreek seeds; ½ tbsp turmeric powder, 1½ cups oil; 6 tbsp salt.

Khatta Nimbu Pickle

Method:

1. Extract the juice from 10 lemons, add a pinch of salt and set aside.
2. Boil some water. Add a pinch of turmeric powder, add the rest of the lemons, and boil for 2 minutes. Remove the lemons from water, wipe dry with a clean cloth and allow to cool.
3. Dry roast the mustard, fenugreek, onion and cumin seeds. Roast the chillies with a tsp of oil. Pound all these along with the garlic into a rough powder and set aside.
4. Cut the lemons into fours. Mix the spice powder with some oil and add the salt, making it into soft dough. Stuff the lemons with this mixture and put them in a glass jar. If any spice powder is left over, sprinkle this over the lemons.
5. Heat and cool the oil. Pour into the jar along with the lemon juice. Cover the mouth of the jar with a muslin cloth and let the lemons soak for 3-4 days after which they should be ready to use. Here the lemons are cut into 4 pieces and not kept whole for the practical purpose.

Prawns Pickle

Prawn Pickle

Ingredients:

½ kg shelled prawns; 2 pods garlic; 4 onions; 12 dry red chillies; 1 tsp turmeric powder; ½ tsp peppercorns; 1 cup gingelly oil; 1 cup vinegar; 2 inch piece ginger; ½ tsp mustard seeds; ½ tsp cumin seeds; 10 green chillies; 1 sprig curry leaves; 1 tbsp sugar; salt to taste.

Method:

1. Grind the onions, red chillies, pepper, and 4 cloves garlic to a smooth paste.
2. In a saucepan, put in the prawns, the *masala* paste, salt and 1 cup water. Boil over low heat. Simmer till water evaporates. Remove from heat.
3. Heat half the oil and fry the cooked prawns till well browned. Remove from oil and set aside.
4. Grind with 2 tbsp of vinegar, 1½ inch piece of ginger, 12 cloves garlic, mustard seeds, turmeric powder and cumin seeds to a paste. Slice the remaining ginger, garlic and green chillies.
5. Add remaining oil to the oil in which the prawns were fried. Fry the sliced ingredients in this. Add curry leaves and ground paste and fry stirring constantly.
6. Pour in the vinegar, season with salt and bring to boil. Add fried prawns and sugar, and simmer. Keep stirring till the oil floats to the top. Cool and bottle in airtight jars.

Mutton Pickle

Ingredients:

1½ kg mutton; ½ kg onions; 350 gms ginger; 1 pod garlic; ¾ cups mustard oil; ¾ cups vinegar; 1 tbsp chilli powder; 2 tbsp mango powder (*amchur*); 2 tsp cumin seeds; 12 green cardamoms; 15 cloves; ¼ tsp nutmeg powder; 4 tbsp salt.

Method:

1. Cut the meat into 1½ inch pieces and wash well. Put in a large saucepan to simmer without adding any water, till all the liquid dries up. Keep aside.
2. Grind onion, garlic and ginger to paste.
3. Heat oil and fry the onion paste till brown. Add meat pieces, mix well and fry. Add ½ cup vinegar, all the remaining spices and cook for 5 minutes, stirring constantly.

Mutton Pickle

4. Remove from heat. Pour in the remaining vinegar and cool. Put in airtight jars and keep for a week before use.

Chutneys

There are three varieties of chutneys. First, those that can be preserved for a long period. Second, those that can be preserved only for a few days. The third variety includes fresh chutneys made from fresh coriander, coconut, mint leaves with slices of raw mangoes or a squeeze of lemon juice, green chillies, a little garlic and ginger, salt, a little sugar, and a little onion, all ground into a fine paste. This is the most popular green chutney or the '*hari chatni*' of North India, which accompanies all barbequed food and fried snacks.

Those made to be preserved for a longer period, are either hot and sweet, or sweet and sour. These are made from fruits or vegetables or a mixture of the two, cooked with vinegar, sugar and spices and has the consistency of a jam. Some chutneys are reduced to a puree. Others retain recognisable pieces of their ingredients. All are characterised by a syrupy and sometimes highly spiced juice that coats the ingredients. Cooked for about two hours, chutneys are put in glass jars and kept for a long time like jam. They enliven an insipid meal. They can also be used as a delicious sandwich spread. Chutneys, sold in jars under various trade names,

Coconut Chutney

may contain exotic fruits like mango, coconut, pineapple, tamarind pulp, or temperate ones like aborigine, tomato, onion, melon, grapes, cherries, apples, etc.

If you visit a South Indian restaurant, you will recollect that there are three or four kinds of chutneys that are served with food. The coconut chutney enjoys a place of prominence. Its presence at every south Indian meal is imperative. This chutney is freshly ground with the tender flesh of the coconut. In the lesson on 'South Indian Dishes' you have already learnt how this famous chutney is made.

Another favourite chutney is made from tomatoes and is very popular amongst the Bengalis. No festive meal is complete without it.

Tomato Chutney

Ingredients: 1½ kg large ripe tomatoes; 2 tsp raisins; 8 green cardamoms; 6 tbsp sugar; 1½ tsp salt; ½ cup vinegar; 1 tsp red chilli powder; 2 bay leaves. Chop finely: 6 cloves garlic; 1 inch piece ginger; 1 small onion.

Tomato Chutney

Method:

1. Drop the tomatoes in boiling water, cover and let stand for 2 minutes. Drain, peel and chop fine.
2. Mix chopped garlic, ginger, tomatoes and onion; cook in a little oil and keep stirring till soft.
3. Add vinegar, sugar, raisins, ground cardamoms, salt, chilli powder and bay leaves. Keep stirring till the chutney thickens.
4. Remove from heat and cool. Discard the bay leaves and store the chutney in a sterilised bottle. It will keep well for a week in the refrigerator.

Note: This savoury chutney is particularly loved by children and is one of the favourite chutneys eaten in Bengal. No festive meal is complete without it.

Raitas

Raita, a traditional Indian cold dish is *dahi*/curd/yogurt based, where *dahi* is beaten and seasoned; and chopped fruits or semi cooked grated vegetables are added to it. Sometimes while garnishing it is tempered too. Raita and *Dahi* are Hindi words. Curd or curds is of English origin.

It is also believed that Yogurt, both the product and the word, is of Turkish origin. However, the product is also traditional in India, Arabic countries, Central Asia, and countries of the former Ottoman Empire, whose people attribute their health and longevity to it.

Yogurt is slightly laxative, easily digested and replenishes the intestinal flora. Natural yogurt contains only 37-46 calories per 100 gms, 0.2-1.5 percent fat (according to the milk used), 3.5 percent protein, mineral salts like calcium and phosphorus, and vitamins.

Boondi Raita

The tropical climate in India necessitates the use of coolers, especially during the hot summers. Even in winters their popularity diminishes only slightly. The ideal coolers are the raitas prepared from well-beaten yogurt to which a variety of fruits, vegetables and even fried ingredients are added. The mixture is garnished with roasted and coarsely powdered cumin seeds, a pinch of chilli powder and *chaat masala*. These days readymade raita *masala* is also available in packets. A sprinkling of fresh coriander or mint leaves garnishes the dish, which is chilled before being served with the meal. Not only is raita a perfect companion to a hot and spicy meal, it is also an ideal accompaniment to all kinds of biryanis with salad, and to a variety of stuffed parathas. No North Indian menu is complete without raita.

Raita is prepared with a variety of ingredients and herb garnishing. These ingredients include fruits like apples, pineapples, grapes, bananas, mangoes and guavas, or vegetables like cucumber, tomatoes, onions, radish and carrots. Sometimes gram flour droplets deep-fried in oil (*boondi*) is used.

To make '*boondi* raita', it is practical to buy a packet of *boondi* from the nearest sweet shop or from your grocery store. You can empty the packet in a plastic container with a tight lid and store for a fortnight. Beyond this period, the *boondi* turns rancid. When you want to make the raita, just soak a handful of *boondi* per cup yogurt being used, in tepid water. Beat the curd creamy with a fork or a beater. Add a little salt. If the yogurt is tart, add a little sugar as well and 2-3 tbsp of milk. This will take away the tartness. Blend well. Remove the *boondi* from the water and squeeze out the excess liquid. Add to the beaten curd and garnish with coarsely ground cumin seeds, a pinch of chilli powder and chopped fresh coriander or mint leaves.

When using fruits like apples, pineapples, banana and mangoes, always peel them and dice into tiny pieces. Cucumber and carrots are peeled and chopped into tiny bits or grated into the beaten curd. Onions and tomatoes are finely chopped. Boiled and diced potatoes also make a fine raita.

Let us learn how to make unique raita with mangoes.

Ripe Mango Raita

Ripe Mango Raita

Ingredients:
3 ripe mangoes; 1½ cup curds; ¼ coconut; ½ tsp mustard seeds; 4 green chillies; 1 small onion; ½ tbsp ghee; salt and sugar to taste.

Method:

1. Peel and chop mangoes into small cubes. Beat curds/yogurt to a creamy consistency. Add salt and sugar. Grind the coconut and chillies to a paste and add to the beaten curd.
2. Add the mango cubes to the curd mixture and mix well.
3. Heat ghee in a saucepan and crackle mustard seeds in it. Add to this the curd mango mixture and remove from heat. Cool and then chill before serving. This is a South Indian recipe. The spicy and sweet flavours blend well to give a unique taste.

Mango Raita is also made in the following way:

Beat 2 cup thick curds with ½ cup milk, 3 tbsp sugar, 2 tsp levelled salt and 1 tsp levelled white pepper; add 2 to 3 chopped ripe mangoes to it; chill and serve it cold garnished with 1 tsp green cardamom powder and 2 tbsp chopped cashew nuts.

Tempered Brinjal Raita

Ingredients: 2 cups lightly beaten yogurt; 1 cup thinly sliced and deep-fried brinjal pieces, 2 green chillies, de-seeded and chopped; salt and pepper to taste; 1 tsp cooking oil; ½ tsp mustard seeds; a few curry leaves; ¼ tsp asafoetida; 1 tbsp chopped fresh coriander.

Method:

Brinjal Raita

1. Put yogurt in a bowl, add fried brinjal, salt, pepper and chopped green chillies to it. Mix well and chill.
2. Heat oil in a tempering ladle, crackle mustard seeds in it; add asafoetida and curry leaves; and fry for 2 seconds.
3. Pour this tempering over the yogurt mixture just before serving.
4. Garnish it with chopped coriander and serve it cold.

STORING PICKLES AND CHUTNEYS

All pickles and chutneys, except those that are freshly consumed, should be kept in glass jars with tight fitted lids. These jars should be of good quality, as they have to be sterilised. Cheap quality jars will crack due to the heat.

Wash the jars well with plain water and detergent. Rinse thoroughly. Pour in boiling water and invert them on a rack and let them stand for 30 minutes or so. Dry the jars inside and out with a piece of clean cotton cloth and then store the pickles or chutneys in them.

Before screwing on the lid you could melt some paraffin wax in a pan and pour over the pickles and chutneys on top (it will harden at once forming a scaling film of wax on top, which can be removed when you want to use preserves), it will prevent impurities and moisture from getting into the pickles and chutneys, thus saving them from spoiling.

Practical things to be done

1. Ginger Chutney

Utensils used: A saucepan; a skillet or frying pan; a bowl; an earthenware or glass jar; a knife; chopping board.

Gadgets: Food processor, or mortar and pestle.

Ingredients: 8 tbsp jaggery; 1½ cup vinegar; 4 x 4 inch pieces ginger; 3 cloves garlic; 12 tbsp raisins; 4 tbsp dry red chillies; 1 tsp fenugreek seeds; 2 tbsp salt.

To make ginger chutney, follow this simple procedure:

1. In a saucepan, boil jaggery with 1 cup vinegar to make syrup.
2. In the skillet or frying pan, roast the chillies and fenugreek seeds, cool and powder.
3. In a food processor or a large mortar, pound together the peeled ginger, garlic, stoned raisins, chillies and fenugreek.
4. Mix together the jaggery syrup, the remaining vinegar, pounded spices and salt. Put into a large earthenware or glass jar and place in the sun for a fortnight. After that it will be ready to use.

2. Cucumber Raita

Utensils used: a mixing bowl; a peeler; a knife; a fork; a grater; a colander.

Gadgets: A hand-blender.

Ingredients: 3 cups yogurt, lightly beaten; salt and sugar to taste; 2 medium-sized cucumber; 2 tsp fresh soya, finely chopped (optional); ½ tsp lightly roasted, coarsely ground cumin seeds, one green chilli, de-seeded and finely chopped.

To make cucumber raita, follow this simple procedure:

1. Take out the bitter juices from the cucumbers (you have already learnt how to do this in the lesson on 'Salads'). Peel and finely chop or grate them. Sprinkle salt over the cucumbers and keep in the colander to drain for 15 minutes.
2. Meanwhile, beat the yogurt in a bowl with a fork or hand-blender until creamy. Mix in sugar and salt.
3. Squeeze out the excess liquid from the cucumber. Fold into the beaten yogurt. Stir in the soya and the chopped chillies. Chill.
4. Sprinkle cumin powder over the raita and serve. You can also add ginger powder to this raita.

TIPS

If the curd is tart / sour, add 3-4 tbsp of milk while blending. This will take away the tartness.

Expert cook suggests...

1. To store chutneys for a longer time, soak an almond overnight. Peel it and grind it along with the chutney. The almond acts as a preservative.
2. Peels of apples and tender cucumbers are rich in vitamins. Do not throw them. Grind them with coriander leaves, green chillies, ginger and coconut; add salt and sugar according to taste and dilute it with yogurt. It makes a fine nutritious raita.

Gobhi ka Achar

Tomato Chutney from Bengal

Angoor Kele ka Raita

Gajar Raita

DAY 21

Juices, Punches and Refreshers

The object of your taking this course in cookery is to gain culinary expertise. It is not confined only to cooking. You must also learn the art of entertaining your family, friends and relatives. This entertainment must begin with offering your guests a glass of water on their arrival, followed by snacks and drinks.

The guest in an Indian household is next only to God and commands reverence. Just as we celebrate our numerous festivals with great pomp and show, revering our deities, making offerings of flowers and '*prasad*', in the same tradition we offer our guests the best that our household can provide.

Whey Pineapple Drink

If your guests are to have lunch with you, then you may only serve them drinks and move on to the lunch table. If they are teatime guests, then serving snacks and drinks is in order. The dinnertime guests could well be satisfied with drinks and a couple of tidbits with dips so that their appetite is not impaired.

Whey Rose Drink

Pomegrenate Refresher

Even though teatime requires tea or coffee with the spread of snacks, the summer months act as a deterrent to hot beverages. This is where your expertise in making unique juices, fruit punches and refreshers is to be put to test.

Cold Dishes

Heat is not the only fuel used to cook. Some of the finest food is served cold. There is no limit to the variety – appetizers, cold salads, soups, main dishes and desserts. Cold dishes are always welcome in the hot summer months.

Whereas, heat is ideal to kill harmful bacteria in food, one needs to be careful about hygiene and cleanliness when serving cold dishes. Freezing restricts the development of bacteria, but it does not kill them. The moment the temperature increases, it becomes ideal for the harmful bacteria to grow.

Many dishes can be made directly without any preliminary use of heat, but when used, it helps sterilise the food before it is chilled.

Low temperatures tend to reduce the sensitivity of the taste buds, and one may desire stronger flavours, seasoning and higher sugar content.

Juices

Juice is the liquid extracted from fruits and vegetables such as carrots, beetroots, cabbage, tomatoes and spinach. This is done by pressure or by centrifugal force. An electric juicer is ideal as it separates the pith and seeds, giving you a clear juice. However, a variety of manual juicers and hand-held presses are available in the market to make your task easier.

Fruit juice is a refreshing drink, rich in vitamins. You can drink it plain or diluted with water or soda water, for example, orange juice is very beneficial when taken at breakfast time. Concentrated fruit juices are available in the market, either in liquid form, or as crystals. These can be diluted to taste. The calorie content of the juice depends on the fruits from which it was extracted. It also depends upon the proportion of added sugar, though many people prefer unsweetened juices.

Mixed Fruit Juice

The most widely consumed fruit juices include those of apple, grapes, oranges, pineapple, grapefruit and tomatoes. Juices of other fresh fruits like apricots, mangoes, pears or those that are more acidic like raspberry, have a larger portion of added water and sugar.

Fruit juices are used mainly as drinks. They are also used to make ices and sorbets and for general cooking, for example lemon juice has its special uses particularly in cooking. In many diets, natural fruit juices are complemented by vegetable juices and served as non-alcoholic starters, for example, carrot juice, red cabbage juice, and spinach juice are often mixed together.

Let us learn how a fermented juice is made.

Punches and Refreshers

Punches are iced or hot drinks, sometimes flamed. They can be made either with tea, sugar, spices, fruits, and rum or brandy, or with rum and sugar syrup. The word 'punch' originally describes a British colonial drink, which had five ingredients. In Hindi, '*panch*' means five. The drink was made in a large punch bowl and served in small bowls. Stemmed or fluted glasses have replaced the bowls. In about 1830, a ban on importing rum into France from West Indies was lifted; it was done so as not to compete with cognac. At the same time, an attraction for English things helped make punches popular.

Fruit Punch

A forerunner of the cocktail, it has been made according to various recipes. English punch consists of boiling tea poured over slices of lemon, with sugar, cinnamon, and rum. It was flamed before drinking it. In the French punch, the quantity of tea is less and the rum is replaced by brandy, poured in the end and flamed. Roman punch is a sorbet made with dry white wine or champagne, with orange or lemon slices, mixed with Italian meringue over which a glass of rum is poured at the time of serving.

We are going to learn how to make different kinds of fruit punches and refreshers called 'mocktails', which are totally non-alcoholic. You can combine a horde of ingredients to produce some delicious concoctions. Let us see how they are made. Before that, here are a few tips to make the task easier for you.

Some tips on making punches:

- You must always use simple garnishing. An elaborate one makes your cocktail striking, but it makes it difficult to drink. A slice of lemon, a cherry on a toothpick, or a strawberry or pineapple chunk or an olive on a trendy striver stick or stuck to the rim of glass should be fancy enough. You can add a touch of class by buying a bunch of decorative stirrers.
- Fluted glasses or tall stem glasses should preferably be used to serve cocktails. A stirrer or a swizzle stick should be served in long glasses but squat glasses would need a garnish stuck to the rim or on a toothpick.

- If you are using fresh or tinned fruits to make the drink, you must slice them into tiny bits and put them in an electric blender to give a smooth texture. This way you do not need to strain the drink. Just add little fruit syrup or water to blend the fruits with crushed ice and serve.
- Since all cocktails are coolers and refreshers, ice is an important ingredient. Get dry ice from the market or freeze your own ice preferably with mineral water or purified water. These days ice trays with decorative shapes are available to add a touch of class to your drink. Chill the soda bottles and the juices you are using, much before the preparation time.
- To crush ice, put ice cubes in a clean dish and beat lightly with a rolling pin.

Rain Forest

Ingredients: ¾ cup khus syrup or sherbet; 2½ bottles chilled soda; 4-5 tsp lemon juice; ¼ tsp pepper; ½ tsp salt; ice cubes; cherries and sweet lime (*mousambi*) slices for garnishing.

Portions: To serve 4 people.

Method:

1. In a large pan combine the khus syrup/sherbet and the lemon juice. Add salt and pepper.
2. Add the chilled soda to the khus mixture.
3. Fill the glass with crushed ice. Pour in the prepared mixture.
4. Stick a thin slice of unpeeled sweet lime to the rim of the glass. Float a cherry stuck on a toothpick in the cocktail and serve.

Purple Rain

Ingredients: ½ kg black grapes, 2 tsp lemon juice; 4 tbsp crushed strawberry or raspberry; 4 tsp double cream or ice cream; ¾ bottle chilled soda; ice cubes; grapes and sprigs of mint for garnishing.

Portions: To serve 6 people.

Method:

1. Set aside a few grapes for garnishing. In a blender, combine all the grapes with ¾ cups of water. Strain to get 2 large glasses of juice. Refrigerate it.
2. When you are ready to serve, blend grape juice, lemon juice, strawberry crush and the cream/ice cream in a blender.
3. Add soda to the mixture. Fill ¾ of the glass with crushed ice and top with the blended mixture.
4. Slit a grape and stick it to the rim of the glass. Float a few mint leaves on the cocktail and serve.

Lemon and Honey Cooler

Ingredients: 4 lemons; 1 litre water; 125 gms honey; ice cubes; sprigs of mint for garnishing.

Portions: To serve 6-8 people.

Method:

1. Pare the rind from a lemon. Put it in a pan with water.
2. Bring it to the boil. Remove from heat. Stir the honey and the juice extracted from the lemons.
3. Put the mixture into a bowl, cover and let it cool.
4. When you are ready to serve, strain into a chilled glass jug.
5. Pour into tall glasses. Top with crushed ice. Float a mint sprig on top. Put in a stirrer and serve.

Banana and Honey Milkshake

Ingredients: 2 ripe bananas, chopped; 850 ml chilled milk; 3 tbsp honey.

Portions: To serve 4 people.

Method:

1. Combine and blend the milk, bananas and honey in a blender.
2. Blend until the mixture turns smooth and frothy.
3. Pour into four tall glasses. Top with crushed ice if required. Put in a colourful, flexible drinking straw and serve.

Moroccan Mint Tea

Ingredients: 4 tsp green tea leaves; 4 sprigs of fresh mint or 1 dried mint; 125 gms castor sugar; 850 ml boiling water; sugar to taste.

Portions: To serve 6 people.

Method:

1. Pour a little boiling water over the tea leaves in a teapot. Swirl around and drain out the water leaving the tea leaves inside the pot.
2. Add the dried or fresh mint leaves and castor sugar. Pour rest of the boiling water over this mixture. Leave to infuse for 5 minutes.
3. Add sugar to taste and stir to dissolve the sugar.
4. Fill ¼ of a tall glass with crushed ice and strain the tea into the glass and serve decorated with a mint sprig.

Let us now do some practical work. We are going to learn how to prepare two traditional Indian coolers, which are all time favourites.

Practical things to be done

1. Thandai

Utensils used: An assortment of mixing bowls, a big glass jar; tall glasses; stirrers; a long-handled spoon; muslin cloth. (These are common to both the recipes).

Gadgets: An electric blender/a mortar and pestle.

Portions: To serve 6-8.

Ingredients: 1½ litres milk; ½ cup almonds; 2 tbsp broken cashew nuts; 1 cup watermelon seeds (*magaz*); 8 tbsp *khus-khus* (poppy seeds); 15-20 peppercorns; 6-8 green cardamoms; few dried rose petals; 10-12 tbsp sugar; a few strands of saffron (*kesar*) soaked in warm water for garnishing.

To make *thandai*, follow this simple procedure:

1. In a small bowl soak the almonds for 3-5 hours. Alternatively, you could drop them in hot water. The skin will shrink and you can peel them easily.
2. In another bowl soak together the watermelon seeds, *khus-khus*; cashew nuts, peppercorns, cardamoms and rose petals for 3-4 hours.
3. Peel almonds and add to the other ingredients. Combine all of them in a blender and blend to a paste adding a little water or milk if needed. Alternatively, you could use a mortar and pestle. However, this way the paste does not become very smooth.
4. Add the paste to the cold milk. Add sugar and mix well.
5. Strain the mixture through a muslin cloth and discard the residue.
6. Pour into tall glasses. Add crushed ice. Serve garnished with strands of *kesar* and a rose petal.

2. Panna

Gadgets: A blender; a pressure cooker.

Portions: To serve 6-8.

Ingredients: ½ kg raw green mangoes; ¾ cup sugar; ½ cup fresh mint leaves; 2 tsp roasted cumin seeds, coarsely ground; 2 tsp salt; a few mint sprigs for garnishing.

To make *panna*, follow this simple procedure.

1. Wash and peel the mangoes. Place in a pressure cooker with 6 cups of water. Cook till it gives 2-3 whistles. Remove from heat.
2. When cool, extract the pulp of the mangoes by squeezing with your hand. Discard the mango stone.
3. Mix the pulp and water in a blender. Add the mint leaves ground to a paste with a little water. Powder the sugar.
4. Add cumin powder, powdered sugar and salt to the mixture and blend some more.
5. Strain the mixture through a sieve. Adjust seasoning and chill.
6. When you are ready to serve, put crushed ice to fill ¾ of a tall glass and pour in the panna. Garnish with a mint leaf.

This coolant is a great favourite during the hot summer months because it wards off heat stroke.

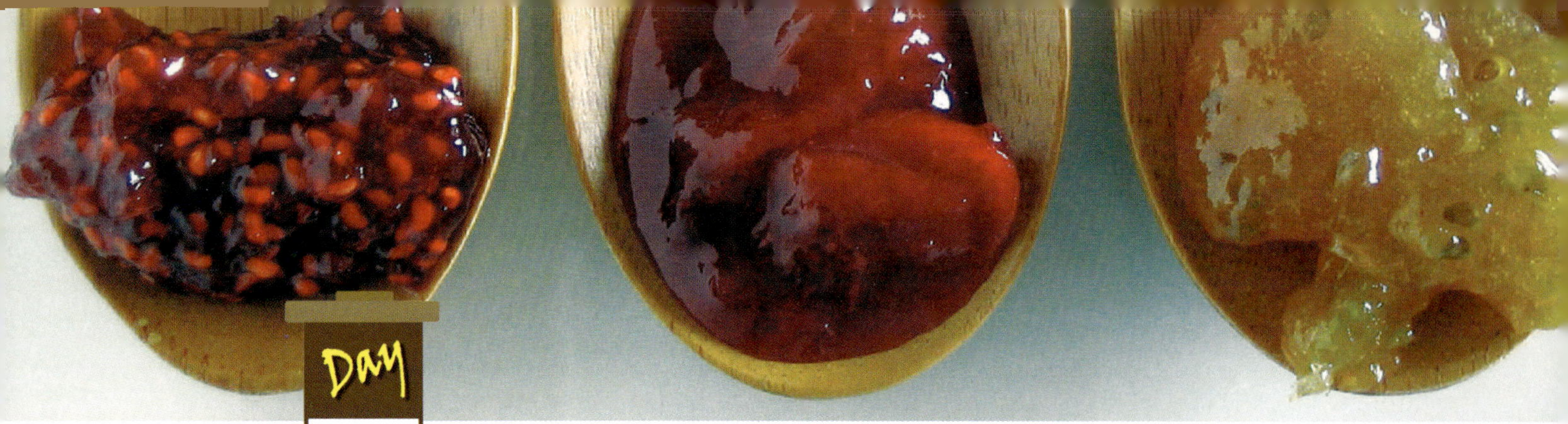

Day 22

Jams, Jellies and Marmalades

Jams, jellies and marmalades are made from fruits boiled with sugar to gel point. These are eaten with bread or toast. They can also be used to sandwich cakes, or as an icing with a sprinkling of castor sugar. Children love to eat them with parathas or puris. They are also used in desserts such as bread pudding, poached fruits, iced desserts, pancakes, waffles, to coat cookies, to flavour yogurt, and to make sweet sauces for desserts.

Most fruits contain acid, some sugar and the natural setting agent pectin. Together they help jams, jellies and marmalades to set properly. The acid, sugar and pectin must be in the right proportion.

Pineapple Jam, Mixed Fruit Jam, Orange Marmalade

- Jam is made with whole or cut fruits.
- Marmalade is made with citrus fruits.
- Jelly is made with strained fruit juice boiled with sugar.

Jam

Fruits with a lot of acid make the best preserves. Fruits that are barely ripe are ideal because at this stage the pectin content is the highest. Pears, peaches, apricots, strawberries and raspberries should be slightly underripe, while plums and cherries should be just ripe but still full-flavoured. Spices like vanilla and cinnamon, or caramel for apples can improve the flavour of jams. Fruits with strong flavour such as peaches, strawberries, cherries and mixed citrus fruits also help improve the flavour of jam. Adding raspberries to peaches and melon helps deepen the colour. Some less common fruits such as watermelons or tomatoes, as well as exotic fruits like mango, guava and coconut can also be used.

Pectin, which is the setting agent, is found mostly in the skin, seeds and core of fruits. Long cooking time destroys pectin. This is why it is prudent to make jams and jellies in small, rapidly cooked batches. If the fruit is low in pectin, you will need to add lemon juice. The ideal proportion is 2 tablespoons of lemon juice for 1.5 kg fruit. A good alternative could be the strained and reduced juice of sour apples.

The sugar content in preserves should be a minimum of 60 percent to prevent mould. For a dark, rich taste, especially in marmalades, you can substitute up to a quarter of the sugar with brown sugar. If the proportion of the sugar is insufficient or the jam is not sufficiently cooked, the jam may ferment and will not keep. If there is too much sugar, the jam is too concentrated and tends to crystallise.

Jam-Making Season

- December to March – oranges, grapefruit, guava
- July – strawberries, raspberries, cherries
- August – apricots
- September – peaches, tomatoes, plums, raspberries
- October – apples, pears, figs, grapes
- November – oranges, apples

EQUIPMENT FOR JAM-MAKING

- Paring knife for stoning the fruit; nutcracker.
- Stoneware pot for storing the fruit. A thick glass jar would also do.
- Weighing scales.
- A heavy-bottomed large saucepan made of stainless steel or a pressure cooker without the lid. Whatever you are using, make sure it is thick enough to prevent the jam from burning. Its capacity should be twice that of the fruit to be cooked in it when boiling rapidly. This will prevent overflowing and facilitate evaporation. It should be thoroughly cleaned before use.
- A stainless steel ladle for skimming the scum during cooking.
- A long-handled wooden spatula or spoon.
- Ladle with an insulated handle to pour the preserve into bottles.
- Jam jars, not too large as the contents can deteriorate before they have been used up.
- Waxed paper, paraffin, or cellophane paper.
- A very fine strainer or a clean dish towel to strain the juice to make jelly.
- A wide mouthed funnel to fill the bottles with jam, jellies and marmalades.

STERILISING AND SEALING JARS

Use only heat proof bottles, as sterilising is done at high heat. Ordinary bottles may crack. The bottles used to store preserves must be sterilised to kill germs. Wash the bottles with detergent and water, and then boil them in water for 10 minutes. Dry them upside-down in a warm oven. You must fill the bottles with preserves within 1/8 inch of the top. Bottles without screw-top lids need ½ inch headroom for sealing.

There are three methods to seal the bottles filled with preserves:

- For hot or cold jams, cover the bottle with a piece of moistened cellophane paper pulled tightly across the opening and held in place by an elastic band.
- For cold jams, pour over the surface of the jam a very thin layer of paraffin wax that has been melted in a pan. Turn the bottle so that the wax covers the complete surface and sides giving an airtight seal. This is the most common and successful method.
- Place a circle of paper soaked in alcohol or waxed paper on top of the bottle. This is the oldest method.

SEALING WITH PARAFFIN

Paraffin is available in slabs in the market. You could also use white, unscented household candles. Melt the paraffin wax over a very low heat or in a water bath. Put the wax in a small pan and hold it in boiling water in a large vessel. Pour a thin layer of tepid paraffin over the hot preserve. If the paraffin is too hot, it will shrink away from the sides of the bottle when it cools. Prick any air bubbles that appear in the paraffin before they have time to set and burst the seal. When first layer has set, pour in another layer. Repeat the process till the paraffin layer is 1/8 inch thick.

COOKING JAM

Wash the fruits and remove peel, pith, stems, stones and any damaged flesh. Cut the fruits into small pieces. If you are using berries and grapes, leave them whole. The fruit may be cooked whole, and then chopped and seeded. If you want a fine textured preserve, cut the rind into julienne and add to the cooking fruits. The seeds should be tied in a muslin bag and added to the cooking fruit to extract the pectin. Put the fruits in the cooking pan or a pressure cooker with the correct amount of water and cook till they turn pulpy. Test for pectin. If you are making jelly, strain the fruit through a very fine strainer or a dish towel. To keep the jelly clear, do not squeeze the dish towel or work the fruit pulp through the strainer. Let the juice strain out by itself. Test the juice for pectin.

Strawberry Jam

Add the right amount of sugar to the fruit pulp or the juice. Stir to dissolve and bring to boil. Keep boiling till gel point is reached. Remove from heat and test by placing a spot of preserve on a cold plate. If it is ready, a skin will form on the surface as it cools. Skim off the scum from the top of the preserve with a ladle. Cool for 10 minutes to prevent the juice from rising to the top of each bottle. Using a ladle and a funnel, fill the bottles with hot preserves. Wipe the rim and seal, leaving appropriate headroom in each bottle. Label and store in a cool, dark and dry place. It will keep for a year. Do not refrigerate otherwise the preserves will crystallise.

Testing for Pectin

Mix one tablespoon of cooked unsweetened fruit juice with one tablespoon of rubbing alcohol in a bowl. Swirl the mixture for a couple of minutes till it starts to clot. Then, push your finger into the solution. If there are large clots formed in the solution, the pectin content is high. Small lumps indicate low pectin level. Throw away this mixture as the alcohol is poisonous.

Testing Setting Point

To cook preserves rapidly, they must be boiled over high heat. When the cooked fruit becomes tender, it is tested to see if it is set or gelled sufficiently. To do this, follow this method:

1. With a ladle, keep skimming off the scum that rises to the top as the fruit is cooking. This will ensure a shining and clear preserve.
2. Cooking food normally reaches setting point, or gel point at 220°F. When you feel that the fruit is sufficiently cooked, lift some of the mixture on the spatula. It should fall from the spatula in a sheet of drips.
3. You could also test by pouring a few drops of the preserve on a cold plate. Wait for it to set. Push gently with your finger. If the surface of the preserve wrinkles, it means the fruit has reached gel point.

Expert cook suggests...

Apple is a rich source of pectin that helps set jams. Add a few pieces when making a jam. The jam will set well.

Problem Shooting

Here are a few common problems. Once you know the cause, take care.

- If the fruit discolours, the preserve was cooked too long. To shorten cooking time, warm the sugar in the oven first.
- If the whole fruit has risen to the top of the jar, the syrup was not properly boiled and has too much liquid. Cooked jam was not allowed to rest in the pan before bottling.
- If the jam ferments, crystallises, or forms a mould, the equipment was not properly sterilised.
- If the jam ferments or becomes fizzy, it was insufficiently cooked, or pectin, sugar and acid were not in the right proportion.

Some Remedies

- **Mouldy jam:** Remove and discard every trace of mould from the jam, together with the underlying jam to a depth of ½ inch; use the remaining jam immediately. Store the jam in a cool, dry place and check occasionally.
- **Fermented jam:** This will happen if the jam has been cooked insufficiently, or the fruit used is of poor quality, or not enough sugar has been added. Reheat and add some more sugar and cook. Test for setting point.
- **Crystallised jam:** Reheat and add lemon juice or a little citric acid and water. Pay special attention to the temperature and density.
- **Unset jam:** This happens either due to under boiling, to a lack of pectin, or to the use of too much sugar. Finish this jam as soon as possible and make a fresh batch, with a little more care this time.

Jellies

Jelly based Sugar-Coated sweets

Only fruits rich in pectin are good for making jellies. Such fruits are mulberries, apples, mango and guava. Alternatively, one of these fruits can be combined with a strong-flavoured fruit that is low in pectin. The acid content of the fruit and the sugar concentration are also important. To extract the juice, first the berries are cooked with a little water until the skins break. In the case of citrus fruits and apples, the prepared fruit is presoaked with the cores and seeds collected in a muslin bag and cooked in water. The liquid is then put through a very fine strainer. Sugar, equal to the weight of the juice obtained, is added to the juice. The boiling time will vary according to the fruit used, for example, for berries 3-4 minutes and for apples 20-30 minutes. To test whether or not the jelly has begun to set, use the setting point test. If the drops of preserve dropped on a cold plate solidify in a few minutes, the jelly is ready for bottling.

If you master the techniques described above, you will then find making jams, jellies and marmalades an easy task. Let us now learn to make a few items.

Practical things to be done

1. Apricot Jam

Utensils used: A large pressure cooker; a long-handled ladle; a wooden spoon or spatula; a ladle with an insulated handle; a large funnel; a fine strainer or a dish towel; measuring scales; a small saucepan; a paring knife; a peeler; sterilised bottles; paraffin; cellophane paper; wax paper (These are common to all jam, jelly and marmalade making).

Ingredients: 1 kg ripe stoned apricots; 1 kg granulated sugar, 6 tbsp water.

Follow this simple procedure to make apricot jam:

1. Dissolve sugar in water in a pan or a pressure cooker, bring to boil for 5 minutes, skim off the top.
2. Add the apricots and cook until the setting stage is reached. This will take about 30 minutes. A few half-kernels from the apricot stones may be added to the jam when it has finished cooking.
3. Pour into sterilised bottles and seal.

2. Apple Jelly

Ingredients: 1 kg slightly acidic apples; 1 kg granulated sugar; juice of 2 lemons; 1 litre water.

Follow this procedure to make apple jelly:

1. Wash and quarter the apples without peeling or coring. Place the quarters in the pressure cooker or a large heavy-bottomed pan, with the water. Boil gently for 50 minutes.
2. Pour the contents into a strainer a little at a time. Let the juice run through without pressing the fruit.
3. Pour the juice back into the cooker. Add 1 kg granulated sugar and the lemon juice. Bring to a boil. Cook for 40 to 45 minutes or till syrup coats the spoon. Test for setting point.
4. With the help of the funnel, pour the preserve into sterilised bottles. Seal and store in a cool, dry place.

3. Orange and Lime Marmalade

Ingredients: 2 oranges; 4 limes; 1 kg sugar; 3 litre water.

To make marmalade, follow this simple procedure:

1. Wash the oranges and limes, cut off and discard the ends. Peel the fruit and discard the pith.
2. Cut the peel into fine shreds. Remove the seeds and tie in a muslin bag.
3. Slice the fruits and put in a pressure cooker with the peel and seeds. Add the water, bring to boil and simmer for one hour.
4. Strain the fruit pulp through muslin. Allow to drip into a clean vessel. Do not press with hand.
5. Heat sugar in the oven at very low temperature. Stir it into the clarified fruit pulp. Add a few pieces of thinly cut orange peel. Boil rapidly to setting point, stirring often.
6. Let the mixture cool slightly. Pour the marmalade into sterilised bottles and seal.

Day 23

Indian Sweets and Desserts

India is a land of 4 Fs – Food, Feasts, Fairs and Festivals. They say that there are more festivals in India than there are days in a year. Indian civilisation is 5000 years old. Right from the Vedic period of Aryans, references to festivals to honour five natural elements i.e., sun, rain, rivers, trees, the coming of monsoons, end of winters and dawn of spring, etc; the Gods/Goddesses representing each of them were honoured and worshipped. Celebrations not only included fasting and prayers, but also events of social interaction, where along with cultural and dramatic activities, the display of physical strength, valour and virility were equally important. Therefore, lavish display of food, according to the season and occasion becomes an integral and important part of the festivities. The celebration of fairs and festivals form a wondrous and joyful events.

These events are the moments of remembrance and commemoration of birthdays, great deeds of innumerable Gods and Goddesses, heroes and heroines, prophets and saints, etc; sacred, secular, seasonal and personal, each of these occasions has a special spirit which brings the families, friends and communities together to enjoy the sharing of gifts, festival, food, etc.

India is a complex panorama of religious, linguistic, geographic and artistic diversity, hence, diversity in unity and unity in diversity can be easily traced in each of India's many religious groups; Hindus, Muslims, Christians, Sikhs, Buddhist, Jains, Parsis and others have their own special days to celebrate. In spite of this diverse culture, the spirit to celebrate drives them together.

Beetroot Halwa

Out of innumerable festivals celebrated by Indians, the most festive is **Diwali**. It is the most spectacular festival and is called the festival of lights. Diwali falls usually in the month of October/November. It is indeed a festival of joy and all the communities come together in the Diwali celebrations.

Preparations for Diwali begin weeks in advance. Large quantities of flour, rice, sugar, coconuts, nuts and other ingredients used in making sweetmeats are bought, and the kitchen hums with activity. The choicest family sweets are prepared for the occasion. The traditional sweets served on Diwali are a variety of *laddoo, barfi, masoorpak, gulab jamuns* and *jalebis*, etc. *Nimkis/Namkeens* (salted snacks made of refined flour and gram flour) are also prepared.

Indian sweets and desserts, however, are not confined to festivals or weddings. As a normal practice too, in the households they are served at the end of a meal. They are either served cold as *rasgulla, phirni, kheer, kulfi, sandesh, barfi* or served hot as *jalebi, gulab jamun* and *halwa*, etc.

The basic ingredients for most Indian desserts are milk and milk products such as *mawa, paneer* and ghee, sugar, dry fruits, besides other food items like *suji (rawa)*, wheat flour, gram flour, rice flour, rice and *sewaiyan* (vermicelli). Rose water, *kewda*, cardamom and essences are used for flavouring and silver foil is used for decoration.

Kulfi

Ras malai

Phirni

Indian desserts can broadly be classified into two categories:

- Solid forms include a variety of *halwas, laddoos, barfi, sandesh, gulab jamuns, jalebi, pinni, kulfi, rasgulla,* besides others.
- Semi-liquid includes dishes like *phirni*, which is made from milk and rice flour, garnished with chopped pistachio and almonds.

Gajar Halwa

Gajar Halwa

Halwas are made with *suji (rawa)*, wheat flour, gram flour, pumpkin, carrots, beetroot and a variety of other foods. The wheat flour *halwa* is made of flour or semolina fried in ghee. Constant stirring is important as all flours tend to scorch easily. The flour is fried on low heat until it begins to turn brown. Meanwhile, sugar is dissolved in water. It is added to the fried flour. Constant stirring at this stage ensures that no lumps are formed. The mixture thickens to the consistency of loosely kneaded crumbly dough. This is garnished with chopped almonds and cashew nuts. A sprinkling of powdered cardamom adds flavour to the *halwa*.

Sewaiyan

Sewaiyan

To make *Sewaiyan*, the readymade packet of *Sewaiyan* is best; roasted in a little ghee in a *kadhai*. Warm milk is added to the browned *Sewaiyan*, and cooked on medium flame till the dish is done. Sugar is added and stirred well. The mixture is simmered till it becomes thick like the batter for fritters. A little rose water or *kewda* water is sprinkled over the mixture for flavour or the dish is flavoured with green cardamom powder. A garnishing of almonds, pistachio and raisins finally makes it an appetizing and delicious dessert. This speciality is one of the prominent desserts served on Id-ul-Fitr.

The nuts used to garnish sweets are usually roasted in a little ghee, cooled and cut into thin slivers. Sometimes the recipe requires raw chopped cashew nuts and almonds. In that case the almonds are soaked in warm water for a couple of hours and peeled. In *kheer* and *sewaiyan*, the raisins are added when the mixture is boiling. This way they swell up and become soft.

Let us now take a look at how some of the other desserts are prepared:

Rasgullas

Ingredients: 3 cups milk, 1 tbsp flour, 1½ kg sugar, 1 cup sour whey.

Method: Make *chhena* (*paneer*) from the milk and whey. Add flour to the *chhena*. Knead it with the palms of the hands until it is smooth and pliable. Divide the dough into small portions. In each portion put a grain or two of sugar candy and roll to form a ball. Make thin syrup by combining the sugar and 4 cups of water. Cook over low heat. Add 2 tablespoons milk to the boiling syrup. Boil for 10 minutes sprinkling water on the boiling syrup every 2 minutes. Remove from the heat and cool. Add the balls to the syrup. Flavour with rosewater, if desired.

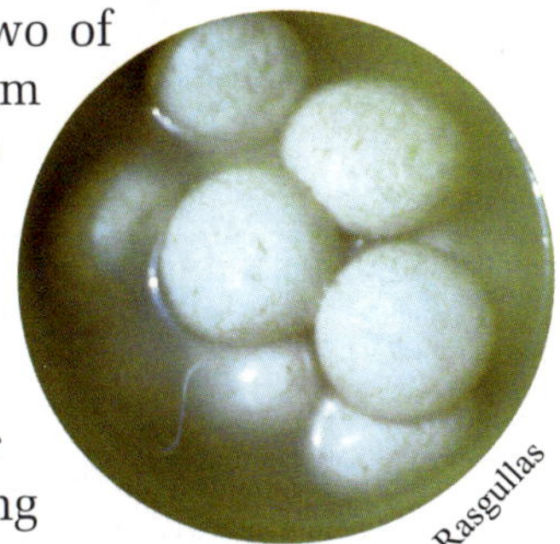

Rasgullas

Sandesh

Ingredients: 2 cups milk, 8 tbsp castor sugar, 1 cup sour whey, flavouring like lemon, rose, or any other preferred by you.

Method: Make *chhena* from the milk and whey. Combine it with sugar. Knead well until very smooth. Place a *kadhai* on the fire. Stir the mixture in it with a spatula till all the water dries up. Remove from the fire. Keep stirring with the spatula. Cool. Add food colouring of your choice.

Divide into equal portions. Press each portion in a pastry mould to give it shape. Remove from the mould. *Sandesh* can also be made from date-palm *gur* (jaggery) instead of sugar.

Suseum

Ingredients: 500 gms sweet potatoes, ½ tsp salt or to taste, 2 pods cardamom (powdered), 2½ tbsp rice flour, 1 tbsp grated coconut, 3 tbsp water, 4 tbsp sugar or jaggery, 1 tsp turmeric powder.

Method: Boil the sweet potatoes; peel and mash them. Mix cardamom, sugar, coconut and salt with the potatoes. Make small balls from this paste. Mix flour, turmeric and salt with a little water and make a thick batter. Dip the small potato balls into the batter and fry in oil. Serve hot.

Kalkass

Ingredients: 5 tbsp flour (maida), 700 gms sugar, 1 coconut, 1 tsp cardamom powder, 8 tbsp ghee.

Method: Grate coconut and grind it. Squeeze out all the milk adding a little hot water if necessary. Mix flour and coconut milk and knead to soft dough. Take marble-sized pieces of the dough, flatten out on a fork, roll it off so that the fork mark is imprinted on it. Make as many little rolls as possible. Heat the ghee in a pan. When hot, fry all the rolls to a golden brown. Make thick syrup of the sugar. Put all the rolls in a bowl and pour syrup over them. Shake the bowl a little so that the syrup covers all the rolls. Sprinkle with cardamom powder and cool.

Chana Dal Kheer

Ingredients: 8 tbsp chana dal, 1 tbsp ghee, 1 coconut, a few cardamoms, 700 gms jaggery.

Method: Wash, clean and soak dal in water for 10 minutes. Add water and cook it well. In the meantime, take a small piece of coconut, cut it into small pieces and keep it on one side. Grind the rest of the coconut and extract milk. Grind the gratings again and extract milk a second and a third time. When the dal is nearly done, add the thinner milk and jaggery. Stir and cook on a low heat for 20 minutes. When cooked well, remove from the heat and let it cool for 5 minutes. Then add the thick coconut milk. Fry the coconut bits in ghee till brown. Add to the *kheer* along with crushed cardamoms. Serve cold.

Badam Kheer

Ingredients: 60 almonds, powdered cardamoms, 6 cups milk, a pinch of saffron, 8 tbsp sugar (or to taste).

Kheer

Method: Soak almonds in hot water for a few hours. Peel and slice them. Soak saffron in 2 tbsp hot milk. Heat milk in a large saucepan, add sugar and boil till slightly thickened. Add almonds, saffron and cardamom powder. Serve hot with fresh hot puris.

Malabar Banana Dessert

Ingredients: 6 ripe Malabar bananas, 8 tbsp grated coconut, 2 eggs, 2 tsp raisins, ½ cup milk, vanilla essence, 2 tbsp sugar, 2 tbsp butter, 1 tbsp crushed almonds, 12 cloves.

Method: Wash bananas. Steam them without removing their skin till they are soft. Cool, peel them and cut each lengthwise. Carefully remove the strings of seeds. Mash with a fork to a smooth dough adding a little butter. Shape into 12 balls. Beat the eggs and stir in milk, sugar and almonds. Blend well with the coconut and raisins. Melt a little butter and scramble the egg mixture till frothy. Add a dash of vanilla essence. Take each banana ball and flatten it in the palm of your hand. Pile a tsp of the egg mixture in the centre. Cover the stuffing carefully and roll into a ball again. Stick a clove into the top. Place in a dish and chill overnight. Serve with cream. If desired, the balls can be dipped in a thin batter of refined flour and fried in hot ghee. Serve hot.

Pumpkin Halwa

Ingredients: 1 large ripe red pumpkin, 4 tbsp almonds, ½ cup milk, 4 tbsp pistachios, 500 gms *khoya* (solidified milk), 4 tbsp pumpkin seeds, 1 cup cream, a pinch of saffron soaked in a little water, 8 tbsp ghee, 500 gm sugar, rose essence or cardamom powder.

Method: Peel pumpkin; remove the pith and seeds and grate the flesh. Mix and boil with the milk. Cook gently till all the milk dries up. Heat ghee in a large saucepan and fry the pumpkin mixture till it turns reddish in colour. Add sugar. Dry fry *khoya* in a separate pan. Mix it with pumpkin mixture and fry gently on a low heat. Blanch the nuts and chop fine. Pour the mixture onto a large plate and spread evenly with a wooden spoon. Sprinkle the saffron water, rose essence and nuts on top. Whip the cream and make an even pattern on the surface with dollops of cream. When cool, cut in squares so that you have a dollop of cream on each piece.

The recipe mentions large pumpkin, definition of large can vary from person to person, therefore, when you try the recipe, keep in mind that large pumpkin must yield the flesh (after peeling) about 2.5 kg to 3 kg in weight. Otherwise, first you may try half the recipe. Health conscious people may omit cream from the recipe.

Practical things to be done

1. Sugar Syrup

Utensils used: A large stainless steel saucepan with a heavy bottom; a long-handled wooden spoon.

Gadgets: None.

Ingredients: 1 kg sugar; 750 ml water.

Follow this simple procedure to make sugar syrup:

1. Dissolve the sugar and water completely by stirring, taking care to see that all the sugar has dissolved.
2. Heat the mixture over very low heat and stir gently. The sugar should be completely dissolved when the mixture comes to a boil. If crystals remain, they will make the syrup cloudy and inclined to crystallise.
3. Once the sugar dissolves, stop stirring and bring the syrup to boil. When it is sparkling clear, it is ready. This should take about 10 minutes.

Using and keeping the syrup:

- This syrup is used for soaking the *rasgullas* and *gulab jamuns*, for poaching and glazing fruits and as a base for sorbets.
- Sugar crystals form easily, so the sugar should be completely dissolved before boiling the syrup.
- Light syrup can be refrigerated for 2-3 days, medium syrup for 8-10 days, and heavy syrup for up to 2 weeks.

2. Sugar Syrup (Thick)

To make thick sugar syrup, follow this simple procedure:

1. The initial process is the same as described above. The boiling time is longer. Keep boiling the syrup. Skim off any grey foam that rises to the top.
2. When the sugar has dissolved, increase the heat to boil the syrup rapidly.
3. Keep boiling, till the desired consistency is reached. Test for consistency.
4. Keep scraping the sides of the pan to remove crystals as these can burn, discolouring the syrup.
5. As soon as the desired density is reached, dip the base of the hot pan into a vessel of cold water to stop cooking.

Using and keeping the syrup:

- This syrup is used to make coconut *barfi*, *besan ki barfi* and *laddoos*.
- If you happen to burn yourself with the syrup, immediately plunge the burn in cold water, and wash off the syrup.
- Boiling syrup crystallises if it is stirred and the sides are not scraped, or if the sugar contains impurities and it is allowed to boil to too high a temperature. In that case, add a little cold water.
- You can store it for about 2 weeks in the refrigerator.

Testing sugar syrup:

- Sugar syrup will need to be tested for desired density. If it begins to caramelise, never test it with hand. It is dangerous.
- Dip a tsp into the boiling syrup. Allow it to cool. Knead between two fingers to test for consistency.
- If a thread forms, the density is right for light sweets like *rasgullas*.
- If a hard ball is formed, the syrup is right for coconut *barfi* and *laddoos*.
- If it is brittle and sticks to the teeth, it is right for certain caramels and toffees.

3. Praline (*Chikki*)

This is a favourite sweet sold in slabs. It is made from caramelised sugar with almonds/ peanuts. The nuts are roasted well to develop their flavour. Equal quantity of nuts and sugar is used. The quantity will depend on the amount of praline required.

Chikki is also made with jaggery, walnuts, roasted and powdered sesame seeds, mixed dry fruits and roasted gram dal, etc. After roasting the nuts, they are either coarsely powdered or added full to the sugar or jaggery syrup and then set in a flat plate. Try it with 1 cup grated jaggery, 1 tsp butter and ½ cup roasted and pounded peanuts.

Utensils used are the same as that for the previous recipe.

To make praline, follow this simple procedure.

1. Put the roasted whole almonds, peanuts or hazelnuts and sugar in the saucepan. Heat gently over low heat till the sugar melts. Stir often. Continue to cook, stirring lightly, till the sugar changes to deep brown and the nuts begin to pop.
2. Remove the pan from heat and pour the content onto a lightly greased, clean marble slab or baking tray.
3. Spread out the mixture with a wooden spoon, to form a thick slab. Garnish with thin slices of dry coconut and allow it to cool. Mark it into pieces with a knife when still warm.
4. Cut the praline into pieces. Store in an airtight jar. You could keep it whole too. The whole slab will easily come off thc marble top, or the tray.

Expert cook suggests...

1. Crumble a few *gulab jamuns* and add them to the coconut while making coconut *barfi* for added taste.
2. If *gulab jamuns* do not turn out soft and fluffy, steam them with the syrup in a pressure cooker.
3. Add a few drops of lemon juice while making sugar syrup. It prevents it from crystallisation.

Gulab Jamun

Imarti

Aam Rus

Jalebi

DAY 24

Ice Creams and Cold Desserts

Ice creams, sorbets and other cold desserts are a favourite treat for the young and the old alike, especially after a rich and elaborate meal. The oppressive heat of the summer months makes their popularity significant.

Primarily western in origin, ice creams are popular all over the world. Indians can have an ice cream anytime, anywhere. The famous Indian *kulfi*, a legacy of the Mughal period, is perhaps the only product similar to ice cream.

Freezing can create a wide range of desserts. Frozen desserts fall into two main categories:

- **Sorbets** are made of a combination of fruit juices or puree, wine or liquor, combined with sugar and other flavourings.
- **Rich mixtures** made with egg, milk or cream. The most common of this variety are custard-based ice creams that are made from milk thickened with egg.

Ice creams and sorbets

The success of ice creams and sorbets depend on their smoothness. Great care must be taken not to allow any ice crystals to form during freezing. This is easily done by stirring the mixture constantly, by hand or by machine. Good sorbets and ice creams are light in texture due to the air that is incorporated during churning. You could further lighten a sorbet by adding whipped egg white or meringue halfway through freezing.

Always remember that cold blunts the taste. The flavours must be strong with the addition of sugar, some acid, lemon or alcohol. Fruits such as berries, passion fruits, also the taste of coffee, chocolates and vanilla are preferred for ice creams. With ice creams you could liberally use a sprinkling of nuts and praline (see lesson on Indian Desserts), as well as tint them with food colouring, but with caution.

Ice creams

The most delicious of all ice creams is the one made with egg custard. The standard proportion to be followed is 500 ml milk, 135 gms sugar and 6-8 egg yolks, plus 250 ml cream. There are a number of variations to this traditional recipe. For an extra richness you could use cream instead of milk. The French variety uses more egg yolks.

If you are using milk or light cream, or a mixture of both, you could freeze the mixture without cooking it, as is normally done in the custard-based ice creams. However, the cream should be boiled to reduce and enrich it.

In mixtures like frozen yogurt or ice creams made with soft cheese, you could drop the egg yolk custard, as its thickening quality is not required. You could thicken mixtures made of fruit puree by adding gelatin.

Ice creams need flavouring. This differs from nation to nation.

- The **French** love pistachio and praline.
- The **Italians** use lots of hazelnut.
- The **British** enjoy chocolate ripple. Flavourings are available in abundance, from the traditional

chocolate chip, butter pecan and rum raisins to chocolate with nuts and marshmallow.

- The **Indians** love fruits and dry fruits based ice creams.

Always use pureed fruit to thicken fruit ice creams so that the custard does not thin down. The fruit must be at its peak of ripeness for its aroma to survive the chilling process. Otherwise, it is better to poach the fruit in syrup before using it. Fruits with too much acid may curdle an egg custard. The rind of lemon and orange is used in ice creams with little or no juice.

You can transform a plain ice cream into an exotic and spectacular creation by using a variety of toppings, sauces and accompaniments. Vanilla ice cream could be decorated with the poached peach halves or with pureed raspberries. Pears, chocolate sauce and vanilla ice cream make an interesting combination too. You could slice a banana into halves, pour hot fudge sauce over it and top it with whipped cream and you have the famous 'banana split'.

Ice cream variations

Use your imagination to serve ice cream in a variety of ways. Here are a few examples.

Dusty Roads is made by serving one scoop each of chocolate and coffee ice cream in a serving dish. Add 60 ml each of chocolate and butterscotch sauces. Top with whipped cream, chopped and toasted almonds and cocoa powder.

Peach Melba can be made by putting a scoop of vanilla ice cream in a serving dish, set two poached peach halves on each side and top with 60 ml Melba sauce, sprinkle with chopped and toasted almonds.

Mixed Delight is made by layering one scoop each of vanilla and peach ice cream in a dish, decorated with 125 gm sliced strawberries and 30 ml brandy (optional). Topped with whipped cream and a fresh whole strawberry, it makes an excellent dessert.

The various sauces and methods to prepare them have already been discussed in detail in the lesson on 'Chutneys and Sauces'.

Expert cook suggests...

1. Surplus milk chocolates, if added to the ice cream mix will give the ice cream a smoother and creamier texture.
2. To ensure that ice cream does not melt quickly when served, chill the ice cream bowls in the refrigerator a few minutes before use.

Sorbet

We call it ice, water ice or the commercial variety is called a 'drink stick' since it is often frozen round a wooden stick. It consists of sugar or sugar syrup and flavouring but there are countless variations too.

We have fruit sorbets, which are made from either a single fruit or a mixture, pureed or frozen. Chopped herbs like mint, or spices like cinnamon may be added to the fruits. Thyme, rosemary, and other infused herb sorbets are usually served as refreshing first courses or in between the courses to clear the palate. In our country we consume it as and when we want to.

Arriving at the right balance of flavour and sweetness in a sorbet is a matter of tasting and adjusting ingredients until the combination is just right. The proportion of sugar is critical. It can vary with every batch of fruit. It is best to taste the mixture after mixing sugar gradually, a little at a time.

The sorbet can be made light in texture by adding lightly whipped egg whites halfway through churning. Egg whites can, however, mask the pure flavour of sorbet. Nowadays, chefs prefer to lighten the texture by substituting glucose for up to a quarter of the regular sugar in the recipe.

Ingredients for making ice creams, sorbets and frozen desserts

The common ingredients that are generally used to make ice creams, sorbets and frozen desserts must be fully understood. It helps follow the guidelines of a recipe and you can never go wrong.

Milk and cream:

Milk

The smoothness and richness of an ice cream is directly related to the fat content in the milk and cream. The higher the fat content, the smoother the ice cream. Milk is the preferred base for ice cream custards because cream with a high fat content tends to curdle or form granules of fats while churning. Though, some cream is added halfway during churning, to give a richer texture.

Condensed milk can be substituted for cream. However, it lends a flavour that cannot be masked with another flavour.

White Sugar

Brown Sugar

Sugar:

This is generally used in syrup form. Both the white and brown variety of sugar prevents the formation of ice crystals and adds smoothness to the ice cream. Sugar, however, lowers the freezing point resulting in the mixture taking longer to freeze. If you add too little sugar, the ice cream may be grainy. If you add too much sugar, the mixture may not freeze at all.

Glucose

Glucose:

This gives a smoother texture to sorbets without being too sweet. It is a natural sugar but less sweet than regular sugar.

Soft Cheese

Yogurt, soft cheese:

Yogurt never loses its flavour even when frozen. It can be used alone or with milk as the main ingredient in a variety of mixtures. Fresh cream cheese gives body to ice creams and a variety of frozen desserts.

Potato Flour

Cornflour, potato flour and other thickeners:

These are used to make ice cream but they detract from the true flavour. They should be sparingly used, if at all.

Eggs

Eggs:

One of the most indispensable ingredients for thickening custard ice creams is egg, both whole and the yolk. Whole egg or egg yolk is whisked with sugar to the ribbon. Egg whites are added to sorbets for lightness. Raw egg yolk can harbour bacteria that are not killed by freezing. Therefore, whenever a frozen mixture has to be stored, the egg yolk must be cooked, either by custard or by whisking with sugar over heat.

Honey, maple syrup and other sweeteners:

Honey

They have a strong, cloying flavour though they act like sugar syrup when frozen. However, artificial sweeteners do not have the quality to produce a smooth mixture.

Fruits:

Fruits

Fruit juices and purees are often used for sorbets and to flavour ice creams. They also add acid in sorbets to balance the sugar and enhance the flavour, especially citrus fruits. Fruits like berries, can be pureed to be used raw. The flavour of many fruits like peaches, plums and pears improves when poached in syrup. Pineapple and kiwi must also be poached before use to destroy certain enzymes that prevent freezing. Figs and gooseberries are mealy even after poaching.

Nuts:

Pistachio

Walnuts

Peanuts

Almond

Cashew Nut

Chopped or sliced nuts offer a contrasting crunchiness in ice cream especially those with caramel toppings. The most commonly used nuts are almonds, pistachio, cashew nuts, walnuts and peanuts. They are traditional favourites with other cold and frozen desserts as well.

Red Wine

Liquor and wine:

These are used to flavour frozen desserts and to make sorbets. In India, we have yet to develop the art of using liqueurs and wines in food. For freezing purposes you must remember that alcohol sharply lowers the freezing point of a mixture and must be used sparingly.

FREEZING ICE CREAM AND SORBETS

All varieties of ice creams and sorbets, except the very rich ones, develop the smoothest texture when churned in an electric motor or by hand. For best results, you must first chill the mixture to reduce the churning time. That way freezing can be completed before the ice melts or the churner gets too warm.

Here are a few simple rules for freezing ice creams.

1. The container must be filled not more than two-thirds full, as the mixture will expand when frozen. The churning time required until the mixture begins to stiffen depends on the quantity, ingredients and temperature. If churned in less than 7-8 minutes, the texture may be grainy. If mixture has not frozen in 30 minutes, remove the mixture and refreeze the container and add more salt to the ice.
2. When the mixture begins to stiffen, add whipped egg whites (to sorbets) or flavourings like chocolate chips (to ice creams). Continue churning until stiff. Remove the paddle. Press down on the mixture and pack it in the container itself, or transfer it to a chilled container or mould, and store in the freezer till you need it. Alternatively, using the stirring method, freeze ice creams and sorbets directly in the freezer. To do this, pour the mixture into ice trays, preferably metal ones as they conduct the cold better. Freeze until half frozen. Then take it out into a chilled mixing bowl and whisk until smooth. Return the mixture to the trays and continue freezing, whisking once or twice more, until the mixture is stiff.

A Gelatin Dessert

Problem Shooting

As with other things, there can be problems. For a better understanding, the common problems that you may encounter are discussed as follows:

A **lumpy product** could be due to:

- Mixture, particularly fruit puree, was not smooth before being frozen.
- Paddle did not scrape the sides of the container during churning.

A **granular texture** could be due to:

- Excess water or alcohol in the mixture.
- A low amount of sugar or fat.
- The mixture was insufficiently churned, or churned too slowly.
- The mixture was frozen too quickly at very low temperature.
- The cream could have curdled during churning.
- The container could have been too full.
- The finished dessert was stored for too long.

A **poor flavour** could be due to:

- Not enough sugar.
- Too little acid such as lemon juice was used in a sorbet.

Storing Ice Cream and Sorbet

Both should always be kept aside for an hour or two after churning to allow the flavour to mellow. The richer the mixture, the longer you can store it before ice crystals begin to form. Sugar and gelatin slow down the formation of crystals. You can freeze homemade yogurt mixture for up to a week, while plain ice cream can be frozen for a fortnight. Light sorbets are best eaten within two or three hours, though you can freeze them, too, for a week. All frozen mixtures to be stored must be sealed tightly as they easily pick up other flavours. A fresh-frozen mixture thaws quickly. Handle it as little as possible. For ice cream or sorbet that has been frozen for over 12 hours, transfer it to the refrigerator section half an hour before serving or until it softens. The mixture should be soft enough to be scooped.

Gelatin

Gelatin is an important ingredient for setting moulded desserts and for other cold desserts. The recipe determines the amount required. To get 500 ml of clear liquid like fruit juice, 1 tablespoon of gelatin is sufficient. Soft, fluffy mixtures need less, while heavy, creamy ones may need more.

There are two kinds of gelatin. Natural gelatin, which is extracted from bones and skin, and commercial gelatin. Natural gelatin is found chiefly in the knuckle bones of calves. It is extracted by simmering in liquid for up to 8 hours. Commercial gelatin is available as a powder or granules. Both are tasteless and easy to use. You can measure powdered gelatin with a spoon.

Gelatin can be softened in a cold liquid, usually water, then dissolved in a pan over low heat and allowed to cool. The mixture to which gelatin is added must be warm enough to prevent the gelatin from setting immediately. You must stir the mixture thoroughly so that it is evenly distributed. As it cools, gelatin will separate from a fluffy mixture, and must be stirred gently but frequently while cooling.

Always use a metal bowl or container to chill a gelatin mixture. The bowl is set over ice. It sets rapidly once it is cold. Remove the bowl from ice as soon as mixture begins to thicken. Fold in any whipped ingredients such as cream or egg whites. Pour the mixture into the mould. If the mixture sets before being poured into the mould, you can melt it over very low heat. Those that contain egg will curdle and whipped cream will melt.

When the gelatin mixture is set, it must be put in the refrigerator for at least two hours to become firm. Since gelatin crystallises and separates easily in a freezer, it is not advisable to chill it quickly. Gelatin desserts keep well for two to three days but they stiffen. After 12 hours and more, leave them to soften for half an hour at room temperature before serving. An all-time favourite dessert is the homemade fruit gelatin mould, which is made by clarifying fruit juice with egg whites to make a transparent glistening mould. Fresh fruit juice set with gelatin and then whisked into opaque foam just before it sets, is another delicious cold dessert.

Moulded Gelatin Desserts

The addition of gelatin gives form and body to desserts by trapping air within whipped cream and eggs, thus sustaining their lightness. A gelatin mixture will not set firmly enough to hold its shape if too little gelatin has been added or it has been incorrectly mixed. Gelatin based desserts are mostly set in fancy moulds. To set soft foamy mixtures you must always use shallow, simple shapes, but creams can set firmly in tall peaked moulds and patterned ring moulds. A variety of moulds are available in the market. The more complicated the design of the mould, the more likely it is that the gelatin mixture will stick during unmoulding. You can decorate gelatin desserts with whipped cream or a ring of contrasting sauce around the base. Tall moulds can be decorated with a dollop of cream sprinkled with fresh berries or toasted nuts.

Unmoulding Gelatin Desserts

When the moulded gelatin dessert is firmly set, it needs to be loosened from the mould and inverted onto a plate for serving. Care has to be taken not to damage the shape as the presentation will be tarnished. Follow this procedure for unmoulding:

1. Gently lower the mould into a bowl of warm water till the water reaches the rim of the mould. Leave for a couple of seconds. Lift out the mould and dry the base.
2. Slowly tilt the mould sideways and gently pull the mixture away from the edge with your fingertips.
3. Rinse the serving plate with water to make it slippery so that if the mould does not land centrally, it can be pushed into the centre. Holding the plate upside down on the mould, quickly turn over both together, holding them firmly. Tap on the base of mould gently with your knuckles.

Cherry Jelly

4. Give a quick forceful shake sideways and down. The dessert will fall onto the plate. If it sticks, give several taps and shakes. If it still sticks, place a hot, wet cloth over the mould for 10-15 seconds. This will dislodge the mixture.

Note: To soften and melt powdered gelatin, sprinkle it over a small quantity of cold liquid. Leave the gelatin for 5 minutes without stirring till it swells to a spongy mass. Put the pan in a large vessel half filled with water and heat over low heat till the gelatin has melted, shaking the gelatin gently without stirring.

Meringue

This is a cold dessert made with a mixture of whipped egg whites and sugar.

There are three varieties of meringue:

- Folding castor sugar into whipped egg whites makes the simple meringue.

- The Italian meringue is made with sugar syrup mixed with whipped egg whites so that they are partially cooked, holding their shape longer. This is a more stable variety.
- The most robust of all is the cooked meringue. To obtain the lightest, finest texture while whisking egg whites, always use a copper bowl. After it has been beaten properly, you must not leave the meringue into the copper bowl for more than a few minutes as it may discolour. You could stiffen the whites by adding a pinch of salt or a little cream of tartar. Meringue is stiff enough to be piped or spread directly on a baking tray. You do not need any moulds for them. Always bake meringue at a very low temperature. It should retain its whiteness or acquire only a light colour. The ideal texture is crunchy on the outside but soft enough to collapse at the prick of a fork. Crisp meringue can be filled with whipped cream, fruit or ice cream. A layer of meringue set inside an iced dessert adds a unique touch but, once mixed with other ingredients, meringue tends to soften within an hour or two.

Simple meringue

It is easy to make a simple meringue. Egg whites are whipped until very stiff, and then a tablespoon of sugar for each egg white is beaten in so that the whites stand in short peaks. More sugar is lightly folded in. The first addition of sugar stabilises the egg white foam, but if the second, larger addition is over mixed, the egg whites lose their form and turn watery. Last of all, the flavouring is added. This mixture can be baked and sandwiched with cream, or spread on a cake or ice cream. Mixed with ground almonds or hazelnuts, it can be the basis of delicious cakes. Meringue can also be poached in water or milk.

To make 600 ml of Simple Meringue you need:

4 egg whites at room temperature; 200 gms castor sugar; 1 tsp vanilla essence.

Method:

1. In a copper mixing bowl, beat the egg whites until stiff. Use a balloon whisk. Add 4 tablespoons of sugar, one at a time.
2. Keep beating until the egg whites and sugar mixture forms short peaks when the whisk is lifted.
3. Using a wooden or plastic spatula, fold in the remaining sugar.
4. Last of all, fold in the vanilla essence. Continue folding for a minute until long peaks are formed. A sprinkling of sugar added just before baking lends a sparkle and crispness to simple meringue.

Cooked Italian meringue

This is made by beating hot sugar syrup, boiled to the hardball stage, (see lesson on 'Indian Desserts'), into stiffly whipped egg whites. The heat of the syrup partially cooks the egg whites. They hold their shape well for as long as two days. It is baked to be more melting, less crisp and frothy than simple meringue. Cooked meringue is stiffer than these two varieties. Whisking unbeaten egg whites with sugar over a pan of steaming water till a smooth fluffy paste is obtained. Whisking it by hand is definitely hard work. It can be stored for a week.

Both Italian and cooked meringues are basis of small cakes, often made rich with nuts. While baking, you can set aside a little of the meringue mixture to use as a filling. Both of them hold their form even when mixed with other ingredients. You can mix Italian meringue with butter to obtain a version of butter cream or added to sweeten whipped cream or to lighten sorbets. It can be mixed with pureed fruit and cooked as a hot dessert soufflé.

To make 600 ml of Italian Meringue you need:

4 egg whites; 200 gms castor sugar; 125 ml water; 1 tsp vanilla essence.

Method:

1. In a pan, heat sugar and water over low heat till the sugar dissolves. Bring to a boil and continue boiling without stirring till the hardball stage (see 'Indian Desserts').
2. Beat the egg whites till stiff. You could use an electric mixer for best results. Gradually add the sugar syrup, a little at a time, beating constantly. Pour the syrup directly into the eggs or it will stick to the sides of the bowl.
3. Keep beating the mixture till it is cool. By now it will be very stiff. Beat in the vanilla essence.

To make 600 ml of Cooked Meringue you will need:

4 egg whites; 200 gms castor sugar; 1 tsp vanilla essence.

Method:

1. Take a copper mixing bowl. Put the egg whites, sugar and vanilla essence into this bowl and whisk with a balloon whisk or an electric whisk till everything is well mixed.
2. Place the bowl over a pan of steaming water and keep whisking till the mixture forms stiff peaks when the whisk is lifted. This will take about 10-15 minutes. Remove from heat and keep whisking till cool.

Besides the cold and frozen desserts just discussed, there are many more.

- A great favourite is the pudding made of egg custard thickened slightly with flour, cornflour or arrowroot.
- Other popular flavours are coffee, chocolate and vanilla. Desserts made with chocolate and cheese set firmly enough to be unmoulded. Chocolate is often mixed with a selection of nuts and set into simple round shapes or into loaf shape.
- Pureed fruits folded into whipped cream, or thickened custard and whipped cream make an excellent fruit cream to be served partially chilled. Desserts need a light hand, a sweet disposition and a lot of imagination with which you can combine various ingredients to make your own special finale to a meal.

In the practical session you will learn how to make ice cream and sorbet to give you a hands-on experience in dessert making.

Practical things to be done

1. Vanilla Ice Cream

Utensils used: A selection of mixing bowls; a balloon whisk; measuring spoons; a scoop.

Gadgets: Ice cream churn or freezer.

Portions: To serves 6 persons.

Ingredients: Vanilla custard (see lesson on 'Sauces') made from 500 ml milk, 6 egg yolks, 1 tsp vanilla essence and 125 gms castor sugar; 250 ml double cream.

To make vanilla ice cream, follow this procedure.

1. Prepare the custard following the procedure explained in the lesson on 'Sauces'. Freeze the custard in an ice cream churn or freezer until it is semisolid.
2. In a mixing bowl, lightly whip the cream. Add this to the custard and mix thoroughly. Freeze again till set.
3. If using a churn, lift out the paddle and pack down the ice cream in the churn, or pack it into a chilled container. Cover tightly and store in the freezer. Serve when you want to. If the ice cream has been kept in the freezer for more than 12 hours put it in the refrigerator section for 30 minutes to soften it and then serve. For added decoration, spoon some chocolate sauce or fudge sauce (see lesson on 'Sauces') over the ice cream when serving.

Vanilla Ice Cream with Hot Chocolate Sauce

For variety, you could try some of these variations.

- Adding 250 gms chopped chocolate chips to vanilla ice cream when you are mixing in the whipped cream can make **chocolate chip ice cream**.

Blackcurrant Ice-cream

- Making a puree of 500 gms fresh strawberries and stirring it into the chilled vanilla custard with 1-2 tablespoon lemon juice can make **strawberry ice cream**. Sweeten the mixture to taste.
- **Banana ice cream** can be made by peeling and pureeing 3 bananas with the juice of 1 orange, adding icing sugar to sweeten the mixture to taste. Stir this into the chilled vanilla custard.
- **Coffee ice cream** is made when you add 3 tablespoons instant coffee in place of the vanilla essence in the custard. Stir in the coffee into the custard while it is still hot.
- Adding 1 tablespoon peppermint essence instead of the vanilla essence, and a few drops of green food colouring to the custard when it is cool can make **peppermint ice cream**. You could also add some chopped chocolate chips to this ice cream.
- **Peach or plum ice cream** is made when you poach 1 kg peaches or plums halved in sugar syrup (see lesson on 'Indian Desserts') made with 1 litre of water and 300 gms sugar. Drain and puree the fruit and strain it through a sieve. Stir this puree into the chilled vanilla custard with a few drops of almond extract for peaches, or 1-2 tablespoon lemon juice for plums.

2. Raspberry Sorbet

Utensils used: A saucepan; a sieve; a selection of mixing bowls; a wooden spoon.

Gadgets: Ice cream churn or freezer; food processor.

Portions: To serve 6-8 persons.

Ingredients: 500 gms fresh raspberries; juice of 1 lemon; 250 ml water; 200 gms sugar; a few raspberries and mint leaves for decoration.

To make raspberry sorbet, follow this simple procedure.

1. Put the sugar and water into a saucepan. Heat till the sugar dissolves. Bring to a boil; simmer for 2-3 minutes and cool. Puree the raspberries in a food processor. Work the puree through a sieve to remove the seeds. Mix the sugar syrup, lemon juice, a little water and the raspberry puree thoroughly. Taste the mixture adding more sugar or lemon juice if required. Chill the mixture. Taste it again as chilling diminishes the sweetness.
2. Using an ice cream churn or a freezer, freeze this mixture. Then store it in the freezer packed in a container with a tightfitting lid. When you are ready to serve, scoop out three scoops of the sorbet per serving into a stemmed glass, decorate with fresh raspberries and sprig of mint leaves.

Similarly you can prepare 'strawberry sorbet'. Raspberry and Strawberry both are seasonal fruits, use whatever is available in the market when you want to make the sorbet.

For variety, you could try some of these variations.

- **Blackcurrant sorbet** can be made by substituting blackcurrants for raspberries in the recipe and following the instructions. Simmer the currants with the sugar syrup till they turn soft. Puree and sieve them. Serve decorated with blackcurrants.
- **Lemon sorbet** can be made by substituting 175 ml lemon juice and finely grated rind of 3 lemons for raspberry puree in the recipe. After freezing, pack into chilled hollowed shells and top with the lid or simply scoop out into stemmed glasses adding a thin lemon slice stuck to the rim of the glass for decoration.
- **Orange sorbet** can be made by substituting 500 ml fresh orange juice for raspberry puree and water. After freezing, pack into chilled fruit shells as for lemon sorbet, or serve scoops of the sorbet in stemmed glasses decorated with an orange segment.
- **Champagne or wine sorbet** can be made by substituting 750 ml champagne or wine for raspberries and water. When serving, pour a few spoonfuls of wine or champagne over the sorbet and top with dry lemon or orange peel.

All these ice creams and sorbets will add an exotic touch to your meals. You can serve them anytime. Numerous varieties of cold and frozen desserts are available in the market. Those made at home have the personal creative touch, which is always appreciated by everyone. ■■

PROGRESS CHECKLIST # 4

Do not skip this checklist. Answer all the questions. They are based on what you learnt in the last six days. Whenever in doubt, go back to the appropriate lesson and reread the relevant section. Your sincere efforts will make you a great cook.

1. Did the family members appreciate the 'vanilla custard' cooked by you?

   ☐ Yes ☐ No

2. Did you try making a 'raita' other than cucumber 'raita'?

   ☐ Yes ☐ No

If not, try making other 'raitas'. They are simple to make. When garnished well, they are immediately appreciated.

3. Did everyone appreciate the *'Thandai'* made by you?

   ☐ Yes ☐ No

Experiment with other drinks, particularly fruit based drinks made like *'Panna'*.

4. Which of these three jams did you make?

   A. Apricot jam.

   B. Apple jelly.

   C. Orange marmalade.

Try other fruits like plums, guavas and pineapple.

5. Were you able to make good 'praline' (*chikki*)?

   ☐ Yes ☐ No

Try making other Indian sweets like *'barfi'* and *'halwa'*.

6. Did everyone appreciate the vanilla ice cream made by you?

   ☐ Yes ☐ No

7. Did you make a fruit sorbet?

   ☐ Yes ☐ No

8. How do you rate your personal cooking confidence?

   ☐ Low

   ☐ Average

   ☐ Good

9. How do you rate your personal progress in cooking?

   ☐ Low

   ☐ Average

   ☐ Good

10. List items that you will cook again after completing the course.

■ ■

COOKING METHOD # 8

Cooking Method # 8.1

Baking and Roasting

Baking and roasting refers to cooking in hot air in an enclosed place as in a tandoor or an oven. Roasting is applied to meat and poultry, and baking is done with fish, vegetables and casseroles. Cakes and cookies are also baked.

In baking and roasting, both the temperature and timing are critical factors. If you fail to be precise, it can make the difference as between a good dish and a disaster! It was never easy to control temperatures in clay ovens, but experience has taught people how to make a fine 'tandoori chicken'. Electricity and gas-operated ovens can be very precise and are ideal for baking cakes and cookies. Opening the oven door can drastically bring down the temperature. Follow cooking instructions precisely.

Baking and roasting are fine arts. Understand the technique. Follow the recipe precisely. Keep a record of your successes and failures. This will take you up the ladder of success.

TIPS

A few tips to follow while baking and roasting:

- When using the oven for roasting or baking, preheat it.
- Leave space for air circulation.
- Keep the door closed as far as possible and rotate the food.
- Place meats and poultry on a rack to drain fat, prevent the bottom from cooking in the pan juices. Allow heat to circulate around the meat.
- If basting the food, use lemon juice, fruit juice broth or marinade without adding fat.
- To bake vegetables, wash, prick skins and place on a baking sheet in the oven.

Cooking Method # 8.2

Grilling

This is done on an open grid over a heat source, which may be an electric or gas element, hot coals, burning wood or a gas tandoor. Grilling is commonly used to prepare meat, poultry, fish, and even vegetables. It is a low-fat method of cooking as the fat drips away from the food. Be sure to baste the food or marinade it, without fat.

Basting Food While Grilling

TIPS

A few tips to follow while grilling:

- Trim fat from meat. Use lean meat to prevent flare-up of flames and to reduce calories.
- Baste food as it cooks to prevent drying out. Use lemon juice, fruit juice, both low-fat Italian dressing, or wine for flavour.

If you are using a charcoal grill, be sure to choose one that works on the least amount of coal. Coal may flavour your grilled foods.

The best grilling temperature is when the charcoal has been burning for 30–45 minutes and is grey in colour.

Sprinkle aromatic herbs such as thyme, sage or rosemary over the coals as they add light flavour to grilled foods.

Clean the grill after use with a wire brush and apply a coating of vegetable oil. Do not let black residue build up on your grill.

Cooking Method # 8.3

Broiling

This is to cook with direct heat from above. Broilers may use gas or electricity. It is a high-heat cooking method that does not require fats and cooks foods quickly. Steaks, chicken, fish, and certain vegetables such as onions, zucchini and tomatoes are foods that are commonly broiled.

A few tips to follow while broiling:

- Always preheat the broiler.
- Use a broiling pan or rack set in a shallow pan to allow fat to drain away.
- Marinade tender meats for 30 minutes, tougher meats for up to 24 hours. Marinade fish fillets or steaks for only 30 minutes.
- Thinner foods can be placed closer to the heat than thicker foods. If thicker foods are placed too close to the heat, the outside will be cooked while the inside may remain only semi-cooked.
- Turn thick foods once for more even cooking. Fish less than 1 inch thick, and similar thin foods do not need to be turned.
- Watch foods carefully. The side turned towards the heat in the end cooks in much lesser time (about half) than the one you begin with.

Cooking Method # 8.4

Pan-broiling

To pan-broil, you cook food uncovered in a sauté pan or skillet without adding any fat or liquids. Fat is drained off as it accumulates. Bacon and hamburgers are two examples of foods that can be pan-broiled.

A few tips to follow while pan-broiling:

- Do not use too high a temperature.
- Drain off the fat to avoid frying the food.

DAY 25

Baking Basics

The use of cereals is as old as the history of mankind. Over the years, with experimentation and innovation, we have a wide variety of cakes, pies, cookies, and numerous breads that are unique to different parts of the world. Baked goods do not have excessive calories as saturated fat, sugar, or cholesterol. It is possible to make adjustments to many traditional baking recipes, including cakes, cookies, and pies, and have products that are healthy to eat but tasty. When you do your own baking, you can control the amount of sugar, fat, saturated fat, and cholesterol in the finished products.

Baking is a special art and requires several skills. These skills can be acquired with persistence and

Oven Toaster Grill

an understanding of the basic principles of baking. Both the right equipment and the best ingredients are important. Knowledge of equipment and how to use it is necessary. Baking requires precision. One needs to be precise in measuring the exact amount of ingredients to follow a definite procedure in terms of technique and baking at a precise temperature and for a prescribed time. As with all cooking procedures, cleanliness needs special attention. The equipment should be clean. This ensures the best possible product, which is tasty and healthy.

Cooking Equipment

The equipment for baking can be divided into several categories:

Measuring ingredients:

Measuring – Weighing Scale, Jar, Spoons, Cups

The measurement items used for the volume measurement in baking include:

- The standard set of spoons, which are used for either wet or dry ingredients, consists 1 tablespoon, 1 teaspoon, ½ teaspoon, and ¼ teaspoon.
- A set of measuring cups (for dry ingredients) consists 1 cup, ½ cup, 1/3 cup, and ¼ cup measure.
- A 1 or 2 cup measuring jug for liquids.

Scales:

The use of weights for both dry and wet ingredients, as the primary form of measurement is a common practice in bakeries. Weighing an ingredient is much easier and more accurate than the many variables in technique that are possible in volume measurement (commonly referred to as teaspoons, tablespoons, cups, millilitre, litre, etc.). Nevertheless, standard measures of volume are used in most homes. Rather than the use of a scale, with careful technique, you can still prepare a very good product.

Egg and flour beaten together in a mixing bowl

Mixing utensils:

In order to properly blend ingredients you need to use proper utensils. While blending cake batter, remember to use either a spoon (with a specified number of strokes), or when using an electric beater, it must be set at the right speed and for a specific length of time. If the recipes call for 'folding', you need to use a rubber spatula.

Mixing bowls:

Determine which bowl is best for use. They are available in a variety of sizes. Do not use a bowl that is too small otherwise the ingredients will not blend properly.

Baking pans:

Most recipes indicate the type and size of pan that should be used for a particular recipe. If in doubt about the size of a pan, simply measure it to confirm the size. If you have a similar pan but not the exact size, it may be necessary to change the cooking time – making it either longer or shorter.

Baking pans and moulds

The oven:

The oven temperature must be exact and constant in order to achieve a high level of proficiency in baking. Electric ovens are notorious for needing longer preheating and stabilisation times than gas ovens. The oven temperature is a critical part of the success of baking.

Cooling racks:

Freshly baked cake on a cooling rack

Wire racks for cooling are very important. Proper cooling of a baked item ensures an even outer texture and a good appearance.

A detailed description of all equipments has been given in the third section of this course.

Baking Ingredients

A primary rule for all ingredients is that they must be fresh. Buy from a reliable grocery store. Here are a few things to remember about ingredients.

Flours:

The most important ingredient in most baked goods is flour. It provides the structure for baked products. When flour is mixed with a liquid, gluten is formed. This gives the structure to baked goods. Most people use all-purpose flour available in the local supermarket, as well as refined flour, wheat flour or cornflour. The recipe will indicate the flour you will require.

Sugars:

Sugar does much more in baking than just make the product sweet. Sugar contributes in making a fine-textured and tender product. It prevents staling by holding onto water, provides leavening when creamed, and helps the crust to brown. In yeast breads, sugar provides food for the yeast to eat so that they produce carbon dioxide gas that makes bread rise. Sugars used in baking are generally granulated, either white or brown. Other sweetening agents may include the use of syrups, such as honey or molasses.

Liquids:

Liquids such as milk should be fresh and properly measured. Water and a variety of juices are also used. Do not overlook the effect of flavours that liquids can contribute. Liquid is important for gluten development.

Eggs:

In addition to the use of milk as a primary ingredient in many baked products, eggs are commonly used. Eggs provide structure, moisture, flavour, and colour when used in baked goods. Egg whites, when whipped, are important to leaven in products such as angel food cake. Eggs should be fresh and not too cold. Many recipes suggest that the eggs be at room temperature. This does not mean that the eggs must be stored out of the refrigerator.

It is best to remove the eggs from the refrigerator about 2 hours before use and separate them (according to the need) when still cold. It is easier to separate eggs when cold, but it is advisable to use them when at room temperature, especially for baking.

Fat:

Fats are important for making tender baked goods that taste good. They prevent staling of baked goods and provide leavening when creamed with sugar. Common fats used in baking include butter (sweet and salted), shortening, margarine, and vegetable oil. Ensure that the fats are not 'rancid', a condition that does not appear to be spoiled, but causes a poor taste in the end product. Use of fresh ingredients is the best assurance that the fats are fresh.

Baking Ingredients and Equipment

Leavening agents:

Freshness is most important for ingredients used for leavening. Leavening agents include:

- **Yeast** – A live fungi that produces carbon dioxide gas when it feeds on the sugar in a dough. It may be purchased dry (it comes in little foil envelopes – always check the freshness date on them), or compressed (it comes as small moist cakes that must be refrigerated and used within two weeks).
- **Baking powder** – A mixture of acid and alkali (the alkali is baking soda) that reacts with liquid by foaming and creating bubbles that raise the dough; double-acting baking soda has two acids – one that foams at room temperature, another that foams at oven temperatures.
- **Baking soda** – An acid ingredient, such as buttermilk, must be in the dough in order for baking soda to raise the dough.

These leavening agents lose some of their leavening power over a period of time. When you purchase them, mark the date of purchase with a marker on the side of the package. Allow no more than a storage time of 6 months for baking powder in a dry environment, 18 months for baking soda, and up to the date on the label for dry yeast. If you question whether your baking powder is okay to use, simply measure 1 teaspoon into a cup of hot water. If it is still good, the mixture will actively fizz and bubble. If you question whether your yeast is alive, check for bubbles when the yeast is combined with lukewarm water in your recipe.

Other forms of leavening include the use of steam (as in cream puffs) and air (as in the mixing process).

Salt and flavouring:

Salt is a common additive for providing flavour to many baked goods. In yeast breads, salt prevents the yeast from producing too much carbon dioxide gas and possibly ruining the final product. Flavouring may come from other sources – extracts such as vanilla, various fruits, liquids, nuts, and seasonings, to name a few. If you are developing your own recipe (or trying to decipher grandmother's recipe) you will probably have to make the item several times to determine the correct flavour. Keep track of the amounts with accurate measurements to establish the flavour desired.

See the lists of common baking terms and functions and types of ingredients used in baking, given at the end of today's lesson.

YEAST BREADS

Yeast breads are one of the most favourite forms of food that are a great accompaniment with virtually any meal. Most bread is made primarily of flour, water, salt, and yeast, with little or no fat added. For example, French bread usually contains no fat.

There is some bread, however, that use increased amounts of fat, sugar, and sometimes eggs. These include rich dinner rolls, brioche, Danish pastry, croissants, and sweet rolls such as cinnamon rolls. If you follow the basic rules of bread making, you will enjoy many successes in this area and receive many compliments.

Yeast Bread (*Pav*)

Ensure that the ingredients are correctly measured and combined in the proper order. In all cases of using yeast, take caution not to kill the yeast by using water that is too hot. Yeast grows best between 100°–110°F. At a lower temperature, it takes longer for the yeast to grow, and the bread will not rise as much as desired. If the water is too hot, much of the yeast will die and the bread will not rise. You can test the water by placing a little on your wrist just like testing a baby's bottle. The dough is properly mixed when it is no longer sticky. If it is still sticky, more flour (in small amounts) should be mixed in.

After the bread dough is mixed (whether by hand or machine), place the dough on a lightly floured table for kneading. Kneading is the process of working dough into a smooth mass by pressing and folding to develop the gluten and mix the ingredients. If you use a mixer with a 'dough hook' attachment, this will do your kneading, or you can use the food processor for kneading using the plastic dough-kneading blade. To knead by hand, do the following:

- Place the round of dough in front of you and bring the top half of the dough over towards you.
- Turn the dough a quarter turn, and repeat the process.
- Continue turning the dough a quarter turn and repeat the kneading process until the dough is very soft.
- If the dough feels sticky while kneading it, add a sprinkling of flour. The purpose of kneading is to develop the gluten in the dough so that the gas produced by the yeast is captured within. When the dough is not kneaded enough, the gas is not contained, and the resulting bread tends to be heavy and small in volume. The length of kneading time varies. 5 to 8 minutes is usually enough, or until the dough becomes smooth and shiny. The quantity of dough and the type of flour used also affect kneading time.

After the dough is kneaded, transfer into a lightly greased bowl, cover with a damp cloth or cling-film, or place in polythene bag and place in a warm, draft free area. Let the dough rest and rise until double in size This is known as 'proofing'. During proofing, the yeast consumes the sugar and starches in the dough, producing carbon dioxide gas that is the bread's leavening.

- When the dough has sufficiently proofed (it usually takes about 1–1½ hours), it is tested by inserting the fingers in the dough to the knuckle in several places. If the finger marks close very slowly, the dough is ready to be punched. Punching the dough is to pull up the dough on all sides, fold over the centre, and press down. Then turn the dough upside down in the bowl. The dough is punched to keep it at an even temperature, expel the carbon dioxide, further develop the gluten, and bring fresh oxygen to the yeast cells for further growth.
- Once punched, divide the dough (if necessary), shape into desired shapes (rolls, loaves), and place onto nonstick or lightly oiled sheet pans, or other baking dish and proof again, until double in bulk. Fully proofed loaves of dough when touched gently will slowly fill out the dents made by the fingers. Rich dough containing fat should not be allowed to reach full proof. Fat weakens the gluten structure and the dough may collapse in baking if given as full a proof as bread dough.

After the second proofing, place directly into a preheated oven and bake until it sounds hollow when tapped. Oven temperature is an important factor. If bread is placed in an oven that is not hot enough, the bread will not rise in the oven and will be smaller than intended.

After baking, bread is removed from the pan immediately and cooled on cooling racks that allow good air circulation. Do not cool bread in a draft or the crust may crack. Once cooled, store bread in plastic bags, except for hard-crusted breads (the crust will soften if placed in plastic). If the bread is not completely cooled when you place it in a bag, moisture will build up inside the wrapping, making the bread soggy and encourage mould growth.

To save much time, you can purchase frozen bread dough (usually in half-kilo loaves) at the supermarket. It is ready to be proofed and baked. Not only is the dough convenient to make your own loaf of bread, it is useful for making a pizza crust or being cut up to make rolls. For pizza, all you need to do is let the dough rise in a warm spot while you lightly sauté (preferably in a nonstick pan using a light greasing with vegetable oil) some vegetables. Then assemble the pizza by spreading tomato sauce on the crust, sprinkling mozzarella cheese (made from skimmed milk), and spreading the vegetables evenly on top.

Good yeast breads are characterised by an even golden brown colour. The bread should be light for its size. It should have a good shape and have a tender or crispy crust as desired. The interior should be soft and free from large air pockets (evidence of letting the bread proof for too long a period of time). The texture of the bread should be smooth due to the very fine air cells within the interior, the aroma should be pleasing, not strong, and the inner colour should be off-white.

Most yeast breads use minimal amounts of fat, amounting to no more than 1 to 2 grams per slice, and provide lots of nutrients for their calories. Wholet-wheat and other whole grain breads contain more vitamins, minerals, and fibre than white bread. Breads such as richer dinner rolls, brioche, Danish pastry, croissants, and sweet rolls such as cinnamon rolls contain more fat.

Commercially made Danish pastry with little or no fat is available at the supermarket. There are sweet roll recipes that cut dramatically on the fat but still taste great. Dinner rolls do not have to be made from rich dough. They can be made quite easily from regular bread dough. As for brioche and croissants, they rely on fat (it's actually butter) for their flakiness, so lower-in-fat versions are simply not successful.

The amount of salt used in making bread is minimal. Do not change the amount the recipe calls for because salt is very important in controlling the growth of the yeast and production of gases that are important in the baking process.

Quick breads

Quick breads are essentially what the name implies – breads made quickly. While yeast breads require time for rising, the leavening action in a quick bread is caused by baking powder, baking soda, or steam and sometimes a combination of all three. These cause the baked items to rise in the oven. Quick breads include muffins, certain loaf breads (such as banana bread), biscuits, pancakes, waffles, quick coffeecakes, cream puffs, and popovers. Many traditional recipes for quick breads contain more fat and sugar than necessary, but they are very adaptable to some simple modifications. Muffins are a very popular quick bread, available in many different varieties.

Muffins

When making muffins and loaf breads remember these simple rules:

1. Mix dry ingredients in one bowl, and blend liquid ingredients in another.
2. Pour liquid ingredients, all at once, over the dry ingredients. Stir together until blended. The mixture will still be lumpy.

Here are some tips for making and storing muffins and loaf breads:

- Do not over mix the batter or dough. It develops too much gluten. This results in a tough baked product with peaked tops and vertical tunnels running through it. Stir just until dry ingredients are moistened. The batter should be lumpy. The only exception to this rule is popovers – they must be beaten very well before pouring into cups for baking.

- Dried fruits, such as raisins, should be steeped in water before using them in recipes so they are plump and do not rob moisture from the batter during mixing and baking.
- Grease and flour pans, unless using nonstick pans.
- Once the batter or dough is ready, put into pans and bake right away to ensure that they rise as much as possible.
- Bake in the top third of the oven so the bottoms do not burn and they cook evenly.
- Bake until a wooden pick inserted into the centre comes out clean. Overbaked muffins will be dry.
- Let muffins cool for 5 minutes and then remove from pans. Otherwise, they will become soggy. Cool on wire racks. Loaf bread can cool in the pan.
- Store cooled baked goods in plastic at room temperature, where they can stay fresh for up to 4 days. They can also be frozen for 2 to 3 months in airtight packaging.

Variety of Biscuits

Mango Cheese Crepes (Pancakes)

Biscuits are characterised by a rough appearance with a light golden colour and cake-like interior. They use more fat, usually shortening, than most other quick breads. Biscuits generally double in size during the baking process and go well with any meal. Biscuits are made from dough by following these steps:

1. Cut shortening into the dry ingredients until the mixture becomes crumbly. Biscuits can also be made using oil.
2. Combine liquid ingredients.
3. Add liquid to dry ingredients and mix dough only until soft but not sticky and leaves the side of the bowl, forming a ball.
4. Dough is then kneaded gently.
5. Dough is rolled to about half the desired thickness of finished biscuits and cut into desired shapes using round cookie / biscuit cutter.
6. Dough is placed ½ inch apart on baking pan for crispy biscuits or touching each other for softer biscuits. Brush the tops with milk to enhance browning.

Pancakes (also known as griddle cakes) are a form of quick bread that is characterised by a very thin batter that can be poured, and used primarily as a breakfast food. Crepes (also known as French pancakes) are similar to pancakes but have a more velvety appearance and a thinner, smoother batter. Crepes are wonderful for any meal and for desserts. They are commonly stuffed with meat, fish, fruit, and sometimes are served flambé style (flaming with the aid of brandy). The **waffle** is very similar to the pancake batter, but is slightly thicker and somewhat richer. The use of a waffle iron is used to create the characteristic shape. Waffles should be made to order and are served with syrups, fruits, frozen yogurt, and other creations that may be your favourite.

Cornbread is very similar to the muffin mixture, except that it is baked in pans, instead of individual muffins. American style Cornbread is baked in muffin pans.

Popovers are leavened primarily with the use of steam. When pouring them into the greased cavities of a muffin tin, place them directly into a preheated oven without delay. The popovers will rise due to the steam that they produce.

Making Quick Breads Nutritious

Quick breads vary in their fat content. Most of them can be made with less fat, or at least a less saturated fat. Muffins and loaf bread recipes are easily adaptable to using less sugar and fat; biscuits are a little harder. Here are some tips to modify recipes.

- You can decrease the fat in many quick bread recipes by about one-fourth to one-third of the original amount without any significant difference in quality. In recipes for muffins, quick breads, and biscuits, the minimum amount of fat is 1 to 2 tablespoons per cup of flour.
- You can substitute soft tub margarine or liquid margarine for stick margarine or butter in a recipe to ensure less fat, and less saturated fat. You can also substitute oil for shortening a cup oil for each ½ cup of shortening.
- Many quick breads, especially muffins and loaf breads, are ideal for fibre rich ingredients, such as fruits, raisins, wheat or oat bran, whole-wheat flour, and rolled oats.
- Whole-wheat pastry flour can be substituted for white flour in quick breads that use baking powder. Usually whole-wheat pastry flour can replace half the white flour called for in the recipe for good results. Simply substitute

American Style Quick Cornbread

an equivalent amount of whole-wheat pastry flour for white flour. You may find whole-wheat pastry flour at the supermarket; if not, check your grocery store.

- You can decrease the sugar content in muffin and quick bread recipes to 1 tablespoon sugar per cup of flour.
- Decrease the amount of nuts in the recipe by half. Nuts are full of fats and calories.
- When choosing muffin and loaf bread recipes, try to choose those with 5 grams or less fat per muffin or serving. Whereas some muffins can be full of hearty, healthy ingredients such as whole-wheat flour and fruits, other muffins resemble little cakes with high fat and sugar content.
- Biscuits do not have to be made with shortening; oil can be used.
- Also, always remember to use nonstick pans.

Glazes and Topping for Bread

Poppy Seed Bread

Chocolate Glazed Bread

Banana Bread with Cream Cheese Glaze

This is an important part of baking. All breads need some kind of finish before or after baking. If you want to flavour the crust, shape the bread on a board sprinkled with rolled oats, cornmeal, and chopped nuts, or simply with generous amounts of flour. Similarly, coat the baking tins. Egg glaze gives bread a shiny, golden-brown surface; for extra glaze the dough is glazed, left to dry, then given a second coating of the glaze.

Popular and savoury bread toppings include seeds such as sesame and poppy, coarse salt crystals, and chopped or flaked nuts such as almonds. When using nuts, first brush the bread with egg whites to make the nuts stick to the bread. To make a sweet baked topping, brush the dough with water, milk or lightly whisked egg whites and sprinkle with sugar.

Use coarse sugar as that adds a pleasant texture. Some sweetbreads and coffee cakes have sticky toppings. After baking, a sweet glaze made with sugar, milk, butter and honey is poured over the bread while it is still hot. Soft icing is spread on top when the bread is cold.

Problem Shooting for Yeast Breads

If the dough has risen poorly or not at all, the reason could be:

- Yeast was stale.
- Liquid for dissolving yeast was too hot.
- Dough has too much soft flour, sugar, salt, fat or eggs.
- Yeast came in contact with salt or too much sugar during mixing.
- Dough was under or over kneaded.
- Oven temperature was too low.

The reasons for heavy bread with a dark crust and shapeless loaves could be:

- Dough has too much liquid.
- Dough rose too much during first rising.
- Dough did not rise enough before baking (second rising).

In case of soft, puffy bread with a pale crust, flat loaves with loose crumbs having open holes, the reason could be:

- Dough had too much yeast.
- Dough rose at too high a temperature.
- Dough rose too much before baking (second rising).
- Oven temperature was too low.

For yeasty or sour taste, the reason could be:

- Dough had too much yeast or rose too much.
- Dough rose too fast during first rising.
- Dough rose too slowly.

Croûtes, Croûtons and Toast

Both croûtes and croûtons are different shapes of bread that are toasted or fried as a garnish for other foods. A croûte is usually larger than a croûton, often shaped as a hollow container by hollowing out the centre of a thick slice. It is an ideal, crispy container to serve scrambled eggs.

A croûton is a slice of bread cut into tiny squares, triangles, rounds, hearts or teardrops, toasted or deep-fried to serve as a topping for soups. Sometimes, both croûtes and croûtons are added to salads, especially of mixed greens. Fried croûtons are also used to garnish dishes with a sauce or serve as a crispy base for steaks and poached eggs. Toasts are thin slices of bread toasted in a toaster till light golden. This is eaten with a spread of butter or jam. Wafer-thin slices of bread that crush in the oven, called Melba toast, make a good alternative to bread rolls.

Fried Croûtons

Making toasted croûtes and croûtons

Cut white bread in 1 cm slices. Trim it into desired shapes. Crusty rolls or loaves of French bread may be sliced without trimming. Bake the bread at 350°F/175°C till crisp and light golden. If you want to make garlic flavoured croûtes, rub the bread with a cut clove of garlic. Cool and keep in an airtight container. They will keep for two weeks.

Making fried croûtes and croûtons

Cut a white bread in 6 mm thick slices. Dice it or cut into shapes. Discard the crusts. Deep-fry the bread pieces, browning them on both sides over medium heat. Keep stirring constantly so that they brown evenly. Drain on paper towels. cool and wrap them in aluminium foil. They will keep for a day. When you need them reheat in the foil in an oven.

Making toasted cubed croûtons

Toast bread slices. When still warm, brush both sides with butter. Cut into cubes discarding the crusts.

Making Melba toast

Cut bread into thinnest possible slices. Bake at 350°/175°C until crisp and curled and unevenly brown. If you cannot cut the bread into really thin slice, toast sliced bread of medium thickness, discard the crusts and split the slice horizontally. Press the slice with the palm to flatten. Bake until crisp.

Making breadcrumbs

Breadcrumbs come in handy when you have to coat food items such as cutlets and chops for deep-frying. Fresh breadcrumbs are used to bind stuffing, thicken soups and sauces. Dry brown breadcrumbs are sprinkled over some baked dishes for colour and crunch.

To make fresh white breadcrumbs, cut away the crusts from fairly dry white bread. Cut the bread in large cubes. Grind in a food processor or blender, or work it with your fingers through a coarse sieve. Use within two days.

To make **dry white breadcrumbs**, cut away the crusts and dry the white bread in a warm place or in an oven on very low heat till crisp. Crush in a food processor or blender, or with a rolling pin and work through a course sieve – alternatively, you could make dry fresh breadcrumbs in the oven on very low heat so they do not brown. Store in an airtight container. It will stay for a month.

To make dry brown breadcrumbs, follow the same procedure as for dry white breadcrumbs, first toasting the bread at 350°/175°C till golden brown. Cool and store in an airtight container. It will keep for a month.

Baking terms

Cream

It means to beat the fat and sugar together with the back of a spoon to a light and fluffy texture to incorporate air in the dough and batter for cakes, cookies, and icings.

Whip:

It means to beat rapidly to incorporate air and increase volume.

Whip

Cut in:

It means to cut fat into flour using a pastry knife or two knives when making pie crust, so that small pieces of fat are coated with flour.

Fold:

It means to combine a whipped or delicate ingredient with another, using an under and over motion with a flat utensil.

Knead:

It means to manipulate dough with your hands to develop gluten.

Knead

Batter:

It is a semiliquid mixture of flour or other starch, and liquid ingredients used to make baked goods such as cakes, cookies, and quick breads.

Dough:

It is a mixture of flour and liquid, which is stiffer than a batter and is used to make baked goods such as breads, cookies, and pastries.

Dough

Make up:

It means to form or shape a dough or batter into a particular shape and size before baking.

Gluten:

It is the protein that provides structure in baked goods; it forms when flour is moistened.

Baking ingredients

Know your ingredients well. Here is a description of common ingredients used in baking:

Flour:

It provides structure to baked goods, more in breads than in more tender products such as cakes.

Sugar:

They add flavour, help make a fine-textured tender product, prevent staling by holding onto water, provide leavening when creamed and help crust brown. They are available as:

- Fine granulated table sugar.
- Confectioner's white sugar ground to a fine powder, used in icings, toppings, and cream fillings.
- Brown sugar – It is not as highly refined, contains some molasses and caramel, used for its flavour and colour.

Milk and cream:

They add flavour, develop gluten, provide nutritional value and help the crust brown. They are available as:

- Whole, low-fat, and skim milk.
- Buttermilk – Is mildly acid. When mixed with baking soda, it produces leavening and also imparts a special flavour.
- Dry milk – Usually treated as a dry ingredient, which is reconstituted when water is added.

Water:

It combines with flour to make gluten.

Eggs:

They provide structure, moisture, colour and flavour, provide leavening when whipped (egg white), and make batter smooth (egg yolk). They are available fresh, frozen and dried.

Fat:

They help make the product tender, add richness, prevent staling of the product and provide leavening when creamed. They are available in various forms:

- Regular shortening – Has waxy texture and no taste, creams well, and is used in pie crusts, biscuits, many cookies, pastries, and breads.
- Emulsified or high ratio shortening, which is softer and creams better than regular shortening, used in some cakes and icing.
- Butter – Makes the dough hard to handle because it melts at room temperature. It tastes better than shortening because it melts in the mouth.
- Margarine – Can replace butter but lacks the flavour.
- Oils are rarely used in baking. They are used to grease pans and deep-fry doughnuts.

Leavening agents:

They help make baked goods rise by producing bubbles of gas. They are available in several forms.

- Baking powder.
- Baking soda and acid ingredients like buttermilk.
- Yeast – A live microscopic plant that eats sugar and then produces carbon dioxide gas in bread dough.

Seasonings and flavourings:

They help season and lend flavour to the baked products. They include salt, chocolate, spices, extracts, etc.

BAKING SUBSTITUTES

Many times when one ingredient is not available, you may need to substitute it for another. You may also need to do so for dietary reasons. Here are a few popular substitutes you can use.

Instead of:	Use:
1 whole egg	2 egg whites
2 whole eggs	1 whole egg plus 2 egg whites
Regular milk	Skimmed or 1% fat milk
1 cup heavy cream	1 cup evaporated skimmed milk
1 cup light cream	1 cup low-fat yogurt
1 cup whipped cream	Whip 1/3 cup heavy cream and add 2/3 cup non-fat yogurt
1 tbsp butter	1 tbsp margarine or lard
1 cup shortening	2/3 cup vegetable oil
1/2 cup shortening	1/3 cup vegetable oil
1 cup sour cream	1 cup reduced fat sour cream or 1 cup low-fat yogurt
1 tbsp cream cheese	1 tbsp Baker's cheese
1 oz (28.5 g) baking	3 tbsp cocoa chocolate and 1 tbsp vegetable oil

Practical things to be done

Today we are going to learn how to bake crown loaf. Those who have never baked bread before will find this simple step-by-step recipe easy. You will be proud of your achievement the first time that you try.

1. Whole Wheat Buns (Yeast bread)

Ingredients:

Sifted whole wheat flour – 700 gm, fresh yeast – 25 gm, sugar – 1 tsp, salt – 1tsp and sesame seeds.

Preparation and Cooking:

- Soak fresh yeast in a bowl of warm water for 1 hour.
- Place flour in a large mixing bowl; make a well in the centre. Add the yeast water salt and sugar, and stir with a knife, adding enough water to make a stiff but pliable dough.

- Knead with your hands for 20 minutes; cover with a damp cloth and leave for 1 hour in a warm place.
- Knead again, but this time for 10 minutes only and keep it aside covered for 1 hour more or till the dough rises again.
- Now once again knead it for 5 minutes and cut the dough into 20 to 24 portions and shape them. Place them in a baking tray and sprinkle the buns with sesame seeds.
- Leave till the dough doubls in size (approximately 1½ to 2 hour) covered under a damp cloth.
- Preheat your oven to 180 degree celsius heat, 30 minutes before use.
- Place the baking tray in the oven and bake for 30 minutes or till the crust is deep brown.

Cooking time: Almost 3 hours for preparation and 30 minutes for baking.

TIPS

- Do not discard biscuit or snack crumbs. The salted ones can be used to bind cutlets, and sweet ones can be used as a pudding base.
- To make breadcrumbs, cut 2 or 3 slices of bread into small pieces. Add one or two teaspoons of flour to the bread pieces and churn in a mixer.

■ ■

Day 26

Cakes and Cookies

Cakes are a popular form of dessert that are made from a thin batter containing flour, liquid, eggs, fat (in most cases), leavening, and flavouring. Although available in mixes that are usually good with low-fat content, the fun and pleasure of baking your own cake is still a favourite amongst those who take up the challenge.

Although most commercial bakeries were selling cakes that were made from 'scratch', a term which meant that cakes were being made from raw ingredients, the industry has moved to the age of mixes. It may be hard to believe, but many bakeries now use cake mixes in the production of their baked goods.

Cakes are divided into three basic categories according to fat content:

Shortened or Butter Cake:

The shortened cake contains fat. It requires a baking pan that has been oiled and dusted with flour prior to pouring the batter. This group generally includes the layer cakes, white cakes, yellow cakes, and pound cakes, to name a few. A smooth, very lightly browned exterior characterises the shortened cake. The texture is tender and moist.

The following procedure is used to make a shortened cake:

1. Cream fat and sugar together until fluffy. This can be done by hand, using the back of a spoon, or by using a mixer and paddle attachment at moderate speed.
2. Beat in eggs, one at a time, beating well after each addition. Add one-third of sifted dry ingredients at a time into bowl and beat until smooth.
3. Add half the liquid ingredients and beat just until well blended. Repeat with balance two-third of dry ingredients, balance half of liquid ingredients, and end with remaining dry ingredients. Beat until smooth and creamy. Scrape down the bowl with a rubber spatula at least once during this step for even mixing. The reason for alternately adding the flour and liquid ingredients is to ensure that the flour absorbs all the liquid.

Chocolate Cake

Butter Cake

Unshortened or foam cake:

An unshortened cake contains no fat and rises due to the beaten egg white that is part of the recipe. The classic example is the angel food cake. It is delicious, low in fat and calories, and has many varieties. The baking pan for making an angel food cake is usually a tube pan. Sponge cakes are also examples of unshortened cake. They are commonly used to make jellyroll. Unlike angel food cakes, they may have some leavening added. Unshortened cakes are characterised by being very light, free from any cracks, light brown in colour, tender and moist, with an excellent shape.

Follow these steps to make an angel food cake:

1. Warm the egg whites slightly as they attain more volume when they are warm.

Angel Food Cake

2. Sift the flour with half the sugar. This makes it easier for the flour to mix evenly with the egg whites.
3. Beat the egg whites until they form soft peaks.
4. Gradually beat in the sugar that was not mixed with the flour. Continue to beat until the egg whites form soft, glossy peaks. Do not over beat.
5. Fold in the flour-sugar mixture just until it is completely absorbed.
6. Put into ungreased tube pan and bake immediately.

Semi-shortened cake:

The chiffon cake is an example of a cake that has a minimal amount of fat usually oil. It is relatively light and moist and has a nice spongy texture, good volume and taste. Like angel food, it is airy, but its texture is closer to a shortened cake. Unlike angel food cake, it does contain egg yolks and oil. Chiffon cake is easier to make than angel food cake. It also takes less time. It is adaptable to adding fruit flavours such as pineapple or raspberry.

Follow these steps to make a chiffon cake:

1. The dry ingredients are mixed in a bowl. A well is made in the centre.
2. The wet ingredients (except the eggs) are mixed slowly into the dry ingredients.
3. Egg whites are beaten until foamy, and then sugar is added gradually until the whites are stiff (but not dry), glossy, and just hold their shape (they should not droop). If the egg whites are under-whipped, the cake will be tough. If the egg whites are over-whipped, the cake may sink after baking.

4. Stiffly beaten egg whites are folded in gently with the batter.
5. Batter is put into an ungreased tube pan or in layer pans that have had the bottoms (not the sides) oiled and dusted with flour.

Making Cakes and Icings Nutritious

Angel food cake is a good choice, as it contains no fat.

- A sprinkling of confectioner's sugar.
- No-sugar fruit spreads.
- Fresh fruit or berries.
- A glaze made by combining confectioner's sugar and fruit juice concentrate (try 1½ cups confectioner's sugar, 4 tablespoons juice concentrate and 1 teaspoon lemon).
- Fruit sauce (mash raw or cooked fruit with a potato masher or process in a food processor).

Selecting Cake Tins

Cake Tins

The type of tin used directly affects the result of the baked product. You must always use the shape and the size specified in the recipe. Spring form tins are ones with a detachable bottom. They are useful for fragile cakes that need special care. In general, dense, long cooking cake mixtures need thicker tins to prevent scorching.

Preparing and Greasing Cake Tins

We coat cake tins with fat, flour or both to give an even golden surface to the cake. We usually line the tin with greaseproof paper to make it easy to unmould, and to protect the cake batter from oven heat. For cakes made with egg whites, the tin is not greased as the batter is supposed to cling. For moist batters, a nonstick tin is ideal as it does not need greasing unless a coating is required, or a protective paper lining is used.

Greasing a cake tin is essential because it helps loosen the cake. The fat used for greasing should be the same as that used in the batter. Melt or soften the fat, and using a pastry brush, apply an even, thin coating. Be careful to brush the corners and the rim as well. Some cake recipes specify an additional coating of flour after greasing. This second coating could be sugar, breadcrumbs and chopped or sliced nuts.

Flour, Sugar and Breadcrumbs Coating

Generously sprinkle the coating on the greased area of the cake tin. Ensure that it reaches the edges. Turn and shake the tin to coat the surface evenly. Turn it upside down and tap out the excess on the work surface.

Nut coating

Sprinkle your choice of nuts, either chopped or sliced, into the greased tin, shake it and press the nuts onto the sides.

Cake tin liner

Lining a Loaf tin

Lining a round tin

Place the tin upside down with a square of paper on top. Press the paper down with your hands, and with the back of a heavy knife, press against the tin in a stroking motion, cutting the paper into a circle. Brush the tin with fat and press it into the base of the tin. Grease the paper.

TIPS: Easier way to line a round tin is to keep the tin on square paper, draw a line around the mould with a pencil and then cut the circle with a kitchen scissors. Fit it in the tin and brush it with fat.

Lining a Spring Form Tin

To line a spring form tin, follow this procedure:

1. Fold a square of paper to quarters, then in triangular 8ths or 16ths depending on the size of the tin. Set the point of the paper in the centre of the upturned tin and cut the paper level with the edge.
2. In the same way, cut a second circle. Grease the tin, open one circle of paper and place it in the base of the tin. Grease the paper.
3. Cut a strip of paper a little longer and deeper than the circumference of the tin. Fold one long edge and cut slits along it.
4. Press all round the sides of the tin so that the folded cut edge overlaps the base. Set the second round of paper in the base of the tin to cover and hold the overlap in place. Grease the paper.

Lining a Loaf Tin

To line a loaf tin, follow this procedure:

1. Cut out a piece of paper as wide as the base and sides of the tin. Fold it so that it fits the base.
2. Unfold the paper and cut the corners along the folds so that it fits the tin perfectly. After lightly greasing the tin, press the paper into the tin and grease it.

Alternatively, you could follow this method:

1. Cut a strip of paper along the circumference of the tin and 5 inches more than the height of the tin. Grease the tin and press the strip lengthwise into the tin, so the ends overlap the edge. Grease the paper.
2. Cut another strip of paper as wide as the height of the tin and 5 inches longer than the circumference. Press the paper crosswise into the base of the tin and grease it.

Ingredients Used for Cake Making

Correct ingredients and their accurate weight is a basic need for cake baking. Instructions in a recipe should be followed strictly. Both, increasing or reducing quantities of a batter is often risky. Do not substitute, for example, wholemeal flour for plain flour or golden syrup for honey. Never substitute one kind of fat for another.

Eggs: Most recipes assume an egg to weigh 60 gms. Eggs should be taken out and kept at room temperature before mixing.

Salt: A pinch of salt develops the flavour of any sweet mixture.

Flour: Most cakes are made from plain flour, which gives a light texture, while whole meal, semolina, rye and other flours have a characteristic effect. Cornflour, potato starch, arrowroot and rice flour are sometimes used for extra lightness. Self-raising flour contains raising agents and must not be substituted for plain flour. Recipes using plain flour will always specify the raising agents to be used. Flour is most accurately measured by weight. If you are measuring by volume, sift after measuring unless otherwise specified. Sifting is particularly important for lightness in whisked cakes.

Fat: The flavour of butter is incomparable while making a variety of delicate cakes. Recipes often specify the use of salted or unsalted butter. Firm margarine could be substituted for butter, but it lacks flavour. Shortening gives lightness, but no flavour. Oil is a lighter substitute for chiffon cakes. Fat improves the shelf life of cakes, preventing dryness.

Problem Shooting

Cake baking is a simple task when you follow a recipe strictly. However, as in other work, sometimes problems do crop in. A better understanding of these will help you guard against them.

Sunken centre in a cake could be due to one of these reasons:

- Excessive amount of sugar – this becomes apparent by a very brown crust and sticky centre.
- Too much baking powder or other raising agent.
- Excessive liquid, apparent by a sticky layer forming above the bottom crust.
- Too low oven temperature.

Process of Making A Chocolate Cake

1. Mix eggs and sugar
2. Mix and sieve dry ingredients
3. Beat eggs and sugar together
4. Mix oil with eggs mixture
5. Add milk and beat
6. Add dry ingredients spoon by spoon
7. Beat the mixture thoroughly
8. Pour it in the greased mould
9. Ready to be baked
10. Baked cake on cooling rack

- Batter exposed to a draught before it is set.
- Undercooking shown by a sticky central layer.

Peaked top in a cake could be due to one of these reasons:

- Too much gluten developed in mixture, caused either by using too hard a flour or by overbeating.
- Too high oven temperature.

Tough, close-textured cake could be due to one of these reasons:

- Insufficiently beaten or whipped batter.
- Insufficient raising agent.
- Not enough sugar.
- Batter overmixed.

Mixing Batter by Machine

The use of an electric mixer makes the task of cake making easier – whisking whole eggs or egg whites, beating egg yolks and sugar and creaming butter easier. Models vary according to power and speed. Be sure to use the speed and attachments recommended by the manufacturer for specific tasks. During beating, you may need to stop the machine and scrape the sides from time to time. A mixer can help distribute ingredients such as nuts and dried fruit evenly in heavier or richer cakes. All liquid ingredients must be combined before dry ones are added. Heavy ingredients should always be chopped first, added towards the end of the mixing process and combined at low speed.

Making, Icing and Storing Cakes

Here are a few tips on making, icing and storing cakes.

- Always preheat the oven.
- Grease and flour pans if required, or use nonstick pans.
- The most common fault in making sponge cakes is insufficient beating of the eggs and sugar. Beat them until stiff peaks form.
- If using egg whites, they separate easily if cold. They create the most volume when whipped at room temperature. Make sure the mixing bowl and utensils are free of fat, as fat will create less volume. Do not use glass or plastic bowls to whip egg whites – they may also create less volume. A copper bowl and whisk are the best for whipping egg whites.

Cake batter ready to bake

- If creaming fat and sugar, the fat creams better when it is at room temperature. Let it sit on the kitchen counter for about half an hour. Cream until the mixture is of the consistency of stiff whipped cream.
- Do not let cake batter sit around in the kitchen. Get it into the oven, or it will deflate.
- Do not fill a cake pan more than three-quarters full. Otherwise it may overflow during baking. Use a ladle or spoon for filling the pans so that it does not overfill.
- When loading the oven, leave space for air to circulate between pans and the sides and back of the oven.
- Bake at the right temperature. Use an oven thermometer to guide you. If the oven is too hot, the cake will not rise properly. The crust and bottom may brown too much, or even burn. If the oven is not hot enough, the cake will not rise properly and may fall.
- Once in the oven, leave cakes alone until the crust starts to brown. The motion involved in opening the oven door and letting cool air in could make the cake fall.
- To test for completeness, shortened cakes will pull away from the sides of the pan, the centre should spring back when lightly touched, and a toothpick or cake tester will come out clean when inserted in the thickest part of the cake.
- Most cakes require 15 minutes of cooling prior to the removal from the pan. Use a cooling rack so that the cooling air can circulate to the bottom of the pan and reduce the temperature quickly. In the case of un-shortened cakes, you should run a metal spatula along the sides of the pan in order to help remove it from the pan. Then you can put one wire rack on top, and one below the cake. Invert

and remove pan. For angel food cake, cool upside down on something like a soft drink bottle. Once cool, run a metal spatula along the sides of the pan and remove carefully.

Icing Cakes

- Do not attempt to ice the cake until it is completely cool. Otherwise the cake will stick to your spatula and ruin the appearance of the icing.
- Dip the metal spatula into hot water for a few minutes prior to icing the cake. A warm spatula will spread the icing easier, faster, and have less of a tendency of pulling up the crumbs from the surface of the cake.
- If there is a tear in the side of the cake, mix ½ cup icing with 3 tablespoons water to make a very thin mixture. Spread over broken surface to coat evenly. Allow drying before frosting cake.

Storing Cakes

- Shortened or butter cakes stay fresh at room temperature for up to one week or can be frozen (don't ice until later) for up to 6 months.
- Angel, sponge, and chiffon cakes stay fresh only for about four days (although chiffon can last up to two weeks) at room temperature. They can be frozen (don't ice until later) for up to 6 months.
- Cheese cake must be refrigerated and can be held up to 4 days. It can also be frozen up to 4 months.

Soft Icings

When making soft icings for cakes, the idea is to obtain a thin sugar coating, smooth enough to shine and soft enough to slice easily. The key to smoothness lies in maintaining the correct temperature, so that coarse crystals do not form. This becomes possible by the addition of glucose, golden syrup, and cream of tartar and lemon juice.

Glacé icing:

Make glacé icing by sifting 200 gms icing sugar into a bowl and stir in 6-7 tablespoons water with ½ teaspoon vanilla essence. Add enough water to make a soft paste. You could substitute lemon or orange juice for water. This recipe will make 250 ml icing.

Honey glacé:

Make honey glacé by mixing 100 gms sugar, 4 tablespoons milk, 60 gms butter and 4 tablespoons honey in a saucepan. Gently heat the mixture, stir it constantly till melted, and just bring it to boil. Spread this on dough or batter for baking. This recipe will make 250 ml glacé.

Chocolate icing:

Make chocolate icing by combining 250gms sugar and 125 ml water in a saucepan; bringing it to boil, and then cooling. Later on gradually stir 175 gms chopped chocolate into the sugar syrup. Cook it by placing this saucepan into a larger vessel filled with water. Heated water in the large vessel will help cook the sugar-chocolate mixture without scorching it as no direct heat is applied. Cook for 5 minutes; remove it from heat, blend in ½ teaspoon vegetable oil in it and allow the mixture to cool. Stir it gently until just warm and is of coating consistency.

Expert cook suggests...

1. If you do not have candied peel to add when baking a cake, use a spoon or two of marmalade. The cake will taste just as good.
2. To soften a cake after baking, sprinkle a solution of sugar and water over it while it is still warm.
3. Use sunflower oil instead of cream for cake batter. The cake will turn out tasty, and will have low calories.

Cookies

The word biscuit is a French derivative meaning cooked twice. Americans call them 'cookies', a name that popularly refers to homemade biscuits. Cookies are one of the most popular baked goods available in many different varieties. Although cookies can be purchased in dry mixes and in refrigerated, ready to shape and bake forms, the fun of making cookies from scratch will yield a product that is truly unique.

Cookie batters are more liquid than cake batters. They range from liquid to very stiff, and these differences often call for different mixing methods, although the basic steps are much like those for shortened cakes.

For cookie sheets, use heavyweight, flat pans or those with barely turned up edges so that the cookies can cook evenly. Heavyweight pans are less likely to warp, and ones made out of aluminum conduct heat well. Nonstick cookie sheets are fine. Ensure that they are made from a heavyweight metal and are coated with a good nonstick. Insulated cookie sheets (they have air sandwiched between two sheets of aluminum) are helpful to prevent burned cookie bottoms, and cookies bake for the time that the recipe calls for.

When baking cookies, try to find a product known as parchment or baker's paper. This is a heat-resistant paper that is used on top of pans. It requires no greasing (even if the recipe calls for it). The main advantage of using this paper is that it reduces cleanup to a minimum. It is also useful when you need to reuse your pans during baking as you can place the cookie dough directly into the parchment paper and then place the paper onto a cookie sheet. When you put cookie dough onto a hot baking sheet, the dough will spread and start to bake before being put into the oven. Baker's paper is used throughout the commercial baking industry. It is often available at a kitchen supply/cooking store.

There are many different types of cookies. Here are a few of the more popular ones.

- **Dropped cookies** are made from a soft dough or batter and are dropped onto a cookie sheet from a spoon. Two spoons are usually used. One to scoop out the batter and the other to push the batter out onto the cooking sheet. The cookies should be similar in size and shape so that they cook evenly and for the same period of time.

- **Rolled cookies** are cut out from stiff chilled dough with cookie cutters. They tend to be rich cookies.

- **Moulded and pressed cookies** are moulded into the desired shapes by hand or using a cookie mould or cookie press. They also tend to be rich cookies.

- **Refrigerator or icebox cookies** are made ahead of time and stored in the refrigerator in rolls until they are needed. They are cut and baked.

- **Bar cookies**, like brownies, are baked in pans rather than in cookie sheets. They are generally cooled completely in the pan before removing.

Ingredients Used for Cookies

The dough for biscuits or cookies requires a lot of nuts, grains such as oatmeal, and dried fruits such as raisins and dates. Plain butter is the principal flavouring ingredient, while honey, molasses and brown sugar provide colour and sweetness. Chocolate, coffee and spices like ginger, cinnamon or nutmeg are commonly used, as are seeds like sesame or caraway. Occasionally, soda bicarbonate or baking powder is used to make the cookies more crumbly.

Making Cookie Batter by Machine

Using an electric mixer makes the task quite easy. Stiff dough that requires kneading is done well in a food processor or mixer with a dough hook. Softer dough can be beaten in a food processor or with an electric beater. You must be careful not to overwork the dough or the cookies will become tough. If you are using chopped ingredients, use your hands to mix them. This will ensure an even distribution of the chopped ingredients.

Rolling cookie dough

Cookie dough tends to crumble and stick. It should be lightly kneaded after mixing. Chill the dough at least for an hour until firm. Follow these steps to roll cookie dough:

1. Sprinkle flour or sugar generously over the dough and place it between two sheets of greaseproof paper or cling film.
2. Flatten the dough with your hand and gently roll it with a rolling pin to obtain the desired thickness.
3. Peel off the top layer of paper. Using a cookie cutter or a knife dipped in flour, cut out the cookies. Press the dough trimmings together and roll again.

Moulding cookie dough

First try to mould the dough without chilling it. If it is too sticky, chill it until firm. Some recipes call for moistening your hands with water, others for flouring them, before handling the dough. Here are some simple steps to mould cookie dough:

1. Divide the dough into walnut-sized balls. Roll these in icing sugar. Set them well apart on a prepared baking tray.
2. Using a fork dipped in water press the balls, or press them with the base of a drinking glass dusted with icing sugar.

Cooling cookies

Remove the cookies from the baking trays as soon as possible to stop them from cooking further. They remain soft when still warm. This will prevent them from breaking easily. If they stick as they cool, warm them briefly in the oven to release them. Slide the paper off the baking tray, peel the cookies from it and leave them on a rack to cool. Loosen cookies baked on a tray with a sharp flexible knife. For sticky cookies, pour a little water under the paper, onto the hot baking tray. The steam will loosen the cookies so that you can easily lift them off the tray. You could coat baked cookies with cake icings, and glacés based on sugar or chocolate. A sprinkling of nuts, grated chocolate and coloured sugar, or icing or melted chocolate piped with a paper cone may also be added.

You will learn how to make different kinds of pastries in the lesson on 'Western Desserts'. Even though there is a great similarity between cakes, cookies and pastries, most of the time a pastry is just a shell for other ingredients. Cakes and cookies are often treated as teatime snacks. Pastries or the desserts made from the pastry shells are mostly served at the end of a meal. There is, however, no hard and fast rule regarding the appropriate serving time for any of the above. In the West, the meals are often light, rounded off with a selection of cheeses and crackers, ice cream, sorbet or a frozen dessert.

Tips for baking and storing cookies

TIPS

Here are a few tips to ensure happy baking and storing of cookies:

- Preheat the oven. Ensure that the temperature is accurate. Most cookies bake quickly at a high temperature. If the temperature is too high, the cookies will burn on the edges and bottoms. If the temperature is too low, the cookies may spread out across the pan and turn out hard, dry, and without a nice brown colour.
- Your baking pans may or may not need to be greased, as richer cookies often do not require greased pans. Check the recipe. If so, lightly grease with vegetable oil, otherwise the cookies may spread too much. Preferably, use parchment paper.
- Place cookie sheets in the upper half of the oven to prevent burned bottoms. Use the middle rack for one cookie sheet. For two cookie sheets, place side by side on the middle rack, if they can fit with at least one inch of space in the middle. If not, place one on one side of the middle rack and the other sheet on the other side of a rack placed at the top of the oven. With this arrangement, you need to switch the position of both sheets halfway through baking.
- Watch cookies carefully in the oven. They will overbake much quicker than you think.
- When the edges and bottoms of the cookies are golden brown, they are done.
- When cookies are still warm, but firm enough to be handled without breaking, remove them from the pan. Then they won't stick. Recipes will generally indicate the cooking time needed.
- Do not cool cookies too quickly as they might crack.

- Cookies will generally keep well in an airtight container for up to one week, and in some cases, even longer. Store only those cookies that have completely cooled. Store different types separately to avoid sogginess.
- Cookies can be frozen in airtight packages for up to 3-4 months. If cookies need to be frosted or glazed, wait to do so until they are thawed. Brownies also freeze well.

Let us move onto the practical session where you will learn how to bake a cake and how to decorate it with simple icing.

Practical things to be done

1. Pineapple Cake

Ingredients:

Eggs – 2 no, flour – 3 tbsp, sugar – 4 tbsp, pineapple essence 4 drops.

For Icing: Fresh cream – 200 gm, powdered sugar – 4 tbsp, cream of tartar – ¼ tsp, pineapple tit-bits – 1 cup, tinned cherries – 6 no or glazed cherries – 6 no.

Preparation and Cooking:

1. Preheat the electric oven/oven of your cooking range or convection mode of your microwave to 180 °C .
2. Prepare a rectangular or a square baking mould; line it with paper and brush with oil.
3. Keep the cream chilled.
4. Cut pineapple slices into desired shapes and place under refrigeration.
5. Break eggs in a bowl and beat.
6. Heat sugar with 3 tbsp water and cook till fully dissolved. Pour over beaten eggs and churn fast with a rotary beater or a whisker till the mixture is thick and creamy. If tested it forms the shapes.
7. Now add flour and 2 drops of essence and mix fast.
8. Pour the mixture into the prepared mould and bake in a hot oven for 10 to 15 minutes or till golden in colour.

9. Take it out and invert on a wire rack. Cool and remove the lined paper from the cake.

Note:

Just baked cake is an ideal example of a sponge cake where not even a drop of fat is used.

For Fresh Cream Icing:

1. Beat cream; add powdered sugar, cream of tartar and remaining 2 drops of pineapple essence; mix it well and keep under refrigeration.
2. Invert and place cake on a plate/platter, sprinkle it with pineapple syrup and cover with a thick layer of cream icing. Spread icing on the sides of the cake, too.
3. Cover the cake with pineapple pieces and garnish with cherries. If any cream is left, put it in an icing gun and decorate the cake with it.

Serving:

Chill the cake properly before serving. Cut it into desired size pieces and serve at teatime.

Or serve it with chilled pineapple sauce as a dessert.

Tips:

For 'Pineapple sauce': Mix 200 ml pineapple juice with 1 tsp sugar and 1 tsp corn flour mixed with a little juice and boil for a few seconds, stirring once in between. Cool and chill.

Cooking time: 15 minutes baking.

2. Making a Paper Piping Cone

You need a polythene paper cone when you have to write on a cake with contrasting colour icing, or when you have to decorate the cake with a pattern or flowers.

To make a cone, follow this simple procedure:

1. Take 8 x 14 inches of polythene paper and fold the rectangle in half diagonally. Cut along the fold.
2. Fold the short side of one triangle over to the right-angled corner to form a cone.
3. With one hand holding the cone together, wrap the long point of the triangle around the paper cone.
4. Tuck the pointed paper sheet inside the cone to secure it. Snip off a tiny bit from the tip to make a hole through which you can force the icing.

When you need this cone, pour the icing of your choice into the cone, twist the top until there is no air left in the cone. Hold the twisted end taut with one hand. With the other hand, gently press the filling at the top of the cone to make it flow slowly out of the hole. Use to decorate the cake.

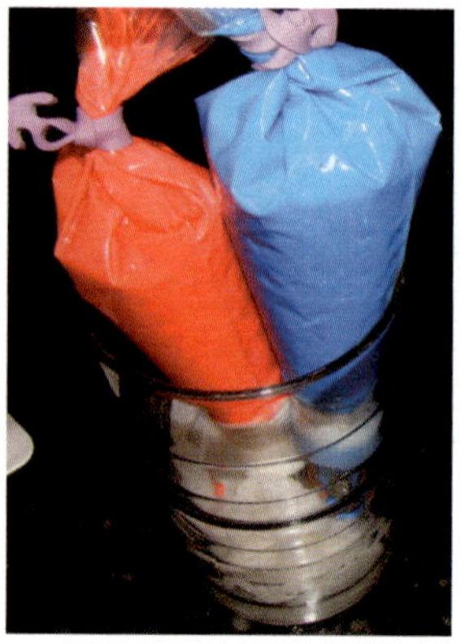

Readymade 'Icing bags' are available in the market and can be bought easily. They are washable and reusable, so they last for many years.

Dates and Walnut Cake

Chocolate Truffle

Pineapple Cake

Cornmeal & Coconut Cake with Custard sauce

Day 27

Western Desserts

Western desserts include cakes, cookies, pastries, pies, puddings and a number of other frozen or cold desserts. You have already learnt 'Baking Basics' and 'Cakes and Cookies' as a forerunner to today's lesson. We presume that you are already familiar with many aspects of this subject. Let us now learn about the desserts that have delighted people all over the world.

When we attempt to control our food intake, the thought of giving up baked goods is somewhat depressing. Although we associate desserts with lots of calories, the reality is that there are many nutritious choices available. Even if they are not nutritious, we can consume amounts that are reasonable. Commercial cakes, pies, and cookies are often high in fat, saturated fat, and calories. In addition, some are quite high in cholesterol. These are some that are acceptable.

Strawberry Mousse

Fruit Medley

Trifle Pudding

- Baked goods specially made without (or with little) fat is a fast-growing section in the supermarket – one that has some good tasting choices.
- Angel food cake or sponge cake (used to make jellyroll) uses little or no fat.

To keep down the amount of fat in baked goods, try to select cakes and pies with 5 grams or less of fat per serving and cookies with 4 grams or less of fat for every 30 grams of the product.

Fruit-based desserts vary from serving cut fresh fruits or canned fruits (use those that are packed in juice to cut down on sugar) to baking fruits into dishes such as baked apples or baked bananas, fruit compote, or crumbles. Crumbles (also called crisps) are made of cut-up fruit placed in a baking dish, topped with a streusel-type topping, and baked until the fruit is soft and the top crunchy. Although streusel toppings are typically high in fat they need not be, as the recipes will show. When baking fruits, it is important not to use too high a heat or to overcook them.

Many fruit based cold desserts like mousse, souffles and jellies with fruits are equally the part of western desserts.

Puddings and custard are also popular dessert items. Puddings are soft desserts with a thick, creamy consistency or a spongy texture. Other kinds of puddings are commonly thickened with cornflour and may include ingredients such as rice or tapioca.

Puddings made mainly of eggs, milk, sugar, and flavourings are called custards. In making custards, use low heat and do not overcook. Cooking at too high a temperature for too long will curdle the milk and toughen the eggs.

All custard puddings, other than bread pudding, should be cooked in a water bath, meaning that the custard cups or pans are placed into a pan of water for baking (the water should be almost at level with the custard in the cup or pan). The water bath prevents curdling of the milk and eggs, which can occur when they are exposed to direct heat for some time.

Dates Pudding

Crumble

To keep down the amount of fat in puddings, it is possible to use skimmed milk. This works particularly well when you are using a pudding mix, and results in a low-fat, tasty dessert. It can also be done when making puddings. Custards can be made with fewer eggs and skimmed milk.

Meringues are stiffly beaten mixtures of egg whites and sugar that are baked in an oven. They make wonderful, fat-free shells in which you can place fresh fruit or fruit sauces for a colourful dessert.

Frozen desserts include dairy products: Ice cream, ice milk, and frozen yogurt. Other frozen desserts include sherbet, sorbet, water ice, and fruit bars. Sherbet is a fruit-based soft dessert that, unlike sorbet and fruit bars, contains some milk fat, generally 1 to 2 percent. Sherbet makes a refreshingly smooth and light dessert and can be served with fresh fruit. Sorbet, a fruity ice, is an international dessert, appetizer, and snack. It is typically made of fruit, fruit juice, water, and sugar. Some recipes call for egg white or gelatin, which are used as thickeners. It contains no milk. It is a fat-free relatively low calorie dessert.

Water ice, such as lemon ice, is basically water, sugar, and flavouring. It contains no fat but quite a bit of sugar (as does sorbet). There are a variety of frozen fruit bars available in the freezer section of your supermarket – fruit and juice bars, fruit-flavoured bars, fruit and cream bars, or real fruit bars. When there are so many varieties, then what is the difference between them? Most contain very little fat (1 gram, if at all) and most are under 90 calories. Where they do vary is the content of sugar. For the least amount of refined sugar, purchase a brand that does not have much refined sugar.

Pies

Pies and pastries are among the most popular desserts. Pies are truly an American treat, with apple pie being the favourite. An important feature of good pies and pastries is the quality of the crust. In all instances the crust should be flaky, tender, and flavourful. Pies comprises two basic parts, the crust and the filling. Many varieties can be created which may include a one or two-crust pie, and a variety of fruit, creams, puddings, or other fillings. The pie dough, also known as the crust, is generally made up of four ingredients and that are flour, fat, salt, and water. Unfortunately, these four ingredients can create a challenge to the novice, ranging from perfection to a total disaster! In order to achieve a level of perfection, it is important not to let the flour develop too much gluten. This happens when the dough is handled too much.

Hot Apple Pie

Here are the basic procedures:

Flour: Flour can either be all-purpose (readily available in the supermarket) or a pastry flour. The flour gives the basic structure to the dough. It should be fresh, without any lumps or bugs. Be careful. The flour is placed into a large bowl.

Puff Pastry Dough

Salt: Salt lends flavour of its own to the dough and helps to colour the baked crust. The salt can be added either to the flour (thoroughly mixed) or can be combined with the water (thoroughly stirred prior to addition).

Fat: Recipes often call for shortening, although a mixture of half shortening and half margarine is quite acceptable. Oil can be used, but the crust will not be as flaky as those using solid fats. Commercial bakeries that make their own dough for pies use a form of shortening known as 'high ratio shortening'. This is designed specifically for baking. The fat, chilled prior to use so it does not melt during handling (resulting in a pie crust that is not flaky), is added to the flour and salt mixture and is incorporated by a method known as 'cutting in'. This can be accomplished in three different ways.

- **Pastry blender:** A pastry blender is a device specifically designed for cutting the fat into the flour mixture. Its purpose is to cut the fat in such a way that the fat is broken into the shape of 'garden peas' and each pea is coated with flour.
- **Two butter knives:** The two butter knives used at a 90-degree angle from one another will perform the same task as a pastry blender. Be careful not to overmix the dough.
- **A metal dinner fork:** Metal dinner fork performs the least of the three methods. With practice, it can be equally effective to make pie dough.

Water: The water should be very cold so as not to melt the fat. If you choose to add salt to the water (instead of the flour), stir the water before adding it slowly to the pie dough as you mix it gently with a spoon or fork. As the water is added, mix just enough to blend the ingredients together into the shape of a ball. If you overmix the dough, it will appear greasy and will yield a tough crust. Wrap the dough with clear wrap and refrigerate it for 20 minutes. It will be easier to roll out.

The metal blade of the food processor can be used to make pie dough in seconds. Simply add small chunks of fat into the flour and salt in the work bowl and pulse 3 or 4 times. Add the water through the feed tube while pulsing very rapidly (about 20-30 times) until it gathers into a ball. Remove and press together. While the dough is chilling in the refrigerator, start making your filling. After making the filling, follow the given procedure to roll the pie dough:

1. If making a double crust pie (top and bottom crusts), cut the dough into half, and place one half back into the refrigerator.
2. Place the dough on top of a piece of wax paper that is very lightly dusted with flour.
3. Push down the dough, keeping it rounded. Place another piece of wax paper on top.
4. Roll out the dough in a round shape so that it is about 1-2 inches larger than the pie pan.
5. Place the dough into the pie tin (glass is best, metal, aluminium, disposable, etc.) and pour in the filling.
6. To finish the edge of the piecrust, trim the edge within ½ inch of the rim. You can press the tines of a fork around the entire rim of the pie plate for a decorative finish.

When using a pie filling that is soggy, such as custard, or when the filling does not need to be cooked, the piecrust is partially or fully baked before it is filled. Follow your recipe carefully.

When making a two-crust pie, roll out the second piece of dough a little thinner than the first. Place the top crust on the filled pie, press the edges to seal with your fingers, and trim the edge to within ½ inch of the rim. You can now flute the edges using your thumb and forefinger.

To bake the pie, brush the top of the pie with milk (to help brown the crust) just prior to baking. Place the pie into a preheated oven (usually 400-425°F) and bake for the prescribed time (usually until golden brown).

Leftover pie dough pieces can be reused to make miniature tarts (with leftover fillings). Once again, be careful not to overmix the dough or it will become very tough. Besides the traditional pie shells, there are crumb crusts, such as graham cracker crust. They are easy and quick to make and are used only for unbaked pies, such as cream pies. Crumb crusts may also use vanilla or chocolate wafer crumbs, or gingersnap crumbs.

Making pies nutritious

The traditional pastry dough recipes use a significant amount of fat. Those that use shortening are higher in saturated fat than they need be. As the Healthier Pie Crust recipe indicates, it is possible to have a flaky crust using less total fat, and substituting half the shortening with margarine. You can also use 1 cup of flour to 3-4 tablespoons of stick margarine and 3 tablespoons of cold water. Oil can also be used to make a crust for the pies, although oily crusts tend not to be as flaky as regular crusts.

Now that you have learnt how to make a better crust, let's take a look at fillings. Fruits make excellent fillings. To cut down on sugar in fruit pies, use sweet fruit and six tablespoons sugar or less per pie. If you love custard or cream filled pies, low-in-fat recipes are available. For a tasty cream-style pie, fill the graham cracker or vanilla wafer crusts with pudding made with low fat or skimmed milk. Top with 1 cup heavy cream whipped with plain low-fat yogurt. Or make a pie by blending yogurt, fresh or frozen fruit, and 1 cup whipped cream. Pour into pie shell and freeze.

Pastry

Both cakes and pastries have flour as the main ingredient. The difference lies in their mixing.

The dough for bread is kneaded till elastic to develop the gluten, but the opposite effect is needed when making pastry. To achieve a pastry, which is rich and yet light, with a crumbly or flaky texture, you need to take great care in mixing and baking. The dough is folded into hundreds of layers.

Chocolate Pastry

The classic pastry field is dominated by three kinds of dough – plain, puff and choux.

- Prime examples of plain pastry dough are the English plain pastry dough short crust and American pie pastry.
- Puff pastry challenges even the most experienced cook. The strudel is an example.
- The 'odd-man' out is the choux pastry, which depends on eggs for its lightness.

Ingredients for pastry

You must understand how each ingredient contributes to make a fine product.

Flour: The best flour for pastry is the fairy soft wheat flour as it develops less gluten. Hard flours develop strong gluten, making pastry difficult to roll and shape. Tasty but heavy, wholemeal flour can be used in short crust pastry where groundnuts may be substituted for part of it.

Fat: While vegetable shortening lightens the pastry, butter gives it a delicious flavour. Some special dough may call for sour cream, or oil, which yields a less flaky crust. The fat used for greasing your baking tray or mould should be the same as that used in the dough.

Eggs: Egg yolk makes the dough crumbly and rich, and provides colour. Whole eggs bind the dough and makes it pliable; in choux pastry, eggs make it rise like a cake.

Water: This moistens the dough and makes shortcut pastry crumbly and produces steam so that choux and puff pastry will rise in the oven. In some dough, milk can be substituted for water, producing softer dough that browns well.

Salt: A pinch of salt adds flavour to the pastry.

Sugar: We usually add castor sugar to pastries, with icing sugar giving a particularly fine grain, and brown sugar adding colour and sweetness. Pastry containing a high proportion of sugar will scorch easily.

Raising agents: Baking powder or soda bicarbonate is occasionally added to lighten pastry dough.

Vanilla: This is the usual flavouring for sweet pastry and biscuit dough, though grated lemon rind and spices such as cinnamon, nutmeg or ginger are good alternatives.

PREPARING PASTRY DOUGH

The final goal of pastry making is a light, crisp finish. The high fat content of most pastry dough has a beneficial shortening effect, separating starch granules and gluten strands within the dough itself. The dough must be mixed quickly otherwise the gluten that develops will make the dough elastic and thus difficult to roll, inclined to shrink during cooking and tougher when cooked.

Kneading by machine: You can knead the dough, in small batches, in a food processor or in an electric mixer. Take care not to overwork the dough. The electric mixer is ideal for the job of cutting the butter into flour. As soon as the dough begins to form a clump, it should be taken out of the work bowl and kneaded with the heel of the hand until pliable. While working with machine, never let the dough form into a ball. The dough made in a machine should be allowed to rest thoroughly to relax the gluten.

Chilling the dough: Pastry dough must be tightly wrapped in cling film or greaseproof paper, otherwise the edges may dry and crack when it is rolled. It should be chilled for 30 minutes. Chilling helps the gluten 'relax' and separates the gluten and the fat in the dough, ensuring a light texture when baked. You can store this kneaded dough, except that for choux pastry, for two to three days in the refrigerator. The dough for choux pastry can be stored for 12 hours. Plain and puff pastry dough also freezes well after being rolled and shaped, ready for baking. They can be transferred directly from the freezer to the oven. However, they will need a few minutes' extra baking time.

Rolling the dough: The dough must be of the right consistency when you are ready to roll it. If too soft, chill the dough to set the fat. If too firm, strike it a few times with a rolling pin, until the butter starts to soften and becomes pliable. A cold surface, such as marble, is ideal for rolling pastry. Granite counters will do as well. Dust the surface lightly with flour to prevent the dough sticking to it. You could also use two layers of cling film or greaseproof paper to roll the pastry.

PROCESS OF MAKING SHORT CRUST PASTRY

Short crust pastry

This is the easiest and the most versatile of all dough. The ingredients are mixed quickly, and the fat is rubbed into the flour with fingertips. Chilled water is added to make the dough that should be soft but not sticky. Egg yolk is added sometimes for a richer dough. You can give it a flaky texture by rolling, folding and rolling again for one or two times. For this process the dough has to be chilled thoroughly.

The initial oven temperature for short crust pastry is high so that the dough keeps its shape. It is then lowered to complete cooking. To prevent dough from becoming soggy in pies and tarts with a moist filling like pureed apple, pastry cream or molasses, a shell may be baked ahead, then filled and again baked. You should always preheat the baking

1. Ingredients for Pastry ; 2. Horten flour (sifted with salt) and butter;
3. Knead with chilled water; 4. Roll dough into 1.4" thick circle;
5. Fit the circle in pastry mould. Prick surface and bake;
6. Cool pastry shell and pour chilled filling

tray and bake the pie on a low shelf. You could sprinkle the base of a pre-baked pastry shell with breadcrumbs, brush the sides with egg whites and bake again for a few minutes. This will prevent moisture soaking into the shell. Brush the pastry with jam glaze (see apricot glaze) after baking. If you are using juicy fruits for a filling, first spread a layer of pastry cream over the pastry.

Fillings: There are a variety of ingredients, which you could choose to fill your pastry shell. It is here that you have to be imaginative. A favourite filling is apple, which could be chopped, sliced or pureed and would look nice in an open tart with a shiny glaze. Fruits like peaches and pears are poached before being arranged in a baked pastry shell and glazed with poaching syrup. You could use nuts with custard to fill your pastry shell or a mixture of eggs, cinnamon and sugar. Pastry fillings are, by no means, limited to sweet ingredients. Other savoury pies and tarts are filled with minced meat, cooked vegetables, fish, meat mixed with sauce or egg and cheese. But these pies and tarts are usually served as a part of the main menu in a Western-style meal or as a teatime snack.

Choux pastry

This is also known as cream puff pastry and is cooked twice. First, the butter is melted in water and brought to a boil. Then, it is taken off the heat and flour is beaten in. The flour is cooked to a ball of dough due to the warmth of the butter and water mixture. This dough is dried over the heat for half a minute. Next, eggs are mixed, one by one, into the dough, which should be warm enough to cook them slightly. The only tricky part in making choux pastry is gauging the amount of eggs to be used. In the beginning, the dough thickens but after a while, it becomes thin. At this point lightly beaten egg is gradually added till the dough is of dropping consistency and can easily fall from the spoon. This pastry is too soft to be rolled and is always piped or spooned onto the baking tray.

As it bakes, choux pastry puffs up, but it must cook further to become dry and crisp. Leave plenty of space between the pastries on the baking tray allowing it to expand. To help it rise evenly, score the dough with a fork before cooking. The dough lets off a lot of steam while baking. If you are cooking it in an electric oven, the door should be propped open slightly after 10 minutes' cooking. Do not open the door completely as partly cooked choux is liable to deflate in a cold draught.

Puff pastry

Puff/Flaky Pastry

This is the most difficult kind of pastry to make. It challenges the expertise of even the most experienced of cooks. It is raised by literally hundreds of layers of butter interspersed with flour and water dough. When it is put in the oven, the butter melts, detaching the dough layers, while the water turns to steam, raising the pastry to three or four times its original thickness.

The exact proportion of dough and butter is judged by weighing the dough after mixing, then adding half its weight in butter. The flour is sifted onto the work surface, water, salt and 30 grams of butter is added and a teaspoon of lemon juice to help cut the gluten. Everything is mixed to form soft dough, which is slightly sticky. This is wrapped around the additional butter, which is made soft by pounding it with a rolling pin. Then the dough is rolled and rerolled till the dough becomes elastic. This is the most important part of making puff pastry as elasticity ensures lightness. Before popping the pastry into the oven, the top is scored with a knife, otherwise it will dry and crack. A finish of egg glaze is sufficient, with a light sprinkling of sugar lightly baked till it caramelises. This pastry is an ideal container not only for sweat fillings for dessert but also for a variety of other fillings like cooked vegetables, minced meats, ham, mushrooms and spinach, to make it into a teatime snack.

The ideal way to begin baking puff pastry is to give it a quick blast of heat so as to melt the butter layers and at the same time to convert the water in the dough to steam, making it rise in the oven. When the dough has risen, the heat can be lowered for a thorough cooking. The pastry should be well browned as toasting adds crispness and flavour. To prevent the base from scorching during cooking, you could put a cold baking tray under the hot one halfway through cooking. To prevent the top from browning too much, cover it loosely with foil. After baking, scoop out and discard any uncooked dough from the hollow shells. If you do not want the pastry to rise too much, prick the base before baking.

Sweet fillings: Pastry cream is the most common sweet filling used in pastries. It is a mixture thickened with enough flour or cornflour to hold its shape without making the pastry soggy. Pastry cream can be refrigerated for a day or two. It blends well with a wide variety of flavouring from chocolate to coffee or even a stiff fruit puree. The cream tends to be heavy and is often mixed with an equal quantity of butter cream or whipped cream.

Butter cream: This is made with egg yolks beaten with hot sugar syrup to a light mixture, and then mixed with creamed butter. You use egg whites for a lighter version. The butter cream can be flavoured with any ingredient from coffee to chocolate to pureed fruit. Take care to use only unsalted butter. Beat it thoroughly for lightness. It could also be made light by mixing an equal quantity of pastry cream.

Butter icing: This is made by thoroughly beating together equal weights of creamed butter and sugar. Icing sugar gives a smooth filling, granulated sugar adds crunch while brown sugar gives more taste.

Glacés for pastries: Glacé, as the name suggests, is used to give a shine and colour to the pastry. One kind is applied before baking and the other after the pastry or biscuit has been baked. The glacé also acts as a protective layer when the pastry is filled with a moist filling. An egg glacé, made by whisking a whole egg with a large pinch of salt, is the best one for raw dough. The salt breaks the albumen in the egg white, making it easier to brush the glacé smoothly. For a more golden but less shiny effect, glacé the dough with egg yolk, salt and a tablespoon of water beaten together.

Egg based glacés hold the dough together, seal the edges of leavened dough and lids of pies. Other glacés that are applied before baking, include sugar syrup, water sprinkled with sugar or even milk for a golden colour. Richer glacés with honey or nuts are more commonly used for breads and cakes. Glacés that are added after baking are usually fruit based. Red currant jelly glacé is a favourite for tarts filled with berries and plums. Other fruits are coated with apricot jam glacé (see lesson on 'Cakes and Cookies') or a glacé of a similar colour. While poaching fruits in syrup, you could make fruit syrup glacé by reducing the poaching liquid, then thickening it with cornflour or arrowroot. Fruit glacé protects the pastry and helps prevent the juice of ripe fruits from saturating it.

Caramel

This is a substance, light or dark brown in colour, obtained during the last stage in cooking when all the moisture has evaporated. Caramel is liquid when hot, but sets when cool to become crisp and brittle. Light caramel made at 160°C has little flavour and is used much like sugar syrup boiled to the hard crack stage for coating sweets or fruits. Medium caramel, which is medium to dark brown in colour made at 175°C, has a nutty, sweet flavour, which becomes increasingly bitter as the temperature rises and the colour darkens. It is used to line moulds for desserts such as caramel custard. If the caramel sets too quickly, warm it gently in the pan until it melts, taking care not to cook it further. If you dissolve this in water, it forms a simple sauce that can be served with ice cream and a variety of desserts.

Note: A whole range of instant mixtures for caramel, cakes, pastries and other desserts are available in the market but the taste of homemade ones is definitely better. Now, let us learn how to make caramel, pastry cream and butter cream.

Practical things to be done

1. Making Caramel

Utensils used: A heavy-bottomed saucepan and a wooden spoon.

Portions: You can make the quantity you need. Here we shall make 1 litre of caramel.

Ingredients: 1 kg sugar; 2 litre water.

Follow this procedure to make caramel:

1. Heat the water and sugar in the saucepan over low heat, stirring gently. The sugar should

dissolve completely by the time the syrup begins to boil. Let it boil for a minute till it is sparkling clear.

2. Keep boiling this syrup till it starts to brown around the edge of the pan. Lower the heat and continue to cook, stirring gently all the while. Swirl the pan once or twice so that the syrup colours evenly.
3. To check the colour of the caramel, tip the pan sideways during cooking, to see the caramel run off the bottom of the pan. At this stage, you will get a light caramel.
4. If you wish to make a really dark caramel, continue to cook the syrup, stirring gently. When smoke begins to rise out of the saucepan, your caramel is done. Plunge the base of the saucepan in a bowl of cool water to prevent the caramel from cooking further in the heat of the pan.

Note: To caramelise sugar without making it into syrup, spread the sugar in the base of a heavy pan. Cook over medium heat till the sugar begins to melt. Stir gently till the sugar melts evenly, and then cook it till you achieve the desired thickness and colour.

2. Making Pastry Cream

Utensils used: 2 large saucepans; a mixing bowl; a balloon whisk.

Portions: Makes 625 ml pastry cream.

Ingredients: 500 ml milk; 1 tsp vanilla essence; 6 egg yolks; 100 gms castor sugar; 30 gms flour.

To make pastry cream, follow this simple procedure:

1. Pour the milk into a saucepan and bring it to boil. Cover the pan and simmer over very low heat for 5 minutes. Whisk together the egg yolk and sugar in a mixing bowl. When it becomes thick and light, mix in the flour and whisk some more.
2. Strain the milk into this mixture. Stir to mix well with the whisk till the mixture is smooth and homogenous. There should be no lumps.
3. Pour the mixture into another pan, return to heat and bring to a boil, whisking constantly. If lumps begin to form during cooking, take the pan off the heat at once and whisk till the mixture becomes smooth, then return to heat again.
4. Cook the mixture gently, whisking all the while, till it softens slightly and the flour is completely cooked. This will take about 2 minutes. Add the vanilla essence now. Transfer the cream to a bowl. Rub a lump of butter over the surface as it cools. This will prevent a skin forming on top of the cream. Cover the bowl and cool.

Here are a few variations you can try:

- Light pastry cream used for pastry tarts, puff pastry desserts, and cream puffs is made by folding whipped cream, made with 250 ml double cream, into any flavour of pastry cream.

- Chocolate or coffee pastry cream used for choux pastry, especially éclairs is made in this manner: Melt 150 gms chocolate on a heatproof plate over a pan of hot water and beat into the pastry cream. For coffee, dissolve 2 tablespoons dry instant coffee in the milk.

3. Making Butter Cream

Utensils used: A selection of mixing bowls; a saucepan; a balloon whisk; a wooden spoon.

Portions: To make 375 gms butter cream.

Ingredients: 100 gms sugar; 90 ml water; 4 egg yolks; 250 gms unsalted butter; ½ tsp vanilla essence.

To make butter cream, follow this simple procedure:

1. Heat sugar with water in a saucepan till the sugar is dissolved. Boil the mixture till it reaches the softball consistency (see lesson on 'Indian Desserts').
2. Beat egg yolk in a bowl till just mixed. Gradually add to this the hot sugar syrup, beating with

a whisk or a wooden spoon. You have to beat as fast as possible till the mixture is cool and thick. This will take about 5 minutes.

3. Cream the butter well and beat it into the cool yolk mixture a little at a time. Add vanilla essence and beat the mixture again.

You can try these variations.

- To make raspberry butter cream, puree 250 gms fresh or thawed, frozen raspberries, strain and beat into 375 gms butter cream.
- To make orange or lemon butter cream, beat grated rind of 2 oranges or lemons, 4 tablespoons orange or lemon juice into 375 gms butter cream.
- To make chocolate or coffee butter cream, melt 175 gms chopped plain chocolate or dissolve 2 tablespoons instant coffee in 2 tablespoons hot water, cool slightly and beat into 375 gms butter cream.

Baked apple served with ice cream

4. Baked Apples

Ingredients: ¼ cup or less brown sugar; 1 tsp cinnamon; 1 tbsp vegetable oil; 1/3 cup raisins; 6 medium baking apples, cored.

Portion: Makes 6 servings.

Follow this simple procedure to make baked apples:

1. In a bowl, mix sugar, cinnamon, oil, and raisins. Fill centre of apples and place upright in a baking dish. Pour 1 cup water around apples.
2. Bake at 375°F for 45-60 minutes, basting frequently.

5. Raisin Whole-Wheat Bread Pudding

Ingredients: 1½ cups whole-wheat bread, cut into 1 inch cubes; 1/3 cup raisins; 2 tbsp sugar; ¾ tsp ground cinnamon; 1 egg; ¼ tsp vanilla, 1¼ cups skimmed milk.

Raisin whole-wheat Bread Pudding

Portions: To serve 4 persons.

To make raisin whole-wheat bread pudding, follow this simple procedure:

1. Preheat oven to 325°F (slow).
2. Place bread cubes in large casserole. Sprinkle with raisins.
3. Mix sugar and cinnamon. Stir in egg. Add vanilla.
4. Heat the milk. Slowly stir into egg mixture. Pour over bread.
5. Bake until tip of knife inserted in centre comes out clean – about 40 minutes.

Apple Custard Merinague

Mushroom Chicken Pie

Banana Paneer Splendour

Day 28

Chinese Food

China is a country where reflections and discussions about nutrition and cookery have been a focal point since centuries. Innumerable rituals are associated with Chinese meals. The serving of braised turtle at the table would signify long life. Success in a venture would inspire a ragout of stag with mushrooms to be served.

Harmony is very important to Chinese cuisine. This is achieved through a contrast of dishes. A crisp dish precedes a creamy preparation, and a hot spicy dish would have a sweet garnish.

Four basic flavours, namely salt, sour, bitter, and sweet blend remarkably well in Chinese foods. The vegetables are finely diced or thinly sliced to enable them to be cooked in the shortest possible time. The finely cut foods do not only cook easily and quickly, but also absorb flavours of the seasoning.

The cooking methods in China were originally conditioned by the acute lack of fuel, which prompted the cooks to innovate dishes that cooked even on embers in 10-15 minutes.

The Chinese have a great aesthetic sense and present food artistically. The dish must appeal to the guest through sight and smell, and sometimes through touch and hearing. A soup of shrimps, ham, mushrooms and bamboo shoots is garnished with rice croûtons that distinctly crackle.

Ingredients are cut into cubes, thin strips, dices, small sticks, round slices, or 'grains of rice', depending on the type of food being cooked. The ingredients are often cut into decorative shapes like spring onion feathers, tomato petals, and trumps or carrots shaped into stars.

The basic ingredients of Chinese food are eggs, a great variety of noodles and vermicelli made from flour and rice along with a variety of vegetables and meats. "To the Chinese, food is an art form and in the preparation of dishes, great care is taken to provide contrasting flavours, textures both crunchy and soft, a pleasing variety of colour and shapes in which vegetables play an important part; that is why their dishes are as appealing visually as they are satisfying to the appetite."

"The essence of Chinese cooking is that very small amount of any expensive food such as meat, is used to enhance and 'lift' a much larger amount of fairly bland, relatively inexpensive food such as rice. Economy has always been of paramount concern to the Chinese, but nutritionally, their dishes are excellent because, whichever method is used, the ingredients are cooked quickly, and, therefore, retain their natural goodness," says Mr. H.K. Lee in his book '*Chinese Cooking*'.

A variety of Chinese food

Vegetables include dried mushrooms, red, green and yellow peppers, carrots, green peas, cauliflower, broccoli, spring onions, ginger, garlic, Chinese cabbage, spinach, etc. Other main ingredients are soy beans, bean curd, bean curd cheese, bean sprouts and as an oil or sauce; lotus seeds, leaves and roots; red dates; water chestnut; bamboo shoots, glutinous rice and rice flour, oyster sauce, black bean sauce, sesame seed oil, sesame paste, soybean paste, soy sauce, sweet bean paste, chillies, rock sugar, Chinese rose dew, Chinese snow pickle, chow chow, monosodium glutamate and five spice powder made from a mixture of star anise, anis pepper (Szechuan peppercorns), cloves and cinnamon, etc. Along with these ingredients fish, shellfish, poultry, pork, lamb and beef are equally important to them as most of their dishes are based in combination of meats and vegetables.

Dishes are often steamed. Steaming and stir frying are two favourite methods of cooking, though a few items are partly deep-fried, too. Ajinomoto, commonly known as 'Chinese salt' is used to season foods in Chinese cuisine. Its chemical name is 'monosodium glutamate'. It improves the flavour of foodstuffs. Researchers claim that it may cause cancer and should be used sparingly. The recipes are designed to facilitate eating with chopsticks.

Chinese cuisine was one of the first foreign cuisines to be introduced globally. Every country has Chinese restaurants. In India, too, Chinese food became popular in the late 60s but became a household favourite only in the 80s. Now most of the fast food joints specialise in Chinese food. Chinese soups, the chop suey, noodles and fried rice are the most common dishes on a Chinese menu.

Here, you will learn about them.

Chop Suey

This dish was innovated in the end of 19th century in the United States by immigrant Chinese cooks for their American customers. It includes a mixture of chopped, simmered vegetables, sometimes accompanied by strips of meat.

To prepare chop suey, cut juliennes of young and tender seasonal vegetables like carrots, leeks, onions and peppers, etc. Place them in a shallow frying pan with 2-3 tablespoons of oil for 500 gms vegetables. Stir well, cover and cook gently for 4-5 minutes on high flame. During the cooking time, cut some spring onions into small sticks. Scald some bean sprouts, cool and drain. Chop finely one clove of garlic and dice some skinned and deseeded tomatoes. Mix with 1½ tablespoons of soy sauce, and a little salt if necessary. Mix and serve hot. You could also use 1 teaspoon of sesame oil to season this mixture.

Noodles

Noodles are thin strips of paste made from flour, eggs, and water and cut into thin flat strips or piped into thin, long strands. The best noodles are made with egg yolks. Whole eggs produce tough noodles. Noodles can be used fresh or dried. They are cooked in a large quantity of boiling salted water to which a teaspoon of oil has been added to prevent the noodle strands sticking together. When the noodles turn opaque, remove from fire, put into a big colander and rinse under cold running water. Then, add a teaspoon of oil, mix well and set aside for further cooking with vegetables and meats of your choice.

Noodles are extensively used in Chinese and Vietnamese cuisine. Yellow noodles are made from eggs and wheat flour to which a little ajinomoto is added. Rice noodles include very fine vermicelli, which is steamed and served with stir fried vegetables and meats, or chop suey, as well as ordinary flat noodles. You could make your own noodles using refined wheat flour, eggs and water, using a drawing machine. However, it is best to buy packets available in the market. Both flat noodles and the long rounded ones are available.

Hakka Noodles

Homemade noodles

To make noodles, follow this recipe:

1. Sift 500 gms of refined flour and arrange as a small mound on the work surface. Dissolve 2 teaspoons of salt in 2-3 tablespoons of water. Pour it on the flour. Then add 3 whole eggs and 6 egg yolks.
2. Using your fingers, work the flour gradually into the liquid. Knead the dough thoroughly, working it with the heel of the palm until smooth and firm. Wrap it in a cloth and leave for 1 hour so that it loses its elasticity.
3. Divide the dough into pieces about the size of an egg. Roll these into balls. Roll out each piece into the shape of a very thin chapatti.
4. Spread these chapattis on baking sheets covered with sheets of paper and leave them to dry for 50 minutes.
5. Lightly dust each chapatti with dry flour. Roll it up. Cut into strips 2-3 mm wide, then gradually unroll the strips on a flat surface or hang them on a rod to dry for 10-15 minutes.

Fried rice

Chicken Fried Rice

Fried rice is made of the easily available short or long-grained rice. The rice is boiled in salted water, but left a little undercooked. Then it is washed under cold running water to separate the grains. After this, it is stir fried with a variety of vegetables, meats, fish, poultry and even scrambled eggs.

It is garnished with a little soy sauce and green chilli slit lengthwise. The fried rice is a popular dish not only in Chinese cuisine but also all over the world. The Chinese also serve plain boiled rice or steamed rice with a variety of other dishes.

Chinese soups

The Chinese serve a variety of soups, which are always cooked over brisk heat. Their garnishes are never allowed to become sticky. They are either clear, unthickened soups, or those thickened with cornflour. Out of many the most popular ones in India are the Sweet Corn Soups, which are made with vegetables, poultry, fish, or a combination of all. They contain vegetables/ chicken simmered in vegetable or chicken stock, and sweet corn kernel are added (which are available fresh or canned). While the soup is simmering, a well-beaten egg is poured into it and the content is stirred briskly so that strands of cooked egg float on top. To this is added a little water and the soup is served piping hot. You can garnish it with soy sauce and a mixture of vinegar and chopped green chillies.

Chinese Chicken-Crab-Corn Soup

Chinese Egg-drop soup

Along with above mentioned Chinese dishes, other popular dishes are Sweet-n-Sour Vegetables or Chicken or Seafood, Chilli-Garlic sauce based veg or non-veg dishes and Manchurian veg and non-veg dishes that are mainly eaten with fried rice and steamed or fried noodles. For more information refer to the recipe section.

Using chopsticks

Learning to use chopsticks is quite simple and easy. Place one chopstick in the hollow between thumb and index finger and rest its lower end below the first joint of the third finger. This chopstick remains stationary. Hold the other chopstick between the tips of the index and middle finger. Steady its upper half against the base of the index finger. Use the tip of the thumb to keep it in place. To pick up food, move the upper chopstick with index and middle fingers. The strongest chopsticks are made from bamboo, but they can also be made from lacquered wood, plastic, or ebony.

Practical things to be done

1. Chicken Chowmein

Chowmein literally means 'stir fried noodles'. It is a very popular dish. A variety of ingredients such as fish, meat, poultry or vegetables can be added to suit individual taste. When served cold, it makes a tasty salad.

Chicken Chowmein

Utensils used: A nonstick wok; a wooden spatula; chopping knife; few bowls.

Portions: To serve 4.

Ingredients: 250 gms egg noodles; 4-5 tbsp vegetable oil; 125 gms French beans; 250 gms chicken breast meat; 2 tbsp light soy sauce; 1 tsp salt; ½ tsp sugar; 1 tbsp Chinese rice wine or dry sherry (optional); 2 spring onions, finely shredded; a few drops of sesame oil; chilli sauce to serve.

To cook chowmien, follow this simple procedure:

1. Cook the noodles in salted water to which a teaspoon of oil is added. When they turn opaque, are tender but a little undercooked, remove from fire. Drain. Wash under cold running water and drain again. Then toss with 1 tablespoon of oil and keep aside.
2. Slice the chicken breast into thin shreds. Cut the tops and tails of the beans.
3. Heat 3 tablespoons of oil in a preheated wok or a nonstick *kadhai* until hot, add noodles and stir fry for 2-3 minutes with 1 tablespoon soy sauce. Remove to a serving dish. Keep warm.
4. Heat the remaining oil. Stir fry the beans and meat for about 2 mins. Add salt, sugar, wine (if using it), the remaining soy sauce and about half the spring onions.
5. Blend the meat mixture well and add a little stock or water if necessary. Pour this on top of the noodles. Sprinkle the sesame oil and the remaining spring onions on top. Serve hot or cold with chilli sauce.

2. Chinese Egg Fried Rice

Ingredients:

Rice parboiled – 2 cup, vegetables parboiled – 2 cups, eggs – 3 no, cooking oil – 3 tbsp or chilli oil, onion chopped – 1 no, soy sauce – 1 tbsp and salt – 1 tsp.

Preparation and Cooking:

1. Heat oil in a micro safe large bowl for 1 minute on high; add a chopped onion and cook on high for 1 minute.
2. Add beaten eggs and ½ tsp salt to the oil; cook for 2 minutes on medium, stirring once.
3. Mix boiled vegetables with the egg mixture and cook on medium for 3 minutes, stirring once.
4. Add rice and salt; sprinkle soy sauce and stir gently again, sprinkle 2 tbsp water or stock; cover the dish with a lid and reheat for 5 minutes so that the rice is very hot.

Serving:

Serve the fried rice with any of the Chinese dishes.

Variation:

Instead of vegetables, use cooked and chopped chicken or shrimps.

Tips:

If you have to par-boil rice in a microwave, put 1 cup raw rice and 5 cups water in a large dish and boil for 13 minutes on high. Drain the water immediately through a colander and place the rice under tap water. Drain well and use.

Fried rice turns out very well if the par boiled rice is cooked in advance and kept under refrigeration for a few hours. You may cook them in the traditional way of a gas stove too.

Cooking time: 11 minutes micro cooking.

Italian Food

Italian cuisine is one of the oldest in Europe. It is derived from traditional Greek cooking which was influenced greatly by oriental cuisine. Over the centuries, these culinary traditions were firmly entrenched in the Italian way of life, to become one of the best known foods across the world. The cooks in Italy perfected the skills learnt from the Greek. Food like the pasta, spaghetti, risotto, fissto missto and pizza are enjoyed worldwide. They are served in combination with Parma ham, salami, and cheeses like Parmesan and Gorgonzola. The fine quality of Italian ice cream and water ices is also widely acknowledged.

Italian Food

The secret of Italian cuisine is in the quality and variety of its ingredients, which include rice and pasta, olive oil, wheat flour, beans, a variety of vegetables, herbs, cheeses and olives, fish, ham and poultry among others.

Rice and Pasta

Connoisseurs of rice and pasta appreciate that the Italians have developed the preparation of these dishes to a fine art. They use herbs, especially basil, thyme, sage, oregano, rosemary and parsley extensively. The herbs flavour the hearty minestrone soup as well as the delicate chicken dishes. Rice, which absorbs any flavour, is cooked in stock, flavoured with saffron and uses ingredients like chicken, white truffles, tomatoes and peppers. Garlic is a favourite seasoning.

Herbs used in Italian cooking

Italian pasta is recognised worldwide. In Italy, it is served as a first course, sometimes mixed with butter and Parmesan cheese, or smothered in a thick tomato sauce. It is also served differently with a meat sauce, a sauce made with ham, eggs, fresh cream, pepper and grated cheese, or with any of the variety of sauces that are an integral part of Italian cuisine. The famous pesto sauce made with basil, parsley, and marjoram pounded with oil, Parmesan cheese, and garlic is eaten with pasta and spaghetti.

Ingredients for Pasta

Classic pasta is made only with wheat semolina and water. The best quality has a translucent, amber appearance. The taste varies with the shapes that range from elbows, shells, macaroni to tagliatelli. They are usually classified as:

- Soup pasta, Long pasta, Short pasta.
- Egg pasta is made with 2-3 eggs per kg semolina. It is especially popular in Paris.
- Milk pasta contains at least 6 gms dried milk powder per 450 gms pasta.
- Flavoured pasta is made with a vegetable like spinach or flavouring like tomato, added during the manufacturing process. No artificial colouring is used.

- Whole-wheat pasta contains more vitamins and minerals than others. It has more dietary fibre, too.

Good quality pasta will have a dry, smooth and even appearance. The colour is translucent ivory, verging on yellow. It breaks easily and cleanly, and quadruples in volume on being cooked. Some Pastas, especially Lasagne, Cannelloni, and Ravioli, are sold fresh or frozen, ready stuffed with a filling.

An average 60 gms portion of pasta provides 230 calories and protein equivalent to that in beef. To make pasta into a well-balanced diet for the family, serve pasta with a little butter, fresh tomato sauce, and grated cheese. This will provide proteins, fats, carbohydrates, vitamins and dietary fibres.

Pasta and bean soup

Varieties of Pasta

Pastas can be divided into four broad groups:

Tagliatelli pasta

1. **Pasta for soup is very small and made in various shapes**. These include vermicelli, linguine (small grains), pennette (small quills), stelline (little starts), risoni (rice grains) conchigliette (little shells), and anelline (little rings), which are sometimes serrated.

Penne pasta

2. **Pasta for boiling has the greatest variety**. Some are flat such as tagliatelle, trenette; others are cylindrical like spaghetti, spagettini, and fideline. There are also hollow pasta such as macaroni, rigatoni, and penne, which are straight, pasta shells, nests, butterflies, spirals, etc.

Shell pasta

Spaghetti

3. **Pasta for baking must first be boiled in water**. It includes lasagne, tortiglioni, bucatini conchiglie, and cravattine.

Elbow

4. **Filled pasta of which cannelloni and ravioli** are the commonest forms, have a stuffing folded in. Other types in the same variety include tortellini, torlettoni, agnolotti, lumache, and manicotti.

Cannelloni

Ravioli pasta

Cooking Pasta

Pasta, whatever its quantity, should be cooked in plenty of water. Use a large pan. The water is needed to make the pasta swell and move freely. Otherwise, the released starch makes it sticky. Add a tablespoon of oil and salt to the water to prevent the stickiness. Sprinkle small pasta briskly into boiling water. Long pasta like spaghetti is gradually pushed into the boiling water without breaking the strands, cooked until it softens and bends.

1. Boiling pasta

2. Boiled pasta being stir fried

3. Baked pasta

The cooking time for pasta varies according to the quality of the pasta, its size, and the hardness of the water. Even if the cooking time is specified on the packet, it is better to test the pasta for doneness before draining it. Vermicelli takes about 4-5 minutes, flat pasta and spaghetti takes 10-12 minutes, and large macaroni takes 15 minutes. In each case the time is counted when the water comes to the boil after the pasta has been added. If you are using the pasta in a cold salad, drain at once. Rinse under cold running water. Mix immediately with a little oil, so that it does not stick on cooking.

If you are serving it hot, the sauce of choice should be poured boiling hot onto the hot pasta. Stir quickly and sprinkle grated cheese on top. Serve immediately on a hot serving dish. If the pasta is not to be used immediately, drain it, and keep it hot mixed with a tablespoon of oil. When you are ready to use, plunge it into boiling water, drain once again, and add the ingredients.

To make Italian pasta, dried wheaten flour preparation, mostly made from durum wheat is used. The flour is well kneaded into a stiff dough and forced through specially perforated cylinders from which it comes out in various shapes known by different names (macaroni, spaghetti, vermicelli, crescioni, ditalini, ravioli, tagliatelli and tortellini, etc.) The variety of pasta is made by kneading vigorously hard wheat with boiling water. Then the paste is put in a bronze cylinder equipped with die and pressure is applied to it by a hydraulic press. Egg pasta is made by adding dry or fresh eggs to the same mixture.

Pasta, an excellent staple, is essentially an energy food providing the body with 350 calories per 100 gms pasta. The food value of pasta products is the same as that of the cereals from which it is made. It contains carbohydrates and mineral salts but only very small amounts of protein, fats and vitamins.

PIZZA

In its simplest form, the pizza consists of a medium thick slab of bread dough spread over with thick tomato puree and parmesan or Mozzarella cheese, seasoned with herbs and garlic, and baked in an oven. There are numerous varieties of pizza, garnished with vegetables like peas, olives, peppers, mushrooms, capers, etc. It is also topped with slices of smoked sausages, ham, seafood, mussels and chicken. It can be served as a starter, a savoury or as a snack. In India, pizza makers also use mutton kebabs, chicken *tikkas* and *paneer* for toppings to suit the Indian taste. Miniature pizzas are used as cocktail snacks.

Italian Pizza

PIZZA DOUGH

The basic pizza dough is made in the following manner:

Yeast risen pizza dough:

1. Crumble 15 gms of fresh baker's yeast in 3 tablespoons of warm water to which a little sugar has been added. Leave this in a corner until frothy.
2. Sieve 350 gms flour, make a well in the centre and pour in 1½ cups warm water and 4 tablespoons olive oil. Add the yeast and 1 teaspoon salt.
3. Work the dough with your fingers. Knead on a flour board until the dough is smooth and elastic.
4. Roll the dough into a ball, dust with flour, and leave in a covered bowl in a warm place away from draught until it doubles in size.
5. Knead for one minute. Roll out into a circle about 8-10 inches in diametre. Raise the edges with the thumb to form a rim. The pizza is ready for filling and baking.

Yeast-free Pizza Dough:

Place 1½ cups plain flour, 1 tablespoon baking powder and ½ teaspoon salt in a bowl. Make a well in the centre and add ½ cup water and 2 tablespoons olive oil. Combine gradually incorporating the flour into the olive oil and water, adding a little extra water if necessary. Transfer the dough to a floured board and knead until smooth and elastic. It should take 5-7 minutes.

Sour-dough Pizza Dough:

To make the starter: Combine 1 teaspoon active dried yeast and 1 cup water. Whisk in 1 cup all purpose plain flour. Cover with plastic wrap and set aside at room temperature for 3 to 24 hours, until frothy. The longer the souring time, more sour the dough. Add ½ teaspoon salt and 2 cups or 250 gms all-purpose plain flour to the starter. Knead until pliable. It should take about 5 minutes.

Making Pizza Dough

The most important ingredient for making a pizza is the sauce used to coat the rolled out pizza base. Let us learn about two popular varieties.

Italian Tomato Sauce

Utensils Used: Saucepan bowl, a knife, a wooden spoon.

Ingredients: Two large onions, 2 cloves garlic, 1 tablespoon olive oil, 1 kg ripe tomatoes.

Method:

1. Peel and finely chop the onions and garlic. Sauté in the olive oil over low heat for about 10 minutes, or until transparent. Roughly chop the tomatoes and add to the onions.
2. Cook the mixture over medium heat for about 40 minutes or until it begins to thicken. Cool it.
3. This mixture can be stored in the refrigerator for up to 3 weeks.

Practical things to be done

1. Cheese Pizza

Utensils used: A big trough for kneading.

Ingredients:

1 quantity yeast-free pizza dough; ½ cup (125 ml) Basic tomato sauce; 60 gms Romano cheese, grated; 60 gms provolone cheese, sliced; 30 gms grated parmesan cheese; 60 gms grated Mozzarella cheese.

Cheese Pizza

Portions: 2-4.

To make cheese pizza, follow this procedure:

1. Place an unglazed terracotta tile or baking sheet in the oven. Preheat oven to 450°F.
2. On a floured surface, press out the pizza dough using your fingertips into a 9½ inches circle, always pressing from the inside of the dough to the outside.
3. Place the pizza dough on the heated brick, tile or baking sheet. Spoon on the tomato sauce and arrange the cheeses on top.
4. Bake for 15 minutes, or until the pizza is golden on the edges and crisp underneath.

2. Bow -tie Macaroni Baked in Cheese Sauce

Ingredients:

Macaroni boiled – 3 cups, cheese sauce – 1 and ½ cup to 2 cups, carrots chopped – ½ cup, green peas shelled – ½ cup, green pepper sliced 1 no, milk – ½ cup (if required), cheese grated – ¼ cup, fresh herbs – ¼ cup or oregano – 1 tsp and tomato – 10 to 12 slices.

Preparation and Cooking:

1. Grease a micro safe dish and keep aside.
2. Boil carrots and peas in a steamer for 3 minutes on high.
3. Combine cheese sauce, oregano and fresh herbs together and mix with boiled macaroni and vegetables. If you find the mixture too thick, add ½ cup milk and check the seasoning.
4. Spread half the pasta mixture in the greased dish; arrange half of the tomato slices and sliced pepper on top and cover with the remaining pasta mixture.
5. Arrange the rest of the tomato and pepper slices on top of the dish and sprinkle grated cheese.
6. Bake on combination mode. Press combi-1, set time and start. Bake the dish for 10 minutes. If the top is not golden brown, then put the dish under grill for 5 minutes. Remove and serve.

Day 30

Garnishing and Presentation

There is a famous saying; "The taste of the pudding is in its eating". This may have been true at one point of time. Today appearances count a lot for everything. A brightly wrapped package attracts the eye, as does a well laid table with food. The display has to be tempting to attract the attention and to set the salivary glands working. This is why most cooked dishes require special serving dishes and platters, bowls, glasses and tureens.

Garnishing

A single ingredient or a combination of several ingredients can be used to garnish or decorate a dish. The garnish can be placed over and around meats, chicken, fish and vegetables, rice dishes and desserts, too.

Dinner Served on Table

Whether simple or composite, the garnish should always blend with the flavour of the dish. The range of garnishes is the most diverse in French cooking. Blending of flavours makes it necessary to use traditional garnishes like:

- A roast leg of mutton with small kidney beans.
- Poached fish with boiled or steamed potatoes.
- Venison with chestnut puree.

The **Indian menu** relies on simple garnishing using dried herbs, fresh coriander and mint leaves, tomato and onion slices and rings, lemon slices and wedges, tomato flowers, cucumber flowers, shredded cabbage and lettuce, and fried dry fruits. Sliced, hard-boiled eggs and chunks of boiled potatoes, deep-fried to a light brown are also used as garnishes.

- A typical **Indian curry** both vegetarian and non-vegetarian, looks appetising with a sprinkling of chopped fresh coriander.
- Rice *pulaos* and biryanis are often garnished with sliced crisp fried onions, mint leaves, dry fruits and hard-boiled eggs.
- To make salad look appetising, you can use thinly sliced onion, tomatoes, carrots and radish. Lay them in circles of different coloured vegetables with a tomato rose in the centre. A few lemon slices and spring onions with leaves cut to a length of 3-4 inches, sliced into two lengthwise can decorate four sides of the salad. If you are serving a mixed chopped salad, serve it on a bed of cabbage or lettuce leaves. Heap the salad tossed in salad dressing, in the centre. Surround with slices of cucumber and radish, perch a carrot flower or a tomato flower on top.
- Raitas look attractive with chopped fresh mint or coriander on top of the usual garnishing of coarsely ground, roasted cumin seeds and chilli powder. The same garnishing makes *dahi bhallas* particularly inviting.

- The **kormas**, if they are the non-vegetarian variety, are garnished with halved hard-boiled eggs.
- The vegetarian kormas look nice with onion rings and fried boiled potato chunks.
- **Roasts of all kinds** are served surrounded by onion rings, lemon wedges and hard-boiled eggs cut into fours. If you are serving gravy or sauce along with the roasts, pour it in a tureen and serve on the side.

Throughout the course, garnishing and decoration for finished dishes has been suggested. In this last lesson we will discuss specific techniques for certain specialised dishes. It will help you to make your cooking look appetising.

Presenting Soups

Creamy Cauliflower Soup

Ham and Pork Noodle Soup

- Ideally, there should be harmony between the type of soup and the kind of bowl in which it is presented, for example, the clarity of consommé calls for a simple, shallow porcelain soup plate to display the sparkling liquid.
- Broth-based soups are suited to pot-bellied terrines or rustic earthenware bowls, which double up as baking dishes for bread-thickened soups that are cooked partly in the oven.
- Opinions differ on whether creamy and pureed soups look more attractive in plain or coloured bowls. It is a matter of personal taste.
- Garnishes can transform soup. A swirl of cream, a sprinkling of herbs or a small ingredient such as a shrimp or a piece of tomato adds extra colour and flavour.
- Hot soups should be served very hot.
- Similarly, cold soups should be cold, though extreme chilling may dull the flavour.

Accompaniments of Soups

- Small pastries such as cheese straws can be served separately.
- Rice and noodles are added to the soup.
- Small choux puff may be added just before service so that they stay crisp.
- The simplest accompaniment and yet the most frequently used, is the croûton. When properly made, it is a welcome addition to a variety of soups, from rustic fish and broth-based soups to velvety bisques. Croûtons can be the traditional fried cubes of bread or simply cubes of toast.
- Alternatively, whole slices of French bread or rolls can be dried or toasted in the oven to make croûtes. These can be rubbed with a clove of garlic, in the style of Mediterranean cooking, for fish soups such as bouillabaisse.
- Tiny cocktail biscuits are a quick alternative for almost any soup. Crusty bread is an excellent accompaniment to any soup.

Presenting Eggs

- A plain boiled or poached egg cries out for a cosmetic touch of sauce, be it béchamel, cheese sauce, veloute, butter sauce, or even brown sauce. Mayonnaise is the top choice for salad eggs, often with a touch of tomato, herb, or a single slice of jet-black truffle.

- Omelettes can be garnished with a spoonful of flavouring or a ribbon of tomato sauce around the dish.
- Many eggs benefit from an edible container such as a pastry tartlet shell, or a fried or toasted croute of bread. Lighter alternatives include a bed of spinach, sliced tomatoes, or artichoke bottoms.

- When neatly sliced, hard-boiled eggs add colourful appeal to cold dishes like spinach salad or fish mousse, while fluffy sieved yolk forms a pretty garnish.
- Soft-boiled eggs are often eaten in the shell served in an eggcup, or the contents can be scooped into a warm dish accompanied by slices of toast.

Presenting fish

The presentation of fish is an integral part of the cooking method.

Baked Whole Fish

- A grilled or baked whole fish, for example, slashed along the sides with its skin toasted a crankily brown, can look perfect on its own or adorned simply with wedges of lemon and sprigs of watercress.
- Vegetables such as tomatoes and sweet peppers, grilled or baked with the fish, add extra colour.
- For small whole fish served individually, the head should be left on and the tail and fins trimmed. Once again, little garnish is needed other than some lemon wedges and sprigs of greenery. Traditionally, the fish is set on the plate with its head facing left, so that the flesh is easy to remove for a right-handed person.
- Whether hot or cold, a large poached fish should be served on the bone, trimmed and the skin removed.
- Classically, hot fish is displayed on a white napkin on a silver platter. Nowadays, greens of some kind often replace the napkin. The sauce should be served separately so that the fish is displayed in all its glory.
- Presentation of cold poached fish can be as elaborate as a coating of aspic with decorations of stuffed eggs, tomato baskets and cucumber boats.
- Fish curries go well with a sprinkling of chopped fresh coriander and tomatoes cut in fours.
- Deep-fried fish could be decorated with lemon slices and onion rings.
- Fillets and pieces of fish pose a greater presentation problem. Colour should be exploited. For example, the pink flesh of salmon or trout looks attractive. Fish with brilliant skins like red snapper, red mullet or bluefish may be cooked with the skin on and presented skin side up. Fillets can be cut and folded in a variety of shapes, as can whole boned fish. The classic decoration for a fish platter includes semicircles of sliced lemon.

Presenting shellfish

- Shellfish are highly decorative items in their own right. The colour of a lobster, let alone its complex structure, would be hard to dream of. Even the humble prawn is made handsome

by its whiskers and curly tail. Whether they are served hot or cold, lobster shells, split lengthwise, form a natural container for stuffing.
- Smaller crustaceans such as prawns, shrimps and crayfish, preferably with their heads left on, adorn the edge of fish dishes and peep temptingly over the rim of a bowl of soup. In salads, shellfish add to the appearance as well as to the taste of the dish.
- Curried prawns could be garnished with fresh coriander leaves and green chillies slit lengthwise.

Presenting Poultry

- A bunch of fresh watercress or a few potatoes are sufficient decoration for a whole bird that has been trussed and is golden brown from roasting.
- A bird, braised or pot-roasted with vegetables, needs no embellishment other than a sprinkling of chopped parsley.
- For a grander display, the birds can be carved, reshaped on the bone and displayed with a rich white or brown sauce for flavouring, surrounded by a panoply of stuffed vegetable and decorated with garlands of flowers cut from egg white, truffle, tomato and leek.
- More challenging is the presentation of poultry when cut into pieces. During cooking the meat shrinks, often exposing pieces of the joint and rib that should be trimmed for serving dish, the bird should be arranged in a fan shape, starting with the legs and leading inward to the breast pieces. When breast meat is off the bone, it is often carved in neat diagonal slices that are arranged in a fan shape on the plate, making an attractive frame for a fruit or vegetable garnish. The sauce is spooned under rather than over the meat.

Some poultry recipes dictate their own presentation:

- Deep-fried chicken should come in a basket.
- American potpie in a deep dish.
- While poultry stuffed with pasta or tortillas rarely needs decoration.

Fried Chicken Legs

- Curried poultry can be garnished with hard-boiled eggs cut into halves and a sprinkling of chopped fresh coriander.

Presenting Meat

- The presentation of meat depends on the way it is cooked. Traditionally, grand roasts such as sirloins of beef, barons of lamb and suckling pigs are displayed brown and crisp on the bone.
- Here, as with smaller roasts like leg of lamb, the meat is often carved, before being reshaped on the bone for guests to help themselves. The garnish – stuffed tomatoes, oven-roast potatoes, Brussels sprouts are clustered around the meat.

Shammi Kebab

- A bouquet of glacéd vegetables such as carrots, green beans, onions and peas, is a universal favourite.
- For boned roasts and pot-roasts, the meat is sliced in the kitchen and arranged down the centre of the dish, with vegetables on either side.
- Smaller pieces of meat such as steaks and chops may be arranged overlapping on bones on top pointing serving dish, outwards.
- Watercress is a popular garnish for grilled or pan-fried meats.
- Chopped parsley is used when the meat is moist with curry. As with roasts, vegetables that complement the meat should be added to the plate as a garnish.
- Individual plate presentations of meat and accompaniments are popular, particularly for meats like kebabs or chops that form their own decorations. Presenting meat dishes on individual plates simplifies service and looks attractive.
- Apart from parsley, fresh coriander, fried chunks of boiled potatoes and slices of hard-boiled eggs go well with meat curries.

Presenting Vegetables

- Most Indian dishes made from vegetables are simply garnished with coriander and

Mixed Veg Fry

mint leaves, slit green chillies, ginger cut into juliennes or fried chunks of *paneer*.

- Coarsely ground, roasted cumin and the vibrantly red chilli powder are sprinkled on top to add colour to the dish.
- Dry fries of okra and boiled potatoes are often better with a touch of *amchur*. The agreeable shapes and vibrant colours of vegetables make them a good choice for eye-catching presentations.
- A dull-looking dish that lacks life can often be saved by the addition of a garnish of shiny glacéd carrots or neatly arranged green beans.
- Modern plate presentations set great emphasis on display of assorted vegetables at the peak of freshness, all carefully cut to shape.
- A more traditional garnish for great platters of roast meats and poultry is an assortment of stuffed vegetables. The fillings may be flavoured with herbs and lemon – a vivid, eye-catching contrast. Potatoes are most often used. Carrots, sweet potatoes, turnips and even green beans also pipe well.
- In vegetable salads, appearance plays an even more important role. The crispness of the leaves of a fresh green salad or the balanced colour of a cooked vegetable salad make the dish attractive.

Presenting Sorbets, Ice Creams, and Frozen Desserts

- For a simple presentation, ice cream may be set into a square or round mould with an indented design, then easily unmoulded onto a chilled serving dish.
- Sorbets can be served in stemmed glasses.
- Hollowed out shells of lemons and other citrus fruits offer handy containers that may be frozen. Just before serving, add a decorative green leaf. To serve more than one flavour at one time, ice cream and sorbet may be formed into balls with a scoop and piled in a coupe glass. They can also be shaped into ovals with two spoons and set in a star shape on a cold, flat plate against a background of brightly coloured sauce. Sliced fruits may be added as garnish with a sprig of mint or frosted fresh fruit.

Strawberry Ice Cream

- Many pretty frozen desserts – such as the multi-coloured slices of frozen soufflé – need no additional decoration.
- A layer of icing sugar or cocoa sprinkled thickly on top of parfaits and frozen desserts adds a simple finishing touch. A sprinkling of browned chopped nuts or crushed caramel may be preferred, contributing texture as well as colour.
- Alternatives include shredded coconut, candied citrus peel, chopped crystallised fruits, grated chocolate or ornamental chocolate leaves. Decorative rosettes of whipped cream must be added just before serving. When frozen, they acquire the texture of butter. The grandest finish of all for frozen desserts is a cloud of spun sugar or a cage of caramel that must be cracked to reach the dessert itself.
- Accompaniments are equally traditional. The intense flavour of a sorbet demands at most a spoonful or two of liqueur.
- The flavours of ice cream invite a variety of sweet sauces from fruit to butterscotch to chocolate. Richer frozen desserts, however, require macaroons or wafers as accompaniments. They are good also with ice cream.

Lemon Sorbet

Presenting Fruit

- Like all other food items, fruit can be presented in many interesting and attractive forms. The colour of the fruit, its shine and flavour make it a welcome addition to many dishes, particularly cold desserts where it is served in combination with ice cream, custards and soufflés.

- Even when fruits are served directly, rather than just be peeled and diced, it can be presented in interesting shapes.
- Muskmelon can be cut into flower like halves where the pulp can be scooped with a spoon and eaten. Similarly, mango pieces can be made attractive by presenting them as dices still attached to the peel.

Fruit Tart

Expert cook suggests...

1. When roasting *papads* put them in a small stainless bowl when still hot and press the sides. When cool the *papads* will take the shape of the bowl. It is a novel way of serving *papad*.

Masala Papad

2. To have creaseless '*papads*', iron them with an iron set on 'hot' and store them in an airtight container.
3. Powder dry mint leaves. Store in an airtight container. Use it to garnish salads and raitas.

Salted Cashew Nuts

4. Serve salted cashew nuts and almonds without frying them. Put the required quantity with some salt in a *kadhai*. Roast them over a low flame till evenly browned. Sieve the salt, which can be used again.

Crushed dried Mint Leaves

5. Add a few drops of food colours to the water when freezing ice cubes. They look attractive when added to cold drinks.

With this chapter we come to the end of our lessons. Our effort was to guide you step-by-step towards developing a familiarity with different kinds of foods. We hope we have been able to help dispel the initial fears that everyone feels before emerging in a new field. We hope we have been able to assist you in developing your culinary skills. We also hope that the kitchen shall never be an awkward territory for you. We are confident that you have found happiness in taking up this course in the comfort of your home.

Learning is never complete. This is the end of the course. However, for you it is the beginning of a fascinating study of food. We have covered a vast territory in the past 30 days. It may have fulfilled the objective of acquainting you with this vast field. If you want to become a super-cook, you will need to keep referring to the study material repeatedly. A large number of recipes are included in the Selected Recipes section of this course. Try those that you find attractive. A vast storehouse of information is included in the third section, which is a reference section. Read it to update your kitchen. You will also get to know where to find important information when you need it.

True knowledge comes from experience; problems come to add to your experience and you will continue to find the solutions within this course material.

Be honest with the problems you faced during the practical sessions; don't be disappointed and discouraged if you go wrong. Instead, note down the mistakes you made; refer to the text carefully whenever you need it; follow the instructions intently, so that you can find the solutions and rectify your mistakes during the next trial. There is a saying, "Experience is another name of the mistakes we committed in (past) life." Shun your ego, take the mistakes positively in your stride and learn from them.

Presentation Table:

Stuffed Chicken Rolls

Fish Cutlets Baked

Grapes & Raspberries display

Fruit Medley

Tomato Soup

Cherry Jelly with Fruits

Ice Cream

Fried Prawns in Garlic Sauce

Strawberry Sorbet

Burger Pattice

50 Selected Recipes

Rice

Lazizan (Vegetable and Nut Pulao)

Ingredients:

Basmati rice – ½ cup, cauliflower – ½ cup, carrot – 1 no, potato – 1 no, peas shelled – ½ cup, capsicum – 1 no, ginger juliennes – 1 tbsp, oil – ¼ cup, black cumin – 1 tsp, whole spices – 2 tbsp, lemon juice – 1 tbsp, black pepper powder – 2 tsp, almonds – 20 no, cashew nuts – 15 no, raisins – 20 no, turmeric – 1 tsp (opt), water – 3 and ½ cup, salt to taste.

Preparation and Cooking:

1. Wash and soak rice for 30 minutes.
2. Clean and cut all the vegetables into ½ cubes.
3. Boil or steam all the vegetables except capsicum.
4. Heat oil in a deep pan and fry all the nuts in it to a golden brown colour and remove. In the same oil, crackle cumin and spices. Drain rice and fry with spices for 1 minute.
5. Add water, salt, turmeric, pepper powder and lemon juice to the rice. Cover and cook till rice is half done. Open the lid and add vegetables and half the nuts; stir gently and cover again. Cook for 10 minutes more on medium flame or till rice is done.
6. Let the dish stand for 5 minutes. Loosen the rice with fork and serve.

Serving:

Garnish 'Lazizan' with the rest of the nuts and ginger juliennes & serve with plain curd, papad and pickle etc.

Variation:

Cook peas / cauliflower or potato pulao the same way.

Cooking time: 25 to 30 minutes.

Boneless Mutton Pulao

Ingredients:

Basmati rice – 2 ½ cup, mutton boneless – 500 gm, brown onion – ½ cup, ginger-garlic paste – 1 tbsp, tomato puree – ¼ cup, oil – ¼ cup, black cumin –1 tsp, peppercorns –15 no, brown cardamoms – 3 no, cinnamon – 4 small pieces, chilli powder – 1 tbsp, turmeric – 1 tsp (opt), mint powder – 1 tsp, lemon-juice – 2 tbsp, water – 3 cups, milk – ½ cup, ginger juliennes –1 tbsp, onions crisp fried 3 tbsp for garnishing and salt to taste.

Preparation and Cooking:

1. Marinate the boneless mutton pieces with lime juice / vinegar, salt and red chilli powder and keep aside for 2 hours.
2. Soak rice for 30 to 40 minutes.
3. Boil mutton in a micro safe bowl with ½ cup water, ginger-garlic paste and whole spices for 20 minutes, covered. Cook for the first 5 minutes on micro high and the next 15 minutes on medium. Stand the dish for 10 minutes and strain. Save the liquid.
4. Or boil mutton in a pressure pan or a kadai till it becomes tender but not soft.
5. Heat oil in a large pan or kadai and crackle cumin seed on high flame. Add brown onions and rice; stir and cook on high flame for 2 minutes, uncovered.
6. Mix turmeric, chilli salt and mint powder with rice mixture.
7. Lift the mutton pieces and mix with rice. Mix the saved liquid, tomato puree and water to make 5 cups and add this to the mutton and rice mixture.
8. Cover the dish and cook for 20 minutes, for the first 10 minutes on a high flame, and the next 10 minutes on medium heat. Open the lid after 15 minutes of cooking and insert ginger juliennes into the rice. Stand the dish for 10 minutes.

Serving:

Loosen the rice with a fork and serve hot with curd / burani or mutton-coconut shorba.

Tips: Burani is a thin onion raita, spiced and flavoured with salt, pepper, green chilli and coriander leaves.

Mutton Coconut Shorba is a mutton stock and coconut milk spiced soup, often eaten with biryani and pulao in Hyderabad.

Cooking time: 43 minutes micro cooking.

NUTRI CHAWAL

Ingredients:

Basmati rice – ½ cup, soya chunks – 1½ cup, brown onion – ¼ cup, tomato puree – ½ cup, peas and carrot cubes –1 cup, cooking oil – ¼ cup, ginger-garlic paste – 1 tbsp, red pepper juliennes – ¼ cup, dried methi leaves – 2 tbsp, chilli powder – 2 tsp, turmeric powder – 1 tsp, peppercorns – 10 no, cumin – 1 tsp, bay leaf –1 no, cloves – 6 no, garam masala powder – 1 tsp, red chilli whole – 2 no, water / veg stock – 4 cups and salt to taste.

Preparation and Cooking:

1. Soak rice for 30 minutes.
2. Soak soya nuggets in water for 1 hour; drain and squeeze; add 2 cups fresh water and 1 tsp salt. Cook for 10 minutes. Stand the dish for 5 to 10 minutes; drain water and keep the boiled chunks warm.
3. Heat oil in a large pan and crackle cuminseeds, red chilli whole, peppercorns and cloves; add dry fenugreek leaves, ginger-garlic paste, brown onion, chilli and turmeric powder as well as tomato puree and boiled soya chunks. Stir well to coat the chunks with prepared masala; add shelled peas and carrot cubes. Cover and cook for 3 minutes.
4. Switch off the fire; remove soya chunks from the pan and keep them warm.
5. Add water/stock, rice, bay leaf and salt to the same pan. Stir well. Cover and cook for 10 minutes on high flame.
6. Open the lid and mix soya chunk masala gently with the rice. Cover and cook on low flame for another 10 to 12 minutes. Add red pepper juliennes and stand the dish for 5 minutes.

Serving:

Mix 'Nutri Nuggets Pulao' lightly with a fork and serve it hot with curd or any raita.

Tips: The food value of this dish is the same as of mutton pulao, because soya nuggets and granules are high protein products with fiber. Hence, they are excellent for vegetarians. This preparation of rice is almost a complete meal in itself and should be considered as one of the main dishes.

Cooking time: 36 minutes micro cooking.

Spices

CHAAT MASALA

Ingredients:

Mango powder – 1 tbsp, roasted cumin powder – 1 tbsp, rock salt – 1 tsp, black salt – 1 tsp, salt – 1 tsp, red chilli powder – 1 tsp, pepper powder – 1 tsp, ginger powder – ½ tsp, clove-cardamom-cinnamon powder – 1 tsp.

Mixing:

Mix all the ingredients in a clean dry bottle; shake well and use as and when required.

Tips:

This masala can be used to make fruit chaat or to add flavour to dahi vadas and other chaat dishes.

Some people like to sprinkle it over plain salad also.

Mixing time: 5 minutes.

Pulses

KABULI CHANNA DRY (CHIC PEAS PREPARATION)

Ingredients:

Kabuli chana – 250 gm, cooking soda – ½ tsp, pomegranate seeds – 1 tbsp, coriander seeds – 1 tbsp, cumin – 2 tsp, red chillies whole – 3 no, cloves – 4 no, cinnamon – 1" stick, black cardamoms – 3 no, ginger powder – ¼ tsp, tomato puree – ¼ cup, oil – 3 tbsp, ginger thinly sliced – 1" piece, coriander chopped – 3 tbsp.

Preparation and Cooking:

1. Wash and soak chanas with 3 cups of water and baking soda for 6 hours or overnight for the same.
2. Discard the water in which chanas were soaked and wash them. Cook in a pressure cooker with 1 tsp salt and 2½ cups water for 20 minutes.
3. Remove from fire and let the pressure fall down.
4. Combine all dry ingredients in a paper bag and roast on micro high for 2 minutes, shaking the paper bag once in between. Or roast the dry

spices in a pan and follow the same process. Cool and powder them.

5. Heat oil in a pan on high flame, lower the heat and add powdered spices; mix well and cook for 1 minute.
6. Put boiled chanas and tomato puree in the pan and mix well with the spices. Cover and cook for 3 minutes on medium flame. Let the dish stand for 5 minutes and then transfer it to the serving bowl.

Serving:

Garnish 'Kabuli Channa' with thinly sliced ginger juliennes and coriander; and serve the dish hot with Poories/Parathas.

Variation:

Add 2 cups of water to the cooked chanas; adjust the seasoning and proceed the same way to get a gravy to be eaten with rice.

Boil chanas with lotus stem roundels and cook with the same spices. You may add ½ tsp turmeric to the dish.

Tips:

It is essential to soak all the legumes (whole dals, channa, rajma, raungi, dry peas, etc) for the period specified in the recipe before cooking, because these ingredients take a long time to cook. If you do not have time to soak legumes for that long a period, boil them in a pressure cooker. Side by side roast dry masala in the microwave and grind; and make tempering for the whole dals on top of the gas stove. This way you can plan cooking your meals within your specified period in the kitchen.

After all microwave is a time saving device, and not only an appliance in the kitchen to depend upon. In fact, it is fun to use the new and traditional methods of cooking side by side.

Cooking time: 30 minutes if the chanas are presoaked.

Sabut Masoor (Dal Tadka)

Ingredients:

Masoor whole – 1 cup, ginger-garlic paste – 1 tbsp, green chillies – 6 no, onion – 1 no, tomatoes – 2 no, oil / ghee – 2 tbsp, cumin – ½ tsp, butter – 1 tbsp (opt), chilli powder – ½ tsp (opt), fenugreek leaves – 1 tbsp (dried), water – 4 cups and salt to taste.

Preparation and Cooking:

1. Soak dal for 2 hours.
2. Chop green chillies, onion and tomatoes.
3. Put dal in a pressure cooker. Add 4 cups water, ginger-garlic paste, half of the chopped chillies and 2 tbsp salt. Pressure cook for 35 minutes. Reduce the heat after the first whistle.
4. Let the dish stand till the pressure of the cooker comes down.
5. Meawhille, heat oil/ghee in a pan and crackle cumin in it. Add chopped onion and green chillies and fry till pinkish in colour. Add chopped tomatoes and dry fenugreek leaves and fry till oil separates. Add red chilli powder to the masala being fried.
6. Open the lid of the pressure cooker; stir dal with a wooden spoon and pour the tempering masala over it. Simmer for another 10 minutes on slow fire.

Serving:

Garnish 'Masoor Dal Tadka' with butter and serve hot with chapaties/phulka or naan etc.

Variation:

Cook sabut moong absolutely the same way.

Cook mixed dal chilmili. Combine ¼ cup each of whole moong, whole urad, whole masoor and chana dal; soak them, cook in a pressure cooker and temper with onion-tomato paste.

Tips:

In Aryan literature, the famous trio of pulses: the three M's, find mention. These are masha (urad /black gram), mudga (moong/green gram) and masura (masoor, lentil). These three dals are consumed in India since the Vedic era and are used in various forms in our day-to-day life.

Dal Makhani (Black gram preparation)

Ingredients:

Urad whole (black gram) – 1 cup, rajmah (kidney beans) – ¼ cup, ginger-garlic paste – 1 tbsp, onion chopped finely – 1 large, tomatoes chopped finely – 2 no, green chillies chopped – 2 to 3 no, ginger juliennes – 2 tbsp, cumin – 1 tsp, red chilli powder – 1 tsp, ghee – 2 tbsp, white butter – 2 to

3 tbsp, cream – 2 tbsp (opt), coriander chopped – 2 tbsp (opt), salt to taste.

Preparation and Cooking:

1. Wash and soak urad and rajmah for 2 hours minimum.
2. Put them in a pressure cooker; add 4 cups of water, ginger-garlic paste, red chilli powder and 2 tbsp salt. Pressure cook for 45 minutes. Reduce the heat after first whistle.
3. Let the dish stand till the pressure of the cooker falls down.
4. Meantime, heat ghee in a pan and crackle cumin in it. Add chopped onion and green chillies and fry till pinkish in colour. Add chopped tomatoes and fry till oil separates.
5. Open the lid of the pressure cooker; stir dal with a wooden spoon and pour the onion tomato masala over it. Simmer it for another 15 minutes on slow fire.
6. Add ½ to 1 cup water if dal is too thick. Add cream if you like . Check the seasoning.
7. Transfer dal to a serving bowl and place white butter on top of it. Stir slowly.

Serving:

Garnish dal with ginger juliennes and coriander; and serve hot with tandoori roti/naan or phulkas/chapaties.

Tips:

This preparation is called 'Dal Makhani' because it is served with butter. Moreover, it is cooked so soft that it's texture is compared to the smoothness of butter. Though, it originated from North India, it is one of the favourite dals of hotels, restaurants and roadside eating joints (dhabas) all over the country.

Cooking time: 60 minutes.

Vegetables

SAUCY BRINJAL ROLLS

Ingredient:

Black brinjal – 1 no large, tomato – 1 no large, tomato puree – ½ cup, chilli-garlic sauce – ¼ cup, corn flour – 1 tbsp, coriander powder – 1 tsp, cumin powder – 1 tsp, cashew nut powder – ¼ cup, onions – 2 no large, garlic – 8 flakes, coriander chopped – ¼ cup, pepper – 1 tsp, clove-cinnamon powder – 1 tsp, green chillies – 3 no, salt to taste, cooking oil – 2 tbsp, butter – 1 tbsp, water – 1 cup, cheese grated – 1 tbsp and flour – 2 tbsp.

Preparation and Cooking:

1. Cut the brinjal into very thin slices lengthwise. Sprinkle them with 1 tsp salt and pepper each to avoid discolouraton. Keep them aside for 30 minutes.
2. Blanch tomatoes. Put a cross across the stem side of a tomato and micro cook on high for 2 minutes. Peel the skin when cold and cut it into small pieces.
3. Chop onions, garlic and green chillies very fine.
4. Heat cooking oil in a micro safe bowl for 1 minute on high and add chopped onions, chillies, garlic and tomato. Micro cook on High for 3 minutes, uncovered. Add coriander and cumin powder, 1 tsp salt, chopped coriander and cashew nut powder. Mix it well and keep aside.
5. Place brinjal slices in the steaming basket and cook them for 2 minutes on micro high so that they become limp. Stand them for 3 minutes.
6. Mix flour with ¼ cup water and keep aside.
7. Now divide the onion mixture according to the number of brinjal slices. Place each slice on the chopping board and spread one portion of onion stuffing on it.
8. Roll it; dip in the flour mixture and place in a shallow micro-proof dish.
9. In this way, finish: stuffing, rolling, dipping and placing rest of the slices in the micro safe dish. You may stick a tooth pick in each roll to secure and avoid opening.

10. Combine tomato sauce, chilli-garlic sauce, butter, clove-cinnamon powder, ½ tsp salt and water in a micro safe bowl; cook on micro high for 3 minutes, covered. Mix corn flour with 3 tbsp water and add to the tomato sauce; cook for 1 minute more on high and remove the dish. Let it stand for 5 minutes.
11. Slowly pour the sauce over brinjal rolls and garnish with 1 tbsp grated cheese.
12. Cover and cook for 5 minutes on micro High just before serving.

Serving:

Serve the hot spicy rolls with any Rice dish or Dinner rolls.

Variation:

Instead of onion stuffing use 200 gm precooked Mutton/Chicken mince stuffing.

Tips:

This is one of my prize-winning recipes sent to the '*Femina*' years ago where certain ingredients were already given and you were supposed to add 2 more ingredients and complete the dish.

Cooking time: 30 minutes for preparation and 16 minutes microwave cooking.

Sarson- Ka- Saag (A pungent and tasty relish of Brassica leaves)

Ingredients:

Sarson leaves – 2 bundles of 500 gm each, spinach/ cholai – 1 bundle of 500 gm, onion – 1 no large, tomato – 1 no large, ginger – 1 piece of 2", garlic paste – 1 tbsp, green chilli – 4 no, red chilli powder – 1 tsp, pure ghee – 3 tbsp or butter – 4 tbsp and corn meal – 2 to 3 tbsp.

Preparation and Cooking:

1. Clean the sarson (mustard) leaves and peel the stems. Wash and chop the leaves roughly. Cut the stems into small pieces.
2. Clean and wash spinach or cholai leaves and chop them.
3. Chop onion, tomato and green chillies very fine.
4. Grate ginger and keep aside.
5. Put chopped mustard leaves and stems in a large micro safe bowl and cover with a lid. Cook on micro high for 10 minutes, stirring after five minutes. Let the dish stand for 10 minutes and cool slightly.
6. In another bowl, cook spinach or cholai for 5 minutes on micro high and cool. Mix them together and pass through a liquidizer for attaining a paste. Do not add extra water.
7. Or put chopped sarson and spinach in a pressure cooker; add ½ cup water and cook for 30 to 40 minutes. Cool and pass through the liquidizer.
8. Meanwhite, heat 3 tbsp ghee or 4 tbsp butter and add chopped onions and garlic. Cook till light brown in colour and add chopped tomatoes, chillies and ginger; cook for 2 minutes, or till well blended.

   Add corn meal and chilli powder; mix thoroughly and cook for 1 minute.
9. Mix the mustard and spinach leaves paste with the tempering masala. Add salt; cover with the lid and cook on micro high for 15 minutes, stirring once in between. Or cook in the pan only for 30 minutes or so on low fire till the liquid dries up.
10. If after tempering you have placed saag in a microwave, remove the lid and stir. If the preparation seems a little watery, cook it uncovered for 5 minutes on micro high and let it stand uncovered for 30 minutes. You may reheat it before serving.

Serving:

Add 2 tsp extra ghee or butter on top of 'Sarson-ka-saag' and serve it piping hot with 'Corn meal bread' (Makki-ki-Roti) or Wheat chapati, etc.

Variation:

Instead of spinach mix other greens like turnip and radish leaves with the mustard leaves and cook the same way.

Tips:

Cooking 'Sarson ka Saag' is quite practical in the microwave. In conventional cooking, you spend almost 2 hours to cook this pungent and tasty dish. If you prepare tempering on the top of the gas stove (as done in the recipe) and then mix, your work is finished side by side when saag is being micro cooked. The final 10 minutes cooking can be done just before serving.

It is believed in North India that this Saag cooked a day earlier, stored under refrigeration and then tempered next day again before eating is tastier. Therefore, many people temper it again just with finely chopped garlic/thinly sliced and fried onion before serving.

Information:

'ACARANGA SUTRA' has mentioned that the use of pungent brassica leaves as a tasty relish (now consumed as Sarson Ka Saag), was first noted around 500 BC.

During winter season, this dish is very popular in Northern India and particularly in Punjab, Haryana and Himachal Pradesh. Since it is a winter green vegetable, people from these areas cook it in a large quantity, store properly under refrigeration and then keep taking it out according to need. During winters this dish is included daily in the menu as a main dish or a side dish. Inhabitants of this region consume home made white butter and clarified butter i.e. ghee with it in great measure. In other regions also people do consume this pungent relish but their preparation is a dry stir-fried vegetable dish cooked in pungent mustard oil.

It is believed that since North Indians consume so much of green leaves in the form of saags; their bodies get a good dose of chlorophyll through out. And we all know very well how important chlorophyll is for the human system.

Cooking time: 30 minutes for preparation and 35 minutes micro cooking.

Buttered Beans

Ingredients:

French beans – 500 gm, butter – 1 tbsp, ajwain – 1 tsp leveled,pepper powder – ½ tsp (opt) and salt to taste.

Preparation and Cooking:

1. Wash and string beans.
2. Cut them in any desired shape and steam in a microwave for 4 minutes. Stand for two minutes.
3. Heat butter in a pan and sauté steamed beans in it for 2 minutes; sprinkle salt and pepper and serve.

Serving:

Serve crunchy 'Buttered Beans' with any Indian meal as a side dish.

Or serve the dish as a salad.

Cooking time: 6 minutes.

Khatte-Meethe Mutter (Sweet-n-sour Peas)

Ingredients:

Green peas shelled – 2 cup, fresh pomegranate seeds 1½ cup, cooking oil – 2 tbsp, peppercorns – 1 tsp, dry pomegranate seeds – 1 tsp (Anardana), sugar – 1 tsp and salt to taste.

Preparation and Cooking:

1. Dry-fry anardana and peppercorns; cool and pound them.
2. Boil green peas with a pinch of cooking soda and keep aside. Or steam them in a microwave for 4 minutes without cooking soda.
3. Heat oil and fry pounded spices.
4. Add boiled green peas and cook for 2 to 3 minutes; sprinkle salt and sugar and mix well. Remove from fire and cool.
5. Mix with fresh pomegranate seeds and serve.

Serving:

Serve sweet-n-sour peas as a snack, a side dish or as a salad.

Tips:

This dish is an ideal example of sweet-n-sour preparation of fresh ingredients or of fruit and vegetable.

Cooking time: 8 minutes.

Milk

Green Chilli Gravy Paneer Squares

Ingredients for Green Chilli gravy:

Cashew paste – ½ cup, almond paste – ¼ cup, curd – ½ cup, fresh cream – ½ cup, lime juice – 1 tbsp, ginger paste – 1 tbsp, butter – 100 gm, green chillies – 100 gm, bay leaf – 1 no, sesame seeds – 3 tbsp, red chillies whole – 2 no, tamarind – a ball of lemon

size, gud (jaggery) – a ball of lemon size (optional), coriander – a few sprigs, water – 2 cups.

Whole Spices: Black cumin – 1 tsp, cloves – 4 no, green cardamoms – 4 no, white peppercorns – 1 tsp, asafoetida – ¼ tsp.

Tempering: Oil – 2 tsp, mustard seeds – 1 tsp, curry leaves – 1 sprig.

Preparation and Cooking:

1. Pound whole spices except cumin.
2. Heat 1cup water and soak tamarind in it for 15 minutes and take out the pulp.
3. Grate jaggery; deseed red chillies and roast sesame seeds for 1.30 minutes on high in a microwave.
4. Chop green chillies and coriander and grind with ½ cup curd along with sesame seeds.
5. Heat butter in a micro safe bowl for 1 minute on high. Add cumin in it and cook for 1 minute on high.
6. Add green chilli paste and ginger paste to the butter and cook on high for 2 minutes, stirring once.
7. Now mix almond and cashew paste, asafoetida, pounded spices, red chillies and salt; stir well and cook for 2 minutes on high, stirring once.
8. Add 2 cups of water. Mix well and cook, covered, on high for 4 minutes and then on medium for 8 minutes, stirring once in between.
9. Add tamarind and jaggery and cook for 2 minutes, covered.
10. Finally add cream and lime juice to the gravy and check the seasoning.
11. Heat oil in a ladle on top of the gas; crackle mustard in it. Add curry leaves and switch off the heat. Pour tempering over the gravy and cover with a lid. Reheat for 2 minutes while serving.

Cooking time: 15 minutes for preparation and 13½ minutes micro cooking for the gravy.

Ingredients for Paneer squares:

Paneer crumble – 1 and ½ cup, corn flour – ¼ cup, rice powder – 2 tbsp, cheese grated – ¼ cup.

Stuffing: Thick green chutney – ¼ cup, almonds chopped – 6 no, cashew chopped – 6 no, raisins chopped – ¼ cup, chillies chopped – 2 no, pepper powder – 1 tsp, cardamom powder – ¼ tsp, ginger powder – ½ tsp, mawa grated – ¼ cup and salt to taste.

Preparation and Cooking:

1. Combine paneer crumble, corn flour, rice powder and cheese in a bowl. Add ½ tsp salt and pepper to each portion; mash together to soft dough and divide into 12 portions.
2. Mix together all the ingredients for stuffing and divide into 6 portions.
3. Take 2 portions of paneer mixture; flatten them with your palms. Place one portion stuffing on one of the flattened paneer ball; cover with the other one, seal and shape like a square.
4. Finish making all the squares this way and place them on a baking tray. Brush with a little oil and cook in the moderately hot oven for 20 to 30 minutes or till just pale yellow in colour. Remove from the oven.

Serving:

Arrange the squares in a serving dish and serve with 'Green Chilli Gravy'. The dish tastes excellent with any type of roti/paratha or naan.

Cooking time: 15 to 20 minutes for baking.

Paneer Koftas

Ingredients:

Homemade paneer – 1½ cup, khoa – ½ cup, mixed nut powder – ¼ cup, corn flour – 2 tbsp, basil – 8 to 10 leaves, white pepper – 2 tsp, chillies chopped – 3 no, salt to taste and oil for frying.

Preparation and cooking:

1. Chop basil very fine.
2. Mix all the ingredients for koftas and add basil, divide the mixture into 12 to 16 equal sizerd portions. Roll them and keep aside.
3. Heat oil for frying koftas. Fry 2 to 3 koftas at a time on medium fire.
4. Remove and place them on kitchen paper.

Serving:

Serve hot with any sauce or chutney as starters or in any gravy of your choice and serve with rice or chapati.

Cooking time: 30 minutes.

PANEER PHAL UNGLI KABABS

Ingredients:

Raw banana – 2 no, homemade paneer – 1½ cup, roasted gram powder – ¼ cup, coriander chopped ¼ cup, green chillies chopped – 4 no, clove powder – ½ tsp, pepper powder – 1 tsp, mint powder – 1 tsp, mixed nut powder – ¼ cup, salt to taste and oil for frying.

Preparation and Cooking:

1. Boil bananas in salted water; peel, mash and cool.
2. Mix together paneer, mashed bananas, chillies, coriander, salt, roasted gram, clove, mint, pepper and nut powder. Mash all the ingredients very well. If the mixture is dry, sprinkle a few drops of water.
3. Divide the dough into 20 to 24 equal sized portions. Roll each portion into a ¾ inch thick finger. Finish rolling all the portions.
4. Heat oil for frying in a kadai and fry 2 to 3 fingers at a time on medium fire till golden brown in colour.
5. Remove them with a slotted spoon on the kitchen oil absorbent paper.

Serving:

Line a serving plate with shredded lettuce or cabbage and arrange the fingers on it. Serve with green chutney or tomato sauce.

Cooking time: 20 minutes for preparation and 20 to 30 minutes for frying the fingers.

Beverages/Tea

KASHMIRI CHAI

Ingredients:

Water – 6½ cups, Kashmiri tea leaves – 2 tbsp, almonds – 6 no, green cardamom powder – ½ tsp, cinnamon powder – ¼ tsp and sugar to taste.

Cooking:

1. Pound 3 almonds and slice the rest.
2. Boil water and add pounded almonds, cardamom and cinnamon powder. Simmer it for 10 minutes.
3. Add tea leaves and simmer for another 5 minutes and strain.
4. Pour kehva (kashmiri chai) in a cup and add 1 tsp sugar in each cup.

Serving:

Garnish kehva with sliced almonds and serve hot. Add one teaspoon of sliced almonds to each cup.

Cooking time: 20 minutes.

HERBAL TEA

Ingredients:

Basil/Tulsi – ¼ cup leaves, ginger grated – 1 tbsp, peppercorns 10 to 15 no, ajwain or aniseeds – 1 tsp, jaggery syrup/honey – 1 tsp each cup, water – 5 cups.

Cooking:

1. Combine all the ingredients except jaggery or honey in a micro safe jug/kettle and cook for 20 minutes, first on micro high for 8 minutes and then on micro low for 12 minutes.

   Or boil all the ingredients in a pan with 1 cup extra water for 30 minutes on high flame of gas stove.
2. Take out the jug/kettle and let it stand for 30 minutes, covered.
3. Strain and pour into individual cups and add 1 tsp jaggery syrup or honey to each cup.
4. Do not throw the ingredients, but keep them under refrigeration.
5. They can be boiled once more with 3 cups water to give you a second herbal extract.

Note:

You may reheat each cup for 30 seconds before consuming it.

Serving:

Serve it hot morning, mid-day, evening or at night.

Variation:

Use a few leaves of fresh mint or a strand of lemon grass with basil and other ingredients.

Tips:

This herbal drink is considered very good for health. Believers of Naturopathy / Nature Cure advise you to consume this beverage daily in place of tea.

From the health point of view:

- It is good for curing Cough and Cold.
- It is ideal for the people suffering from Arthritis and Joint pains.
- It is good for Digestion.
- It is good for children and infants when their chest is congested. Give them a few spoons twice a day.

Cooking Time: 20 minutes microwave cooking.

Eggs

NARGASI KOFTA

Ingredients:

Mutton minced – 500 gm, ginger–garlic paste – 1 tbsp, garam masala – 1 tsp, green chilli paste – 1 tsp, dry mint powder – 1 tsp, hard boiled eggs – 6 to 8 no, flour – ¼ cup, oil for frying, salt and pepper to taste.

Preparation and Cooking:

1. Mix together minced meat, ginger-garlic paste and chilli paste in a mixer grinder and churn for a while. Take out the contents and mix dry ingredients, except flour, with it.
2. Shell the eggs and dredge them with flour evenly.
3. Divide the minced meat according to the number of meat; cover each egg with one portion of minced properly and keep aside for 30 minutes.
4. Heat oil for frying to the smoking point and then lower the heat. Fry eggs one by one on medium fire and remove on kitchen paper.

Serving:

Cut each egg into half; arrange in a shallow serving dish and serve with any gravy of your choice.

Cooking time: 40 minutes.

EGG OMELETTE SQUARES FOR CURRY

Ingredients:

Eggs – 6 no, gram flour – 2 tbsp, green chillies chopped – 4 no, coriander chopped – ¼ cup, milk – ¼ cup, pepper powder – 1 tsp, ginger powder – ½ tsp, salt – 1 tsp, oil – 2 tsp.

Preparation and Cooking:

1. Smear 1 square dish with 1 tsp oil and keep aside.
2. Break eggs in a bowl and mix with milk; beat it nicely. Add gram flour, salt, pepper and ginger powder; beat the mixture smooth till no lumps of gram flour are left. Add 1 tsp remaining oil, chopped chillies and coriander; mix well and pour into the greased dish.
3. Cook on micro high for 6 minutes or till the batter comes up properly. Stir the centre once in between as egg starts setting very fast.
4. Remove and cool the dish. Cut omelette into squares and keep aside covered.

Or

5. Cook 1 or 2 thick omelette with above mentioned ingredients in a non-stick pan on slow fire. Cool and cut them into squares.

Serving:

Add omelette squares to any curry; cover and heat throughly; temper with curry leaves and serve with plain boiled Rice or hot Chapati/Paratha.

Cooking time:
21 minutes.

Snacks

SPINACH ROUNDELS

Ingredients:

Homemade paneer – 1¼ cup, spinach puree – ½ cup, cheese grated – ½ cup, refined flour – ½ cup leveled, cashew nuts – 16 no, baking soda – ¼ tsp leveled, pepper powder – 2 tsp and salt – 1 and ½ tsp leveled.

Preparation and Baking:

1. Sieve together flour salt, pepper and baking soda.
2. Coarsely grind 10 cashew nuts and divide the rest into halves.
3. Preheat oven for moderate heat.
4. Mix together paneer, flour, cashew powder and spinach puree.
5. Knead to a pliable dough. If by chance, the dough feels hard; sprinkle a few drops of milk and knead again.
6. Divide the dough into 12 or 16 equal sized portions. Roll each portion into a ball and then flatten it on your palm. This way finish rolling and flattening all the portions.
7. If the dough sticks to your hands while rolling or flattening, smear your hands with a little cooking oil or butter. Roundels should be crack free.
8. Now place all the flattened roundels in a baking tray at a distance of 3 to 4 inches. Decorate each with cashew nuts and bake in the centre of the oven for 20 to 25 minutes. Remove the tray from the oven and stand it for 10 minutes. Remove the roundels with the tip of a palate knife and serve.

Serving:

Serve them with tomato sauce as a snack or with any cheese-cream salad at meal time as a substitute for cutlets.

This preparation is an excellent accompaniment to any continental meal. Roundels taste cheesier when cold.

Tips:

For perfect baking, it is important that all the ingredients used for a dish are at room temperature while mixing. For instance; paneer, spinach puree and cheese should not be very cold. If refrigerated, take them out at least 2 hours before use. Spinach puree should not be watery.

Cooking time: 15 minutes for preparation and 30 minutes for baking.

MIXED CHAAT PLATTER

Ingredients:

Potatoes boiled – 2 cups, moong dal pakodi – 2 cups, papdi – 32 no, sev – 2 cups, curds – 4 cups, dry boondi – 1 cup or boiled chick peas, sweet–n–sour chutney – 1 cup, green coriander chutney – 1 cup, roasted cumin powder – 1 tsp, rock salt – 1 tsp, chaat masala – ¼ cup, coriander chopped – ¼ cup, green chilli chopped – 2 tbsp (opt).

Preparation:

1. Boil water with 1 tsp salt and put pakodies in it; keep aside for ½ an hour; squeeze water and keep them covered under refrigeration.
2. Beat curd with 2 tbsp powdered sugar and keep under refrigeration.
3. Chop potatoes and keep them aside.

Assembly:

1. Take a big platter or a shallow serving dish.
2. Cover the surface with papdies, saving few for the top.
3. Crumble a few moong pakodies over papadies evenly.
4. Sprinkle a few handfuls of sev, boondi or chick peas and half of the coriander on top.
5. Pour about one cup curd evenly, covering the surface.
6. Sprinkle some chaat masala, green chutney and sweet-n-sour chutney.
7. Spread a layer of boiled potatoes, then sprinkle boondi generously and crush the papdies on top.
8. Once again spread curd generously on top; sprinkle chat masala sev and chutneys.
9. Crush a few more papdies on top and garnish the platter with the rest of coriander and chilli powder.

Serving:

Serve 'Mixed Chaat Platter' immediately.

Tips:

The recipe of Moong Dal pakodi has already been written in 'Moong Dal Pakodi in Curd'.

Assembling time: 15 to 20 minutes.

Salads

Chicken and Pineapple Salad

You Require:

Boneless chicken fillets from – 1 breast, pineapple slices – 6 to 8 no, mayonnaise sauce – ½ cup, fresh cream – ½ cup, mustard sauce – 1 tbsp (optional), celery sticks – 2 no, spring onion with greens – 3 no, lemon juice – 1 tbsp, fresh crushed pepper – 2 tsp, salt to taste.

Preparation and Cooking:

1. Wash chicken and smear it with lemon juice and ½ tsp salt. Keep aside for 30 minutes.
2. Wash and chop spring onions, greens and celery sticks.
3. Mix mayonnaise and fresh cream and chill.
4. Place chicken in the steaming basket with ¼ cup water underneath and cook on high for 8 to10 minutes, turning once after 5 minutes. Let it stand for 5 minutes. Remove and cool slightly. Cut it into cubes or thin strips.

Note:

You may boil chicken in a pressure cooker for 15 minutes. Cool and cut into pieces.

1. Cut pineapple also in the same fashion.
2. Mix chicken, pineapple, celery, spring onion and chilled mayonnaise + cream mixture in a serving bowl and toss.
3. Adjust salt and pepper and store under refrigeration till used.

Serving:

Serve cold 'Chicken Pineapple Salad' as a main dish or as a side dish in the hot summer months with any Continental meal.

Variation:

Make chicken salad with nuts. Omit pineapple and add 1 cup soaked and chopped cashew nuts or walnuts. Soak nuts in lukewarm water for 5 to 6 hours before use.

Tips:

Soaked nuts get revived and become like fresh fruits; they are also healthier and easier to digest.

In India, fresh pineapple is available in abundance. When in season, it can be cleaned, sliced, cooked and preserved under refrigeration in the deep freezer compartment. Cook 1 pineapple slice with 1cup sugar and ½ cup water in a microwave on high for 15 minutes. Cool and preserve. Or cook pineapple with sugar and 1cup water on a gas stove.

Cooking time: 30 minutes for preparation and 10 minutes micro cooking.

Apple, Carrot and Nuts Salad

Ingredients:

Apples – 2 no, carrots – 2 no, lemon-juice – 1 tbsp, raisins – 2 tbsp or black grapes – ½ cup, cashew nuts – 12 no, walnuts – ¼ cup, simple French dressing – ½ cup, lettuce leaves – 8 no, chicken balls – 16 to 20 no (opt).

Preparation and Cooking:

1. Soak cashew nuts, walnuts and raisins in warm water for 2 to 3 hours in separate bowls.
2. Cut carrots; steam and place them in a large bowl.
3. Core and cut the apples without peeling into cubes and sprinkle with lemon juice to avoid discolouration.
4. Mix carrots with apple, chicken balls and soaked raisins.
5. Pour French dressing over the mixed ingredients and toss lightly. Chill.
6. Chop cashew nuts and walnuts. Serve cashew nuts and mixed walnuts with the rest of the salad.

Serving:

Line a platter with lettuce; pile up salad in the centre and garnish with chopped cashew nuts. Serve with any meal.

Preparation time: 30 minutes for chopping and assembling.

Stuffed Parathas

MUTTER KACHORI

You require:

Wheat flour – 1 cup, refined flour – 1 cup, ghee – 2 tbsp, salt – 1 tsp, green peas shelled – 4 cups, green chilli paste – 1 tsp, garam masala – 1 tbsp, mango powder – 1 tsp, asafoetida – ½ tsp, ginger powder ½ tsp, rock salt – 1 tsp, gram flour roasted – 2 tbsp, salt – to taste and oil for frying.

Preparation and Cooking:

1. Sieve together wheat flour, refined flour and 1 tsp salt; add 2 tbsp ghee and make a stiff dough with water.
2. Knead it well; cover with a wet napkin and keep aside.
3. Steam green peas or boil them till soft. Mash with a potato masher and cool.
4. Add the rest of the ingredients except oil for frying and knead peas stuffing well.
5. Heat oil for frying to the smoking point and lower the heat.
6. Once again knead the dough and divide it into lemon-sized portions.
7. Divide the peas mixture also into the same number of portions.
8. Roll each portion into 3-inch discs and place one portion stuffing in the centre.
9. Gather all the ends together and re-roll the stuffed disc (kachori) to 3 to 4-inches in diameter. Thus finish stuffing and rolling all the balls.
10. Increase the flame under oil and fry the kachories one by one on medium fire; turn the side and fry till crisp from both the sides. Remove with a perforated spoon on kitchen oil absorbent paper.

Serving:

Serve 'Mutter-Kachori' hot with Sweet-n-Sour Chutney or fresh Green chutney.

Tips:

Avoid deep-frying on low fire.

Cooking time: 30 minutes for preparation and 30 minutes for frying.

South Indian dishes

RICE POLI

Ingredients:

Rice powder (chawal-ka-atta) – 2 cups, salt – a pinch, hot water to make dough.

Equipment used:

Tawa

Preparation and Cooking:

1. Mix rice flour with salt and knead with hot water to smooth dough.
2. Divide it into equal sized balls; roll each ball into a thin disc and cook on hot tawa like a chapatti. Store in a casserole.

Serving:

Serve Rice Poli with any vegetarian/non-vegetarian dish.

Cooking time : 30 to 40 minutes.

Soups and Stocks

CHICKEN BALLS AND VEGETABLE SOUP

Ingredients:

For Chicken Balls: Chicken minced – 250 gm, vinegar – 1 tbsp, salt – 1 tsp, pepper powder – ½ tsp and ginger-garlic paste – ½ tsp.

For Soup: Chicken stock – 7 cups, butter – 1 tsp, spring onions – 2 no, carrot – 1 large, red pepper – 1 small, capsicum – 1 small, tomato – 1 no, cabbage leaves – 2 no, corn flour – 3 tbsp, chilli-garlic sauce – 1 to 2 tsp, cheese grated – ¼ cup, parsley chopped – 2 tbsp and salt to taste.

Preparation and Cooking:

1. Combine chicken minced, vinegar, salt, pepper and ginger powder in an electric blender and mince it with a mincing blade for a minute or two. Remove.
2. Form small marble sized balls out of the minced meat of the chicken.
3. Clean, wash and chop all the vegetables finely.
4. Heat 3 cups stock in a big micro safe bowl for 6 minutes on micro high and drop the

formed balls into it gently. Now cook them on micro high for 6 minutes, uncovered. Take out the bowl and keep it covered for the next 10 minutes.

5. Heat butter for 1 minute on high; add chopped vegetables, stir them and cook on high for 2 minutes uncovered.
6. With a slotted spoon lift the chicken balls gently out of the stock and keep aside.
7. Put 3 cups stock, vegetables, salt and chilli-garlic sauce in the same bowl containing liquid from the cooked balls and boil on high for 8 minutes, covered.
8. Mix corn flour with ½ cup stock; pour in the vegetables and soup and boil for 3 more minutes on micro high.
9. Remove the bowl and add chicken balls, grated cheese and chopped parsley.
10. You may reheat the soup for 2 to 3 minutes if you prefer it boiling hot.

Serving:

Serve 'Chicken Balls and Vegetable Soup' hot with crusty Garlic Bread or Cheese Croissants.

Variation:

Combine 1 tbsp Soya sauce, 1 tbsp Chilli or Chilli-Garlic sauce, 1 tbsp Tomato sauce and 1 tsp butter. Heat on micro high for 1 minute and toss the chicken balls in it. Cover and just heat through for 1 minute and serve them as starters on toothpicks.

Combine chicken balls with salads.

Tips:

Chicken meatballs can be cooked in advance and stored in the deep freezer but should be taken out 2 hours in advance before use, so that they are at room temperature.

Cooking time: 30 minutes for preparation and 26 minutes micro cooking.

Cream of Tomato

Ingredients:

Tomatoes – 800 gm, carrot – 1 no, ginger – 1" piece, garlic – 6 flakes, béchamel sauce – 1½ cup, water – 3½ cup, pepper powder – 1 tsp, salt to taste, fresh cream – ¼ cup and bread croutons or fried phool makhanas.

Cooking:

1. Cook roughly chopped tomatoes and carrot with ½ cup water on micro high for 5 minutes.
2. Cool and liquidize to a puree consistency. Mix 2 cups stock and strain through a sieve.
3. Mix béchamel sauce with the tomato mixture in a blender and churn.
4. Place the mixture in a deep micro safe bowl and add 1cup stock, salt and pepper powder to it. Stir well with a rotary beater.
5. Cook on micro high for first 5 minutes and then on medium for 10 minutes. Remove and mix cream in it.

Serving:

Serve 'Cream of Tomato' hot in individual soup bowls/cups garnished with fried Phool Makhanas or roasted Bread Croutons.

Phool Makhanas are roasted Lotus seeds.

Variation:

Cream of Spinach: Spinach puree + White Sauce + Stock + fresh Cream + Seasoning.

Cream of Pumpkin:

Cooked and pureed Pumpkin pulp + Asafoetida powder + Bechamel Sauce + Seasoning. Serve it garnished with roasted Sesame seeds.

Cream of Mushrooms:

Mushroom Sauce passed through a liquidizer + veg / non-veg stock + chopped mushroom + seasoning + cream.

Cream of Mixed Veg:

Cooked and pureed mix vegetables + ginger powder + water + seasoning +coconut milk. Add a bouquet garnishing while cooking vegetables.

Cooking time: 20 minutes micro cooking.

Red Meat

Mutton Seekh Kababs

Ingredients:

Mutton mince – 500 gm, lime juice – 1 tbsp, ginger -garlic paste – 1 tbsp, red chilli powder – 1 tsp, cumin powder – ½ tsp, pepper powder – ½ tsp, roasted poppy seeds – 1 tbsp, garam masala – 1 tsp, clove powder – ¼ tsp, cream – 1 tbsp, coriander chopped – 1 cup, black salt – ¼ tsp, salt to taste and metal skewers – 6 to 8 no.

Preparation and Cooking:

1. Pass minced meat twice through an electric grinder and add ground masala to it. Mix chopped coriander and knead well.
2. Roast over the open charcoal flame of a grill/ under the grill of a cooking range or in a hot tandoor.
3. Turn them from time to time and bwat with oil till done.
4. Wait for 3 to 4 minutes and then slide the seekhs gently.
5. Cut them into desired sizes diagonally.

Serving:

Serve the Mutton Seekh Kababs with onion rings or pickled onions etc. Rumali Roti is the best accompaniment.

Tips:

Avoid too hard or too wet a mix of mutton for seekh kababs.

Cooking time: 45 minutes to 60 minutes.

Poultry

Chicken Tikka Tandoori Style (Roasted)

Ingredients:

Chicken – 800 gm or chicken breast – 600 gm, hung curd – 2 cup, ginger-garlic paste – 1 tbsp, red chilli powder – 1 tbsp, salt – 2 tsp, cumin powder – 1 tsp, coriander powder – 1 tsp, ginger powder – 1 tsp, pepper powder – 1 tsp, garam masala – 1 tsp and red tandoori colour – ½ tsp.

Preparation and Cooking:

1. Wash and cut chicken into 12 pieces or cut boneless chicken into 1½" pieces.
2. Mix all the dry ingredients with hung curd and rub on the chicken pieces. Thus marinate chicken and keep aside for 2 to 3 hours.
3. Preheat convection mode of your microwave to 200 degree celsius. Arrange the marinated chicken pieces in a baking tray and bake for 30 to 35 minutes. In between, change sides and bake the chicken pieces with oil once at least once. Use a brush for this. Take out chicken tikkas and serve them hot.

Or

4. Arrange the marinated chicken pieces on the outer side of a micro safe platter and cook for 6 minutes on micro high and then on micro medium for next 4 minutes.
5. Take them out and check if the chicken is done. If done, serve them hot. Boneless chicken pieces should be booked within 6 to 7 minutes.

Serving:

Serve the 'Chicken Tikkas' on a platter of fresh salad with green Chutney and Onion rings as starters.

Variation:

Add mint powder or kasoori methi to the curd mixture before marinating the chicken pieces.

Cut Paneer into 2" cubes and marinate in the same curd mixture and bake in the same manner in an electric oven for 15 to 20 minutes.

Tips:

To get hung curd; Put 3 cups of curd in a muslin cloth, tie and keep in a sieve, or hang it with something for 2 hours. Remove and use as required.

Note:

Don't throw the nourishing whey. Collect it; chill it and consume it as a refreshing drink. You may flavour it with salt-pepper or rooh afza etc.

Cooking time: 10 minutes for preparation and 30 minutes cooking in convection mode or 10 minutes micro cooking.

Seafood/Fish

Garlic Fried Prawns in Chilli Sauce

Ingredients:

Large prawns – 500 gm, lemon juice – 3 tbsp, salt – 1 tsp, pepper powder – 1 tsp leveled, chilli sauce – ¼ cup, tomato sauce – 2 tbsp, garlic slivers – 2 tbsp, egg whites – 2 no, refined flour – ¼ cup, ajinomoto – a pinch and oil for frying.

Preparation and Cooking:

1. De-vein the prawns; wash and drain them. Marinate with lemon juice, salt and pepper. Let them stand for 30 minutes and strain.
2. Heat oil for frying; bring a to smoking point and lower the heat.
3. Beat egg whites very stiff and fold in flour; add ajinomoto and a pinch of salt.
4. Hold each prawn from the tail; dip in the egg batter and fry in hot oil till golden brown in colour. Remove with a slotted spoon and place on kitchen paper.
5. Heat 1 tbsp oil in a pan and fry garlic slivers in it and remove.
6. Add chilli sauce and tomato sauce in the same oil; stir and place fried prawns in it. Stir gently and coat the prawns well with the sauce.

Serving:

Transfer the prawns to a serving plate and garnish with fried garlic and serve.

Cooking time: 30 minutes for preparation and 30 minutes for cooking.

Baked Fish Fillets

Ingredients:

Pomfret / any other fish – 500 gm, tomatoes – 2 no large, mushrooms – 100 gm, onions – 2 no, butter – 2 tbsp, cheese grated – 2 tbsp, lime – 1 no, pepper powder – 2 tsp leveled and fresh breadcrumbs – ½ cup.

Preparation and Cooking:

1. Preheat the electric oven or convection mode of your microwave oven to moderate heat.
2. Fillet the fish and skin it. Wash in cold water.
3. Burn the tomato skins on direct flame; cool and peel the skin. Slice into thin slices.
4. Clean, wash and slice onions and mushrooms.
5. Heat butter in a non-stick pan; add chopped onions and mushrooms and cook for 3 minutes on high flame, uncovered.
6. Grease a heatproof dish and line the bottom with thinly sliced tomatoes. Place the fillets on top; sprinkle salt and pepper over the fish and spread a layer of cooked onions and mushroom.
7. Repeat the layers till the dish is full. The top layer should be of tomatoes.
8. Mix grated cheese, breadcrumbs and 1 tbsp butter and sprinkle over to cover the top.
9. Bake in a hot oven for 35 to 40 minutes.

Serving:

Serve the dish hot with any Continental meal.

Tips:

Fillet is a boneless cut of uncooked meat or fish.

Cooking time: 20 minutes for preparation, 6 minutes micro cooking and 35 minutes baking in convection mode.

Fish Cutlets in Mustard Sauce

Ingredients:

Fish – 500 gm, vinegar – ¼ cup, potatoes boiled – 3 no, corn flour – ¼ cup, green chilli paste – 1 tbsp, ginger paste – 1 tsp, pepper powder – 1 tsp, butter/ oil – 2 tbsp, salt to taste, white sauce – 1½ cup, mustard powder – 2 tbsp, parsley chopped – 1 tbsp.

Preparation and Cooking:

1. Clean and marinate fish with salt and vinegar and keep aside for 30 minutes.
2. Steam fish for 7 minutes on high; remove the skin and bones and discard.
3. Mix together steamed fish flakes, boiled potatoes, corn flour, green chilli paste, ginger paste, salt and pepper. Mix thoroughly; divide into equal portions and shape into cutlets. If you like fancy cooking, you may shape cutlets into fish shapes.

4. Option: Bake them in a moderately hot oven for 15 minutes and serve with mustard sauce.

Or

5. Heat fat in a square dish, place cutlets in it and roll to be coated with fat.
6. Micro cook on high for 2 minutes.
7. Combine white sauce and mustard powder; check seasoning and pour the sauce over the fish.
8. Cover with cling film and heat thoroughly on micro high for 3 minutes.

Serving:

Garnish the fish cutlets with Parsley and serve hot with additional Mustard sauce and crisp unbuttered Toasts and plain Soup.

Cooking time: 12 minutes micro cooking.

Sauce

Chilli Garlic Sauce

Ingredients:

Dry red chillies (broken and deseeded) – 2 cups, garlic peeled – 1 cup, vinegar – 1 cup, salt – 4 tsp and oil – ¼ cup.

Preparation and Cooking:

1. Heat 2 cups water in a micro safe bowl for 2 minutes.
2. Wash and soak broken red chillies in this hot water for 1 hour.
3. Cook them in the same water, covered, for 8 minutes on micro high. Let them stand for 2 to 3 minutes Remove from oven. Mix garlic and cover again. Cool.
4. Put salt, vinegar, chillies and garlic in a blender and blend till smooth.
5. In a small bowl heat oil for 2 minutes on micro high and mix with the smooth chilli-garlic paste.
6. Transfer the sauce into a clean and dry glass bottle and store under refrigeration.
7. Use as and when required. Under refrigeration it lasts almost a month.

Usage:

Chilli-Garlic sauce is used for a variety of things while cooking.

1. It can be mixed with gravies and can be added to flavour dry vegetables.
2. You may mix with a sandwich spread to make yummy sandwiches.
3. You may use it along with salad dressings to flavour vegetable salads.

Variation:

Omit garlic and make 'Chilli sauce'.

No preservatives are added as this sauce is meant to be kept for a short duration.

Cooking Time: 12 minutes in microwave.

Chutneys

Almond and Coriander Chutney

Ingredients:

Coriander chopped – 2 cups, mint chopped – 1 cup, almonds blanched – ½ cup, green chillies – 3 no, capsicum – 1 no, raw mango – 1 no small, pomegranate seeds – 1 tbsp, sugar – 1 tsp and salt to taste.

Preparation:

1. Wash coriander and mint leaves.
2. Chop green chillies, capsicum and raw mango.
3. Roast pomegranate seeds and pound them.
4. Place all the ingredients in a liquidizer; add ¼ cup water and grind to a smooth paste. Store under refrigeration.

Serving:

Serve this chutney with any snacks or use to make sandwiches.

Tips:

This special relish is one of our family recipes. It is very soothing in summer months. Almonds in the recipe act as a stablizer and a preservative, Therefore, it can be stored in the chill tray of a refrigerator for 8 to 10 days.

Preparation time: 30 minutes for preparation and 10 minutes for assembling and churning, etc.

Apricot Chutney

Ingredients:

Dried apricots – 250 gm, jaggery – 250 gm, vinegar – 150 ml, black pepper powder – 1 tsp, garam masala – 1 tsp and salt to taste.

Preparation and Cooking:

1. Wash and soak apricots overnight.
2. Grate jaggery and keep aside.
3. Mash apricots and remove the stones. Break stones with a hammer; take out the kernels/ nut meat and chop.
4. Mix together apricot pulp with the water in which apricots were soaked. Cook on medium fire; add vinegar and simmer till soft; add grated jaggery and cook till well blended.
5. Sprinkle salt pepper and garam masala. Mix well. Cook for a while and remove from fire. Add half of the chopped nut meat and mix well.

Serving:

Garnish the chutney with the remaining nuts and serve with any Indian meal. Or store under refrigeration.

Cooking time: 30 minutes.

Punches and Refreshers

Black Grapes' Refresher

Ingredients:

Black grapes – 2 cups, sugar – 1 tbsp, water – 1 cup and curd – 2 cups.

Preparation:

1. Mix all the ingredients together and keep overnight.
2. Morning mash it and strain through a fine sieve.
3. Mix it with 1½ cup of thick curd and churn.

Serving:

Serve it chilled.

Tips:

This drink is supposed to be very good for maintaining 'good skin'.

Preparation time: 15 minutes.

Indian Sweets

Badam Halwa

Ingredients:

Almonds – 250 gm, sugar – 500 gm, cashew nuts – 15 no, Cardamom powder – 1tsp, ghee – 250 gm, saffron – a few strands, milk – 2 tbsp and water – 375 ml.

Preparation and Cooking:

1. Wash and soak almonds overnight; blanch and grind them to a fine paste.
2. Make a thin syrup with sugar and water. To dissolve sugar well, first cook the mixture on slow fire and later bring it to a boiling point. Once the sugar is dissolved and the syrup clear; switch off the fire.
3. Dissolve saffron in lukewarm milk. Chop cashewnuts.
4. Mix almond paste and sugar syrup.
5. Heat half of the ghee and fry almond paste in it. Cook on medium fire, stirring all the while. Keep stirring and adding 1 tbsp ghee at a time and frying almond paste till ghee finishes.
6. When the mixture starts thickening, add saffron, cardamom powder and chopped cashew nuts.
7. Cook the mixture till it starts leaving the sides of the pan. Remove from fire.
8. Pour on a greased plate.

Serving:

Serve Badam Halwa garnished with rose petals or silver vark, lukewarm or cold.

Tips:

This dish is very nourishing and good for the winter months when our appetite is at its best and the body needs warmth.

Cooking time: 35 minutes but the preparation time is 12 hours.

Gulab Jamun

Ingredients:

Milk powder – 100 gm, refined flour – 1/3 cup, semolina – 1 tbsp leveled, baking powder – ½ tsp, clarified butter (ghee) – 2 tbsp, cardamom powder

– ¼ tsp, water for mixing – ½ cup, ghee or oil for frying, sugar – 2 cups and water – 1 ½ cup.

Preparation and Cooking:

1. Sieve together milk powder, refined flour, semolina and baking powder.
2. Rub into ghee and add cardamom powder.
3. Add water and knead dough. If needed, you may sprinkle drops of water to make the dough.
4. Cover it with a damp cloth and let it stand for 20 minutes.
5. Meanwhite make sugar syrup of 2 thread consistency.
6. Divide the gulab jamun dough into 20 to 24 equal sized portions and roll them. The balls should be crack free.
7. Heat ghee to the smoking point and switch off the fire. Add 10 to 12 balls in warm oil and shake them gently with a knife. Put ghee back on fire and fry gulab jamuns on medium fire till nicely browned from all sides. Drain them and place in warm syrup. Let them simmer for 5 minutes and stay immersed for 30 minutes.

Serving:

Serve 'Gulab Jamun' hot as a sweet or a dessert.

Tips:

Avoid frying them on very hot fat.

Cooking time: 30 minutes for preparation and 30 minutes for frying.

Falooda

Ingredients:

Corn flour – ½ cup, water – 1¼ cup, sugar 1 tbsp (opt), chilled water – 1000 ml and small pressing machine.

Note:

Small wooden/brass pressing machine and its perforated plate for making Gram flour Savian is ideal for making Falooda noodles.

Preparation and Cooking:

1. Wash pressing machine and its plate and keep aside.
2. Pour chilled water in an open bowl.
3. Mix corn flour, sugar and water in a micro safe bowl and cook on high for 2 minutes, uncovered, stirring once after 1 minute.
4. Cook for 3 to 4 minutes on medium, stirring every 1minute or till the mixture is thick and transparent.
5. Immediately, fill the pressing machine ¾ with the hot mixture and press it slowly into the chilled water for making falooda noodles. Repeat the process fast till the corn flour mixture lasts. Corn flour mixture should be warm. If it gets cold due to the weather, warm it for a few seconds.
6. Keep falooda in water itself under refrigeration.

Note:

Do not freeze falooda, otherwise it will become brittle.

Serving:

Serve 'Falooda' with 'Kulfi' or turn it into a tasty drink.

For Falooda Drink: Soak 2 tbsp Sabja Beej in water for 30 minutes; chill 3 cups of milk; keep handy some crushed ice, rooh afza or rose syrup and vanilla ice cream.

Assembly:

In a tall glass place 1 tbsp full of Falooda noodles; Put in 1 tbsp soaked sabja beej; and pour ¾ cup chilled milk over it. Add 1 to 2 tsp rose syrup or rooh afza and top it with a dollop of Vanilla ice cream. Serve it immediately individually.

Tips:

This delicious falooda drink is very soothing in the hot summer months. Sabja Beej is regarded as a cooling agent and good for reducing body heat in the summers. They are black in colour when we buy, but the moment we soak them, they start burning gray and translucent. They are easily available in any grocery shop. Buy and store them, they do not get spoilt easily.

Cooking time: 5 to 6 minutes micro cooking and 5 minutes for pressing falooda noodles.

Ice Creams

LEMON ICE CREAM WITH WALNUTS

Ingredients:

Fresh cream – 1½ cup, eggs – 3 no, sugar – 1 cup, lemon juice – 2 tbsp, glucose biscuit crumbs – 1 ½ cup, crushed walnuts – ¾ cup and salted butter – ¼ cup.

Preparation:

1. Beat 1 whole egg and 2 yolks. Save the whites.
2. Add lemon-juice and sugar to the eggs and beat till creamy. Cook on a double boiler till the mixture thickens.
3. Beat saved egg whites till they stand on peaks and mix with cooked egg mixture and whipped cream.
4. Mix together the biscuit crumbs, butter and crushed walnuts well.
5. Press half the crumb-walnut mixture in the ice cream tray; pour the lemon cream mixture on top and spread evenly. Now spread the rest of the crumb mixture on top and press lightly, so that the surface appears smooth.
6. Place the ice cream tray in the deep freezer for 3 hours minimum.

Serving:

Cut into bars or cubes and serve cold.

Preparation time: 4 hours.

Cakes and Cookies

EGGLESS CAKE

Ingredients:

Flour – 150 gm, butter – 100 gm, milkmaid – 200 ml, Baking powder – 1 tsp, baking soda – ½ tsp, vanilla essence – 1 tsp and medium sized micro safe glass dish or a ring mould.

Preparation:

1. Sieve flour, baking powder and baking soda together.
2. Combine butter and milkmaid and beat well.
3. Add rest of the ingredients and mix well.
4. Add ½ cup water to make the batter of dropping consistency.

Baking:

1. Preheat the oven for 15 minutes.
2. Line the mould with paper and grease it before putting the cake batter in it; or prepare the cake mould first smearing it with oil and then dusting it to with flour evenly. Now pour the mixture in it and bake the cake for 30 minutes or till done on 180 to 200 °C.
3. Insert a needle in the centre of the cake, if it comes out clean, that means the cake is ready, otherwise bake it for another 5 minutes.
4. Remove and let it cool thoroughly before serving.

Alternative:

If you are baking this egg-less cake in the micro mode, then put the cake batter in the glass dish and bake on combi – 2 for 6 to 8 minutes; remove and check if its done by inserting the needle into it. Let the dish stand for 10 minutes or till the cake cools down. Cut the cake into pieces and serve.

Variation:

Eggless Chocolate Cake: Reduce 2 tbsp flour and add 2 tbsp leveled cocoa powder and 1 tbsp powdered sugar; follow the same procedure and bake cake in any oven.

Tips:

In an egg-less cake, milkmaid is used to make it, so sugar is not required at all.

Cooking time: 30 to 35 minutes in the convention oven. Or 6 to 8 minutes for micro cooking.

DARK CHOCOLATE CAKE

Ingredients:

Flour – 2¼ cups, baking powder – ¼ tsp, cooking soda – 1¼ tsp, cocoa powder – ¾ cup, sugar – 1¾ cup, cooking oil – ¾ cup, eggs – 2 no, milk or milk & water – 1¼ cup and vanilla essence – 1 tsp (opt).

Preparation and Baking:

1. Preheat oven for moderate heat.
2. Sieve together flour, baking powder, soda and cocoa twice.
3. Powder sugar and beat it with oil.

4. Add eggs and beat again.
5. Heat milk to lukewarm and mix with the beaten content a little at a time. Keep beating with a rotary beater.
6. Add flour spoon by spoon and keep beating till the flour is used up.
7. Pour in a ring mould made of glass or prepared mould of aluminum.
8. Bake for 50 to 60 minutes.
9. Check after 50 minutes by the needle test.
10. Remove from the oven, wait for 5 minutes and invert on wire rack for cooling.

Serving:

Cut the cake into wedges or slices and serve with Tea or Coffee. Or serve it with Vanilla ice cream and Chocolate sauce. Or serve it with Custard sauce.

Baking time: 50 minutes.

Western Desserts

Fruit Cream

Ingredients:

Strawberries – 10 no, kiwis – 5 no (opt), apples – 2 no, pineapple slices (tinned) 6 no, grapes black or green – 1 cup, bananas – 3 no, chikoo – 3 no, cherries (tinned) – ½ cup (opt), mango cubed – 2 no (opt), fresh cream – 300 ml, sugar – 2 tbsp, lemon – 1 no.

Note:

You can combine fruits of your choice or those available in season. For example: strawberries, mangoes, kiwis and cherries are not available throughout the year. You can mix oranges too, but after removing the piths from the segments.

Do not add guava as it does not lend a pleasant feeling to the dish.

Preparation:

1. After cutting apples and bananas, immediately sprinkle lemon juice on them to avoid discolouration of the fruits.
2. Combine all the fruits in a serving bowl, sprinkle sugar over them; cover with a lid or cling film and keep under refrigeration.
3. Keep cream also under refrigeration and add to the fruits 15 minutes before serving, so that it stays creamy and does not turn semi solid.

Serving:

Serve 'Fruit Cream' cold but not chilled with any Continental or Indian meal.

Variation:

You may add 1 cup soaked dry fruits like Almonds, Cashew nuts, Walnuts and Raisins, etc. Dry fruits should be well soaked for 5 to 6 hours, so that they are well revived. Make your own combinations of fruits and add 1 odd dry fruit.

Tips:

Always cut fruits with stainless steel knives.

Avoid cutting fruits with iron knife.

Preparation time: 20 to 30 minutes.

Chinese Food

Manchurian Sauce with Steamed Vegetable Balls

Ingredients for Manchurian sauce:

Onion finely chopped – 1 no, ginger finely chopped – 1 tbsp, garlic finely chopped – 1 tbsp, green chilli chopped – 2 no, vinegar – ½ cup, tomato sauce – ½ cup, water/stock – 1½ cup, soy sauce – 3 tbsp, oil – 2 tbsp, chilli powder – 2 tsp, pepper powder – 2 tsp, sugar – 2 tsp, ajinomoto – a pinch, salt to taste and corn flour – ¼ cup.

Preparation and Cooking for Manchurian Sauce:

1. Heat oil in a micro safe bowl for 1 minute on high; add chopped onion, ginger, garlic and green chillies and cook on high for 2 minutes, stirring once.
2. Add water, vinegar, tomato, soy and chilli sauce along with salt, pepper, chilli powder, sugar and ajinomoto to the bowl and cook on high for 6 minutes, uncovered, stirring once.
3. Mix corn flour with ½ cup water and pour into the sauce; mix well and cook for 3 minutes on high. Take it out and adjust the seasoning.

Note:

The sauce should be of dark brown colour with a prominent taste of soy sauce and pepper. Keep it covered.

For Steamed Vegetable balls:

1. Combine ½ cup grated cauliflower, ¼ cup finely chopped carrots, ¼ cup finely chopped cabbage, ¼ cup finely chopped spring onions with greens, ¼ chopped capsicum, 2 chillies chopped, 1 egg, 2 tbsp flour, 2 tbsp corn flour, 1 tsp pepper powder, a dash of soy sauce, a dash of chilli sauce and salt in a bowl; make lemon sized balls and steam them in a steaming basket for 4 minutes on high. Stand them for 5 minutes.
2. In another bowl add 2 tbsp oil; heat it and roll the steamed balls in it. Pour in the Manchurian sauce.
3. Cover and cook on reheat for 3 minutes before serving.

Serving:

Serve 'Manchurian sauce with steamed vegetable balls' with any variety of Chinese fried rice or Noodles.

Variation:

- Add chicken, mutton or prawns, etc, to the Manchurian sauce. Follow the method explained in the recipe for Chinese Sweet and Sour vegetables.
- Add meatballs or chicken balls to the Manchurian sauce and serve.

Cooking time: 16 minutes micro cooking.

Chilli Chicken with Chilli Garlic Sauce

Ingredients:

Boneless chicken from 1 chicken breast, chilli sauce – 1 tsp, soy sauce – 1 tsp, Worcestershire sauce – 1 tsp, salt – 1 tsp, vinegar – 2 tbsp, tomato sauce – 1 tbsp, chilli-garlic sauce – 1 tbsp, garlic finely chopped – 1 tbsp, corn flour – 3 tbsp, capsicum cut into roundels – 1 no, ajinomoto – a pinch, chicken stock – 1 and ½ cup and oil – 3 tbsp.

Preparation and Cooking:

1. Marinate chicken pieces with vinegar, chilli sauce, soy sauce, salt, ajinomoto and worcestershire sauce for 2 hours.
2. Strain and save the liquid.
3. Sprinkle 2 tbsp corn flour over the chicken pieces and mix well.
4. Place chicken pieces in a shallow micro safe dish; pour oil over them and mix with your hand. Cook on high for 4 minutes, stirring once. Cover and let it stand for 5 minutes.
5. Meanwhile in another bowl add oil, chopped garlic and capsicum rings. Mix and cook on high for 2 minutes, uncovered; lift the capsicum pieces and keep aside for garnishing.
6. In the same bowl, combine 1cup stock, liquid from the chicken marinade, tomato sauce and chilli garlic sauce, and cook on high for 3 minutes, stirring once after 2 minutes. Mix corn flour with ½ cup stock and pour in the hot sauce. Mix well and cook for 1 minute on high.
7. Check the seasoning; Pour this sauce over the cooked chicken. Stir well; cover and cook on micro high for 6 minutes.

Serving:

Garnish 'Chilli Chicken' with capsicum rings and serve hot with Rice/Noodles.

Variation:

Deep fry chicken pieces in hot oil. Sprinkle more flour on the chicken pieces before frying.

Cooking time: 12 minutes micro cooking.

Momos

Ingredients:

Flour – 100 gm, olive oil – 1 tsp, egg yolk – 1 no, salt – a pinch, 1 cup any veg or non-veg well flavoured stuffing.

Preparation and Cooking:

1. Combine flour, oil, egg yolk and salt with water and make a dough; keep it covered for 2 hours. Divide into three parts.
2. Roll one part into a thin square shaped chapatti and cut into 4 equal portions.

3. Place 2 tsp filling in 1 portion; hold all the 4 corners and carefully give a twist to seal the momo. In this way, finish stuffing all the 4 portions. Repeat the process with the second and third parts.
4. Place all the momos in a steaming basket with ¼ cup water underneath and steam on micro medium for 6 minutes. Let the dish stand for 5 minutes.

Serving:

Serve the 'Momos' warm or at room temperature with Szechuan sauce or Tomato sauce.

Plain veg or non-veg clear soup is also served with it to nullify the effect of hot Szechuan sauce.

Variation:

For momos without egg: combine together 100 gm flour, a pinch of salt and baking powder each; make a dough with water and leave overnight. For the rest, follow the same instructions. Steam them in a traditional way for 10 minutes.

Tips:

Momos, a popular snack from the North-Eastern part of India is gaining importance these days and becoming a popular dish that is available commercially but at selected outlets only. A simple recipe is given here to steam your own momos at home. This recipe will give you 10 to 12 momos.

Cooking time: 6 minutes micro cooking.

Spring Rolls

Ingredients for Pancakes:

Flour – 1 cup, milk or buttermilk – 1 cup, egg – 1 no, salt – ½ tsp, oil – 1 tsp.

For filling: Leftover noodles – 2 cup or stir-fried vegetables for noodles, eggs – 2 no and oil for frying.

Preparation and Cooking:

1. Sieve flour and salt together in a bowl; make a well in the centre and break 1 egg for pancakes in the centre; add oil and milk and beat with a rotary beater till lump free. Let it stand for 30 to 40 minutes.
2. Heat a non-stick tawa or pan and wipe it.
3. Once again mix the batter. Add one ladle batter is the hot tawa and tilt it in a round motion to spread evenly and cook for a few seconds on high flame; turn the sides immediately and remove after a few seconds. Keep it covered and warm. Repeat the process and finish making all the pancakes.
4. Beat eggs with a pinch of salt and keep aside.
5. Heat oil for frying.
6. Spread 1 pancake on the chopping board, brown side up; spread noodles over it. Apply beaten egg on the sides of the pancakes and fold the left and right sides over the vegetables (like a parcel) roll it from 1 side into a parcel. Then dip in the beaten egg and deep fry in moderately hot oil till golden brown. Remove with a perforated spoon on oil absorbent paper.
7. Repeat the process with the rest of the pancakes.
8. Cut each parcel into 4 to 5 pieces and serve.

Serving:

Serve Spring Rolls as a starter with Szechuan sauce.

Tips:

Mix the batter and keep for standing; prepare a veg or a non-veg filling. Cool it; stuff in pancakes and deep fry side by side. Don't stuff and keep.

Many people use rolled out noodle dough instead of pancakes for making spring rolls.

How to make noodle dough?

Sieve 1 cup flour and a pinch of salt in a bowl; make a well in the centre and break 1 egg and beat with a rotary beater. Sprinkle just enough water to make a stiff dough. Knead with hand thoroughly and roll out as thinly as possible. For making spring rolls, roll them into 4 to 5 inch diameter rounds and stuff with any veg or non-veg stuffing roll and seal the edges with a beaten egg and deep fry.

Cooking time: 30 minutes for preparation and 15 minutes for frying.

Mughlai Food

BIRYANI BADSHAHI (MUGHLAI)

Ingredients:

Mutton – 1/2 kg, Rice parboiled – 250 gms, Lemon Juice – 311/2 tblsp, blanched Almonds (Badam) – 10, Mint Leaves (Pudina Leaves) – 1/2 tblsp, Butter – 1 cup, 1 handfuls chopped Coriander Leaves (Dhania Patta), Cumin Seed (Jeera) – 1/2 tblsp, large sliced Onion (Kanda Pyaaz) – 2, Brown Cardamom (Elaichi Moti) – 2, Oil – 1 tblsp, Garlic (Lasun) – 4 pods, Cloves (Lavang) – 2, piece Ginger (Adrak) – 1 " long, Saffron (Kesar) – 1/2 tblsp, Green Chilly (Hari Mirch) chopped – 1/2 tblsp, Red Chili Powder (Lal Mirchi) – 1/2 tblsp, Cinnamon (Tuj/Dalchini) – 1/2", Curd (Dahi) – 1/2 kg, Milk – 125 gms, Water – 3 cups.

Preparation and Cooking:

1. First wash and soak rice.
2. Then fry sliced onions to a golden brown colour.
3. Soak saffron in water.
4. Now grind ginger, red chillies, garlic and almonds and fry these in butter.
5. Add it to the mutton and salt and stir for 5 minutes.
6. Now add water and cook on low flame till meat becomes tender and about 1 cup of gravy is left.
7. Boil rice with salt in another pan.
8. Put curd into a piece of muslin cloth and let the water drain away.
9. Add cloves, cardomoms, cumin seed, mint leaves, chopped chillies and coriander in drained curd.
10. Strain the saffron water and add lemon juice.
11. Add all this to mutton.
12. Sprinkle half of the boiled rice over the mutton and then spread a layer of fried onion and then of rice again.
13. Now pour milk and some butter and cover the vessel.
14. Seal the edges of the pan with flour paste.
15. Place the can on flame for one hour.
16. Serve it very hot with some curry.

Italian Food

LASAGNA

Ingredients:

Tomato-meat sauce – 3 cups, cheese sauce – 1 recipe, grated parmesan cheese – 1 cup, lasagna sheets – 6 to 8 sheets or pancakes – 8 no, oil – 1 tbsp and a large rectangle/square micro safe or ovenproof dish.

Preparation and Cooking:

1. Boil 6 cups water in a large pan. Drop in the lasagna sheets and pour oil; cook till lasagna sheets are soft. Drain the water and rinse pasta with tap water. Keep them warm.
2. Oil a micro safe dish and spread half of the tomato meat sauce evenly to cover the base.
3. Cover it with boiled lasagna sheets.
4. Spread cheese sauce over it and sprinkle a little grated cheese too.
5. Repeat the process one more time and end with a lasagna sheet or a pancake. Sprinkle grated cheese on top.
6. Cook on micro medium for 20 minutes or till the cheese is melted and the sauce is bubbling.
7. Or bake in moderately hot oven for 35 to 40 minutes.

Note:

The recipe of tomato-meat sauce has been given in 'Pasta in Italian meat sauce'.

Serving:

Serve it hot with an Italian meal or any other Continental meal.

Variation:

Cook vegetarian Lasagna: Take 2 cups Spinach puree + ½ cup tomato puree + 2 tsp ginger garlic paste + 1 tsp Italian herbs + 2 tbsp brown onion + 1 tbsp butter + 1 tsp chilli garlic and salt-pepper to taste. Mix all the ingredients together and add ½ cup cream/malai. Use it in place of meat sauce and follow the same process for the rest.

Tips:

You can make your own lasagna sheets with the basic noodle dough; roll the dough into very thin rectangle sheets and cut them into the desired size of your baking dish. Wait for 30-minutes and then boil them.

Basic Noodle dough: Mix together 100 gm flour, 1 tsp olive oil or any other cooking oil,1 egg yolk and a pinch of salt. Knead well and use it.

Note: Personally, I like to cook Lasagna with pancakes that are very light and make an excellent dish. Since these days, all kinds of ready pasta is available, and working people have less time at hand to plan the meals and the party menus; this simple recipe given here can be very handy.

Cooking time: 36 minutes micro cooking time.

Pizza (Pitza)
(Italian Bread)

Ingredients:

Pizza shells – 4 no, capsicums thinly sliced – ½ cup, black olives halved – 8 no, baby corns halved – 12 no or mushroom slices – ½ cup and red–green pepper strips – ½ cup, or boiled and shredded chicken, mozzarella cheese grated – 1½ to 2 cups and pizza sauce – 1½ cup.

For Pizza Sauce: Onion–tomato paste – 1 cup, tomato puree – 1 cup, chilli–garlic sauce – 1 tbsp, butter – 1 tsp, oregano – 2 tsp, pepper powder – 2 tsp, ajwain – 1 tsp, sugar – 1 tsp, finely chopped capsicum – ¼ cup, chilli powder – 1 tsp (opt), parsley chopped – 2 tbsp, bay leaf – 1 no and salt to taste.

Preparation and Cooking:

1. Heat butter in a pan and add ajwain (carom seeds) to crackle.
2. Add chopped capsicum and cook for 1 minute on high fire.
3. Now add all the other ingredients for a pizza sauce to it except parsley.
4. Mix well and cover with the lid. Cook for 3 to 5 minutes.
5. Take out the bay leaf and sprinkle chopped parsley.
6. Preheat the convection mode of your microwave oven for 15 minutes on 200 degree celsius or any electric oven or oven of a cooking range for 20 minutes.

Assembly:

Apply pizza sauce generously on the pizza shells. Sprinkle some cheese over them; arrange sliced vegetables or meat artistically and finally top with grated cheese. Cover the shell nicely from all sides.

Baking:

Bake pizzas in a hot oven one by one for 10 minutes or till the cheese melts.

If you own a cooking range, 3 to 4 pizzas can be baked at a time.

Serving:

Cut the prepared Pizza into wedges and serve hot with Mustard/Tomato Sauce as a starter or as a part of the meal with a soup, salad and any of the 'Italian or Continental' baked dishes.

Tips:

If your microwave has no convection mode or you do not have OTG, then first crisp one side of the pizza shell under the grill of your microwave for 2 to 3 minutes, then apply pizza sauce and veggies / meat and finally grill each shell for 5 minutes or till the cheese melts. Repeat the cooking process with rest of the shells.

Note:

Prepared Pizza can be reheated very well in the micro mode. Place 1 full pizza of room temperature on a paper plate or kitchen paper towel and reheat on high for 1.30 to 2 minutes.

Avoid:

Having too much of pizzas without salad or soups. Enjoy junk food as a mini meal and cultivate a habit of consuming nutritious soups and salads along, as a healthy diet should include fibrous food like vegetables, fruits and dry fruits along with other food items.

Interesting information:

"The name Pizza originated from the area around Naples (South west Italy). It is not certain, however, that the nearby village of Pizza, where the flour for the best pizza dough is grown and ground, can claim to be its creator. A pizza may first have been made to use up left-over bread dough and tomato sauce, plus whatever sausage, ham or cheese happened to be available" says the *Cordon Bleu* book on '*Cheese and Savouries*'.

Cooking time: 10 minutes for cooking Pizza sauce and 10 minutes each for baking pizzas.

Rajasthani Food

DAL-BAATI-CHURMA

Ingredients:

For the panchmel dal: chana dal (split Bengal gram) – 1/3 cup, toovar (arhar) dal – 1/3 cup, moong dal (split green gram) – 1/3 cup, urad dal (split black lentils) – 1 tbsp, whole moong (whole green gram) – 1 tbsp, chilli powder – 3 tsp 1/4 tsp turmeric powder (haldi), coriander (dhania) powder – 1 tsp, garam masala – 1/2 tsp 3 cloves (laung / lavang), bayleaves (tejpatta) – 2, cumin seeds (jeera) – 1 tsp, green chillies, slit – 2, a pinch of asafoetida (hing), dried mango powder (amchur) – 2 tsp, tamarind (imli) pulp – 2 tsp, ghee – 3 tbsp, salt to taste.

For the baatis (for 10 baatis) : whole wheat flour (gehun ka atta) – 1 cup, semolina (rava) – 1/2 cup, besan (Bengal gram flour) – 2 tbsp, milk – 8 tbsp, melted ghee – 4 tbsp, salt to taste.

For churma:

Chapati Flour / Atta – 1/2 cup, Baking Soda – 1/8 tsp, Oil – 1 tsp, Warm Water – 2 tbsp + 2 tsp Oil – few drops, Ghee – 2 tbsp, melted, Powdered Sugar – to taste.

For serving : melted ghee, churma

Preparation and Cooking:

Panchmel Dal

1. Clean and wash the dals and add 4 cups of water. Pressure cook for 2 to 3 whistles or till the dals are cooked.
2. In a bowl, combine the chilli powder, turmeric powder, coriander powder, garam masala with 3 tablespoons of water and mix well. Keep aside.
3. Heat the ghee in a pan and add the cloves, bay leaves, cumin seeds, green chillies and asafoetida. When the cumin seeds crackle, add the prepared masala paste and saut for 1 to 2 minutes.
4. Add the cooked dals, amchur, tamarind pulp and salt and simmer for 5 to 7 minutes. Adjust the consistency of the dal before serving and if required, add some water.

Baatis

1. Mix all the ingredients and knead into a firm dough. Knead well for 5 to 7 minutes.
2. Divide the dough into 10 equal portions and shape each portion into an even sized round. Flatten the rounds lightly using your thumb to make an indentation in the centre of the baati.
3. Boil water in a broad vessel and drop the baatis in the boiling water. Cook for 15 to 20 minutes over a high flame.
4. When the baatis are done, drain and keep aside.
5. Heat a gas tandoor and put the baatis on the grill of the tandoor. Cook them on a medium flame for 20 to 25 minutes. Cooking the baatis over a medium flame will ensure that the baatis are cooked on the insides also.
6. Arrange the baatis on a serving plate, break each baati into two pieces and pour melted ghee on the baatis.

Churma

1. Pre-heat oven to 350°F/ approx 180 °C.
2. Sift the Flour and Baking Soda. Add oil and incorporate into the flour. Add Warm Water to form a stiff dough.
3. Knead for 2-3 minutes. Drizzle a few drops of oil, rub and cover the dough. Allow the Dough to rest for 15 minutes.
4. Make golf-size round balls and transfer into a baking tray or a pizza stone. Bake for 15 min., turn and bake for another 10 min.
5. Once done, dip into melted ghee, roll, pull out and keep aside. Allow them to cool a bit, crumble by hand or in a Food processor.
6. Add additional melted ghee and mix. Add Powdered Sugar and mix in.

Serving:

1. Pour hot panchmel dal over the baatis.
2. Serve hot with churma.

Kitchen Designs & Planning

THE MAGIC IN KITCHEN AND HOW YOU CAN CREATE IT

A kitchen holds a vital place in the layout of a house and can be compared to the bone marrow in a human being. Kitchen planning is based on the most functional aspect, supplemented with a cheerful atmosphere, which is achieved with inspiring colours, good natural light and ventilation. As we all know, the primary function of a kitchen is to help produce meals in the most efficient manner. In short, a good kitchen should ensure smooth functioning with all the basic requirements located at appropriate places for convenience and speedy working with less effort.

While planning your kitchen, these tips may be of immense help:

- Try to keep the workspace free of obstacles and maintain a distance of 5 to 7 feet between different areas of function.
- Remember that it is not the amount of storage space provided but its correct placement that makes for the efficiency of a kitchen. Categorise your items into ones that are daily used and otherwise. Items used daily, termed as mobile storage items, should be handy and convenient to use. Locate them on the left of the working space.
- Avoid putting the cooking range in front of the window as that may cause accidents; and avoid any storage immediately above the cooking range. It should be nearer to preparation area and with ample light.
- Placement of the dish rack should be above the sink for easy drainage.
- As a refrigerator opens from left to right, place it on the right side corner preferably with a platform on the left side for convenient use. Leave sufficient space for the door to open at 120 degree to ensure easy movement of vegetables and chiller trays.
- Electrical points should be away from the wet area.
- Provide pullout storage or trolley below the platform for proper cleaning.

Kitchen

- Cover kitchen walls with ceramic tiles up to 7 feet, if not full.
- The area where the gas cylinder is placed should have proper ventilation for detecting any gas leakage. Gas tube should be about 2 inches above the platform.
- Avoid ceiling fans, instead use exhaust fan at a higher level to remove accumulated heat and to ensure proper air circulation.
- Use materials that will ease cleaning and which are maintenance-free, for example, granite, ceramic glazed tiles and laminates for shutters, metal racks and trolleys.
- Avoid use of marble on flat surfaces as marble stains easily and is porous.
- Lighting should be a combination of natural and fluorescent, with emphasis on aesthetic.
- Once you are sure about these answers, you are absolutely clear about what you want your kitchen to be. Now remodelling your kitchen or even designing a new one won't be such a pain after all.

Kitchen Layout

- An improperly planned kitchen can be a miserable place to cook. This is why in a kitchen remodelling project, one must first analyse the existing layout. Poor planning is responsible for an unexciting and unfriendly kitchen and simple re-planning can help you make the best use of the existing space, while also giving you a good-looking and well-functioning kitchen.

The Work Triangle

- The chief rule for any successful kitchen plan is that it should always follow a work diagram based on the sequence of operations. You don't need a time-and-motion study of your kitchen habits to tell you that work centres comfortably closed, will save both time and energy. You will also save extra steps if your work centres fit the logical sequence of food storage preparation, cooking, serving and cleaning-up.
- The main work centres in food preparation are the refrigerator, the sink and the stove and it is the placement of these three, in respect to each other, that has to be carefully planned. The work triangle is the arrangement of these work centres such that they form a triangle. And this has been proven to be the most efficient layout in a kitchen.
- Of course, for optimum advantage, the distance between any two work-centres must be within the specified limits. Increasing the distances will add needless kitchen mileage and fatigue. Cutting the measurements short of these limits will cramp your kitchen to the point where it will stop functioning efficiently. The three sides of the work triangle should total between 12 and 22 feet. The distance between the sink and the refrigerator should be 4 to 9 feet. The distance between the refrigerator and the cooking gas should be 4 to 7 feet.

The Six Basic Layouts

Every kitchen has the same basic ingredients—the three main work centres comprising of the refrigerator, the sink and the cooking range, and also the cabinets, countertops and appliances. It's how you arrange these 'givens' that make the difference in the way your kitchen functions. There are several tried and tested arrangements based on the 'work triangle' and these will often be dictated by the shape of your room. However, over the years, six basic layouts have evolved, which can be adapted to suit kitchen of any shape and size.

U-shape

If you have the space and the right room architecture, the U-shape kitchen layout is the most efficient. Besides offering a logical sequence of work centres with minimal distances between, the U-shape gives you three full walls of working kitchen. However this layout is suitable only in a kitchen that has at least 8 feet along both its length and width.

One Wall

The one-wall kitchen usually makes most sense in spaces where width is limited. Though its layout does not incorporate the work triangle, it can still be efficient; particularly, if the sink is between the range and the refrigerator.

L-shape

With two adjacent walls used for work centres, an L-shape layout forms a natural triangle. It also permits a lot of flexibility in the arrangement of appliances, storage and counters. Where units turn on to a second wall, the corner space becomes highly inaccessible. This dead space can be utilised by fitting revolving shelves, swivelling baskets and Lazy Susan corner units. Also, the L-shape layout can be more easily adapted to square spaces than long, narrow ones.

Gallery

The gallery corridor plan places appliances and cabinets along opposite walls. This arrangement works most efficiently when the sink and refrigerator are on one wall and the range on the opposite wall. Though a compact work triangle will be created only if the counters are reasonably close, there should be a minimum distance of 4 feet between them.

Island

An island in a kitchen can shorten the distance between the sink, range and refrigerator. It is particularly good in very spacious kitchens, where it adds efficiency to the workflow and visual interest to the vast, open space. The usual function of an island unit is to hold a cook-top, closed shelf and extra worktop space, but it can also incorporate an extra small fridge, and extra sink, a dishwasher or an eating counter.

Peninsula

When you have run out of wall space, but still have floor space available, a peninsula can increase your kitchen's workability. A peninsula extends into the open floor space perpendicular to the wall cabinets; and it can be used to accommodate the range or the sink. By planning the proper size and position of the peninsula, you can create a work triangle that is highly efficient.

POSITIONING OF YOUR KITCHEN

- Now, let us take a look at the positioning of your kitchen if you are planning to go in for construction work. Today, Vaastu Shastra is being applied to designing commercial buildings, industries and even houses. Hence, it is important for you to understand the exact placement of your kitchen. A Vaastu expert can assign the kitchen, chimneys, furnace, boiler etc., to certain positions on the basis of wind directions to prevent the smoke and cooking fumes from blowing into the dining area.
- Vaastu ensures peace, prosperity and progress to the owner and inmates. According to the Vaastu Shastra, it is advisable to make your kitchen in the South-East of your house because the South-East is the region of the Agni Dev or the God of Fire. In addition to this, South-East gets a lot of light from the Sun between December and May. This keeps the kitchen both bright and dry, preventing the breeding of cockroaches that thrive on dampness and moisture.

VENTILATION AND LIGHTING

- It is important for a kitchen to be well ventilated. The windows should have double doors, one with wire mesh on it. This way you can keep the window open while the wire mesh will keep out insects and flies. An exhaust fan or a chimney is also essential. A wall-mounted rotating fan could make life easy for you in summers when it becomes unbearably hot in the kitchen.

Chimney

- When you are cooking, it is important for you to be able to see properly and hence, lighting is important. Tube lights should be placed above the cooking area. If your kitchen is big, you could fix a second tube light at another convenient point. A couple of bulb fixtures would take care of the time when the voltage is too low for the tube lights to function well.

Cleanliness

- It is imperative to keep your kitchen as clean as possible because this is the place where bacteria, flies and insects cause the most damage. The doors and windows should have wire meshing. The kitchen must be swept and mopped at least twice a day so that there is no mess. The garbage pail/bin should be a covered one and should be kept under the sink to facilitate easy cleaning. Line the garbage bin with a garbage bag. Keep your kitchen clean and remain healthy.

Kitchen Apron

U-Shaped Kitchen

THE KITCHEN EQUIPMENTS

There is a surfeit of kitchen equipments available in the market to make your work in the kitchen a cakewalk, but being 'prudent' will pay you dividends in the long run. Even though different pieces of cooking equipments exist for every purpose, there may be some with little or no utility value. Hence, when you venture out to equip your kitchen, 'utility' and 'quality' are the two watchwords. This chapter will be of immense help in guiding you to buy the most useful cookware for your kitchen.

The Best Material For Cookwares

- Although glass and plastic are often in use, metal is the most suitable material for cooking equipments. Metals conduct heat quickly to the food and retain for a long time helping in slow cooking. Let us get to know what products we have on hand.

Ceramic, glass and earthenwares

Though these materials are not good conductors of heat, once hot, they retain heat well and so, are suitable for long simmering and braising. All these materials are widely used today both in the oven and on stovetop. Flameproof glass, like the Borosil carafe and ceramics can be used over a low direct flame, but earthenware is best set on a heat diffusing mat or a hot plate. Stoneware being less porous than earthenware, can withstand higher temperatures.

Enamelware

They are only good for boiling and poaching since the steel used is an inexpensive thin variety. It chips easily and is a poor conductor of heat. The food often gets scorched.

Aluminium

This material is used for making saucepans, casseroles, sauté pans, frying pans and stockpots. It is lightweight and a good conductor of heat. Aluminium, however, may react with foods containing acids giving the food an unpleasant taste. This is why aluminum utensils are often coated with stainless steel, nickel or nonstick plastic.

Steel

- It is tough, durable, and does not warp over high heat, although it can rust. This material is used for a variety of frying pans, omelette pans, deep-fryers, *kadais* and woks, but before use, all these pans need to be seasoned.
- To season steel pans: Pour 1.5 cm oil in the bottom of the pan. Throw handful of coarse salt and leave it overnight. Next morning, heat gently on the stove or in the oven till the oil is almost smoking. Remove from heat and let it cool. Throw away the oil and salt mixture and wipe dry the pan with a cloth. Your pan is ready for cooking.

Stainless steel

This is non-reactive metal even when used with strong acids but it is not a very good heat conductor and so, very often we find the bottom of the utensil scorching in places. This is why some utensils have a copper or aluminium lining to improve conductivity. Stainless steel is often used to make saucepans casseroles, frying pans, roasting pans and a plethora of kitchen bowls and utensils.

Copper

Copper is used for saucepans, saute pans, gratin dishes, casseroles and other cook-and-serve dishes. This is the best conductor of heat. Good quality copper pans are heavy and lined with nickel, tin or stainless steel. However, copper must not be used for acidic ingredients, which may react with the copper and form toxic substances.

Cast iron

Utensils made from this are very sturdy and heavy but can crack if dropped. This metal is used for making flameproof casseroles, griddles, skillets, *tawa* and even *kadhai*. These utensils are ideal for long, slow cooking but need to be seasoned just like the utensils made from steel.

Nonstick plastic

Commercially known as 'Teflon', which is actually a coating of poly-tetra-fluoro-ethylene (PTFE) that prevents food from sticking. This cookware is definitely easy to clean and requires minimal oil for cooking healthier food, but after constant use, the coating wears off. The idea is to use liquid cleansers and a sponge to clean this cookware for a longer life.

Pots And Pans

- For all kinds of stovetop cookware, weight is the key. The heavier the pans the better they cook and the longer they last. For quick cooking and for sautéing, we need a cookware with a large cooking surface while a tall, slim pot is best for long cooking as it guards against over evaporation. We must take care to use the right sized pot for the job at hand. If too little food is cooked in a large pan, not only may the pot scorch but also it is a waste of cooking gas. On the other hand, if the pot is too small, the content may overflow. Let us examine the kind of cookware most essential for your kitchen.

Stock pot

An ideal size would be 12 inches in width to enable you to stir even the most cumbersome bones with ease. This pot should be taller than it is wide, with two sturdy handles. A narrow base will ensure an even spread of heat and the tall sides will facilitate gradual evaporation of stock.

Saucepan

A copper saucepan would be an ideal one since it will ensure that the contents do not scorch during cooking. However, stainless steel is the second best choice. A sloping sides pan would be an advantage as it facilitates a spill-proof pouring out of the liquid.

Frying pan or skillet

Copper and cast iron are the materials of choice for this kind since both these metals are good conductors of heat. Do not get misled by an enamel-coated floral design. The lovely coating will often chip due to repeated exposure to heat. Non-stick cookware is good since they allow you to cook with minimum oil, but the coating gets scratched or simply wears off after constant use.

Fish frying pan

This is a large oval pan with low sides, ideal for frying whole small fish or fillets. Once again, it is advisable to buy the one made of heavy metal.

Omelette pan

It should have a thick base so that the heat spreads evenly. Made of aluminum, steel or cast iron, the pan should have gently sloping sides. The handle should have a firm grip and should be angled for an easy transferring of the omelette.

Sauté pan

This should have a heavy base, low sides to allow steam to escape and should be made of lined copper or stainless steel.

Deep-fryer

Though in Indian kitchens, frying is often done in a *kadhai*, a deep-fryer is also available in the market. It is made of steel, wide and deep for the oil to bubble without overflowing. These days an electric deep-fryer with a wire basket having a heat-proof handle, is in vogue.

Steamer

With stress on healthy, fat-free cooking, a steamer is essential. It is perforated container that fits over a pan of boiling water, ideal for steaming vegetables and other ingredients. It is a popular item used for oriental cooking.

Griddle or *tawa*

It is heavy, usually made of cast iron and is used for making a variety of parathas, *phulkas, chillaas*, pancakes and even *dosa* and *uttapam*. A griddle has a handle that can be laid flat but a tawa has a handle, straight or curved and is flat with a slight sloping depression in the centre. This is a must in Indian kitchen.

Wok or *kadhai*

This is another equipment that we use for a variety of cooking like deep-frying, stir frying, braising, etc. A wok is a large bowl-shaped steel pan with a rounded bottom, a domed lid, metal handles or one single handle. A *kadhai* is usually made of cast iron on steel and has two round handles.

Pressure cooker

This is one of the commonest cookware found in most kitchens. It has sealed tight-fitting lid in which steam pressure builds up, so that food cooks quickly at temperature above the boiling point. A safety valve releases excess steam. It is very useful for cooking meats, dals, pulses and beans. It comes with separators in which a number of dishes can be cooked simultaneously. A whole range of them is available in the market. They are made from heavy aluminium or stainless steel. These days we have nonstick pressure cookers as well.

- Many companies have flooded the market with an impressive array of cookwares which include:

  Popular Pressure Cookers with an extra thick base. They come in two varieties – the short-handle range and the long-handle range.

  Ultimate Pressure Cooker & Pan is a set of cooker and a pan with a common lid. This combination helps you to not only pressure cook but also deep fry / shallow fry or steam vegetables easily.

Both these sets are made from heavy aluminium or stainless steel and come in different sizes.

- Premium Nonstick Cookwares have a range of *tawas*, fry pans, sauté pans, saucepans, coffee/tea pans and *kadhais*. The handles remain cool in the heat of cooking. The exterior is powder coated for durability. The base is scientifically designed for even heating.
- Manttra, the four-in-one Cooking System is a recent addition. The makers claim that it is the fastest, easiest and healthiest way to cook. The company further adds that it is especially designed inside and out for today's healthy lifestyles. The Cooking System is a Stock Pot, Pasta Cooker / Colander, Shellfish Steamer, Vegetable Steamer and Pressure Cooker, all in one.

Frying Kadai and Perforated Spoon

Aluminium Pans

Tea Strainers and Colander

Stock Pots

All Purpose Pans

Omelette Pans

Tempering Laddle and Kadhai

Rice and Vegetable Strainers

Nonstick Kadhai and Nonstick Pan

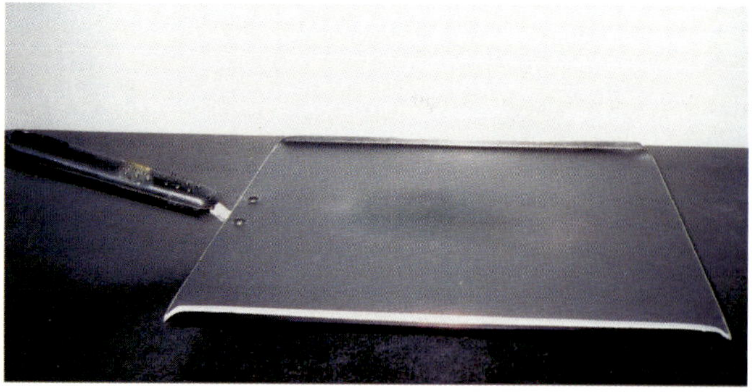

Rice and Vegetable Strainers

Stainless Steel Cookwares

Nonstick Pan and Pressure Cooker

Four Burner Gas Stove

Copper *Kadais* to cook and serve

Kitchen Knives And Other Gadgets

- A selection of carefully chosen cutting tools is essential in the kitchen. In fact, there is a knife for every activity like cutting, peeling, trimming, carving and shaping ingredients. Professional chefs often carry a personal set of knives all the time. The easiest to maintain are those with handles made from heat-resistant plastic. Take care not to buy knives with space between the blade and the handle as bacteria may collect there.
- You must always invest in good quality knives. Keep them in a block or a wall-mounted magnetic strip as knives kept in a drawer go blunt quickly and are a danger to fingers. To begin with, you will need a few select knives along with other gadgets to work with.

• **Carving knife:** This knife has a long, narrow blade ideal for slicing hot cooked meats.

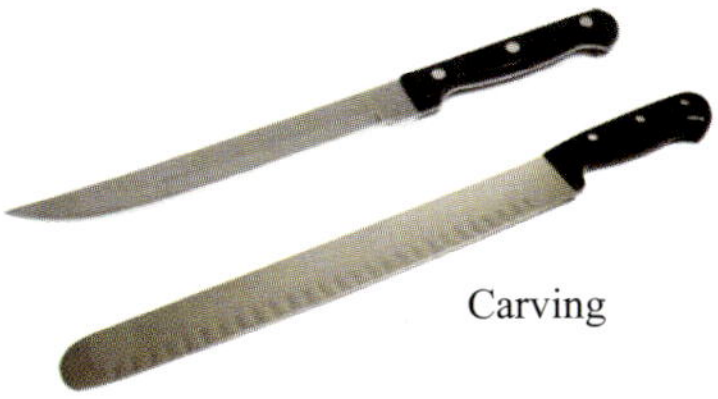
Carving

• **Chef's knife:** This knife is an all purpose kitchen knife that is used for most types of chopping, dicing, mincing, and slicing.

Mini Chef's Knife

Traditional Chef's Knife

• **Chestnut knife**: It is used to score the chestnut prior to roasting. The chestnut knife is short shafted in order to keep the cut confined to the shell without going too deeply to pierce the inner skin.

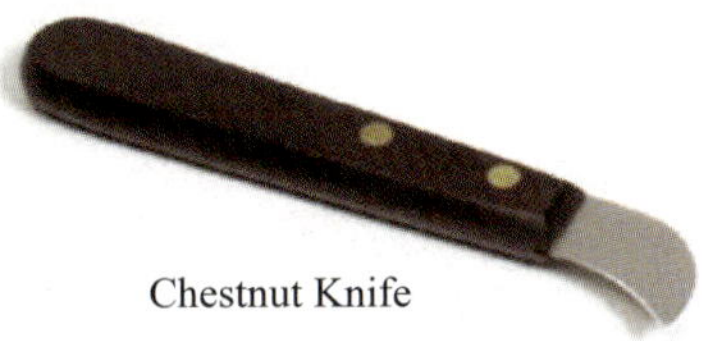
Chestnut Knife

• **Clam knife:** A kitchen utensil that is used to pry open the hard shell of a clam or an oyster in order to remove the meat.

Clam Knife

• **Deli knife:** Designed for thick sandwiches, this knife is made to cut easily and quickly through a variety of sandwich ingredients.

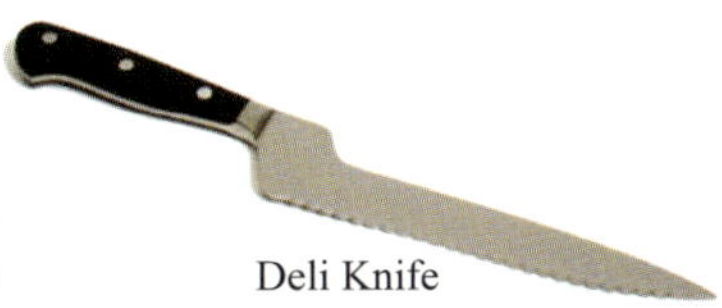
Deli Knife

• **Filet knife:** A knife consisting of a thin flexible blade, typically 6 to 11 inches long, used for filleting fish. The narrow blade enables the knife to cleanly move along the backbones of the fish, in and around areas adjacent to bones, and to evenly slice along the skin, removing it easily from the flesh.

Filet Knife

• **Meat and fish slicers:** Knives designed for slicing meat, such as poultry, ham, and fish.

Meat & Fish Slicer Knife

• **Mincing knife:** A knife that can be used to mince or cut food into smaller bits for seasoning sauces, soups, salads, and other dishes. Mincing knives can be either single or double bladed to cut a variety of foods into very small pieces.

Single Bladed Minicing Knife

Double Bladed Minicing Knife

• **Paring knife:** Used for cutting fruits, vegetables, meat and cheese.

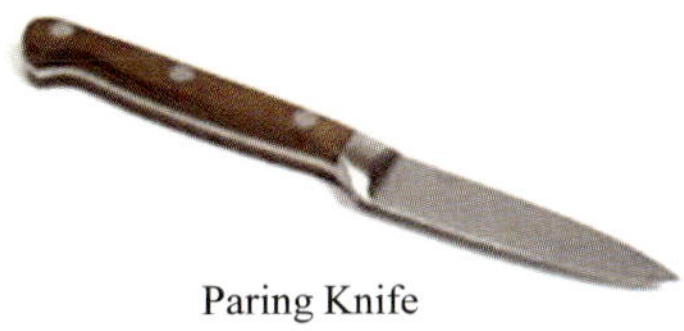
Paring Knife

• **Serrated knife:** Sold in various sizes, the smaller knives, which are usually 5 inches long, are ideal for slicing fruits and vegetables while the large ones cut cakes and breads evenly.

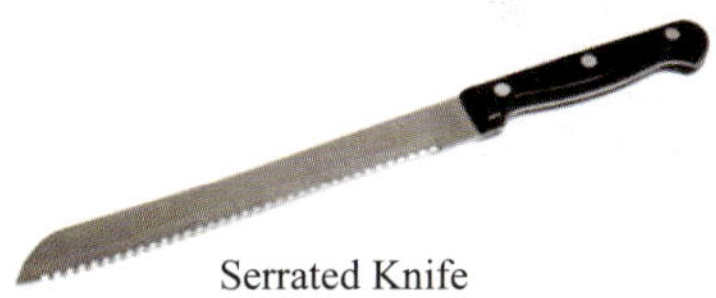
Serrated Knife

• **Utility knife:** A small lightweight knife used for miscellaneous light cutting.

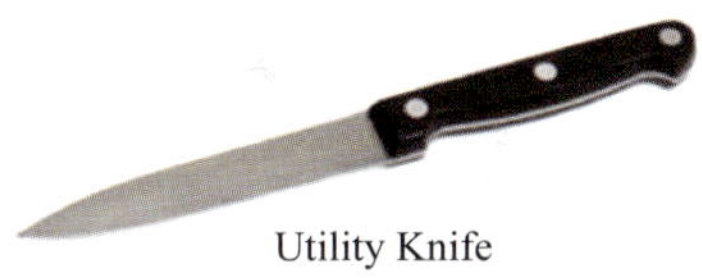
Utility Knife

• **Vegetable peeler:** A vegetable peeler is easier to use than a paring knife for potatoes, apples, carrots and other fruits and vegetables. A swivel blade conforms more to the shape of the ingredient than a fixed blade, so less of the flesh is removed.

Vegetable Peeler

• **Zester:** A zester has a stainless steel rectangular head with five holes that are designed to remove fine shavings of citrus zest when dragged along the surface of the fruit.

Zester

- **Large palette knife:** This has a blunt, highly flexible, flat 21 cm long blade. It is not used for cutting but for spreading icing or jam on a cake or toppings on a pizza or layering butter on bread slices for sandwiches.
- **Small palette knife:** This is blunt, flat and rightly flexible but has a shorter blade used for buttering toast. It is also used for loosening a cake from its tin.
- **Knife sharpener:** The blade of the knife is drawn backwards through the sharpness several times to sharpen it.
- **Chopping board:** These are available both in plastic and wood but wooden boards are the kindest to knives. They are useful in cutting and chopping vegetables but must be cleaned thoroughly after use.
- **Can opener:** This is another necessity for cans of juices, and other canned food. A sturdy can opener will work easily and leave no dangerous jagged edges. Those with cutting wheels and handles that are comfortable to hold, are ideal.
- **Skewers:** A flat bladed skewer is the best because when you turn a *tikka* or a kabab over, the food turns over with it.
- **Scissors:** Keep a pair of scissors solely for the kitchen – they are perfect for cutting the pouches, pasta, milk or any other food packets. You could also use it to trim the snipping herbs or cutting green chillies (it is easier to handle the chillies by cutting with scissors).
- **Bottle opener:** A simple, sturdy bottle opener with a handle that is easy to grip is the best choice.
- **Corkscrew:** This kind of corkscrew has a firm grip on the neck of the bottle and requires a single action to withdraw the cork.
- **Ladle:** This is used for pouring hot liquids from heavy pans. Ideal for serving soups, stews and curries.
- **Serving spoons:** Made of metal, plastic or even wood, these are large spoons used for serving.
- **Strainer:** It is best to have one made from steel though plastic ones are also available. You can use them to strain tea or any boiled food. They come in various sizes. So, it is best to invest in a selection of them.
- **Fish slice:** This is a flat tool used for turning solid food in the pan or for transferring food from the pan to the plate. It is ideal for turning fish which, generally, tends to break.
- **Slotted spoon:** Made of metal, either round or spoon-shaped, it is good for taking out food from boiling water or oil, for deep-frying puris/ *bhaturas* or other fried items.

Using knives safely

1. Cut away from the body.
2. Cut away from anyone near you.
3. Use a cutting board and put a damp napkin folded into four under it to keep the board from slipping.
4. Use the right knife for the job. Don't use a light weight knife for a heavy-duty job.
5. Since a dull knife requires more pressure to cut, keep knives sharp.
6. Always pick up a knife by its handle.
7. Don't use knives to cut string, open cans or bottles, or as a screwdriver.

Cleaning knives safely

1. Do not put a knife in a sink full of water, instead, put on the draining board to avoid cuts.
2. Wipe from dull to sharp edge.
3. Do not put knives in the dishwasher. The heat may harm the blade.

Knife Block

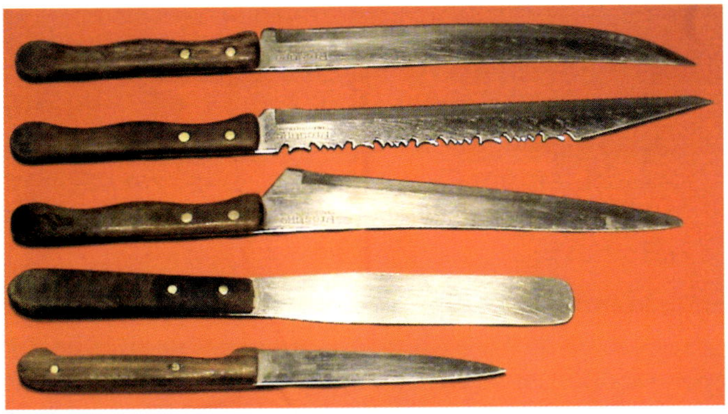

Knives for Different Uses
Top to Bottom:

All-Purpose Knife, Meat Cutting Knife, Bread Knife, Palette Knife, Paring Knife

Serving Spoons

Left to Right :

3 Serving Spoons, 1 Pickle Spoon, Set of Salad Spoons, 2 Serving Spoons, 1 Fish Fork

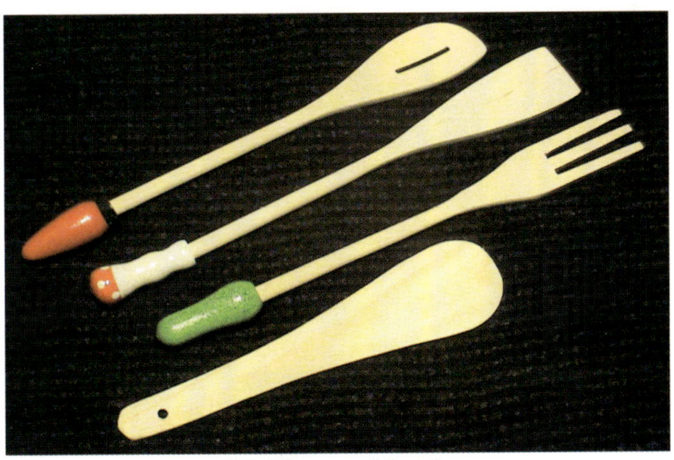

Salad Spoons and Spatula

Set of Knives

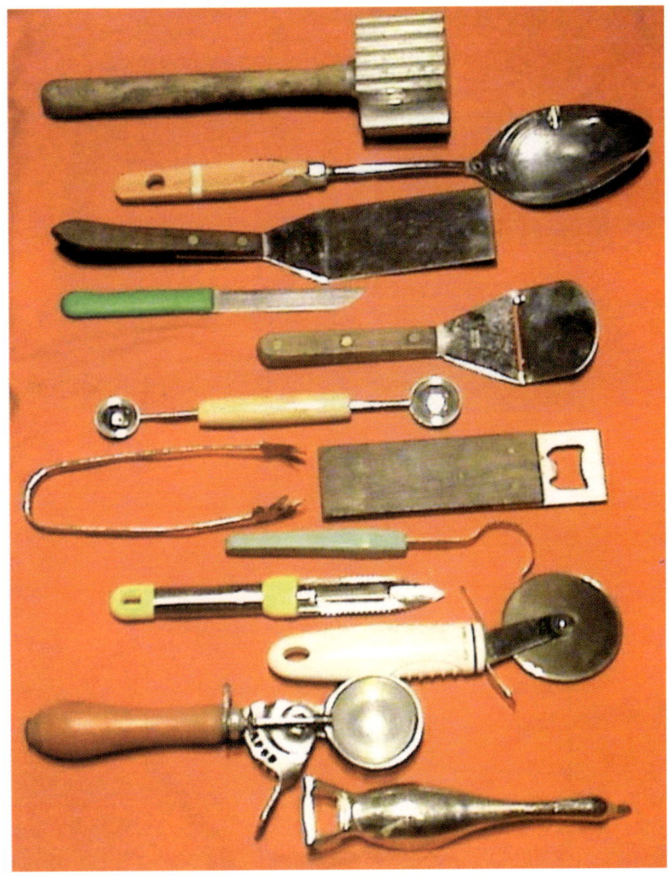

Kitchen Tools

Top to Bottom:

Meat Flattener, Measuring Spoon, Pastry Picker, Fruit knife, Cheese Slicer, Fruit Scooper, Bottle Opener, Tong, Butter Curler, Peeler, Pizza Cutter, Ice cream Scooper, Cork Opener

Cutlery set : Teaspoons, Fruit Forks and Serving Spoons

Cutlery set : Dining Spoons, Forks & Knives and Coffee Spoons

Plastic Serving Spoons

Processing Tools

These tools help you immensely since it is a common belief that good ingredients deserve a good treatment. If you have the right tools, it would automatically mean less wastage of ingredients and time. These are a few that all cooks should have.

- **Mandolin:** This is a flat wooden, plastic or metal frame with adjustable blades for slicing vegetables. Most mandolins have fixed different blades; smooth for cutting chips, matchstick and shoestring potatoes and fluted for waffle potatoes.
- **Box grater:** This is better than a flat grater because it stands up and hence, there is less danger of scraping your fingers. Remember to shake grated ingredients out before they get too compressed. It has two grating surfaces, large and small holes.
- **Potato masher:** Mashing potatoes is quite a tedious job and so, a masher with a comfortable handle, preferably a wooden one, would be ideal.
- **Salt & pepper mills:** For enhanced flavour, freshly ground pepper is a must as pepper loses its aroma soon after crushing. So, a pepper mill is a valuable addition to your kitchen. The salt mill makes up a pair. It uses rock salt or sea salt.
- **Nutmeg grater:** Just like pepper, it is best to buy whole nutmegs and crush or grate them when required.

Graters for Different Purposes

- **Mortar & Pestle:** A variety in marble, metal, wood and porcelain is available but the porcelain or the brass ones are the best. Buy the one you can store.
- **Lemon squeezer:** It is made of rigid plastic and has a bowl to catch the juice. A fitting strainer keeps the pips out. This is also available in the form of a press, made of plastic, wood or metal, with which you can strain the juice directly over the food.

Processing By Machine

It is true that electric machines are labour-saving but, you must also remember that equipping the kitchen with a full range of electric machines is not only expensive but also needs storage space as well as careful handling. Therefore, while buying kitchen machines, take into account what you usually cook, how often and in what quantity. Here are a few to choose from.

- **Hand-held blender:** This is a more portable and less expensive version of the liquidiser. It is used to puree food in the pan. It saves you the trouble of washing-up and storage and is handy for small quantities.
- **Blender:** A liquidiser used to puree foods for soups, dips, batter and drinks. It has a tall, narrow beaker with cutting blades at the bottom. It makes the smoothest purees. For best results, combine some liquid with the solids. Buy the one that has blades set low, so that you can cope with small quantities.

Mixer, Blender and Food Processor

- **Mixer:** The best stationery models have a fixed bowl with a beater that moves across the bottom. Some machines have a meat-mincing attachment, too. You need one with a heavy-duty motor for grinding the batter for *dosa* and *idlis,* mixing yeast dough and thick batters and also for mixing your roti / paratha dough.
- **Food processor:** This is possibly the most essential of all kitchen machines as it not only eliminates the need for a blender combining the blending and grinding along with other activities. It has a fixed bowl with removable cutting, shredding and kneading attachments. Some machines have more than one bowl for different needs. The more expensive the machine, the more sophisticated jobs it will do. Some machines have a separate small jar to cope with small quantities.
- **Deep-fryer:** This has a wire tray that immerses the food in the hot oil bubbling in the body of the fryer. They maintain the proper temperature of the oil with the help of a thermostat, which registers a wide range of temperatures.
- **Electric rice cooker:** It is an implement used to cook rice dishes like *pulao* and biryani, for steaming rice and vegetables as well as for making both vegetarian and non-vegetarian dry dishes, hence, a very useful addition to your kitchen.
- **Hand-held mixer:** This is ideal to use in a pan over the heat. Leaves you with one hand free. Choose one with three speeds detachable beaters for easy cleaning.

Measuring Tools

To achieve perfection in cooking, you must learn to use measuring equipments. This becomes all the more essential when you are baking because a successful result depends on accuracy.

- **Scales:** For best results, it is important to weigh the ingredients. Balancing scales give the most accurate results, especially for small amount. Along with the scales, you must also buy a set of metric weights, large ones made of iron and the smaller ones made of brass.
- **Measuring spoons:** Most of the time you come across the recipes calling for teaspoons or

Weighing Scale, Measuring Jug, Cups and Spoons

tablespoons of ingredients. These should be levelled and measured accurately. Invest in a commercially produced set as ordinary spoons always vary in size.

- **Measuring jug:** This helps in measuring liquids for cooking. A plastic one is safer and lasts longer than the glass one, but a glass one is better for measuring hot liquids. A good jug has both the metric and imperial measurements to help with converting quantities. Buy the biggest that you can store since a large one is more useful for mixing and measuring.
- **Measuring cups:** These are handy where a recipe specifies 1cup,) cup or (cup since ordinary cups vary in size.

Mixing And Sieving Tools

Both the activities are a constant part of cooking. Wooden spoons are the most useful for both. The spatula and the cornered spoon are possibly the most useful.

- **Wooden spoons:** To beat and mix anything by hand, the most useful implement is a short-handled wooden spoon. Long-handled spoons are good for stirring mixtures on the stove. They can withstand heat without burning your hand and do not scratch the pan. A corned spoon will reach right to the edges at the base of the pan.
- **Wooden spatula:** This is flat-sided spoon, ideal for folding mixtures, like egg whites or melted chocolates and cake mixture. It is also used to turn and lift food like an omelette, a paratha or a *dosa*.
- **Bowls:** Choose bowls that fit inside each other so that it does not take up too much of storage space. Glass bowls are the best as they give an all-round view of what is being mixed. Even plastic ones are also good.
- **Sieves:** It is best to buy a couple of sieves, one large and the other small. They have solid steel, metal, wood or plastic frames fitted with a wire mesh. Besides sifting dry ingredients and straining wet ones, you can use a sieve to puree cooked fruits and vegetables, and to make pureed soups.
- **Tongs:** This tool is useful for turning and moving delicate pieces of roasted food, for example, food being grilled on charcoal or your *phulkas*.
- **Plastic spatula:** Made of plastic, it is flexible and useful for getting every last bit of mixture out of the mixing bowl. It is good for folding mixtures, too.
- **Balloon whisk:** This is very useful if you don't have an electric whisk. It is made of steel, with a comfortable handle and a large balloon of

Spoons for various purposes

Top to bottom:

Dal Masher, Cake Mixer, Salad Spoon, Tongs, Wooden Spatula, Churner, Rubber Spatula, Khakra Presser

spring wire. It is ideal for whisking egg whites and for incorporating air into a mixture.

- **Coil whisk:** This is very handy for whisking small quantities of sauce over the heat or in a roasting tin. Never use this in a nonstick pan, as it will damage the coating.
- **Colander:** This is made of steel or aluminium and has perforations to drain out the liquid. Choose a free standing one with handles that is ideal for draining cooked rice, vegetables, noodles, pasta and pulses; and is ideal for washing greens like spinach, fenugreek and mustard greens, etc.

Equipment used for Baking and Biscuit Cutters

Baking And Roasting Tools

- **Piping tube / icing gun:** It is made of metal or clear plastic and comes in a wide range of decorative shapes and sizes. It has a conical nozzle that shapes whipped cream, choux pastry dough and icing. The nozzle needs to be incisively sharp for a clean-cut pattern.
- **Pastry scraper:** Used to cut dough, scrape the sides of bowls and scoop up dough from the work surface; this is made of flexible plastic.
- **Pastry cutters:** Available in plain and fluted, round and oval, as well as in a variety of sizes and shapes. Ranging from animal shapes to letters of the alphabet, hearts and stars etc., they are made of metal. Their edges should be sharp and even, so that the pastry cuts clean. You must press the cutter forcefully and quickly through the dough, to be able to make clean cuts.
- **Muffin tin:** An ideal one should have a nonstick coating. If you are not using a nonstick one, use paper case for muffins and grease the tin well.
- **Sandwich tin:** It is a shallow tin with a loose bottom, 18 cm in diameter. If you plan to make a Victoria cake, you will need two of these. If you make a variety of layered cakes, you must have a number of these tins.
- **Tray bake tin:** This is a nonstick tin, deep-sided and measures 30×25 cm across the top.
- **Loaf tin:** A nonstick, 20×25 cm size tin, it is best for breads, cakes and meat or veg loaves.
- **Ramekins:** These are small, ceramic baking dishes with an average capacity of 150 ml used for individual servings of baked custard and souffles. Keep a selection of these.
- **Spring form cake tin:** Ideal for delicate cakes and cheesecakes that have a tendency to break and once pushed from the bottom, it becomes easier to remove your cake. This need not be nonstick.
- **Baking sheet:** This is used for baking pizzas and cookies, and for providing a heat-conducting base for quiches, pies and tarts. It is a sturdy, inflexible sheet, completely flat. Buy one that will fit easily in your oven.
- **Pie tin:** This has plain, sloping sides and is made of metal. To increase heat conduction, place a very hot baking sheet under the pie tin. You should buy a tin that is 23 cm across the top.
- **Quiche tin:** A metal quiche tin is the best. An ideal size is 20 cm across the base. This tin has fluted edges to help strengthen the fragile pastry shell of a quiche. Buy a variety that lifts out, so that you do not break the quiches while removing it.
- **Baking dish:** A perfect one would be a ceramic one measuring 25×25 cm acorss the top and 5 cm deep. This is used for baking pasta and vegetable dishes and even for roasting. Take care not to pour cold water into a very hot dish or else, it may crack.
- **Roasting tin:** This should be as big as can easily fit into your oven. The best is a deep enamelled one with a pouring lip.

- **Roasting rack:** This is made of metallic bars and helps you to roast meat free of its fat.
- **Casserole:** These are heavy and deep with a light fitted lid, used for braising and pot-roasting in the oven. It retains the moisture generated during cooking.

Now that we have discussed all kinds of oven cookware, it is important to remember two points as far as baking dishes are concerned.

- A cake tin needs to be lined and greased for a good result regardless of the material it is made of or its coating.
- Yeast breads rise less in a shallow tin but pastry cooks best in a shallow tin.

Moulds

We use moulds for various jobs in the kitchen and these moulds are made of various materials depending on what their use is. Ice cream and gelatin dishes are always set in metal moulds. For making chocolates, we use flexible plastic or rubber moulds and for dishes that are served directly from their mould, best mould are earthenware or glass ones.

Ice Cream moulds

Moulds made of metal are best for this as they chill quickly and can be warmed for unmoulding. They may be round, square, conical or brick-shaped with tight-fitting lids to prevent the formation of crystals during storage. The sides must be smooth and the bottom is often embossed, which results in leaving a design on the ice cream when it is unmoulded. Animal-shaped moulds are a great favourite with children.

Baking Tins and Moulds

Bombe mould

Made of metal, spherical in shape with a lid, it can also be cylindrical or square with a rounded top.

Gelatin and pudding moulds

These moulds are designed to display jellies and puddings to the best advantage but need careful handling. An ornate mould with scalloped edges looks beautiful but is very difficult to unmould. Tall moulds are good for mixtures that are to be set firmly as shallow ones are more likely to collapse. The less firm the mixture, the plainer and lower the mould should be. Thin moulds tend to dent and warp. Let us take a look at a variety of these moulds.

- **Charlotte moulds:** This mould is used for ice creams, souffles and puddings. It is bucket-shaped with gentle sloping sides and flat handles near the top.
- **Jelly moulds:** These are made of thin metal, quite ornate in style and are used for aspic fruit jellies or Bavarian creams.
- **Pudding moulds:** These are lidded moulds used for steaming puddings. They come in a variety of shapes from round to really ornate ones shaped like a melon.
- **Aspic egg moulds:** These are small, oval shaped moulds, with a smooth bottom and are used to make individual servings of poached egg in aspic.

Ice Cream Machines

It is usually made of wood and is cylindrical, tub fitted with a handle. The tub is surrounded by ice and coarse rock salt, in the ratio of 1 kg of ice to 100 g salt. The salt lowers the melting point of ice, thus, chilling the mixture in the churn to below the freezing point of water. The paddle has to be turned by hand till the mixture sets, which requires about 10–20 minutes. This machine gives excellent results but the trick is to keep the ice-salt ratio accurate, or else, too much salt with ice will make the ice cream mixture set too quickly making it grainy.

- **Manual Freezer:** It consists of a hand-operated paddle in a sealed metal container of frozen chemical refrigerant. It does not require any ice or salt. It is available in several sizes but a twin container is ideal as you can use the contents of one and store that of the other, as only small quantity of mixture can be frozen at one time. Freezing is quick but the ice cream is a little grainy and lacks creaminess.
- **Freestanding machines:** This is an expensive machine but is essential if you plan to make ice cream and sorbet in large quantities. It has an automatic stirring and cooling mechanism.
- **Wrappers:** These are an essential item in every kitchen, to protect and preserve food, to prevent the food from sticking to baking dishes and moulds and even to serve food.
- **Greaseproof paper:** This paper can withstand gentle oven heat and is used to line cake tins and baking trays. It is thin with a waterproof coating on both sides.
- **Parchment paper:** This is yet another nonstick paper used for lining cake tins.
- **Foil:** This is made of aluminium, conducts heat well and is easily moulded to shape. It is ideal for enclosing ingredients for baking, for covering dishes in the oven and to line baking trays. To prevent food from sticking to the foil, grease it.
- **Cling film:** This is a plastic wrap used more for storage. You can cover containers with cooked food or salads with this but there are brands that can be used in a microwave oven.

Wrapper and Foil

Fuel Saving Tips

A gas stove is the commonest kind of stove that we use in our kitchen. But most of us are not careful enough to use it with prudence, and end up by using more gas than is actually necessary. Sometimes, we tragically pay for our neglect through accidents, which could have been avoided with a little extra care. Just to reiterate the need to save fuel and be safe, a few tips are listed below.

Do you know that you can save over 25% of cooking gas by following a few simple efficiency measures?

There are some to help you make your gas cylinder last for extra seven days.

- Light your stove only after you have kept all the ingredients ready for cooking.
- Always reduce the flame once boiling starts. Experiments conducted reveal a saving of 35% fuel by just taking this simple action.
- A small burner consumes less fuel than a big burner in a gas stove. An experiment on cooking 250 gm of potatoes revealed that the small burner consumed 6.5% less gas but took 7 minutes more than the big burner. Use the small burner more often, especially when you have time to spare.
- Do not use narrow vessels and allow the flame to creep up the sides. Hide the flame with a broader bottomed vessel.
- Surplus water consumes additional fuel, which could otherwise be saved. In an experiment on cooking rice, double the required quantity of water was found to lead to an increase of 65% in fuel consumption.
- A pressure cooker saves both fuel and time. Further savings are possible by cooking various food items all together in the separators of the pressure cooker.
- If all members of the family eat together, frequent reheating of food before serving can be avoided.
- If eating together is not possible store cooked, hot food in insulated containers to serve hot later.
- A coating of undissolved salts is usually found on the insides of kettles and cookers. Even a millimetre thick coating can reduce

USEFUL KITCHEN GADGETS

Toaster

Sandwich Toaster

Charcoal Grill for Barbeque

Electric Oven Toaster Grill

the flow of heat to the vessel's contents and this increases your fuel consumption by as much as 10%. Ensure that the insides of your cooking vessels are always scrubbed clean.

- Cold milk, frozen meat or any other cold foodstuff from the refrigerator should not be taken straight to the cooking pot. Keep it out of the refrigerator for sometime before you put it on the stove. Very cold food uses up a much larger amount of fuel.
- Always place a lid on an open cooking vessel or a pan.
- A bright, steady blue flame indicates efficient burning. If you see an orange, yellow or non-uniform flame, it is time to clean your burner.
- Above all, remember to switch off not only the burner knob, but also the gas valve after you have finished cooking. This will prevent gas leakage.
- Do not keep any oil or inflammable material near the gas cylinder to ensure safety from fire.

- Once your kitchen has been set and you have gathered the know-how of using a gas stove, time has come now to move forward.

Tips for Healthier Cooking

- Substitute whole milk with skimmed or toned milk. You can even make *paneer* and curd with the skimmed milk.
- Use whole-wheat flour with bran since it is rich in fibre. Brown and whole-wheat breads are highly recommended.
- Use minimum amount of water while cooking. Do not discard the water used for soaking and cooking, instead use it in soups, gravies or for kneading dough.
- The skin of the root vegetables like potato, colocasia, yam, turnip, carrot, etc., prevents the leakage of nutrients. Always boil these vegetables with skin to retain nutrients.
- Never chop vegetables into very small size, since smaller the piece, the more loss of nutrients.
- Vegetables and fruits should always be washed and then chopped.
- The skin of vegetables should be peeled as thinly as possible.
- Avoid the use of soda bicarbonate in your cooking to prevent loss of thiamin.
- Repeated heating destroys many nutrients. It is always better to consume the preparation immediately after cooking or as soon as possible.
- Fats and oils used for deep-frying a number of times should be avoided for cooking as they become toxic. If you have to use the same fat for cooking, mix half of used oil and half of fresh unused oil and then use it without bringing it to the boiling point.
- Use Teflon-coated cooking pans to minimise the amount of oil used.
- Restrict the intake of oil. Some of the best methods of cooking are baking, grilling, roasting, steaming, and pressure-cooking.

Storing Your Food

- The first rule that you must follow while storing food in the home is to refrigerate or freeze the perishables right away. Keep checking both the freezer and the refrigerator temperature periodically. The refrigerator temperature should be 40° to 45°F, and that of the freezer should be zero.
- Poultry and meat that need to be stored in the refrigerator may be stored as purchased in the plastic wrap for a day or two. If only part of the meat or poultry is going to be used right away, it can be wrapped loosely for refrigerator storage. Just make sure that the juices can't escape to contaminate other foods.
- Seafood should be kept in the refrigerator or freezer until preparation time.
- Tightly wrap foods meant for the freezer.
- Don't fill up the refrigerator or freezer so tightly that air can't circulate.
- Leftovers should be stored in airtight containers. Check the leftovers in covered dishes and storage bags daily to check spoilage. Anything that looks or smells suspicious should be thrown out at once. A sure sign of spoilage is the presence of mould, which can grow even under refrigeration. Even though they are not a major health threat, mould can make the food unappetising. Mould is deceptive in that only a small part is visible. The larger part extends below the surface of the food.
- Many foods besides fresh meats, most vegetables and dairy products need to be kept cold. For instance, mayonnaise and ketchup should go in the refrigerator after opening. All ready to cook, homemade spices should be kept in the refrigerator.
- Always check the labels on cans and jars to find out how the contents should be stored. If you have neglected to refrigerate items, it is best to throw them out.
- For foods that can be stored at room temperature, some precautions will help make sure they remain safe. Potatoes and onions should never be stored under or near the sink, because leakage from pipes or moisture can damage the food. Special metal or plastic racks with wire trays are available in the market specially for storing potatoes and onions. Store them in a cool, dry place, never store food near household cleaning

products or chemicals because of the danger of accidental contamination.

- While storing canned foods, move the older ones to the front of the shelf and the new ones in the back row, so that you'll be sure to use the older ones first. Check all cans to see if any of them is sticky on the outside. This may indicate a leakage. Cans that appear to be leaking may contain a deadly bacteria, and should be returned to the store.

If you are freezing foods, do the following to ensure that the high-quality food you put into the freezer is still of high quality when it comes out.

- Freeze foods at their peak quality. Don't wait until they are at or near the end of their useful life.
- Use appropriate packaging to prevent freezer burn and protect flavours. Freezer burn appears as greyish-brown, leathery spots on frozen food. It occurs when air reaches its surface. Although undesirable, freezer burn does not make the food unsafe, merely dry in spots. Cut it away before cooking the food. Supermarket meat wraps, while safe for freezing are permeable to air. Over time, this contributes to freezer burn and rancidity, when fats and oils develop an off-taste and odour. Over wrap these packages with airtight heavy-duty foil, plastic wrap or freezer paper.
- Freeze unopened vacuum packages. When freezing food in plastic bags, push all the air out before sealing. Residual air can change into ice crystals and cause fats to go bad.
- Freeze food as fast as possible to maintain its quality. Ideally, food, 2 inch thick should freeze completely in about 2 hours. If your home freezer has a 'quick-freeze', it prevents undesirable large ice crystals from forming.
- You can make a selection of curries, non-vegetarian dishes, dry vegetable dishes, chapattis and parathas for a whole weak or ten days and freeze them for convenience. This is ideal for working couples.
- Cook the curries, dry preparations and the non-vegetarian dishes; cool them and then store them in special bags that are easily available in the market. These bags are made of thick paper with a coating of aluminium

inside to prevent the food from sticking. Fold and staple the edges and freeze.

- Alternatively, you could store them in foam containers and cover them with cling film. Take them out, heat and serve as and when you need them.
- Cook the chapattis and the parathas on a dry *tawa* till half done. Cook and store in the freezer in thick storage bags. When you need them, just take them out beforehand, reheat on *tawa* or on direct flame, smear with oil / ghee and serve.
- *Dahi bhallas* can be deep-fired, cooled and frozen. Similarly, when you need them, just take them out beforehand, pop them in hot water for a few minutes, squeeze out the water and immerse them in beaten curds.
- Spinach, mustard greens and other vegetables can be boiled, pureed and frozen.

Take them out beforehand; just prepare the tempering / tadka, pour it over the vegetables; simmer them covered for a few minutes, add butter or cream and serve.

- Store roasts wrapped in aluminium foil when sufficiently cool. When you need them, just pop in pre-heated oven for ten minutes and serve.

Storing Vegetables And Greens

It is best to buy your weekly supply of vegetables and greens during the weekends. This way you will have ample time to store or refrigerate them properly. While storing fresh vegetables and greens, there are a few points to remember:

- Never wash vegetables and greens before refrigerating. They will retain moisture and perish.
- Wipe the fresh vegetables with a kitchen towel. Store each one separately in plastic net bags and refrigerate. These plastic net bags are available in the market in various sizes.
- Break off the tails of green chillies and store them in wet bags or a stainless steel perforated container. These containers are also available in the market. Never store green chillies in a plastic box. They will have a lot of moisture, so perish fast.
- Green coriander can be stored for over a week in a brown paper bag. But take care not to cut off the stems. Store them as it is and do the cutting, chopping and washing when you need it.

Vegetables

- Spinach, mustard green, fenugreek greens and all other greens should be cleaned, picked and stored in net bags. Do not chop or wash them.
- Smear a little coconut oil over fresh limes before storing them in the refrigerator. They will not become dry or perish for a fortnight.
- Cut cauliflower into florets and refrigerate in a net bag.
- Chop cabbage and refrigerate in a plastic box or a net bag.
- Shell fresh green peas and store in a net bag. Do not store them in a plastic box as this can develop a rotten smell.
- Carrots and beans can be chopped and stored in net bags in the refrigerator. Wash them before use.

These tips save time and energy and make cooking quite easy. But, of course, you need to keep checking all the while for spoilage. At first, all this may sound too complicated but once you begin, you will gain expertise and soon, by a trial and error method, devise new ways to store and refrigerate your foods and vegetables in a manner most convenient to you.

Preserving Nutrients

There are **five factors** that are responsible for the loss of nutrients in food:

High temperature, Long cooking hours, Baking soda, Exposure to the air, Solubility in water

The fact remains that fat-soluble vitamins (A, E, D and K) are insoluble in water, so they are fairly stable in cooking, but the water soluble vitamins and minerals easily leak out of foods during washing or cooking. Given below are a few tips to retain nutrients in foods in storage and cooking:

- Buy food that is fresh and of high quality. Examine fresh fruits and vegetables thoroughly for appropriate colour, size and shape.
- Store fruits and vegetables in the refrigerator (except green bananas, potatoes and onions), because they contain enzymes that make fruits and vegetables lose nutrients. The enzymes are more active at warm temperatures.

A well laid out Table for a Meal; Table set for four people

Kitchen Wall Clock

- Store canned food in a cool, dry place and limit the time of their storage. In general, the longer the storage period and the higher the storage temperatures, the greater the loss of nutrients.
- Freezing is a good way of retaining nutrients when foods are properly packaged, frozen at peak quality and kept below freezing point.
- Food should be used as quickly as possible because vitamins are often lost in storage.
- Wash vegetables quickly and do not soak them in water. Avoid bruising vegetables as this can cause vitamin loss.
- To retain vitamins when cooking vegetables, steaming, stir frying or cooking in a microwave, works well because the cooking is done quickly. If boiling vegetables, the longer they are cooked, the higher the nutrient loss. Cook vegetables just tender and use as little water as possible.
- Potatoes and other vegetables that are boiled or baked without being peeled, retain many more nutrients than peeled and cut. In general, the smaller the pieces you cut your vegetables before cooking, the higher the vitamin loss.
- Leaking and oxidation increase by having created more exposed surface, therefore, the vegetables and fruits should not be cut more than necessary.
- Frying over high temperatures can destroy vitamins in vegetable. For instance, French-fried potatoes or fried chips lose most of their vitamin C.
- Never use baking soda for retaining the colour of vegetables, as it will cause nutrient loss.
- After broiling and roasting meats and poultry, you can skim off the fat and use the remaining dripping in gravies or pour them directly over the meat. In this way, you recover some of the water-soluble B vitamins.
- Use the cooking water from vegetables to make soups, knead dough or make gravies.
- Try and make everybody sit down at a meal together as frequent heating causes vegetables and curries to lose nutrients. Don't cook food too much in advance before serving.
- Factors that destroy vitamins and minerals often spoil the colour, flavour and texture of food. With the vast selection of tips at your disposal, cooking, storing and preparing food for sudden arrival of guests should not be a problem.

Appendix

GLOSSARY OF FOOD ITEMS

English	Hindi	Uses
Almond	Badam	A nut used as an ingredient in pulaos and curries and to garnish swaeets.
Aniseed	Patlee saunf	An aromatic spice used as an appetiser in cooked dishes.
Apricot	Khumani	Used in desserts.
Arrowroot	Arrowroot	Used as a thickening agent in soups, pie fillings and sauces.
Asafoetida	Hing	A powerful seasoning used to flavour curries.
Baking powder	Khanne ka soda	A raising agent used in pastries and batters.
Banana	Kela	Used in puddings and *raitas*.
Basil	Tulsi	Herb of the mint family used for flavouring.
Bay leaf	Tej patta	Used fresh or dried for flavouring curries and rice.
Bitter gourd	Karela	An iron rich green vegetable makes tasty preparations inspite of its bitterness.
Black cardamom	Badi ilaichi	A fragnant spice used for flavouring curries and pulaos.
Black cumin seeds	Kala jeera	This spice is used to flavour curries and pulaos.
Black gram	Urad (Whole)	Used to make curries.
Black peppercorn	Kali/Gol mirch	Used whole or ground in curries, rice and savoury dishes.
Black salt	Kala namak	A flavouring agent used in *chaats, raitas* and sauces.
Bottle gourd	Lauki	A watery vegetable used in curries and at times in sweets.
Brinjal	Baingan	A widely used vegetable, especially tasty when made into *bharta* or stuffed.
Butter	Makkhan	A fat rich in vitamins A and D used for cooking and table use.

English	Hindi	Uses
Buttermilk	Mattha	Used for making drinks and curried dishes.
Cabbage	Bandh gobi	Used in vegetable dishes and used raw in salads.
Capsicum	Shimla mirch	Used in salads and mirch curries.
Caraway	Shahi jeera	Used for flavouring curries seed and pulaos.
Carom seeds	Ajwain	Used as a part of batters, *masalas* and in savoury dishes.
Carrot	Gajar	Used in salads, curries and sweet dishes.
Cashewnuts	Kaju	Used in garnishing pulaos, curries and sweets.
Cauliflower	Phool gobi	Used in pulaos and curries.
Chickpeas	Kabuli chana	Used in making *chole*.
Chilli	Mirch	Adds a hot, spicy flavour to food.
Cinnamon	Dalchini	Available in powder and stick form; used in curries, pulaos and sweetmeats.
Cloves	Laung/Lavang	Used in sweets, savouries and spice powders.
Coconut	Narial	Used extensively in curries, desserts, and for garnishing.
Coriander leaves	Hara dhania	An aromatic herb used for flavouring and garnishing.
Coriander seeds	Dhania seeds	Used whole and in powdered form as a part of *garam masala*.
Corn	Makai	Used in snacks and some curries.
Cornflour	Makke ka atta	Used in cooking as a thickener.
Cottage cheese	Paneer	Used as a base in sweet dishes and vegetable dishes.
Cream	Malai	Used in desserts and curries for thickening and flavouring.
Cucumber	Kheera/Kakri	Used mostly in salads.
Cumin seed	Jeera	Used whole or ground for flavouring and sautéing.

English	Hindi	Uses
Curry leaves	Kadi patta	An aromatic leaf used fresh or dried for seasoning.
Dates	Khajoor	It is used in sweets and making sweet and sour *chutneys*.
Dried milk	Khoya	Used extensively in sweet and savoury dishes.
Dry mango powder	Amchur	Used in curries and vegetables to give sour and tangy taste.
Evaporated milk	Mawa	Used for thickening curries.
Fennel seeds	Badi saunf	Used extensively to flavour curries and pickles.
Fenugreek leaves	Methi	Fresh leaves are used as a vegetable and in *parathas*. Dried leaves also known as kasuri methi are used for seasoning.
Fenugreek seeds	Methi dana	Used whole or ground in curries and pickles.
Fig	Anjeer	Used as fruit or dried for desserts.
Flaked rice	Poha	Used for snacks, savouries and fried dishes.
Flour	Maida	All purpose flour used in many dishes.
French beans	Fransbean	Used in curries and pulaos.
Garam masala	Garam masala	A mixture of selected hot spices used in Indian dishes.
Garlic	Lehsun	Used whole or in paste form to flavour curries and pickles.
Ginger	Adrak	Used in chopped or in paste form in curries, vegetables and pickles.
Ginger powder	Saunth	Used in place of fresh ginger.
Gram	Bhoora chana	An important Indian food grain.
Gram flour	Besan	Used as a batter for frying and thickening curries.
Green gram	Moong	Used as a whole or sprouted or split. Skinless split gram is used for making sweets and curries.
Groundnut	Moong phali	Used raw or roasted in some special curries.

English	Hindi	Uses
Gauva	Amrood	A delicious fruit used in salads.
Honey	Shahad	Used as a sugar substitute.
Horse bean	Urad Dal	Lentil used as a rising agent for rice cakes and also for making savouries.
Indian gooseberry	Amla	Used in pickles and *chutneys*.
Jackfruit	Kathal	Used in curries and making *koftas*.
Jaggery	Gud	Used as a sugar substitute. It adds a delicate earthly taste to the dish.
Kewda water	Kewda jal	Adds fragrance to puddings, cold drinks and rice preparations.
Ladies' Finger	Bhindi	Should be cooked dry to get best results.
Lemon	Nimbu	A citrus fruit used to add sourness and adds a distinct flavour.
Lentil	Masoor	Used both as whole and split form in curries and stuffing.
Lotus puffs	Makhana	Used in making puddings and savouries.
Lotus stems	Kamal kakdi	A cooling vegetable used in kebabs and cultlets.
Mace	Javitri	Spice bark, used in making spicy rice and curries.
Mango	Aam	The king of fruits, used in different forms.
Millet	Bajra	Used for making breads.
Maize	Makaa	Used for making breads and chapatis.
Minced meat	Kheema	Used for making cutlets, ball curry etc.
Mint	Pudina	Used in curries, *chutneys* for garnishing.
Mushroom	Dhingri	Usually used in combination with green peas or fresh corn.
Mustard oil	Sarson ka tel	A pungent cooking oil.
Mustard seeds	Rai/Sarson	Used for making, pickles, sauces and *chutneys*.
Nigella	Kalongi	A seed used in pickles and stuffed vegetables.
Nutmeg	Jaiphal	Used for flavouring puddings and savouries.

English	Hindi	Uses
Papaya	Papita	Raw papaya is used as a meat tenderiser whereas ripe papaya is used as a base for some jams.
Parsley	Ajmuda ki patti	Used for flavouring and garnishing dishes.
Peas (Dried)	Sukhi matar	Used for making *chaat* dishes and *dals*.
Pigeon peas	Toor dal	Used to make curries and *dals*.
Pineapple	Ananas	Strongly flavoured fruit used in salads, puddings and cakes.
Pistachio	Pista	A nut used in puddings, sweetmeats and biriyanis.
Pomegranate seeds	Anardana	Used in curries especially in preparations to add tanginess and flavour.
Poppy seeds	Khus khus	An aromatic spice used to thicken curries.
Potato	Aloo	The most popular and commonly used vegetable.
Pumpkin	Kaddu	Used to make halwa and in curries.
Radish	Mooli	Used in making parathas and in salads.
Raisins	Kishmish	Used in desserts and fried rice.
Rice	Chawaal	Used in making biriyanis and pulaos.
Rice flour	Chawaal ka aata	It is used as a thickening agent.
Ridge gourd	Turia	It is a green vegetable used in some curries.
Rose water	Gulab jal	An aromatic liquid used in Indian sweets like *gulab jamuns* and *sherbets*.
Saffron	Kesar	A flavouring and colouring spice used in biriyanis, sweets and curries.
Sago	Saabudana	Light granular starch used in puddings.
Semolina	Rava/Suji	Used to make parathas, puris and as a base in some sweets.
Sesame seeds	Til	It is used in some sweets while the roasted paste is sometimes used in thickening and flavouring.
Soya curd	Tofu	Used along with vegetables and in soups.
Spinach	Palak	Used in curries, soups and salads.
Spring onions	Hari pyaaz	A green vegetable used in salads and vegetable preparations.
Sugar candy	Misree	Used in sweetmeats and can be served after a meal with fennel seeds.
Sugar syrup	Chaashnee	Used extensively in sweet dishes.
Sweet potato	Shakarkand	It can be fried, boiled, roasted or cooked in gravy.
Tamarind	Imli	Used in curries, *chutneys*, sauces.
Tomatoo	Tamaatar	Used whole or puree in many dishes.
Turmeric	Haldi	A colouring and flavouring spice. It has medicinal properties and acts as an antibiotic.
Vermicelli	Seviyaan	Used in making pudding.
Vinegar	Sirka	It gives a sour taste as well as adds a distinct flavour.
Walnut	Akhrot	Used in garnishing as well as a ingredient in many Indian sweets.
Wheat flour	Atta	Used as a base to make different Indian breads.
White gourd	Petha	A vegetable of the pumpkin family, often used in sweetameats.
Whey	Chach	A watery part of milk that seperates from curd.
Yam	Jamikand/ Suran	Used widely in South Indian cooking.
Yeast	Khameer	A fermentation agent used usually for raising dough.
Yoghurt/ Curd	Dahi	A digestive milk product used in various dishes and also as a base for *raitas* and snacks like *dahi vada*.

NUTRITIVE VALUE OF FOOD ITEMS

(Amounts given per 100 gms of edible portion)

Food	Water ml	Kcal	Protein gm	Fat gm	Carbo hydrate	Fiber gm	Calcium mg	Iron mg	Vit. A i.u.	B1 mg	B2 mg	Niacin mg	Vit. C mg
1	2	3	4	5	6	7	8	9	10	11	12	13	14
Almond	5	657	20	59	12	1.7	230	4.5	—	.3	.6	4.5	—
Amla	81	55	0.5	.10	14	3.4	50	1.2	—	—	—	—	600
Animal fat	1	891	—	99	—	—	—	—	—	—	—	—	—
Apple	84	61	.3	.4	14	1	4	1	20	.02	.04	.2	5
Apricot	90	36	1	—	8	.4	15	1	2000	.03	.05	.5	5
Bajra (millet)	13	361	11.6	.5	67.5	1.2	42	5	—	.33	.25	2.3	—
Banana	70	116	1	.3	27	.3	7	.5	100	.1	.08	.8	7
Barley	13	336	22.5	1.3	62.6	3.9	26	8	—	.47	.20	5.4	—
Bathua leaves	90	30	3.7	.4	2.9	.8	150	4.2	—	.01	.14	.6	35
Beetroot	87	45	1.8	—	10	.7	15	1	—	.02	.03	3	5
Black pepper	13	347	.12	7	59	4.9	130	10	—	.04	.2	1	—
Brown khandsari	1	389	.2	—	97	—	30	2	—	0.2	.1	.3	—
Butter	16	745	.5	82.5	—	—	15	.2	3000	—	—	—	—
Butter oil pure	8	828	—	92	—	—	—	—	2000	—	—	—	—
Cane juice	81	73	.3	—	18	—	6	2	—	.02	.02	.1	10
Cardamom dried	20	228	10	2	43	20	113	5	—	—	—	—	—
Carrot	90	33	1	—	7	.8	40	.7	3000	.05	.05	.5	.6
Cashewnut	5	590	20	45	26	1.3	50	5	—	.6	.2	2.1	—
Cauliflower	90	33	3	.2	5	1	30	1	20	.1	.1	.7	—
Cumin seed	12	356	19	15	36	12		31	300	—	—	2.6	—
Cinnamon	12	229	12	7.8	28	35	440	17	—	.1	.4	2.4	—
Clove	23	293	5	9	48	10	740	5	—	.1	.2	2	—
Coconut kernel	20	375	4	35	11	4	10	2	—	.05	.02	.6	—
Cucumber	96	12	.6	—	2	.5	15	.3	—	.04	.02	.2	10
Custard apple	75	93	1	—	22	1	25	.5	—	.1	.08	.8	30
Dried dates	20	303	2	—	74	2.4	70	2	50	.07	.05	2	—
Dried pea	10	337	25	1	57	4.5	70	5	100	.8	.2	2.5	—
Eggplant (brinjal)	93	22	1	—	4	1	10	1	—	.05	.03	.8	5
Fig-dried	20	269	4	—	63	11	200	4	100	.1	.08	1.7	—
Fig-fresh	85	49	1.3	—	11	2	50	1	80	.05	.05	.4	2
Fresh beans & peas	70	104	7	—	19	2.5	40	15	500	.3	.15	1.5	25
Fresh mushroom	91	13	2.5	.3	—	1	20	1	—	.12	.5	5.8	3
Garlic	63	139	6	—	29	.8	13	1.3	—	.25	.08	.4	10
Gourd	92	28	.7	—	6	.3	20	.6	—	.04	.03	.6	15
Gram, whole	10	338	22	.5	61	5.3	280	8	40	.4	.15	2.5	—
Mung bean (green)	12	324	22	1	57	4.7	100	8	40	.45	.2	2	—
Grape	80	76	1	—	18	.5	20	.3	50	.04	.02	.3	5
Green pepper	90	37	2	.5	6	1	20	1	130-800	.03	.03	.3	150
Green spring onion	90	36	1.8	.5	6	1	40	3	500	.05	.1	.5	50

Food	Water	Kcal	Protein	Fat	Carbo hydrate	Fiber	Calcium	Iron	Vit. A	B1	B2	Niacin	Vit. C
	ml		gm	gm		gm	mg	mg	i.u.	mg	mg	mg	mg
1	2	3	4	5	6	7	8	9	10	11	12	13	14
Groundnut	6	579	27	45	17	3	50	2.5	—	.9	.15	17	—
Guava	80	58	1	.4	13	5.5	15	1	200	.05	.04	1	200
Honey	23	286	4	—	76	—	5	.4	—	—	.05	.2	—
Jam	29	260	.4	—	69	.6	12	.3	—	—	—	—	10
Lemon	85	55	1.1	0.9	11.1	1.7	70	2.3	—	—	—	—	39
Lettuce	94	19	1.4	—	3	.5	35	2.4	300	.1	.1	.4	15
Lichi	82	71	.9	.5	16	.3	5	.5	—	.04	.04	.3	50
Lobia bean	12	323	24.1	1	54.5	3.8	77	5.9	60	.51	.2	1.3	—
(black kidney bean)	11	329	24	1	56	4.5	150	9	40	.4	.2	2	—
Maize, whole	12	363	10	4.5	71	2	12	2.5	—	.35	.13	2	—
Mango	83	63	.5	—	15	.8	10	.5	600	.03	.04	.3	30
Mustard leaves	85	34	4	.6	3.2	.8	155	16.3	—	.03	—	—	33
Melon seeds (without cover)	6	581	25	45	19	2	50	8	—	.2	.15	1.5	—
Methi leaves	85	49	4.4	.9	6	1.1	395	16.5	—	.04	.31	.8	52
Muskmelon	93	26	.5	—	6	.4	10	.4	500	.03	.03	.5	30
Orange	86	53	.8	—	13	.3	30	.5	30	.08	.03	.2	45
Papaya	89	39	.8	—	9	.7	20	.5	1000	.03	.03	.2	50
Peach	85	56	.8	—	13	.5	8	.5	300	.02	.03	.3	10
Pear	84	59	.3	—	15	.9	7	.4	—	.02	.02	.2	4
Pineapple	85	57	.4	—	14	.5	20	.5	100	.08	.03	.1	30
Pistachio	6	626	20	54	15	2	140	14	100	7	.5	1.5	—
Plum	88	45	.7	—	11	.4	10	.4	30	.02	.03	.3	5
Pomegranate	80	77	1	—	18	.2	3	.7	—	.02	.02	.2	8
Potato	80	75	2	—	17	.4	10	.7	—	.1	.03	1.5	15
Pumpkin seeds (without cover)	4	610	30	50	10	2	40	10	30	.2	.2	2	—
Radish	94	18	1	—	4	.7	30	1	—	.03	.03	.3	25
Red kidney bean	12	346	22.9	1.3	60.6	4.5	260	5.8	60	—	—	—	—
Rice, lightly milled	12	354	8	1.5	77	.5	10	2	—	.25	.05	2	—
Sorghum/*Jowar*	12	353	10	2.5	73	1.5	20	4	—	.4	.1	3	—
Soyabean	8	382	35	18	20	4.5	200	7-11	—	1.1	.3	2	—
Spinach	85	48	5	.7	5	1.5	250	10.9	3000	.1	.3	1.5	100
Sugar white	—	400	—	—	100	—	—	—	—	—	—	—	—
Sweet lemon (*Mosambi*)	84.6	55	1.5	1.0	10.9	1.3	90	.3	26	.04	—	.2	63
Sweet potato	70	114	1.5	.3	26	1	25	1	100	.1	.04	.7	30
Tamarind	20	304	2	—	74	2	50	3	50	.4	.15	1.5	10
Tomato	94	20	1	—	4	.6	5	.4	250	.06	.04	.7	25
Turnip	90	34	1	—	8	.7	30	.4	—	.06	.04	.7	25
Walnut	3	697	15	65	13	2.1	80	2	—	.4	.1	.7	—
Wheat flour	13	341	10	1	75	—	16	1.5	—	.08	.05	.8	—
Wheat, sprouted	13	397	29.2	7.4	53.3	1.4	40	6	—	1.4	.54	2.9	—
Wheat, whole	13	344	11.5	2	70	2	30	3.5	—	.4	.1	5	—
Yam	73	104	2	.2	24	.5	10	1.2	20	.1	.03	.4	10

Calorie Content of Common Food Items in Convenient Measures

A. Raw Foods

Item	Measure	Weight	Energy
		g.	Cal.
Cereals			
Rice	1 Cup (small)	150	520
Wheat flour	1 Cup (small)	90	310
Millet flour	1 Cup (small)	90	300
Pulses			
Bengal gram *dal*	1 Cup (small)	130	485
Other *dals*	1 Cup (small)	135	460
Whole Pulses			
Greengram	1 Cup (small)	140	470
Cowpea (*lobia*)	1 Cup (small)	135	440
Rajma	1 Cup (small)	120	415
Soyabean	1 Cup (small)	130	530
Green leafy vegetables	5 Bundles	100	62
Other vegetables	–	100	105
Nuts and Oilseeds			
Almonds	10 no.	15	85
Cashewnuts	10 no.	15	95
Coconut (fresh)	1 no.	115	510
Coconut (dry)	1/2 no.	45	290
Groundnuts	50 no.	15	85
Sesame seeds	1 tsp.	3	15
Oils/Vanaspati ghee	2 tsp.	10 ml.	100
Spices			
Chilli powder	1 tsp.	7	17
Coriander seeds	1 tsp.	7	20
Cumin seeds	1 tsp.	5	18
Fenugreek (*Methi*)	1 tsp.	6	20
Mustard seeds	1 tsp.	10	5
Garlic	7 cloves	3	4
Onion	1 med.	50	30

Item	Measure	Weight	Energy
Animal foods			
Egg (hen)	One	60	100
Mutton	–	100	194
Fish (lean)	–	100	100
Fish (fatty)	–	100	150

B. Cooked Foods

Item	No. of Serving	Weight gms.	Energy cal.
Cereal preparations			
Rice	1 Cup	100	110
Idli	1 Cup	60	75
Plain *dosa*	1 Cup	40	125
Masala dosa	1 Cup	100	200
Phulka	1 Cup	35	80
Paratha	1 Cup	50	150
Upma	1 Cup	130	200
Sevian upma	1 Cup	80	130
Bread toasted	2 slices	50	170
Poha (Awal)	1 Cup	100	200
Dalia	1 Cup	140	165
Khichidi	1 Cup	100	210
Puri	1	25	80
Pulse preparations			
Plain *dal*	1 Cup	140	170
Sambhar	1 Cup	160	81
Chole	1 Cup	150	115
Vegetable preparations			
With gravy	1 Cup	130	130
Dry	1 Cup	100	115
Bagara baingan	1 Cup	170	230
Vegetable kofta	1 Cup	145	220

Item	No. of Serving	Weight gms.	Energy cal.
Fried snacks			
Bhaji	1	7	35
Samosa	1	65	210
Kachori	1	45	200
Potato *bonda*	1	40	100
Sago vada	1	30	100
Masala vada	1	20	56
Vada	1	20	65
Dahi vada	1	80	170
Vegetable cutlet	1	30	70
Chutneys			
Coconut/Ground Nuts/*Til*/Coriander	1tbsp	25	64
Tomato	1 tbsp	20	10
Non-Vegetarian preparations			
Boiled egg	1	50	86
Omelette	1	65	155
Fried egg	1	50	155
Mutton curry	1 cup	145	240
Chicken curry	1 Cup	125	260
Fish (fried)	2 pieces	85	220
Bakery products			
Biscuits	2	40	220
Cake	1	40	220
Vegetable puff	1	60	170
Pastry	1	50	350
Mathri	2	75	300
Sweets			
Laddu, burfi etc.	1	60	250
Halwa (suji)	1 cup	130	430
Double *ka meetha*	"	105	280
Custard/Puddings	"	110	180
Chikki	2	60	300
Jam/Jelly	1tsp.	7	20
Sugar	1 tbsp	15 ml.	20
Honey	1 tbsp	15 ml.	60
Jalebi	2 pieces	100 gm.	500
Gulab jamun	2 pieces	50 gm.	400
Jaggery	1 tbsp.	15 gm.	56

C. Salads

Item	No.	Weight gms.	Energy cal.
Beetroot	1	65	30
Cabbage	1	250	70
Carrot	1	40	20
Cucumber	1	90	12
Lettuce	6 bundles	100	20
Onion	1	50	25
Radish	1	60	10
Tomato	1	50	10
Turnip	1	100	30

D. Fruits

Item	No./ Quantity	Weight gms.	Energy cal.
Apple	1	100	65
Banana	1	80	90
Grapes	30	100	70
Guava	1	100	50
Jackfruit	4 pieces	100	90
Mango	1	250	180
Mosambi/orange	1	100	40
Papaya	1 piece	250	80
Pineapple	1 piece	100	50
Sapota	1	80	80
Custard apple	1	130	130
Watermelon/ Muskmelon	1 piece	100	15

E. Beverages

Item	Measure	Qty. ml.	Energy cal.
Coffee	1 cup	150	100
Tea	1 cup	150	60
Carbonated beverages	1 bottle	200	150
Fresh lime juice	1 glass	200	60
Squash	1 glass	200	80
Syrups (*sherbat*)	1 glass	200	200
Orange juice	1 glass	200	150

F. Milk and Milk Products

Item	Measure	Qty. ml.	Energy cal.
Milk (buffalo)	1 cup	150 ml.	300
Milk (cow)	1 cup	150 ml.	100
Curd (cow)	1 cup	150 ml.	85
Buttermilk (*lassi*)	1 cup	150 ml.	45
Paneer	1 cup	100 gm.	350
Ghee	2 tsp	10 ml.	100
Butter	3 tsp	15 ml.	100
Khoya (from whole milk)		100 gm.	400
Khoya (butter separated)		100 gm.	200
Skimmed milk	1 cup	150 ml.	45
Cream	1 tbsp	15 ml.	50
Cheese	1 packet	30 gm.	100
Rabadi	1 cup	150 gm.	525

Cholesterol Content of Animal Foods

Item g/100 g.	Fat fatty acids	Saturated mg/100 g.	Cholesterol g/100 g.
Butter	80	50	250
Ghee	100	65	300
Milk (cow)	4	2	14
Milk (buffalo)	8	4	16
Milk (skimmed)	0.1	-	2
Milk (condensed)	10	6	40
Cream	13	8	40
Cheese	25	15	100
Egg (whole)	11	4	400
Egg yolk	30	9	1120
Chicken without skin	4	1	60
Chicken with skin	18	6	100
Beef	16	8	70
Mutton	13	7	65
Pork	35	13	90
Organ meats			
Brain	6	2	2000
Heart	5	2	150
Kidney	2	1	370
Liver	9	3	300
Sea foods			
Prawns/Shrimps	2	0.3	150
Fish (lean)	1.5	0.4	45
Fish (fatty)	6	2.5	45

MEASUREMENTS

Item	Quantity	Weight
Almonds	10-12	12 gms
Asafoetida powder (*hing*)	1/2 tspn	5 gms
Baking powder	1 tspn	3 gms
Black gram (*urad*), split	1 cup	220 gms
Black pepper powder	1 tspn	3 gms
Butter	1 tblspn	12 gms
Cashewnuts	10-12	7 gms
Cashewnut paste	1 cup	140 gms
Chopped coriander leaves	1 cup	55 gms
Coriander (*dhania*) powder	1 tspn	2 gms
Cumin (*jeera*) powder	1 tspn	2 gms
Egg	1	63 gms
Flour (*atta*)	1 cup	115 gms
Fresh cream	1 cup	250 mls
Garam masala powder	1 tspn	2 gms
Garlic	6-8 cloves	5 gms
Garlic paste	1 tblspn	16 gms
Ghee	1 tblspn	7 gms
Ginger	1 inch	15-20 gms
Ginger paste	1 tblspn	16 gms
Gram flour (*besan*)	1 tblspn	10 gms
Grated cheese	1 cup	75 gms
Grated coconut	1 cup	175 gms
Green chillies	5	11 gms
Green peas (frozen)	1 cup	110 gms
Honey	1 tbspn	20 gms
Lemon juice	1 tspn	3 gms
Mawa (*khoya*)	1 cup	200 gms
Medium sized carrot	1	60 gins
Medium sized onion	1	90 gms
Medium sized potato	1	100 gms
Medium sized tomato	1	100 gms
Mustard (*rai*) powder	1 tspn	2 gms
Oil	1 tblspn	13 mls
Pigeon Pea, split (*toor dal*)	1 cup	225 gms
Red chilli (*mirch*) powder	1 tspn	2 gms
Refined flour (*maida*)	1 cup	200 gms
Rice	1 cup	200 gms
Rice flour	1 cup	115 gms
Salt	1 tspn	6 gms
Sugar	1 tblspn	14 gms
Tamarind pulp	1 tspn	6 gms
Turmeric (*haldi*) powder	1 tspn	2 gms
Vinegar	1 tblspn	11 gms
White pepper	55-60	3 gms
Yogurt	1 tblspn	15 gms

Fat Contents of Commonly used Vegetable Oils & Ghee (in %)

Oils & Ghee Fat	Saturated	Monounsaturated Fat	Polyunsaturated Fat		Predominant fatty acids
			Linoleic	Alpha linolenic	
Coconut	90	7	2	< 0.5	Saturated
Palm kernel	82	15	2	< 0.5	Saturated
Ghee	65	32	2	< 1.0	Saturated
Vanaspati Ghee (*Dalda*)	24	19	3	< 0.5	Saturated
Red palm oil (raw)	50	40	9	< 0.5	Saturated + Monounsaturated
Palm oil	45	44	10	0.5	Saturated + Monounsaturated
Olive	13	76	10	< 0.5	Monounsaturated
Groundnut	24	50	25	< 0.5	Monounsaturated
Mustard	8	70	12	1.0	Monounsaturated
Sesame	15	42	42	1.0	Mono and polyunsaturated
Rice bran	22	41	35	1.5	Mono and polyunsaturated
Cotton seed	22	25	52	1.0	Polyunsaturated
Corn	12	32	55	1.0	Polyunsaturated
Sunflower	13	27	60	< 0.5	Polyunsaturated
Safflower	13	17	70	< 0.5	Polyunsaturated
Soyabean	15	27	53	5.0	Polyunsaturated